Lecture Notes in Computer Science   **11358**

Commenced Publication in 1973
Founding and Former Series Editors:
Gerhard Goos, Juris Hartmanis, and Jan van Leeuwen

More information about this series at http://www.springer.com/series/7410

Nur Zincir-Heywood · Guillaume Bonfante ·
Mourad Debbabi · Joaquin Garcia-Alfaro (Eds.)

Foundations and Practice of Security

11th International Symposium, FPS 2018
Montreal, QC, Canada, November 13–15, 2018
Revised Selected Papers

 Springer

Editors
Nur Zincir-Heywood
Dalhousie University
Halifax, NS, Canada

Guillaume Bonfante
École des Mines de Nancy
Nancy, France

Mourad Debbabi 🆔
Concordia University
Montreal, QC, Canada

Joaquin Garcia-Alfaro 🆔
Telecom SudParis
Evry, France

ISSN 0302-9743   ISSN 1611-3349 (electronic)
Lecture Notes in Computer Science
ISBN 978-3-030-18418-6   ISBN 978-3-030-18419-3 (eBook)
https://doi.org/10.1007/978-3-030-18419-3

LNCS Sublibrary: SL4 – Security and Cryptology

This Springer imprint is published by the registered company Springer Nature Switzerland AG
The registered company address is: Gewerbestrasse 11, 6330 Cham, Switzerland

Preface

This volume contains the papers presented at the 11th International Symposium on Foundations and Practice of Security (FPS 2018), which was held at Gina Cody School of Engineering and Computer Science, Concordia University, Montreal, Quebec, Canada, during November 13–15, 2018. The Symposium received 51 submissions, from countries all over the world. Each paper was reviewed by at least three committee members. The Program Committee selected 16 full papers for presentation. The program was completed with one short paper and one position paper, and three excellent invited talks given by Guang Gong (University of Waterloo), Sanjay Goel (University at Albany, SUNY) and Sébastien Gambs (Université du Québec à Montréal, UQAM). At least three reviews were given for each submitted paper. The decision on acceptance or rejection in the review process was completed after intensive discussions over a period of one week.

Many people contributed to the success of FPS 2018. First, we would like to thank all the authors who submitted their research results. The selection was a challenging task and we sincerely thank all the Program Committee members, as well as the external reviewers, who volunteer to read and discuss the papers. We greatly thank the general chair, Frédéric Cuppens (IMT Atlantique); the organization chair, Amr Youssef (Concordia University, Canada); the local organization chairs, Paria Shirani (Concordia University, Canada) and Jun Yan (Concordia University, Canada); and the publications and publicity chairs, Arash Mohammadi (Concordia University, Canada) and Joaquin Garcia-Alfaro (IMT, Paris-Saclay, France). We also want to express our gratitude to all the attendees and volunteers. Last but, by no means least, we want to thank all the sponsors for making the event possible.

We hope the articles contained in this proceedings volume will be valuable for your professional activities in the area.

February 2019

Nur Zincir-Heywood
Guillaume Bonfante
Mourad Debbabi

Organization

General Chair

Frédéric Cuppens   IMT Atlantique, France

Program Co-chairs

Nur Zincir-Heywood   Dalhousie University, Canada
Guillaume Bonfante   Ecole des Mines de Nancy, France
Mourad Debbabi   Concordia University, Canada

Publications and Publicity Chairs

Arash Mohammadi   Concordia University, Canada
Joaquin Garcia-Alfaro   Télécom SudParis, France

Organization Chair

Amr Youssef   Concordia University, Canada

Local Organization Chairs

Paria Shirani   Concordia University, Canada
Jun Yan   Concordia University, Canada

Program Committee

Esma Aimeur   University of Montreal, Canada
Jeremy Clark   Concordia University, Canada
Nora Cuppens   IMT Atlantique, France
Frédéric Cuppens   IMT Atlantique, France
Jean-Luc Danger   Télécom Paris-Tech, France
Mourad Debbabi   Concordia University, Canada
Josée Desharnais   Laval University, Canada
Samuel Dubus   NOKIA Bell Labs, France
Joaquin Garcia-Alfaro   Télécom SudParis, France
Dieter Gollmann   Hamburg University of Technology, Germany
Sushil Jajodia   George Mason University, USA
Bruce Kapron   University of Victoria, Canada
Raphaël Khoury   Université du Québec à Chicoutimi, Canada
Hyoungshick Kim   Sungkyunkwan University, Republic of Korea
Igor Kotenko   SPIIRAS, Russia

Evangelos Kranakis	Carleton University Computer Science, Canada
Pascal Lafourcade	Université d'Auvergne, France
Luigi Logrippo	Université du Québec en Outaouais, Canada
Suryadipta Majumdar	University at Albany, USA
Fabio Martinelli	National Research Council of Italy (CNR), Italy
Paliath Narendran	University at Albany, USA
Guillermo Navarro-Arribas	Universitat Autonoma de Barcelona, Spain
Jun Pang	University of Luxembourg, Luxembourg
Marie-Laure Potet	VERIMAG, France
Silvio Ranise	FBK, Security and Trust Unit, Italy
Indrakshi Ray	Colorado State University, USA
Michaël Rusinowitch	LORIA-Inria Nancy, France
Paria Shirani	Concordia University, Canada
Natalia Stakhanova	University of New Brunswick, Canada
Chamseddine Talhi	École de Technologie Supérieure, Canada
Nadia Tawbi	Université Laval, Canada
Lingyu Wang	Concordia University, Canada
Edgar Weippl	SBA Research, Austria
Lena Wiese	Georg-August Universität Göttingen, Germany
Xun Yi	RMIT University, Australia
Nur Zincir-Heywood	Dalhousie University, Canada
Mohammad Zulkernine	Queen's University, Canada

Steering Committee

Frédéric Cuppens	IMT Atlantique, France
Nora Cuppens-Boulahia	IMT Atlantique, France
Mourad Debbabi	University of Conccordia, Canada
Joaquin Garcia-Alfaro	Télécom SudParis, France
Evangelos Kranakis	Carleton University, Canada
Pascal Lafourcade	Université d'Auvergne, France
Jean-Yves Marion	Mines de Nancy, France
Ali Miri	Ryerson University, Canada
Rei Safavi-Naini	Calgary University, Canada
Nadia Tawbi	Université Laval, Canada

Contents

Invited Papers

Securing Internet-of-Things   3
    Guang Gong

Privacy and Ethical Challenges in Big Data 17
    Sébastien Gambs

Mobile Security

Decentralized Dynamic Security Enforcement for Mobile Applications
with CliSeAuDroid 29
    Tobias Hamann and Heiko Mantel

Mobile Travel Credentials 46
    David Bissessar, Maryam Hezaveh, Fayzah Alshammari,
    and Carlisle Adams

Cloud Security and Big Data

Cloud Security Auditing: Major Approaches and Existing Challenges 61
    Suryadipta Majumdar, Taous Madi, Yosr Jarraya, Makan Pourzandi,
    Lingyu Wang, and Mourad Debbabi

Secure Joins with MapReduce 78
    Xavier Bultel, Radu Ciucanu, Matthieu Giraud, Pascal Lafourcade,
    and Lihua Ye

Daedalus: Network Anomaly Detection on IDS Stream Logs 95
    Aniss Chohra, Mourad Debbabi, and Paria Shirani

IoT Security

Configuring Data Flows in the Internet of Things for Security
and Privacy Requirements 115
    Luigi Logrippo and Abdelouadoud Stambouli

Validating Requirements of Access Control for Cloud-Edge
IoT Solutions (Short Paper) 131
    Tahir Ahmad and Silvio Ranise

Software Security, Malware Analysis, and Vulnerability Detection

Evading Deep Neural Network and Random Forest Classifiers
by Generating Adversarial Samples   143
  Erick Eduardo Bernal Martinez, Bella Oh, Feng Li, and Xiao Luo

Protection of Systems Against Fuzzing Attacks   156
  Léopold Ouairy, Hélène Le-Bouder, and Jean-Louis Lanet

A Comparative Study Across Static and Dynamic
Side-Channel Countermeasures   173
  Yuri Gil Dantas, Tobias Hamann, and Heiko Mantel

Cryptography

Card-Based Cryptographic Protocols with the Minimum Number of Cards
Using Private Operations   193
  Hibiki Ono and Yoshifumi Manabe

Cryptographic Formula Obfuscation   208
  Giovanni Di Crescenzo

Fault Analysis of the New Ukrainian Hash Function Standard: Kupyna   225
  Onur Duman and Amr Youssef

Cyber Physical Security and Hardware Security

When Fault Injection Collides with Hardware Complexity   243
  Sebanjila Kevin Bukasa, Ludovic Claudepierre, Ronan Lashermes,
  and Jean-Louis Lanet

A Study on Mitigation Techniques for SCADA-Driven Cyber-Physical
Systems (Position Paper)   257
  Mariana Segovia, Ana Rosa Cavalli, Nora Cuppens,
  and Joaquin Garcia-Alfaro

Access Control

Mining Relationship-Based Access Control Policies from Incomplete
and Noisy Data   267
  Thang Bui, Scott D. Stoller, and Jiajie Li

Fine-Grained Access Control for Microservices   285
  Antonio Nehme, Vitor Jesus, Khaled Mahbub, and Ali Abdallah

Achieving Mobile-Health Privacy Using Attribute-Based Access Control   301
    Vignesh Pagadala and Indrakshi Ray

Author Index   317

Invited Papers

Securing Internet-of-Things

Guang Gong$^{(\boxtimes)}$ (iD)

Department of Electrical and Computer Engineering, University of Waterloo,
Waterloo, ON N2L 3G1, Canada
ggong@uwaterloo.ca

Abstract. In this survey, we first present some vulnerabilities and attacks on IoT systems, and classification of IoT devices, we then show the evolution of the development of lightweight cryptography for securing IoT, the metrics for the design of lightweight cryptography, and the applications in privacy preserving authentication protocols. We use examples including the development of Simon, Simeck, and sLiSCP/sLiSCP-Light lightweight ciphers to demonstrate those approaches.

Keywords: Internet-of-Things (IoT) · Security and privacy · Lightweight cryptography

1 Introduction

The IoT connects an extraordinarily wide range of computing technologies, spanning from computers and servers through to smart devices. Sensors, actuators, radio frequency identification (RFID) tags, vehicular ad hoc networks (VANETs) and micro-controllers equipped with RF transceivers capture and communicate various types of data related to, for example, industrial and building control, e-health (e.g., wearable devices embedded in our clothing), smart energy grid, home automation (Internet-connected appliances in our increasingly smart homes, such as washing machines, dryers, and refrigerators), self driving cars, and embedded systems. That data is transmitted through the Internet via wireless, wired and/or hybrid to back-end business application/integration servers that receive and process it into meaningful information (such as data analytic services and cloud analytic services). Personal and potentially sensitive information may flow through shared data centres and the cloud, where it can be exposed to multiple shareholders and, more broadly, to countless business partners. A graphic schematic of information flow in the IoT system is shown in Fig. 1.

There is consensus that IoT will continue to grow by approximately 20% per year, and the greatest risks for IoT are security, scalability, and reliability [14]. In 2017, IoT devices outnumbered the world's population! It is expected that there will be 30 billion connected devices by 2020, each with different operational and

Supported by NSERC.

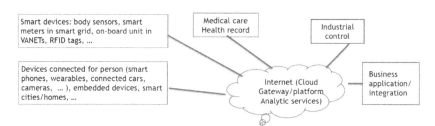

Fig. 1. A diagram of information flow of the IoT

security requirements. Much of the growth in IoT stems from the volume and diversity of data produced by IoT devices. The value of this data has given rise to new economic opportunities, such as *data markets*. At the same time, it also generates new vulnerabilities for security and privacy due to rapidly increasing cyber attacks against the critical infrastructure. According to current developments, the most rapid growing applications of IoT are smart cities ($\approx$26%), industrial IoT ($\approx$24%), connected health ($\approx$20%), followed by smart homes ($\approx$14%), then connected cars, wearables, and smart utilities.

This survey article intents to provide the envisions of vulnerabilities, attacks and countermeasures in securing IoT. The rest of the paper is organized as follows. In Sect. 2, we introduce vulnerabilities and attacks on IoT systems, and some efforts for standardization of IoT security mechanisms. In Sect. 3, we provide the classification of IoT devices according to their communication transmission systems. In Sect. 4, we show the evolution of how lightweight cryptography (LWC) has been merged as a new interdisciplinary research field of electrical and computer engineering, cryptography, and computer science from lightweight cipher suites' design to privacy preserving authentication protocols. Section 5 provides an example of such an evolution for LWC using our work from Simeck to sLiSCP/sLiSCP-light. We conclude this paper in Sect. 6 by presenting some open problems and remarks.

2   Challenges in Securing IoT

The challenges for securing IoT come from security (how to securely share private information), scalability (how to interface different protocols and to optimize connectivity (e.g. 5G cellular systems), and reliability (how much available resources can be allocated to each task).

2.1   Attacks

The complexity, large volume and need for real-time access to data (coined as big data) within IoT systems make it extremely challenging to implement security and privacy protection mechanisms. These challenges are compounded by a historically ad hoc approach to Internet-based security. In the last several decades, since the inception of the Internet, security has been handled as an afterthought and not by design. Quick-fix add-ons developed post-attacks have proven ill equipped to address new security risks presented by an ever-expanding stream of technologies and applications. For example, Wi-Fi service, which is pervasive in today's society, was introduced with serious security flaws. The Wired Equivalent Privacy (WEP) algorithm is now used as the textbook example for how easily security can fail. In current IoT systems, attackers continue to find the simplest, easiest and most cost efficient ways to access secure systems. We can classify the reported attacks on commercial products into the following three categories.

A. Weak Authentication Yields Malware Attacks. In this class, noticeable examples are as follows.

- Weak login password: Mirai malware attack launched in 2016 [22]. Those attacks first exploit the weakness of the password based authentication at login phase of IoT devices like cameras, routers, DVRs, or even baby monitors in order to break in those devices to install malware (e.g., when they connect to the Internet through Telnet or SSH), in sequel the attacker can conduct brute force search for login information since its using only about 60 known default passwords.
- Single master key for updating software: Attacks on Philips Hue smart bulbs which infected millions of ZigBee sensors connected to Internet through WiFi. In those attacks [27], the attacker exploits manufacturers unprofessional practices, i.e., one master key for all bulbs for firmware updates. However, this is just simply repeated an old attack on radio frequency identification (RFID) proximity card in 2005 [18]! The lesson is never learned.

B. Weakness of Underlying Cryptographic Algorithms. Those attacks are launched by observing some weakness of employed cryptographic algorithms and protocols. We list some of them below.

- In 2011, Lockheed Martin networks were breached and, in 2012, the Master Key for Sony Playstation 3 system was leaked. Both used weak pseudorandom bit generators.
- In 2014, compatibility downgrade attacks were demonstrated on TLS (i.e., forcing a connection which runs TLS v1.2 down to SSL v3, where an insecure cipher (i.e., DES) is employed).
- In 2008, MIFARE RFID tag encryption [21] was cracked and, in 2012, HID iClass cards were cloned for which, weak cipher suites are employed (both are privately designed (violating Kerckhoffs' law) publicly released by reverse engineering approaches).
- In 2015, hackers took remote control of Jeep and Chevrolet Corvette vehicles while on route (due to weak authentication).

C. Attacks on Protocols Which Connect IoT Devices. In 2013, we have reported in [29] that message authentication code of 4G-LTE can be forged when it conjuncted with its authenticated key agreement (AKA) protocol. The significant effect of this attack is that it may migrate to future 5G which designates to connect IoT devices, since 5G will adopt 4G-LTE's AKA and cipher suites [4]. The attack works together with the man-in-the-middle (MITM) attacks. An MITM attacker first records all user data messages and control messages, including the authentication and key agreement (AKA) messages. When this attacker observes the package he wants to forge, he shuts down the radio of the victim and then turns it on. The MITM attacker uses the recorded AKA messages to conduct a replay attack. In the AKA protocol, mobile devices are not required to verify whether the random number has been received before or not. They only check the freshness of radio resource control sequence number (RRC SQN). However, in some cases, we can make the RRC SQN wrap around. Thus, the victim believes it is talking to the real network.

Notice that the AKA is claimed to be mutually authenticated. The user equipment (UE) proves its identity to the mobility management entity (MME) by replaying to the challenge from the MME. However, since the UE does not send the challenge to the MME, the MME can prove itself only by transmitting the valid messages protected by the correct session key in the succeeding communication. This enables the replay attack. Such an attack makes the UE accepting the fake MME. Generally, the attacker can get nothing from the replay attack, because he still cannot get the key. However, in this case, it forces the IV to repeat, so a meaningful MAC can be forged.

Four years later, in 2017, Vanhoef and Piessens [28] found that WiFi systems suffered a similar attack to the attack described above for 4G-LTE, i.e., forcing IV repeated in the IEEE 802.1X 4 way authentication and key establishment by applying a man-in-the-middle attack.

2.2 Law and Standardization Efforts

California just became the first state with an *Internet of Things cybersecurity law* (Sep 28, 2018). It states that starting on January 1st, 2020, any manufacturer of a device that connects "directly or indirectly" to the internet must equip it with "reasonable" security features, designed to prevent unauthorized access, modification, or information disclosure. The most improving part is that the law requests a unique password for each device when they will connect to the internet!

The second is the event of NIST Lightweight Crypto Standardization competition for low-end IoT devices, which was initialized in 2017 [24]. It announced the call-for-submission for the standardization of lightweight cryptographic primitives to protect IoT devices in April 2018 where the 128-bit security is minimal requirement and submissions are due in Feb. 2019. Note that ISO has the initiative to standardize lightweight cryptographic primitives for several years now, see [13].

3 Classification of IoT Devices

In this section, we first introduce IoT devices and how they can be connected to Internet. Then we conclude why lightweight cryptography is needed for implementing security mechanisms. According to the complexity of transmitter and receiver (Tx/Rx) structures, we may classify the IoT devices or cyber physical devices [2] into the following three classes.

- Single Tx/Rx pairs, such as GPS receivers, RFID tags [3], cameras, etc.
- Single input and single output (SISO) devices: BlueTooth or BlueTooth Low Energy (BLE), ZigBee [1], NB-IoT, etc.
- More complicated structures, i.e., multiple input multiple output (MIMO) devices, such as WiFi, 4G-LTE, 5G and beyond, Wi-MAX, etc.

In Tables 1, 2 and 3, we provide their communication protocols, operation frequencies, multiple access methods and possible applications. For a more detailed list of IoT devices, the reader is referring to [2, 26].

Table 1. IoT devices with simple Tx/Rx

Communication protocol	Spectrum	Trans. rate and Trans. range	Multiple access	Applications
RFID tags	125–135 KHz	5–98 Kbps, <50 cm	Pure Aloha	Low: smart cards, ticketing, tagging, access control
	13.56 MHz	~106 Kbps, ~1 m	F-TDMA	High: anti-theft, supply chain, indexing
	866–960 MHz	~115 Kbps, ~2–7 m	CSMA/CA	UHF: vehicle ID, supply Chain, indexing, access/security
NFC	13.56 MHz	106–424 Kbps, < 20 cm	Single service coupling	Mobile commerce, bootstrap setups, social networking, identification
Wireless cameras	900 MHz, 2.4/5.8 GHz	1.5–150 Mbps, <4800 m	CSMA/CA	Surveillance, video streaming
GPS	Spectrum: 1575.42 (L1), 1227.6 (L2), 1176.45 (L5) MHz			Location service

3.1 Why Lightweight Crypto?

According to the above classifications, IoT devices are distinguished from general computing platforms in both their structure and behaviour. They have small limited memory and computation resources, compared with their counterpart, servers, and are used in a specific application domain, e.g., automotive on board unit, Electronic Product Code (EPC) tags, and sensors, actuators, etc. They also use specialized network protocols to communicate wirelessly with back-end data-aggregation and computing servers, e.g. RFID (EPC and NFC), ZigBee,

Table 2. SISO IoT devices

Communication protocol	Spectrum	Trans. rate and Trans. range	Multiple access	Applications
ZigBee	2.4 GHz/866 MHz	20–250 Kbps, ~40 m	CSMA/CA	Smart home, physical security, medical devices (including implantable devices) smart meter, home automation
BlueTooth 3.0	2.4 GHz	~25 Mbps, ~10 m	TDMA	Wearable electronics, peripherals, device pairing, vehicle entertainment
BLE	2.4 GHz	~1 Mbps, >100 m	TDMA	Medical devices, wearable electronics, sensor networks, electronic leashing
UWB	>500 MHz	~100 Mbps, ~30 m	TDMA, CDMA	Video streaming, wireless displays, wireless printing/scanning (WPS), file transfers, peer-to-peer (P2P) connections

Bluetooth/BLE, 4G-LTE or 5G, WiFi, etc. (see Tables 1, 2 and 3). In Table 4, we emphasize the security constrains in some applications.

Nevertheless, a standard cryptography aimed for securing Internet communication may not be suitable for IoT applications. We will discuss this deeply in the next section.

4   Evolution of Lightweight Cryptography for IoT

In the literature, metrics for what constitutes a lightweight cryptographic design have been studied. More precisely, researchers have investigated throughput, power consumption, latency, but most importantly hardware area. In fact, it is long commonly set in the literature that an upper bound of 2000 GE (gate equivalents) hardware area is what defines a lightweight design [8,19]. Such a bound is derived from passive RFID tags whose areas range between 1000 and 10000 GE, out of which, a maximum of 20% is to be used for all security functionalities [19]. Note that although lightweight applications span over a spectrum of devices which vary from highly constrained in terms of area and power consumption such as EPC tags [3,19] and implantable medical devices, to less constrained ones such as vehicular embedded system where latency may be the most important metric [20], the 2000 GE bound is one of the design criteria for a lightweight cryptographic primitive.

From those practices, we understand that lightweight cryptography lies in the interdisciplinary areas of electrical engineering, cryptography and computer science. Hence, we single out the criteria below for a cipher qualified as a lightweight primitive [7].

Table 3. MIMO IoT devices

Communication protocol	Spectrum	Transmission rate and Trans. range	Multiple access	Applications
WiFi	2.4/5.8 GHz	50–320 Mbps, ~100 m	CSMA/CA	Internet access points (AP), video streaming, wireless displays, WPS, file transfers, P2P connections
Wi-Max	2–11 GHz	~70 Mbps, ~50 km	OFDMA	Portable internet AP, smart meters, air traffic communications, smart cities, VoIP
3G	700–3500 MHz (UMTS), 450–2100 MHz (CDMA)	<2.4 Mbps, 5–70 km	TD-CDMA, CDMA	GPS services, high-speed data (emails, maps, directions, News, shopping, e-commerce, interactive gaming, etc.)
4G-LTE	400 MHz– 3.5 GHz	300 Mbps (D), 75 Mbps (U), 2–103 km	OFDMA (D), SC-FDMA (U)	Video streaming, mobile Internet, telecommunications, ubiquitous computing with location intelligence
5G and beyond	Up to 90 GHz	Up to 1 Gbps, 2–150 km	Various	Supporting IoT, smart city, industrial automation

D = downlink and U = uplink

Table 4. Bit security, and the corresponding dedicated GE area and cost in applications using common communication protocols

	Trans. rate	Bit security	Sec. area (approx)	Cost (approx)
Internet	10 Gbps	128–512	200 kGE	$50
BLE	1 Mbps	128	40 kGE	$2
ZigBee	20–250 Kbps	128	10 kGE	$0.1
NFC	106–424 Kbps	128	5 kGE	$0.01
EPC	26.7–128 Kbps	80	2 kGE	$0.01

4.1 Criteria of Lightweight Cryptography

Definition 1 *(The requirements of lightweight cryptography (LWC)). A cryptographic primitive is said to be* lightweight *if the hardware area of the implementation is less than 2000 GE, its power consumption is very small and it supports a sustained throughput of 1 bit per clock cycle at a clock speed of 2 MHz. For a cryptographic primitive together with a mode (e.g., authenticated encryption), the GE requirement will be loosened up to 3000 GE.*

From this definition, we may bound how small we can do given the security and throughout requirements.

Definition 2 *(Cryptographic minimal design). A cryptographic algorithm is said to be a* minimal design *if the design with well justified building components has minimal overhead for providing multiple cryptographic functionalities including encryption, hashing, authentication, and pseudorandom bit generation without compromising the security and decreasing the throughput.*

The key point of the design of lightweight cryptographic primitives is to balance trade-offs among three requirements: security strength, the hardware area, and throughput.

4.2   LWC Development and Reverse Engineering

At the earlier time, the effort of the research was concentrated at low-cost implementations of AES (Advanced Encryption Standard), hash-based RFID privacy enhancements, and some non cryptographic approaches, like minimalist. Only in recent years, it is devoted to investigate new cryptographic schemes under the constraints of hardware area, key sizes and power consumption.

Along this approach, there are a number of lightweight ciphers which were designed secretly in the industrial community for low-cost applications (violating Kerckhoffs' principle published in 1883) and publicly released by reverse engineering approaches. Examples include

- Keeloq (Microchip Technologies Inc., designed in 1985) used for car immobilizer and in garage doors (designed in 1985, released and broken in 2007);
- MIFARE RFID tag encryption algorithm (2008), cipher in HID iClass cards (2012);
- GMR (2012) in satellite telecommunication systems;
- A5/1 (1991) in GSM cellular communication networks; and
- RC4 (not lightweight) for web, gmail (used until 2015), and many Internet applications.

All those ciphers, except for RC4, use linear feedback shift register (LFSR) based structures.

4.3   Privacy Preserving Entity Authentication for RFID Systems

RFID systems are the first which demand to use lightweight ciphers for privacy preserving entity authentication. The link between RFID readers and back-end database is assumed to be secured by known security mechanisms (e.g., TLS and IPSec), and wireless links between RFID readers and RFID tags are insecure. An entity authentication protocol is a challenge-response protocol, as shown below.

Privacy preserving authentication in RFID

Reader (K) $\xrightarrow{\quad ch \quad}$ Tag (K)

$\xleftarrow{\quad res \quad}$ $res = Enc_k(ch)$

A general approach for preserving privacy of devices is that device's ID is not sent. In order to verify the validity of the response, the back-end server is required to do an exhaustive search in the space of the pairing ID and key to identify the tag, therefore, verifies the device's response. So, this imposes the request that the implementation of a cipher at server side should be of high speed (see our work [15] for details about this argument). In addition to the protocol design, this puts another dimension of challenges for securing IoT which requests an asymmetric design for underlying cryptographic primitives having the smaller hardware area of the implementation for device sides and high speed software implementation for server sides as well.

The decision of the success of an entity authentication protocol can be implemented by two different methods.

1. *Deterministic verification*: Use an LWC primitive to generate an authentication tag (e.g., ISO/IEC 9798 2 or 3-pass mutual authentication protocol).
2. *Probabilistic verification*: Use a new hard problem, learning parity with noise (LPN), e.g., HB like protocols [17,19] as well as our work [23], which can resist all known attacks on LPN based entity authentication.

4.4   Security Associations in IoT

In order to have a shared key ahead of communication, currently, in the most of IoT applications, a master key is embedded into an IoT device during its manufacture. In near future, elliptic curve cryptography will be deployed as there are four curves that have been recommended for NFC, ZigBee, and VANETs [16] a few years ago. The authentication for establishing an authenticated channel for key sharing is to use the certificate based authentication. This is the same approach as is now used in TLS. However, this requests public-key infrastructure (PKI), which may be not suitable for many IoT applications. Thus, this remains a challenging problem.

5   Examples of LWC

In this section, we introduce an evolutional process from lightweight ciphers Simon and Speck to Simeck to sLiSCP/sLiSCP-light.

5.1   Simon and Simeck

A Feistel structure in block cipher design is a two-stage NLFSR with input. The most noticeable cipher in 2-stage NLFSR is DES, developed in 1976 which has 56 bit key. In 2013, a group of the researchers from NSA (National Security Agency, USA) published a paper, called their ciphers *Simon and Speck* [9]. Simon family is optimized in hardware and Speck, optimized in software (both are submitted to the ISO for possible standardization [13]). Shortly after that, we have found a way to further decrease Simon's hardware footprint with slightly decreasing security, namely, *Simeck* [30] (i.e., the design is aimed at extracting good features from both Simon and Speck).

The round function of both Simon and Simeck is given in Fig. 2 where (x_0, x_1) is an initial state and the feedback function is a simplest quadratic function

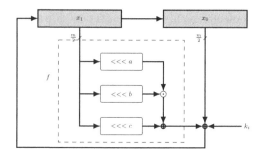

Fig. 2. Simeck round function as an 2-NLFSR with the input key k_i and $(a, b, c) = (1, 8, 2)$ for Simon and $(a, b, c) = (0, 5, 1)$ for Simeck.

where $<<<$ is the (circular) left shift operator. For encryption, (x_0, x_1) is loaded as a plaintext, and the ciphertext is the internal state after r rounds. Simon (2013)/Simeck (2015) have register sizes $m/2$ where $m = 32, 48, 64$ and r varies according to different m. The hardware implementations of the Simeck family are shown in Table 5. Currently, they are the smallest ciphers compared with those having the same parameters including Simon family.

Table 5. Performance of hardware implementations of Simeck

Size Simeck	Tech (nm)	Area (GEs)	Throughput@100 KHz (Kbps)	Power@100 KHz (μW)
32/64	130	**505**	5.6	0.417
32/64	65	**454**	5.6	1.292
48/96	130	**715**	5.0	0.576
48/96	65	**645**	5.0	1.805
64/128	130	**924**	4.2	0.754
64/128	65	**828**	4.2	2.304

5.2   sLiSCP/sLiSCP-light Families

Simeck is a block cipher family. So we need to use modes to provide authenticity. Currently, the main approaches to add authentication to a block cipher are CBC MAC (cipher-block-chain message authentication code) or GCM (polynomial evaluations). Both are very costly. In the search of minimal designs, we find that permutation-based sponge duplexing [10] is well suited for a minimal cryptographic design and thus, we resolve to designing a lightweight family of permutations to efficiently provide multiple cryptographic functionalities with one circuit. This results in the two families of LWC, i.e., sLiSCP: S̲imeck-based Permutations for L̲ightweight S̲ponge C̲ryptographic P̲rimitives and sLiSCP-light. For the details in this subsection, the reader is referring to [6,7].

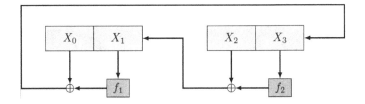

Fig. 3. 2-branches GFS in sLiSCP/sLiSCP-light designs.

Both sLiSCP and sLiSCP-light can be used in a unified sponge duplex construction in order to provide (authenticated) encryption and hashing functionalities. The sLiSCP family of permutations adopts two of the most efficient and extensively analyzed cryptographic structures, namely a 4-subblock Type-2 Generalized Feistel-like Structure (GFS) [11,25], and a round-reduced unkeyed version of the Simeck encryption algorithm [30]. A Type 2 GFS, a general nonlinear feedback shift register (NLFSR) generator in Galois mode, consists of multiple branches of Feistel structures, which is shown in Fig. 3.

Table 6. Branch size: m, state size: $b = 4\,m$, # Simeck rounds: u, and # GFS steps: s.

Permutation (b-bit)	Subblock width m	Rounds u	Steps s	Total # rounds $(u \cdot s)$
sLiSCP/sLiSCP-light-192	48	6	18/12	108/72
sLiSCP/sLiSCP-light-256	64	8	18/12	144/96

Table 7. The performance of hardware implementations of sLiSCP/sLiSCP-light

State size (b bits)	Security (bits)	Process (nm)	Area (GE)	
			sLiSCP	sLiSCP-light
192	80–112	65	2153	1820
		130	2318	1892
256	128	65	2833	2397
		130	3040	2500

In sLiSCP/sLiSCP-light designs, both f_1 and f_2 are identical and implemented by an unkeyed Simeck round function with multiple rounds. Their specifications are given in Table 6.

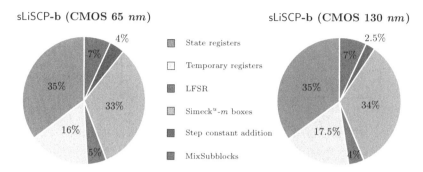

Fig. 4. Resource allocation for sLiSCP/sLiSCP-light

The sLiSCP-light is obtained by turning sLiSCP to a partial substitute permutation network (SPN) structure to get 16% reduction in HW footprint, better diffusion and algebraic properties. We have implemented the sLiSCP/sLiSCP-light instances in the CMOS 65 and 130 nm technology. The performance is shown in Table 7 and the resource allocation for different operations in the implementation is shown in Fig. 4.

We can provide multi-cryptographic primitives using a single sLiSCP permutation as a unified round function in the sponge, i.e., to provide an *all-in-one module* including authenticated encryption, stream cipher, pseudorandom bit generation, MAC and hash function.

6   Concluding Remarks

IoT is bringing an exciting new era of the digital world as well as nightmare due to their security concerns for civilian applications. In this survey, we presented vulnerabilities and attacks on recent IoT products, and pointed out that in all of those attacks, attackers exploited the weakness of the underlying cryptographic primitives including those malware attacks. We have walked through the path for the development of lightweight cryptography for securing IoT. Now we present some possible future research problems.

Future Research Problems

(a) How to balance the tradeoffs between *security, throughout and hardware footprint* for lightweight cryptographic primitives?

(b) How to balance the tradeoffs between *usability and security* (e.g., relay attacks occur because reducing the communication cost for user easiness, in 4G-LTE message authentication in data field is not required, $\cdots$), and *safety and security* (e.g., the emergency case in a smart hospital)?

(c) How to implement *machining learning* for efficiency of IoT as well as for detection of malicious behaviours in IoT?

(d) Can *physical layer security* (i.e., using signals, channels, antennas, ⋯) solve some problems in IoT without using crypto (e.g., in control area networks, see some solutions from our earlier work in [12])?

(e) Recently, there are a number of work to investigate blockchain based IoT security mechanisms (e.g., our attempt on using blockchain to solve ownership transfer problem in supply chains [5]). However, how to solve the *scalability and privacy* of blockchains for IoT applications?

References

1. Zigbee smart energy profile specification (sep) 1.2, revision 4. ZigBee Alliance, December 2014
2. CPS PWG draft cyber-physical systems (CPS) framework. National Institute of Standards and Technology (NIST), September 2015. https://pages.nist.gov/cpspwg/
3. EPC radio frequency identity protocols class-1 generation-2 UHF RFID protocol for communications at 860mhz-960mhz version 2. EPCglobal Inc., Specification documents, April 2015. https://www.gs1.org/sites/default/files/docs/epc/Gen2_Protocol_Standard.pdf
4. 5G-PPP: Deliverable d2.7 security architecture (final) - 5G-Ensure, August 2018. www.5gensure.eu/sites/default/files/5G-ENSURE_D2.7_Security ArchitectureFinal.pdf
5. AlTawy, R., Gong, G.: *Mesh*: a supply chain solution with locally private transactions. In: Privacy Enhancing Technologies, pending revisions (2018)
6. AlTawy, R., Rohit, R., He, M., Mandal, K., Yang, G., Gong, G.: sLiSCP-light: towards lighter sponge-specific cryptographic permutations. ACM Trans. Embed. Comput. Syst. **17**, 1–26 (2018)
7. AlTawy, R., Rohit, R., He, M., Mandal, K., Yang, G., Gong, G.: Towards a cryptographic minimal design: the sLiSCP family of permutations. IEEE Trans. Comput. **67**, 1341–1358 (2018)
8. Armknecht, F., Hamann, M., Mikhalev, V.: Lightweight authentication protocols on ultra-constrained RFIDs - myths and facts. In: Saxena, N., Sadeghi, A.-R. (eds.) RFIDSec 2014. LNCS, vol. 8651, pp. 1–18. Springer, Cham (2014). https://doi.org/10.1007/978-3-319-13066-8_1
9. Beaulieu, R., Shors, D., Smith, J., Treatman-Clark, S., Weeks, B., Wingers, L.: The SIMON and SPECK families of lightweight block ciphers. Cryptology ePrint Archive, Report 2013/404 (2013). http://eprint.iacr.org/2013/404
10. Bertoni, G., Daemen, J., Peeters, M., Van Assche, G.: Permutation-based encryption, authentication and authenticated encryption. In: DIAC (2012)
11. Bogdanov, A., Shibutani, K.: Generalized feistel networks revisited. Des. Codes Crypt. **66**(1), 75–97 (2013)
12. Chai, Q., Gong, G.: BUPLE: securing passive RFID communication through physical layer enhancements. In: Juels, A., Paar, C. (eds.) RFIDSec 2011. LNCS, vol. 7055, pp. 127–146. Springer, Heidelberg (2012). https://doi.org/10.1007/978-3-642-25286-0_9
13. Chen, L.: Lightweight cryptography standards developed in ISO/IEC SC27 (2016). https://www.nist.gov/sites/default/files/documents/2016/10/17/chen-presentation-lwc2016.pdf

14. Columbus, L.: A roundup of 2018 enterprise Internet of Things forecasts and market estimates (2018)
15. Engels, D., Fan, X., Gong, G., Hu, H., Smith, E.M.: Hummingbird: ultra-lightweight cryptography for resource-constrained devices. In: Sion, R., et al. (eds.) FC 2010. LNCS, vol. 6054, pp. 3–18. Springer, Heidelberg (2010). https://doi.org/10.1007/978-3-642-14992-4_2
16. Fan, X., Gong, G.: Securing NFC with elliptic curve cryptography - challenges and solutions. In: RFIDSec Asia 2013, vol. 11, pp. 97–106 (2013)
17. Hopper, N.J., Blum, M.: Secure human identification protocols. In: Boyd, C. (ed.) ASIACRYPT 2001. LNCS, vol. 2248, pp. 52–66. Springer, Heidelberg (2001). https://doi.org/10.1007/3-540-45682-1_4
18. Juels, A.: RFID security and privacy: a research survey. IEEE J. Sel. Areas Commun. **24**, 381–394 (2006)
19. Juels, A., Weis, S.A.: Authenticating pervasive devices with human protocols. In: Shoup, V. (ed.) CRYPTO 2005. LNCS, vol. 3621, pp. 293–308. Springer, Heidelberg (2005). https://doi.org/10.1007/11535218_18
20. Knežević, M., Nikov, V., Rombouts, P.: Low-latency encryption – is "Lightweight = Light + Wait"? In: Prouff, E., Schaumont, P. (eds.) CHES 2012. LNCS, vol. 7428, pp. 426–446. Springer, Heidelberg (2012). https://doi.org/10.1007/978-3-642-33027-8_25
21. de Koning Gans, G., Hoepman, J.-H., Garcia, F.D.: A practical attack on the MIFARE classic. In: Grimaud, G., Standaert, F.-X. (eds.) CARDIS 2008. LNCS, vol. 5189, pp. 267–282. Springer, Heidelberg (2008). https://doi.org/10.1007/978-3-540-85893-5_20
22. Krebs, B.: Hacked cameras, DVRs powered todays massive internet outage, October 2016. https://krebsonsecurity.com/2016/10/hacked-cameras-dvrs-powered-todays-massive-internet-outage/
23. Li, Z., Gong, G., Qin, Z.: Secure and efficient LCMQ entity authentication protocol. IEEE Trans. Inf. Theory **59**(6), 4042–4054 (2013)
24. McKay, K., Bassham, L., Sönmez Turan, M., Mouha, N.: Report on lightweight cryptography (NISTIR8114) (2017). http://nvlpubs.nist.gov/nistpubs/ir/2017/NIST.IR.8114.pdf
25. Nyberg, K.: Generalized Feistel networks. In: Kim, K., Matsumoto, T. (eds.) ASIACRYPT 1996. LNCS, vol. 1163, pp. 91–104. Springer, Heidelberg (1996). https://doi.org/10.1007/BFb0034838
26. Perera, C., Liu, C., Jayawardena, S.: The emerging Internet of Things marketplace from an industrial perspective: a survey. IEEE Trans. Emerg. Top. Comput. **3**, 585–598 (2005)
27. Ronen, E., Shamir, A., Weingarten, A., O'Flynn, C.: IoT goes nuclear: creating a ZigBee chain reaction. In: 2017 IEEE Symposium on Security and Privacy (SP), pp. 195–212, May 2017
28. Vanhoef, M., Piessens, F.: Key reinstallation attacks: forcing nonce reuse in WPA2. In: CCS 2017, October 2017
29. Wu, T., Gong, G.: The weakness of integrity protection for LTE. In: Sixth ACM Conference on Security and Privacy in Wireless and Mobile Networks (WiSec 2013), Budapest, 17–19 April 2013, pp. 79–88 (2013)
30. Yang, G., Zhu, B., Suder, V., Aagaard, M.D., Gong, G.: The Simeck family of lightweight block ciphers. In: Güneysu, T., Handschuh, H. (eds.) CHES 2015. LNCS, vol. 9293, pp. 307–329. Springer, Heidelberg (2015). https://doi.org/10.1007/978-3-662-48324-4_16

Privacy and Ethical Challenges
in Big Data

Sébastien Gambs(✉)

Université du Québec à Montréal (UQAM), Montreal, Canada
gambs.sebastien@uqam.ca

Abstract. The advent of Big Data coupled with the profiling of users has lead to the development of services and decision-making processes that are highly personalized, but also raise fundamental privacy and ethical issues. In particular, the absence of transparency has lead to the loss of control of individuals on the collection and use on their personal information while making it impossible for an individual to question the decision taken by the algorithm and to make it accountable for it. Nonetheless, transparency is only a prerequisite to be able to analyze the possible biases that personalized algorithms could have (*e.g.*, discriminating against a particular group in the population) and then potentially correct them. In this position paper, I will review in a non-exhaustive manner some of the main privacy and ethical challenges associated with Big Data that have emerged in recent years before highlighting a few approaches that are currently investigated to address these challenges.

Keywords: Big Data · Privacy · Transparency · Interpretability · Fairness

1 Introduction

The democratization of mobile systems and the development of information technologies have been accompanied by a massive increase in the amount and the diversity of data collected about individuals, often referred to as *Big Data*. Beyond the technical definition in terms of five "V's" (*Volume*, *Variety*, *Velocity*, *Variability* and *Veracity*), the main promise offered by the analysis of these large-scale datasets is the possibility to realize inferences with an unprecedented level of accuracy and details. Furthermore, in Machine Learning, the Deep Learning revolution [16] coupled with the access to Big Data has enabled a "quantum leap" in the prediction accuracy in many domains.

However, the collection and analysis of Big Data also raises serious privacy and ethical issues. In particular, while privacy risks have existed for a long time due to the sharing of personal data, Big Data magnifies these risks and makes

Sébastien Gambs is supported by the Canada Research Chair program as well as by a Discovery Grant and a Discovery Accelerator Supplement Grant from NSERC.

© Springer Nature Switzerland AG 2019
N. Zincir-Heywood et al. (Eds.): FPS 2018, LNCS 11358, pp. 17–26, 2019.
https://doi.org/10.1007/978-3-030-18419-3_2

them more difficult to grasp and predict due to the possibility of combining data from different sources while also bringing new risks related to the inference attacks that are possible against models learned from Big Data (Sect. 2). Privacy is only one side of the coin as other ethical issues associated to the analysis of Big Data should be addressed such as the Transparency, Interpretability and Fairness of the algorithms that are learned from this data (Sect. 3). Finally, it is also important to acknowledge that these challenges should be tackled in an integrated manner due to the connections between the different underlying ethical values (Sect. 4).

2   Privacy

As we have seen in the wake of the Facebook-Cambridge Analytica scandal, privacy is not only a fundamental right protected by legislations around the world, such as the recent European General Data Protection Regulation (GDPR) as well as the future California Consumer Privacy Act, but also an essential ingredient to democracy. First, *it is important to acknowledge that most of Big Data is actually personal data* that are explicitly produced by individuals or generated by their behaviors online or in the physical world, and thus directly relates to privacy. For example, Big Data issued from existing and emerging technologies include mobility data, health and genomic data, social networks or data captured by IoT (*Internet of Things*) devices. Most of these datasets cannot be shared directly without endangering the privacy of the individuals that have contributed to this data. This limits both our ability to analyze such data to derive useful information and slows down the innovative services that could emerge from such data.

For instance, in the context of large-scale mobility analytics the D4D (*Data for Development*) challenge[1] is a concrete example in which the sharing of mobility data (here in the form of *Call Details Records* - CDRs - generated by phone usage) can be used by scientists to derive useful knowledge. Indeed, these CDRs have a high value [3], not only for scientific research, but also for society in general and for the economy. However, learning the location of an individual is one of the greatest threats against privacy because it can be used to derive other personal information regarding this individual (such as home and place of work, main interests, social network and so forth) [10]. Thus, the sharing of such data is limited and is usually only granted under restricted conditions (*i.e.*, the signature of a non-disclosure agreement), although other models for the privacy-preserving conscientious of mobile data are possible[2].

Genomic data is another paramount example, both due to the sensitivity of this type of data but also the potential for scientific advances in health and related areas [21]. In addition of privacy risks related to the individual concerned, such as inference on genetic diseases, tendency to develop particular health problems or leaking of information about ethnic origin, disclosing his genomic data

---

[1] http://www.d4d.orange.com/en/Accueil.
[2] https://www.nature.com/articles/sdata2018286.

also impact other members of the families through the possibility to reconstruct the genomics of relatives.

The main impacts of Big Data on privacy can be summarized as follows:

1. *Magnification of the privacy risks due to the increase in volume and diversity of the personal data collected and the computational power to process them.* In contrast to the context a few years in which data was siloed and thus the possibility of cross-referencing data were limited, the situation is very much different today as the tendency is more towards the pooling of information coming from different sources into data lakes. For instance, Google has changed in privacy policy in 2012 to enable the sharing of data among the different services it runs while previously the data collected and processed by each service was governed by its own terms of use[3]. In addition, the quantity and diversity of data available has also increased significantly and nourished by phenomenons such as smart cities, the open data movement, IoT or the quantified-self movement.

2. *Often data collected about individuals are "re-used" for a different purpose without asking their consent.* An important use of Big Data is for exploratory analysis in which by definition the data scientist does not know necessarily in advance what he will find in the data. Thus, classical approaches to privacy protection such as consent-based mechanisms do not really make sense anymore as it is impossible to foresee in advance all the possible secondary uses of the data.

3. *The inferences that are possible with Big Data are much more fine-grained and precise than before.* The possibility of inferences as well as their accuracy has significantly increased due to the availability of Big Data to the point that many services can now be highly personalized according to the profile of the user himself, and not simply with respect to the main category he is clustered in. For instance, the analysis of data collected from quantified-self devices opens the possibility to predict the pregnancy of a person or a particular health condition even before this person is herself aware of this.

4. *The massive release of data without taking into account the privacy aspect is likely to lead to a major privacy breach.* Indeed once data is disclosed, it is there forever. In particular, even if privacy legislations such as the GDPR guarantees a *right to erasure* to individuals with respect to the data collected by service providers, there is no magical solution that will remove all the copies of the data that could have been spread around the four corners of the Web once the data is released. As a consequence, caution should be the default approach when disclosing personal data, such as for example when opening the data of inhabitants or citizens.

The relevant literature on Privacy and Big Data is quite extensive considering that privacy has been a very active research domain for the last two decades and it would be illusory to cover it in this paper. In a nutshell, the proposed

---

[3] https://www.theverge.com/2012/3/1/2835250/google-unified-privacy-policy-change-take-effect.

approaches can be split between techniques that have been developed to protect privacy in the online and the offline contexts.

Basically, the *online context considers the real-time analysis of data* in which for instance the data is distributed among several participants that do not trust each other to the point of directly sharing their data but are willing to collaborate to conduct a joint analysis on the data (*e.g.*, by learning a classifier on their joint inputs). Cryptography [12] is one of the fundamental ingredients to implement Privacy Enhancing Technologies (PETs) [11]. For instance, secure multiparty computation can be used for computing data mining tasks in a distributed manner such that only the output of the analysis is revealed and nothing else (including the private inputs of participants) [18]. While the generic techniques in this area were generally costly in terms of computation and communication costs, there has been a strong effort in the last decade to improve their efficiency as well as developing specialized protocols that are dedicated to specific data analysis tasks. Privacy-preserving machine learning is a very important and active area of research, but hereafter we focus on the *offline context, which corresponds to the situation in which the data of users has been collected and must be sanitized before its release* (*e.g.*, before sharing or publishing it) or before it is given as input to an algorithm to limit the subsequent privacy risks.

Since the seminal work of Sweeney more than two decades ago that has shown that 87% of the American population can be uniquely re-identified based on a combination of three attributes (namely date of birth, gender and ZIP code) and the introduction of the k-anonymity privacy model [27], an important part of the privacy research has focused on the development of privacy models and sanitization mechanisms that can reach the guarantees as defined by the privacy model (see [9] for a survey). The main objective of a sanitization mechanism is to modify the dataset (*e.g.*, by introducing some uncertainty or removing some part) before its publication to ensure that breaching the privacy of an individual is harder when working on the sanitized dataset than it is on the original one. The notion of differential privacy [6], which was introduced in the context of private analysis on statistical databases, has gained widespread adoption in the privacy community in recent years. The main guarantee provided by differential privacy is that for any analysis performed on a dataset satisfying this property, adding or removing a single individual from the dataset will not significantly change the probability of an output of the analysis. Thus, the information that the adversary can gain about a specific individual by observing the output of the analysis is limited and can be formally characterized in terms of a privacy parameter ϵ. In addition, differential privacy has been proved to provide compositionality, which allows to bound the global amount of information that will be leaked by several analyses made on the same data. This property is essential within the context of Big Data in which datasets coming from many sources will be gather together.

Challenge 01 (Privacy evaluation of large-scale datasets). *Despite the fact that anonymization has been an active field of research for a long time, for many domains a fundamental question remains on how to evaluate the privacy risks incurred by users before publishing (possibly sanitized) large-scale datasets,* *in particular with respect to the inferences that can be performed on specific sensitive information.*

Most of the current existing privacy models measure the protection level provided in terms of an abstract privacy parameter (*e.g.*, k for k-anonymity [27] or ϵ for differential privacy [6]). However, a complementary aspect that should be investigated more is how to relate the value of a privacy parameter to the possible inferences that can be performed from the disclosed data. In particular, for each type of data (*e.g.*, mobility or genomics data), it is important to conduct a thorough study assessing how well the existing privacy models fare with respect to state-of-the-art inference attacks. Due to their difference in structure and characteristics, each domain often also requires the design of novel inference attacks that are specific both in terms of the information they can predict but also how they work (*e.g.*, inference methods for exploiting the spatiotemporal nature of mobility traces are very different than the ones working on genomic data). Afterwards, based on the findings of this study, novel privacy models integrating the semantic inferences that can be drawn out of the disclosed data should be conceived. To realize this, one possible approach would be to design of a privacy model in which the value of the privacy parameter directly reflects the amount and sensitivity of personal information that can be inferred from the data released (as quantified by the inference attacks). This type of model would really be very useful for practitioners to relate the value of the privacy parameter to the privacy guarantees provided, and thus reduces the gap between the theory and practice of anonymization. Nonetheless, this "meaningful" privacy model should also aim to achieve strong composition properties (like differential privacy) to be able to bound the effect on privacy of several data releases. Another interesting approach for the empirical evaluation of sanitization methods and inference attacks is to organize competitions open to the community in which teams of researchers can propose novel sanitization methods for a particular task as well as inference attacks aiming at countering these sanitization methods (*e.g.*, by re-identifying a record that was previously anonymized).

Challenge 02 (Privacy assessment of machine learning models). *In addition to the inferences that can be made from the data itself, it is also important to understand how much the output of the learning algorithm itself (*e.g., *the classifier) leaks information about the input data it was trained on.*

One possible avenue to tackle this challenge is to evaluate how much of the input data can be reconstructed from the classifier either by reversing the learning algorithm [7] (if its structure allows it) either in the white-box setting (*i.e.*, in which the description of the classifier is known) or the black-box (*i.e.*, in which it is only possible to interact with the classifier by querying with a particular input to receive the associated output). Another possible inference attack against a machine learning model is a membership attack [26] in which the objective of the adversary is to be able to predict whether the profile of a particular individual (which is known to him) was in the dataset used to train the model. Generally, this inference is deemed problematic if revealing the membership of the profile to this database leads to a learning a sensitive information (*e.g.*, that the individual is part of a cohort of patients for a particular disease). This line of research is still in its infancy and much work remains to be done, in particular with respect to how to prevent these inference attacks.

3   Ethical Issues

As mentioned previously, machine learning has now a central role as most of the personalization algorithms are now learnt from data rather than being written by programmers. As a consequence, the machine learning community has also started recently to investigate the concept of Fairness, Accountability and Transparency through the organization since 2014 of an annual specialized workshop dedicated to this issue[4] in more recently through the creation of the FAT* conference[5], which follows a highly multidisciplinary approach to address some of the ethical challenges highlighted in the following.

Challenge 03 (Transparency of personalization processes). *Characterizing the personal information collected about an individual and how this data is transformed before being exploited by the personalization algorithm is the first step before being able to perform algorithm auditing for other ethical values.*

To complement the existing PETs, more recently the concept of TETs (*Transparency Enhancing Technologies*) was introduced to precisely increase the transparency of information technologies [15]. In addition, the study of profiling techniques used to track web users for various recommendation and personalization goals has attracted attention from the computer science community for more than a decade [1]. However, a unified view, driven by privacy concerns, of how the data is exploited by these techniques is missing. Thus, being able to "open the black-box" of personalization algorithms remains a challenging issue [22]. As often the code source of these algorithms might not be directly available (*e.g.*, because it is proprietary or is only accessible as a black-box), some preliminary works have investigated how to lift the opacity of personalization systems starting with the work of data journalists that have investigated how systems such as Uber personalized the price proposed to a customer [4]. Another possible approach is to take a machine learning view of the problem by learning a model (*e.g.*, classifier) approximating how the algorithm works from a training set composed of examples of inputs (*i.e.*, user profiles) and outputs (*i.e.*, personalized service or information). To obtain samples of inputs/outputs, one possibility is to "probe" the personalization system with artificially generated profiles [17] or to rely on a collaborative approach (*e.g.*, through a crowdsourcing platform). Opening the algorithms to the scrutiny of the public is usually not an end but rather only a first step make them more accountable.

---

[4] http://www.fatml.org.
[5] https://fatconference.org.

Challenge 04 (Explainability of machine learning models). *The complex design of machine learning models makes it difficult to understand and explain their predictions, which may lead to a lack of trust if their predictions is used in a decision-making process that has a significant impact on humans.*

Deep learning is a typical example of a opaque model as the structure of the classifier, which is composed of many layers of neural networks, makes the decision of the algorithm difficult to interpret [19]. This is highly problematic as their decisions can have a high impact on individuals, and thus might lead to a lack of control in their digital life, which has been coined as the "governmentality of algorithms" by Antoinette Rouvroy [24]. To ensure the transparency and explainability in algorithmic decision processes, several initiatives have emerged for regulating the use of machine learning models. For instance, in Europe, the new General Data Protection Regulation has a provision requiring explanations for the decisions of machine learning models that have a significant impact on individuals [13].

In the context of machine learning, interpretability can be defined as the ability to explain or to provide the meaning in understandable terms to a human [5]. Examples of interpretable models found in the literature include linear models, decision trees, rule lists as well as rule sets. The explainability requirement can be achieved by two common approaches, namely transparent-box design and black-box explanation. The former consists in building by design transparent models, thus requiring the cooperation of the entity responsible for the training and usage of the model. In contrast, the latter involves an adversarial setting in which the black-box model, whose internal logic is hidden to the auditor, is reversed-engineered to create an interpretable surrogate model. While transparent-box design seems to be the best approach as far as interpretability of decisions is concerned, black-box explanation is sometimes the only available option.

Current techniques for providing black-box explanations include model explanation, outcome explanation and model inspection [14]. Model explanation consists in building an interpretable model to explain the whole logic of the black box while outcome explanation only cares about providing a local explanation of a specific decision. Finally, model inspection consists of all the techniques that can help to understand (*e.g.*, through visualizations or quantitative arguments) the influence of the attributes of the input on the black-box decision.

Once a good representation of how the algorithm works has been learnt, it becomes possible to investigate if this algorithm has a bias and its consequence for users. For example in application domain such as predictive recruiting, one of the main benefit of automating the process advertise by companies is that the recruitment process will become more objective because the machine is not influenced by the biases and stereotypes that a human recruiter could have. However, if the data used to train the learning algorithm is historically biased then there is a good chance that the model outputted by the algorithm will also be biased. For example, in the case of a credit scoring algorithm, some ethnic group in the population might have to pay a higher rate for a loan because they are considered at risk. Even if the ethnicity of a user is not used as an input (anti-discrimination laws might forbid to ask it directly), it might be inferred indirectly from other attributes such as the ZIP code [25].

Challenge 05 (Quantifying and redressing discrimination). *Due to their prevalence in our society, it is important to investigate how to measure and quantify the bias of algorithms learned from Big Data, in particular with respect to the possible risks of discrimination against subgroups of the population, and propose solutions to correct the unwarranted biases.*

The analysis of the algorithms must be performed jointly with that of the data used to learn these algorithms. To quantify discrimination, one possibility is to look at existing metrics that can be found in the computer science literature or to develop new metrics in collaboration with legal and sociological researchers [23]. Discrimination laws that protect specific type of sensitive data (*e.g.*, religion, political opinion or ethnic origin) sometimes specify very concrete criteria that could be used to assess the bias of the algorithm. Moreover, sociological studies enable to better clarify the sometimes "fuzzy" border between legitimate personalization and unfair discrimination. One difficult challenge is the fact that discrimination can also occur in many ways [29]. For instance as mentioned previously, even if an attribute such as the religion is not directly asked to the user, it could be deduced from observing that he visits a place of worship on a regular basis (similarly the ethnic origin can be partially inferred from the genomic data). Discriminatory decisions may also result from mistakes in the data or wrong predictions.

There are many different definitions of fairness in the literature [28] and the choice of the appropriate definition really depends on the context. For instance, one natural approach for defining fairness is the concept of *individual fairness*, which states that individuals that are similar except for the sensitive attribute should be treated similarly and thus should receive similar decisions. This notion relates to the legal concept of disparate treatment, which occurs if the decision process was made based on sensitive attributes. This definition is only relevant when discrimination is due to a prejudice caused by the decision process and therefore cannot be used in the situation in which the objective is to address the biases in the data. In contrast to individual fairness, *group fairness* relies on statistic of outcomes of the subgroups indexed by and can be quantified in several ways, such as the demographic parity and the equalized odds.

Afterwards, the ultimate objective of this key activity is to propose meaningful ways to reduce the bias, and thus the discrimination. In recent years, many approaches have been developed to improve the fairness of machine learning algorithms. Most of these tech-niques can be classified into three families of approaches: namely (1) the *pre-processing approach* in which fairness is achieved by changing the characteristics of the input data (*e.g.*, by suppressing unwarranted correlations with the protected attribute), (2) the *algorithmic modification approach* (also sometimes called constrained optimization) in which the learning algorithm is adapted to ensure that it is fair by design and (3) the *post-processing* approach that modifies the output of the learning algorithm to increase the level of fairness. We refer the interested reader [8] to for a recent survey comparing the different fairness enhancing methods.

4   Conclusion

In this paper, we have discussed separately different privacy and ethical challenges related to Big Data. Nonetheless, in order to achieve a responsible and socially acceptable use of Big Data in our Information Society, it is important to address jointly these challenges due to the existing connections between them. For example, to be able to audit a machine learning model for his potential biases, it is often easier (but not necessary mandatory) to have access to its structure or at least an approximation of the classifier, thus highlighting the strong link between interpretability and fairness. In addition, as we have seen in the previous section one of the proposed approach to enhance fairness relies on the use of anonymization methods thus showing a connection between privacy and fairness.

However, a fundamental open question is to investigate whether the achievements of these different objectives is always a positive sum game. Indeed, as shown by recent works [20], aiming for interpretability can open the door to inference attacks against privacy. In addition, it is possible that under the excuse of making its learning models more interpretable and transparent, a company might be tempted to perform *fairwashing*, which can be defined as promoting the false impression that the models used by the company respect some particular ethical values while it might not be the case. An example of such a risk has been studied in [2] in which the authors demonstrate that it is possible to use black-box explanation to rationalize the decisions of a predictive model that is particularly discriminating towards a particular subpopulation.

References

1. Acar, G., Eubank, C., Englehardt, S., Juárez, M., Narayanan, A., Díaz, C.: The Web never forgets: persistent tracking mechanisms in the wild. In: ACM Conference on Computer and Communications Security, pp. 674–689 (2014)
2. Aïvodji, U., Arai, H., Fortineau, O., Gambs, S., Hara, S., Tapp, A.: Fairwashing: the risk of rationalization. CoRR abs/1901.09749 (2019)
3. Blondel, V.D., Decuyper, A., Krings, G.: A survey of results on mobile phone datasets analysis. EPJ Data Sci. 4(1), 10 (2015)
4. Diakopoulos, N.: Algorithmic accountability reporting: on the investigation of black boxes. Tow Center (2014)
5. Doshi-Velez, F., Kim, B.: A Roadmap for a Rigorous Science of Interpretability. CoRR abs/1702.08608 (2017)
6. Dwork, C.: Differential privacy. ICALP 2, 1–12 (2006)
7. Fredrikson, M., Lantz, E., Jha, S., Lin, S., Page, D., Ristenpart, T.: Privacy in pharmacogenetics: an end-to-end case study of personalized warfarin dosing. In: USENIX Security Symposium, pp. 17–32 (2014)

8. Friedler, S.A., Scheidegger, C., Venkatasubramanian, S., Choudhary, S., Hamilton, E.P., Roth, D.: A comparative study of fairness-enhancing interventions in machine learning. CoRR abs/1802.04422 (2018)
9. Fung, B.C.M., Wang, K., Chen, R., Yu, P.S.: Privacy-preserving data publishing: a survey of recent developments. ACM Comput. Surv. **42**(4), 14:1–14:53 (2010)
10. Gambs, S., Killijian, M.-O., del Prado Cortez, M.N.: Show me how you move and i will tell you who you are. Trans. Data Privacy **4**(2), 103–126 (2011)
11. Goldberg, I.: Digital privacy: theory, technologies, and practices. In: Privacy-Enhancing Technologies for the Internet III: Ten Years Later, December 2007
12. Goldreich, O.: Foundations of Cryptography. Cambridge University Press, Cambridge (2009)
13. Goodman, B., Flaxman, S.R.: European Union Regulations on algorithmic decision-making and a "Right to Explanation". AI Mag. **38**(3), 50–57 (2017)
14. Guidotti, R., Monreale, A., Ruggieri, S., Turini, F., Giannotti, F., Pedreschi, D.: A survey of methods for explaining black box Models. ACM Comput. Surv. **51**(5), 93:1–93:42 (2019)
15. Janic, M., Wijbenga, J.P., Veugen, T.: Transparency enhancing tools (TETs): an overview. STAST, pp. 18–25 (2013)
16. LeCun, Y., Bengio, Y., Hinton, G.E.: Deep learning. Nature **521**(7553), 436–444 (2015)
17. Lécuyer, M., et al.: XRay: enhancing the Web's transparency with differential correlation. In: USENIX Security Symposium, pp. 49–64 (2014)
18. Lindell, Y., Pinkas, B.: Secure multiparty computation for privacy-preserving data mining. IACR Cryptology ePrint Archive 2008:197 (2008)
19. Lou, Y., Caruana, R., Gehrke, J.: Intelligible models for classification and regression. In: KDD, pp. 150–158 (2012)
20. Milli, S., Schmidt, L., Dragan, A.D., Hardt, M.: Model reconstruction from model explanations. CoRR abs/1807.05185 (2018)
21. Naveed, M., Ayday, E., Clayton, E.W., Fellay, J., Gunter, C.A., Hubaux, J.-P., Malin, B.A., Wang, X.F.: Privacy in the Genomic Era. ACM Comput. Surv. **48**(1), 6:1–6:44 (2015)
22. Pasquale, F.: The Black Box Society, the Secret Algorithms that Control Money and Information. Harvard University Press, Cambridge (2015)
23. Romei, A., Ruggieri, S.: Discrimination data analysis: a multi-disciplinary bibliography. In: Custers, B., Calders, T., Schermer, B., Zarsky, T. (eds.) Discrimination and Privacy in the Information Society, pp. 109–135. Springer, Heidelberg (2013). https://doi.org/10.1007/978-3-642-30487-3_6
24. Rouvroy, A., Berns, T.: Gouvernementalité algorithmique et perspectives d'émancipation. Le disparate comme condition d'individualisation par la relation? Réseaux, n 177 (2013)
25. Ruggieri, S., Pedreschi, D., Turini, F.: Data mining for discrimination discovery. TKDD **4**(2), 91–940 (2010)
26. Shokri, R., Stronati, M., Song, C., Shmatikov, V.: Membership inference attacks against machine learning models. In: IEEE Symposium on Security and Privacy, pp. 3–18 (2017)
27. Sweeney, L.: k-anonymity: a model for protecting privacy. Int. J. Uncertainty Fuzziness Knowl. Based Syst. **10**(5), 557–570 (2002)
28. Verma, S., Rubin, J.: Fairness definitions explained. In: FairWare@ICSE 2018, pp. 1–7 (2018)
29. Zliobaite, I.: Measuring discrimination in algorithmic decision making. Data Min. Knowl. Discov. **31**(4), 1060–1089 (2017)

Mobile Security

Decentralized Dynamic Security Enforcement for Mobile Applications with CliSeAuDroid

Tobias Hamann$^{(\boxtimes)}$ and Heiko Mantel

Department of Computer Science, TU Darmstadt, Darmstadt, Germany
{hamann,mantel}@cs.tu-darmstadt.de

Abstract. To date, Android is by far the most prevalent operating system for mobile devices. With Android devices taking a vital role in the everyday life of users, applications on these devices are handling vast amounts of private and potentially sensitive information, as well as sensitive sensor data like the device location. The built-in security mechanisms of the Android platform offer only limited protection for this data and device resources, and are not sufficient to enforce fine-grained policies on how data is used by applications. We present CLISEAUDROID, a runtime enforcement mechanism for Android applications that can enforce fine-grained security policies, either locally within a single application, across multiple applications, or even across multiple devices. We show that CLISEAUDROID can effectively ensure user-defined security requirements that protect sensitive data and resources on Android devices and adds only little runtime overhead to protected applications.

1 Introduction

Over the last decade, the Android platform has gained increasing popularity. To date, it is the most prevalent mobile operating system, with a market share of 85.9% in the first quarter of 2018.[1] Users are entrusting more and more private data to mobile applications, including, e.g., financial data for online banking, calendar entries, or health data. This makes mobile applications also a prime target for attackers. In addition to sensitive user data, mobile devices also expose a variety of privacy-relevant sensors, like the device camera or audio recording.

At the core of the built-in security mechanisms of the Android platform is the Android permission system. Whenever an application tries to access sensitive data or device resources, this access is controlled by the middleware layers of the Android platform. Before such an access can happen for the first time, the device user has to explicitly grant the corresponding permission to the application. Once an application has been granted a permission, however, the further usage of assets protected by this permission is only little controlled. Another challenge for Android security efforts is the fragmentation of the Android landscape into the many active Android versions. The slow migration of existing

---

[1] https://www.gartner.com/newsroom/id/3876865.

© Springer Nature Switzerland AG 2019
N. Zincir-Heywood et al. (Eds.): FPS 2018, LNCS 11358, pp. 29–45, 2019.
https://doi.org/10.1007/978-3-030-18419-3_3

devices to current Android versions means that new security features cannot be incorporated by applications running on older devices. While the current major version of the Android platform, Android 8, has been available for roughly one year, only 14.6% of all active devices are running on Android 8 in August 2018 [1]. Android versions older than Android 6, which introduced major improvements on permission management, are still used by roughly 32% of all active devices.

The shortcomings of the security mechanisms on the Android platform have attracted growing attention by the scientific community over the last years, leading to many security concepts in the area of Android security. Most of these concepts complement the built-in security mechanisms rather than replacing them. These concepts range from static analyses assessing the security of applications before they are installed (e.g., [5, 8, 18]), over adaptations or modifications of the operating system kernel or middleware layers (e.g., [6, 7, 9]), to dynamic approaches hardening applications on the application layer (e.g., [15, 16, 19]).

In this paper, we present CLISEAUDROID, a novel, flexible and light-weight dynamic enforcement mechanism for fine-grained security policies for Android applications.[2] CLISEAUDROID resides completely on the application level, and can be instantiated to address various security considerations not addressed by built-in security mechanisms. Our approach can be used to enforce all of local, cross-application, and cross-device security policies. By local policies, we refer to policies that involve only a single application. By cross-application and cross-device policies, we refer to policies that involve multiple applications on a single device or across devices, respectively. Such policies require coordination between applications and devices for effectively enforcing given security requirements. The capability to enforce cross-device policies for multiple devices of a user is desirable, and is not addressed by previous work on Android application security.

In detail, the contributions of this article are the following:

- We present CLISEAUDROID, a dynamic enforcement mechanism for user-defined, fine-grained security policies for Android applications. CLISEAUDROID can enforce both local policies and distributed policies on the same device or across devices. CLISEAUDROID incorporates the crosslining [11] technique that separates the interaction with the target program from the decision making. Such a separation is crucial for ensuring the reachability of the decision maker in distributed settings, especially on Android, where only one application can actively run in the foreground at a time.
- We evaluate the effectiveness and efficiency of the enforcement capabilities of CLISEAUDROID in case studies involving real, open-source Android applications. We show that CLISEAUDROID can effectively enforce both local policies and distributed policies. Our results indicate that the runtime overhead added by the enforcement are small, leading to no perceivable delay in the

---

[2] The implementation of CLISEAUDROID, all case study policies, and our results are available online. See Sect. 3 for details.

application execution for local enforcement. Distributed enforcement involving network communication shows a mean overhead below one second for up to four devices involved in the enforcement.

2 Android Application Security in a Nutshell

The Android platform provides various security mechanisms that are built into the platform implementation at different levels of the platform architecture. At the core of the security mechanisms for applications are a strong sandboxing mechanism, and a permission system for restricting access of applications to potentially sensitive user data and device resources.

2.1 The Android Security Architecture

The Android software stack is built on top of a Linux kernel. End-user applications run on top of multiple layers of middleware offered by the system architecture, consisting of the Android runtime, libraries, and the Java API framework. These middleware layers manage most of the interaction of applications with lower system levels, including access to protected resources on the device or to implementations of the IPC mechanisms.[3]

All applications on the Android platform are strictly sandboxed. Conceptually, this is achieved by providing distinct Linux UIDs to each application together with mandatory access control enforced by SELinux on the kernel level of the Android platform.[4] This sandboxing also applies for privileged system applications, as well as native code parts of applications. The strict sandboxing ensures that applications cannot access data that is local to other applications. Furthermore, the sandboxing mechanism ensures that access to protected system resources and data is managed by the Android platform implementation for each application, adhering to security policies established at the kernel level.

The core of the Android security architecture that is building on the strong sandboxing is its permission system that restricts the usage of certain designated operations and resources on a device.[5] These permissions are divided into three categories: normal permissions, signature permissions, and dangerous permissions. Data and resources protected by normal permissions are considered as low-risk operations and are granted to applications automatically when they request them, not requiring user confirmation. Signature permissions are granted to each application that requests them, provided that the application defining the permission has been signed with the same certificate as the requesting application. This can, for instance, be facilitated for custom-defined permissions that are shared between applications from the same developer. Dangerous permissions are considered to pose a significant risk for the user's privacy or the device's functionality. Examples for those dangerous permissions are sending

---

[3] https://developer.android.com/guide/platform/.

[4] https://developer.android.com/guide/components/fundamentals.

[5] https://developer.android.com/guide/topics/permissions/overview.

SMS messages (*SEND_SMS*) or accessing the current device location via GPS (*ACCESS_FINE_LOCATION*). Dangerous permissions are not granted to the application automatically, but have to be accepted by the user manually.

Prior to Android 6, permission requests were only posed at installation time of an application. Hence, users had only limited control over the behavior of applications: an installed application either got access to all requested permissions, or could not be installed on the device. From Android 6 onwards, these install-time requests were replaced with runtime requests. When installing an application, users are still presented with all permissions that the application requests. The actual granting of these permissions, however, is performed when the application tries to use them for the first time. Dangerous permissions can be revoked or regranted at any time using the system settings of the device.

Exemplary Shortcomings of Built-in Security Mechanisms. The built-in security mechanisms of the Android platform offer only a limited granularity for controlling sensitive data and resources on devices. For instance, the granting procedure for permissions at the first time of use is not sufficient to provide users with a fine-grained control over sensitive data and resources. Consider, for instance, a simple security requirement stating that an installed application may not send SMS messages to expensive premium SMS services (this requirement has been considered in other work, e.g., by DROIDFORCE [19]). Using the built-in permission system, users have the choice to either grant the application with the permission to send SMS messages when it first asks for it, or can deny it. How the permission is actually used after granting the permission is not controlled by the Android system. In particular, an application requiring the permission to send SMS messages for benign purposes can also abuse this permission to send expensive messages without users noticing.

Naturally, on-device security mechanisms are limited to controlling applications on that very device. However, this can be insufficient to enforce user-specific security policies. Consider, for instance, a variant of the premium SMS requirement stating that multiple installed applications may send SMS messages also to expensive premium numbers, but within each 24-h interval only three such messages may be sent altogether from all devices of the user. In order to ensure this property, global knowledge of the execution history across devices is required. This cannot be achieved by the built-in Android security architecture.

2.2   State of the Art

To overcome the limitations of Android's built-in security mechanisms, a large variety of security solutions has been proposed in the literature, ranging from static analyses that assert application security before installation, to dynamic approaches that enforce security requirements at runtime.

Static Approaches. Static analysis techniques can be used for establishing trust in applications, enabling informed user decisions whether to install a given application or not. A large number of static analysis techniques for Android applications has been proposed. A recent, comprehensive literature survey of static analysis mechanisms for Android has analyzed over 120 research papers on static analysis approaches for Android applications [17]. These static approaches range from tools that build on analysis techniques that are proven to be sound (like, e.g., [8,18]) to tools that aim for a high recall in combination with high precision, but do not build on such formal foundations (like, e.g. [5]).

While static approaches can detect potential security violations in applications, they do not modify application behavior at runtime to make it compliant to a given security policy. In addition, static approaches can be overly restrictive, as they cannot take runtime information into consideration to determine whether sensitive information is actually leaked for a certain program run.

OS-Level and Middleware-Level Dynamic Enforcement. Application security can be ensured dynamically by enforcement mechanisms that are integrated into the operating system kernel or the middleware. Such approaches can offer a high level of protection by providing additional security features on devices. However, such approaches usually require substantial modifications of the platform running on the device, like rooting the device or flashing modified system images.

The Android Security Framework (ASF) [6] provides a module-based mechanism to extend the Android security mechanisms. The ASF resides on multiple layers of the Android platform, providing an API for security module developers. Security modules are provided in the form of code, and can be used to implement security enforcement for applications running on top of the ASF. The CRePE mechanism introduced context-aware enforcement of security policies for the Android platform [9]. CRePE resides in the Android middleware, and provides a hook-based system to detect access to permission-protected APIs of the Android system. It consists of a centralized policy provision and management system that is able to track the current device context, like, e.g., the current location of the device. Similar to CRePE, the Security Enhanced Android Framework (SEAF) provides a modified Android middleware layer that incorporates hooks to detect access to protected resources [7]. It provides both, a more fine-grained access control model for Android and behavior-based enforcement of security policies. This behavior-based enforcement can, e.g., be used to detect suspicious orderings of permission usages that indicate malicious behavior of a target application.

Application-Level Dynamic Enforcement. As an orthogonal approach to modifications of the operating system kernel or the Android middleware, enforcement mechanisms can reside completely on the application level. While such mechanisms are not closely integrated into the low-level parts of the system, they come with the advantage that usually no modification of the platform is required for enforcing security policies. Since this approach does not offer monitoring capabilities on the lower levels of the system (like, e.g., hooks), application-level enforcement mechanisms usually involve application instrumentation.

DROIDFORCE [19] is a tool for enforcing complex, data-centric, system-wide policies for Android applications. Conceptually, DROIDFORCE consists of a policy enforcement point that is inlined into target applications, and a central enforcement decision point on the device. Hence, enforcement decision in

DROIDFORCE are always made centrally, and can consider the state of multiple applications on the same device. For detecting security-relevant program points, DROIDFORCE incorporates a machine-learning approach. The framework presented in [16] provides capabilities to protect data usage on Android devices. The focus of this framework is the enforcement of attribute-based usage control depending on local or remote attributes that may change over time. Data providers embed usage control policies in data, which are then enforced by a central data protection system application on the device. Approaches that build on dynamic taint-tracking systems like, for instance, TaintDroid [10] follow an approach that is focused on data-flow tracking. Such approaches can analyze the flow of sensitive data inside or across applications, e.g., in order to prevent processing of sensitive data by third-party libraries. Many variants of dynamic or hybrid taint-tracking have been proposed, ranging from basic data-flow tracking to more sophisticated analyses that, e.g., consider native code inside apps [15].

3   CliSeAuDroid

With CLISEAUDROID, we present a novel runtime enforcement mechanism that enables the enforcement of fine-grained, user-defined security policies for Android applications both locally (i.e., within a single application), and in a distributed fashion (i.e., across different applications on the same device, or across different devices). CLISEAUDROID operates completely on the application layer, and can be applied to applications running on unmodified and unrooted Android devices. Policies for CLISEAUDROID are provided as Java source code, and are compiled for execution on devices. This approach provides support for using method and field invocations at the target program in the decision-making process, in particular involving the Android application lifecycle. In terms of the Android permission system, CLISEAUDROID offers a more fine-grained possibility to specify permission access, as well as a more sophisticated way to specify how data and device resources may be used after the corresponding permissions have been granted to an application. The implementation of CLISEAUDROID is provided as open-source software and available online. We provide the source code of CLISEAUDROID, sample security policies, and our evaluation results at www.mais.informatik.tu-darmstadt.de/assets/tools/cliseaudroid.zip.

3.1   Architecture

Figure 1 shows the architecture of CLISEAUDROID. It consists of four components: the interceptor, the coordinator, the local policy, and the enforcer. The interceptor component is responsible for monitoring the target application (Arrow 1), and communicating intercepted program events to the coordinator (Arrow 2). The coordinator component, in turn, checks with the local policy component whether the observed program behavior complies with the enforced security requirement (Arrow 3a). In case the observed behavior would violate the security requirement, a suitable countermeasure is determined and communicated to the enforcer component (Arrow 4). Finally, the enforcer component implements this countermeasure at the interaction point with the target application (Arrow 5). CLiSeAuDroid supports the enforcement of distributed, system-wide security policies by communicating with other encapsulated applications. By system-wide policies, we refer to policies that consider all nodes in a distributed system, and that require global knowledge of the system state. This communication might involve other applications on the same device, or applications on a different device. In such settings, the coordinator can delegate the decision-making to other encapsulated applications instead of deciding locally (Arrow 3b).

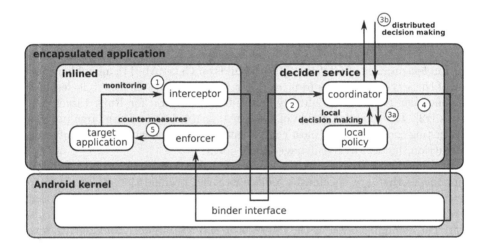

Fig. 1. Architecture of CLiSeAuDroid

All components of the enforcement mechanism are located at the application level, depicted by the upper, dark-gray box in Fig. 1. This is achieved by instrumenting the target application APK file, placing the interceptor component and the enforcer component inlined into the target application code. The decision-making part of the mechanism, i.e., the coordinator component and the local policy component are located in a separate *decider service*. This technique of splitting the enforcement into an inlined entity and an entity outside the original application code, known as crosslining [11], guarantees that the decision making components are reachable for other applications, even if the target application is not actively running. The instrumentation results in an encapsulated application, in which all components of CLiSeAuDroid are included into the target application. The inlined part of the security mechanism and the decider service communicate via the binder interface provided by the Android kernel, depicted by the lower, light-gray box of Fig. 1.

The component design of CLISEAUDROID implements the concept of service automata, a parametric framework for enforcing security requirements in local and distributed systems at runtime [14]. The service automata framework is parametric in the enforced security requirement, the possible countermeasures on the target, and the monitored program events. For all communication within the enforcement and for the decision-making, we abstract from target application events by generating internal events based on the observed behavior. Implementing the concept of Service Automata, CLISEAUDROID enables the decentralized coordination between different target applications running on a single device or across devices, and thus the enforcement of system-wide policies. A decentralized coordination that does not require a central decision-making entity can be beneficial depending on the application scenario, especially in distributed settings involving mobile devices that might not be reachable continuously.

3.2   Implementation Details

The implementation of CLISEAUDROID builds on CLISEAU [11], an implementation of the service automata framework for Java programs. CLISEAU is designed in a modular fashion that already enabled its extension for Ruby target programs [12]. The modular design of CLISEAU enabled us to reuse large parts of the existing codebase, since most components are working with an internal event abstraction that is target-language independent.

In addition to the existing codebase of CLISEAU, we developed software components that are specifically tailored to the peculiarities of the Android platform. The decision-making process is implemented as a background service, that is kept alive even when the target application is not actively running. The communication of the interceptor and the enforcer components with the decision-making service facilitate the Android inter-process communication mechanisms, in particular the Android binder interface using Intents. Different target applications instrumented with CLISEAUDROID communicate over plain Java sockets. Currently, this requires a-priori knowledge of the IP addresses of all targeted devices. However, CLISEAUDROID is designed in a modular fashion that enables its adaptation to different communication strategies. Hence, the socket-based communication can be adapted to a setting that is agnostic of the actual IP addresses of target devices, e.g., using cloud-based communication mechanisms like Firebase Cloud Messaging [3]. Regardless of the actual communication strategy, applications instrumented by CLISEAUDROID require the permission for internet access for distributed enforcement scenarios. We also enhanced the instrumentation infrastructure of CLISEAU to enable the instrumentation of Android applications using the AspectBench Compiler (abc) [4].

3.3   Application Instrumentation

The instrumentation process of CLISEAUDROID operates on the application package file (APK) of the target application. APKs are container files, including the binary files of the application as well as necessary dependencies and application resources. Figure 2 visualizes the instrumentation process of CLISEAU-DROID. The instrumentation operates on three input artifacts: the APK file of the target application, an instantiation of CLISEAUDROID for the target application, and a pointcut specification of the security-relevant program points.

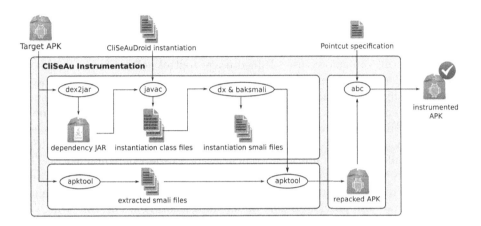

Fig. 2. Application instrumentation

The instantiation of CLISEAUDROID for the target program and policy consists of an implementation of the local policy component, the enforcer component, a factory class for abstracting from intercepted program behavior, and a factory class for creating enforcer objects from decisions. These implementations can be reused between different application scenarios, e.g., when the same policy shall be enforced but different program points are relevant for the monitoring process. The security-relevant program points are specified as AspectJ pointcuts. Program points matching these pointcuts are intercepted during the enforcement and translated to the internal event abstraction by a factory class.

The CLISEAUDROID instantiation for the target application is provided as source code and compiled against a JAR file (generated with dex2jar) containing class information of the target application. In particular, this JAR includes dependencies inside the target application that are required for compiling the policy instantiations. These dependencies include, for instance, information about the fields of classes in the target application, or method signatures of these classes. After compiling the CLISEAUDROID instantiation to class files, they are converted to smali files using the dx and baksmali tools, because regular Java class files cannot be directly used inside APK containers. In order to include the generated smali files into the target APK, we first extract the existing smali files from the APK using the apktool and subsequently repackage all files into a single APK file using the apktool. Finally, the AspectBench Compiler (abc) [4] combines the repackaged target APK that now contains all components required for an enforcement with CLISEAUDROID and the pointcut specification that provides the program points of the target application relevant for the enforcement. The result is an instrumented APK that is monitored by CLISEAUDROID. In case policy violations are detected, suitable countermeasures are taken. Note that the instrumented APK file needs to be signed after the instrumentation, as the existing signature of the APK is not preserved during the instrumentation.

4   Security Evaluation

CLISEAUDROID can enforce user-defined usage control policies for granted permissions and device resources locally, across applications and across devices. We empirically evaluate the capabilities of CLISEAUDROID for enforcing such fine-grained and system-wide security policies using exemplary case study policies highlighting security aspects that cannot be enforced by the Android platform security architecture. The flexible and modular design of CLISEAUDROID enables the enforcement of user-defined policies for a variety of requirements. The policies can reuse existing code from other policy instantiations, or can be developed from scratch to match given scenarios. In this paper, we focus on example policies that we also provide as part of our implementation. For evaluating the effectiveness of enforcing these policies, we target open-source applications publicly available on the F-Droid store [2] that make use of specific permissions that we target in the case study policies.

4.1   Case Study Policies

We present three classes of security policies that we investigate in our case studies. For each of these classes, we present an exemplary instantiation for a specific permission-protected part of the Android API.

Explicit Permission Usage Control. Permissions on the Android platform are granted per application based on user confirmation. Once the permission has been granted, users are not asked for confirmation again when the application accesses an API protected by that permission. While there might be benign reasons for an application to access a permission-protected API at the time a permission is granted, the application can also misuse the permission later.

CLISEAUDROID can be instantiated to ask users for explicit confirmation whenever the target application tries to access an API protected by a permission. We evaluate an instantiation of such a policy for the *SEND_SMS* permission. The SMSUSERCONFIRMATION policy provides users with a fine-grained control over permission usage for sending SMS messages. Instead of granting the *SEND_SMS* permission forever, users can choose to be asked every time the application tries to send a SMS message. When the application first tries to access the permission-protected API method for sending SMS messages, the user is presented with a popup window. In this popup window, the user can decide to grant or deny access for the permission to the application. In addition, the user can choose to remember this decision for the application. If the user does not choose to remember this decision, he will be presented with a popup message asking for permission each time the application tries to send a SMS message. Enforcing this policy for applications running on older devices also provides a backport of the permission model of Android starting from Android 5 in case the user chooses to remember the decision.

Rate-Limiting Policies. Once an application has been granted with a specific permission, there is no limit on the frequency the application can use API methods protected by this permission. While users might be willing to grant applications with a specific permission, they might want to ensure that the permission is not used extensively.

CLISEAUDROID enables the enforcement of user-defined rate limits for accessing permission-protected API methods. We evaluate an instantiation of such a policy for the *SEND_SMS* permission. The SMSRATELIMITING policy limits the amount of SMS messages that can be sent by a specific application. Using the distributed enforcement capability of CLISEAUDROID, this policy can also be applied to enforce rate limits across multiple applications and devices of the user. This enables settings where a user wants to use applications that make use of SMS messaging on more than one device, e.g., on a smartphone and on a tablet device. Note that for both local and distributed rate limiting, we can reuse the same instantiation of CLISEAUDROID. In distributed settings each unit is instrumented separately and installed on the corresponding device. The coordinator components of the different units will handle the decision-making during runtime in a transparent fashion for the end user.

Provision of Fake Data. Denying applications access to permission-protected APIs can lead to application crashes, as the application might depend on the presence of data queried from the APIs. While users might want to deny certain applications access to specific permissions, they might still have an interest in using other functionalities of the application. Hence, avoiding application crashes in such cases is a desirable goal for enforcement mechanisms.

CLISEAUDROID can be instantiated to deny applications access to specific permissions, providing fake data for the application instead. We evaluate an instantiation of such a policy for the *ACCESS_FINE_LOCATION* permission. The FAKELOCATIONPROVISION policy can prevent application crashes by enabling the provision of fake location data to applications. Whenever the target application tries to access the current location of the device, the return values of the API calls are intercepted and modified to show a different location (e.g., in Antarctica). This enables users to still run the application, without providing it with the actual location of the device. Note that the generic architecture of CLISEAUDROID also allows the provision of more sophisticated return data, like, e.g., plausible movement profiles for fake locations. For the evaluation in this article, we limit ourselves to a static return value that is used as fake data.

4.2   Case Study Instantiations

In our evaluations, we target two open-source applications that are publicly available on F-Droid: TinyTravelTracker[6] and ShellMS[7]. The TinyTravelTracker app collects GPS location data in the background in order to provide the user with movement profiles. Naturally, TinyTravelTracker requires access to the *ACCESS_FINE_LOCATION* permission for this purpose. The ShellMS app, in turn, provides a background service that can be used by other applications on the device or by users via the Android Debug Bridge (adb) for sending SMS messages. Naturally, ShellMS requires the *SEND_SMS* permission.

Evaluation Setup. We instantiate the FAKELOCATIONPROVISION policy for TinyTravelTracker. We instantiate both the SMSUSERCONFIRMATION policy, and the SMSRATELIMITING policies for ShellMS. For the SMSRATELIMITING policy, we evaluate four variants: a purely local variant involving only one application instance and device, and distributed variants involving 2, 3, and 4 devices, correspondingly. We evaluated all policy instantiations on Google Nexus 5 devices running Android 4.4.3 in a local WiFi network.

Evaluation Results. The left-hand side of Fig. 3 shows a screenshot of an instrumented ShellMS instance using the SMSUSERCONFIRMATION policy. Our evaluation confirms that CLISEAUDROID can effectively enforce the policy, and will ask users for permission whenever the application tries to send SMS messages. No SMS message was sent without explicit user confirmation in our experiments. We further confirmed in our experiments that the SMSRATELIMITING policy was correctly preventing ShellMS from sending more messages than the quota permits. We were able to confirm this both locally, and in our cross-device experiments. The quota limit was enforced across all involved devices, regardless of where the permitted messages originated before. The right-hand side of Fig. 3 shows a screenshot of an instrumented TinyTravelTracker instance for the FAKELOCATIONPROVISION policy. As can be seen in the figure, the application is correctly prevented from access to the real device location and is provided with a fake location in Antarctica instead. Note that we do not evaluate in full rigor whether all invocations of security-relevant methods are intercepted and handled by CLISEAUDROID. We rely on the automatized instrumentation by abc for ensuring a sound instantiation of the monitoring. Defining suitable pointcuts for given security requirements is part of policy development and controlled by the user of CLISEAUDROID.

In summary, CLISEAUDROID succeeded in enforcing all of our security policy instantiations, both locally on a single device and in distributed settings involving up to four devices. In our experiments, we did not observe any disruption of regular application functionality that was not covered by the security policies.

---

[6] https://f-droid.org/en/packages/com.rareventure.gps2/.
[7] https://f-droid.org/en/packages/com.android.shellms/.

Fig. 3. Screenshots of encapsulated target applications

5 Performance Evaluation

Dynamically enforcing security policies at runtime comes at the cost of a performance overhead. This overhead is caused by the additional time required for monitoring application behavior, the time required for the decision making, and the time required to impose countermeasures on the application. In addition to the runtime overhead, some preprocessing time is required when instrumenting the target application. In this section, we evaluate the performance overhead introduced by CLISEAUDROID in both of these dimensions for the case study policies presented in Sect. 4. We show that the runtime overhead of CLISEAUDROID achieves its goal of achieving a light-weight enforcement without adding extensive runtime overhead, and that the runtime overhead of CLISEAUDROID is not perceivable to end users for local enforcement.

5.1 Instrumentation Overhead

Instrumenting a target application with CLISEAUDROID is a one-time operation. Once an instance of the target application has been instrumented for a specific device, the resulting APK file can be installed on the device like a regular application. The instrumentation process can thus be kept transparent to the end user, who is provided with the instrumented APK file. When instrumenting applications for a distributed setting, one instance of the target application is instrumented per unit of the distributed system.

Figure 4 summarizes the instrumentation times and size overheads for the different target applications and case study policies. Overall, our evaluation shows that the instrumentation time is below three minutes for all our case study policies and applications. Since the instrumentation is carried out only once before installing the target application on a device, we consider this an acceptable overhead. Regarding application size, the instrumentation added less than 1 MB to the original application size for each policy instantiation.

security policy	instrumentation time	size overhead
SMSUSERCONFIRMATION	35s	100.5kB (25.2%)
SMSRATELIMITING	34s	96.7kB (24.3%)
FAKELOCATIONPROVISION	150s	591.9kB (3.3%)

Fig. 4. Instrumentation time and application size overhead (per unit)

5.2   Runtime Overhead

We evaluate the runtime overhead introduced by CLISEAUDROID when running an encapsulated application by measuring the time spent within the enforcement components. For this, we measure the start time when we first intercept a program event that is relevant for the enforced security policy. We measure the end time at the point just before the enforcer applies the determined countermeasure to the target program. For our experiments, we carried out measurements for each policy instantiation, discarding outliers that lie more than three absolute standard deviations from the median. All experiments were carried out on Google Nexus 5 devices running Android 4.4.3. The start and end times, respectively, were logged to the device for evaluation. These log results were extracted from the devices using the Android debug bridge (adb).

Figure 5 summarizes the mean overhead times (with 95% confidence intervals) and the standard deviation introduced by CLISEAUDROID for each policy instantiation. For the policies that do not involve direct user interaction (i.e., the SMSRATELIMITING policy, and the FAKELOCATIONPROVISION policy), we carried out 2,000 experiments. For the SMSUSERCONFIRMATION policy involving user interaction, we carried out 100 experiments. Our results show that for purely local enforcement within a single application, the mean overhead added by CLISEAUDROID is below 6 ms for each runtime check on the invocation of a security-relevant method. For distributed enforcement across devices, our results show a comparably high overhead that is increasing with the amount of network hops performed during the enforcement. In addition to the higher mean enforcement overhead, we can also observe that the standard deviation is significantly higher than for local enforcement. Figure 6 visualizes the distributions of overhead times for local enforcement of the FAKELOCATIONPROVISION and SMSRATELIMITING policies.

security policy	mean overhead	standard deviation
SMSUSERCONFIRMATION	1.6726 ± 0.0232 ms	0.2753 ms
SMSRATELIMITING (local)	5.4051 ± 0.0443 ms	2.3608 ms
SMSRATELIMITING (2 hops)	423.4710 ± 5.3791 ms	287.8840 ms
SMSRATELIMITING (3 hops)	616.0131 ± 7.0449 ms	377.2245 ms
SMSRATELIMITING (4 hops)	712.3791 ± 6.2084 ms	332.2642 ms
FAKELOCATIONPROVISION	3.6122 ± 0.0227 ms	1.1995 ms

Fig. 5. Runtime overhead introduced by CLISEAUDROID enforcement

Our results indicate that the runtime overhead introduced by CLISEAU-DROID is within limits that are not perceivable to the end user for local enforcement. Indeed, during our experiments we did not notice any disruption of application functionality. This observation lines up with the overhead added by CLISEAU for other target languages, and is competitive with other enforcement mechanisms for the Android platform, like, e.g., DROIDFORCE [19].

For distributed policies, we can observe a much higher overhead above 400 ms. This magnitude of runtime overhead can be clearly perceivable to end users. However, depending on the application scenario, the security benefits can still outweigh the overhead. Our experiments show that even with up to four devices involved in the enforcement process, the overhead remains below 1 s. Interpreting the overhead in distributed settings, the biggest part of the overhead seems to stem from network communication overhead. We consider investigations of possibilities to decrease this overhead while still ensuring a sound enforcement as an interesting direction for future work. Decreasing this overhead might involve different communication technologies, or strategies to reduce the amount of communication required for decision making, e.g., by precomputing decisions. Previous evaluations of such precomputation strategies showed a significant potential for reducing overhead [13].

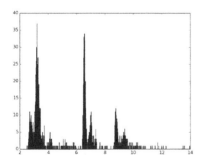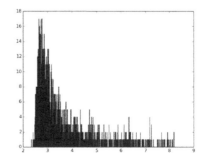

Fig. 6. Runtime overhead distribution introduced by local enforcement for the SMSRATELIMITING policy (left) and FAKELOCATIONPROVISION policy (right)

6   Conclusion

In this article, we presented CLISEAUDROID, a mechanism for dynamically enforcing both local and system-wide security policies for Android applications at runtime. CLISEAUDROID enables the enforcement of fine-grained security policies that cannot be enforced with built-in Android security mechanisms. Our mechanism is implemented completely at the application layer, and can be used on unmodified and unrooted Android devices.

We showed that CLISEAUDROID can effectively enforce realistic, user-defined security policies for applications running on a single device or across devices. Our experimental evaluation indicates that the performance overhead added by this enforcement is small, and within boundaries that are not recognizable by end users for local enforcement. When enforcing distributed policies, the performance overhead is significantly higher, but was still below 1 second in our experiments.

The capability to enforce cross-device security policies adds to our confidence that CLISEAUDROID is not just yet another tool for Android security, but provides a flexible and light-weight solution for security concerns in our increasingly connected world.

Acknowledgments. This work was supported by the DFG under the project RSCP (MA 3326/4-3) in the priority program RS^3 (SPP 1496).

References

1. Android Distribution Dashboard. https://developer.android.com/about/dashboards/. Accessed 3 Sept 2018
2. F-Droid. https://www.f-droid.org. Accessed 3 Sept 2018
3. Firebase Cloud Messaging (FCM). https://firebase.google.com/docs/cloud-messaging/. Accessed 3 Sept 2018
4. Arzt, S., Rasthofer, S., Bodden, E.: Instrumenting Android and Java applications as easy as abc. In: Legay, A., Bensalem, S. (eds.) RV 2013. LNCS, vol. 8174, pp. 364–381. Springer, Heidelberg (2013). https://doi.org/10.1007/978-3-642-40787-1_26
5. Arzt, S., et al.: FlowDroid: precise context, flow, field, object-sensitive and lifecycle-aware taint analysis for Android apps. In: PLDI 2014, pp. 259–269 (2014)
6. Backes, M., Bugiel, S., Gerling, S., von Styp-Rekowsky, P.: Android security framework: extensible multi-layered access control on Android. In: ACSAC 2014, pp. 46–55 (2014)
7. Banuri, H., et al.: An Android runtime security policy enforcement framework. Pers. Ubiquitous Comput. **16**(6), 631–641 (2012)
8. Chen, H., Tiu, A., Xu, Z., Liu, Y.: A permission-dependent type system for secure information flow analysis. In: CSF 2018, pp. 218–232 (2018)
9. Conti, M., Nguyen, V.T.N., Crispo, B.: CRePE: context-related policy enforcement for Android. In: Burmester, M., Tsudik, G., Magliveras, S., Ilić, I. (eds.) ISC 2010. LNCS, vol. 6531, pp. 331–345. Springer, Heidelberg (2011). https://doi.org/10.1007/978-3-642-18178-8_29
10. Enck, W., et al.: TaintDroid: an information-flow tracking system for realtime privacy monitoring on smartphones. ACM Trans. Comput. Syst. **32**(2), 5 (2014)

11. Gay, R., Hu, J., Mantel, H.: CliSeAu: securing distributed Java programs by cooperative dynamic enforcement. In: Prakash, A., Shyamasundar, R. (eds.) ICISS 2014. LNCS, vol. 8880, pp. 378–398. Springer, Cham (2014). https://doi.org/10.1007/978-3-319-13841-1_21

12. Gay, R., Hu, J., Mantel, H., Mazaheri, S.: Relationship-based access control for resharing in decentralized online social networks. In: Imine, A., Fernandez, J.M., Marion, J.-Y., Logrippo, L., Garcia-Alfaro, J. (eds.) FPS 2017. LNCS, vol. 10723, pp. 18–34. Springer, Cham (2018). https://doi.org/10.1007/978-3-319-75650-9_2

13. Gay, R., Hu, J., Mantel, H., Schickel, J.: Towards accelerated usage control based on access correlations. In: Lipmaa, H., Mitrokotsa, A., Matulevičius, R. (eds.) NordSec 2017. LNCS, vol. 10674, pp. 245–261. Springer, Cham (2017). https://doi.org/10.1007/978-3-319-70290-2_15

14. Gay, R., Mantel, H., Sprick, B.: Service automata. In: Barthe, G., Datta, A., Etalle, S. (eds.) FAST 2011. LNCS, vol. 7140, pp. 148–163. Springer, Heidelberg (2012). https://doi.org/10.1007/978-3-642-29420-4_10

15. Graa, M., Cuppens-Boulahia, N., Cuppens, F., Lanet, J.-L.: Tracking explicit and control flows in Java and native Android apps code. In: ICISSP 2016, pp. 307–316 (2016)

16. Lazouski, A., Martinelli, F., Mori, P., Saracino, A.: Stateful data usage control for Android mobile devices. Int. J. Inf. Secur. 16(4), 345–369 (2017)

17. Li, L., Bissyandé, T.F., Papadakis, M., Rasthofer, S., Bartel, A., Octeau, D., Klein, J., Le Traon, Y.: Static analysis of Android apps: a systematic literature review. Inf. Softw. Technol. 88, 67–95 (2017)

18. Lortz, S., Mantel, H., Starostin, A., Bähr, T., Schneider, D., Weber, A.: Cassandra: towards a certifying app store for Android. In: SPSM 2014, pp. 93–104 (2014)

19. Rasthofer, S., Arzt, S., Lovat, E., Bodden, E.: DroidForce: enforcing complex, data-centric, system-wide policies in Android. In: ARES 2014, pp. 40–49 (2014)

Mobile Travel Credentials

David Bissessar, Maryam Hezaveh$^{(\boxtimes)}$, Fayzah Alshammari,
and Carlisle Adams

University of Ottawa, Ottawa, Canada
{dbis020,mheza028,falsh070,cadams}@uottawa.ca

Abstract. The international travel continuum is a highly demanding environment in which the participating entities have goals which are sometimes in conflict. The traveler seeks the ability to plan trips in advance and to travel conveniently, minimizing line-ups and unforeseen problems. Service providers seek to make the most of specialized resources, maximize quality of service, intercept security threats, and enforce the controls appropriate for their zones of responsibility. This paper proposes a system to benefit the needs of these multiple stakeholders: the needs of the traveler for convenience, privacy and efficiency, and the needs of the service provider for security, reliability, and accountability. Today's environment is characterized by paper documents, traditional biometric verification using facial and fingerprint images, and the manual processing of queues of passengers. Instead of this, we present a novel approach centered on fully electronic travel documents stored on the traveler's phone, secured by cryptographic operations that utilize privacy-respecting biometric references. A prototype system has been developed and implemented, demonstrating the intended benefits for all stakeholders.

Keywords: e-Passport · Privacy · Credential · Biometrics · Cryptography

1 Introduction

The current travel environment is characterized by paper-based documents, physical checkpoints staffed with agency personnel, and a medium level of systems integration between collaborating agencies. Traveler identity is largely verified based on the e-passport (a paper-based document augmented with a chip that stores traveler data) [1]. System integration occurs between immigration authorities, airlines, border control, and agencies such as Interpol [2]. Self-serve kiosks at airports perform traditional biometric verification and check identities against operational databases [3, 4]. Sharing of traveler data between airlines and border agencies is common practice, occurring in a controlled and regulated manner [5]. The system proposed in this paper builds on much of this practice, but introduces electronic credentials in such a way that convenience and efficiency is enhanced, while simultaneously enhancing privacy and security. The focus of this paper (and of the prototype system that was implemented) is to describe the credential issuance and credential verification processes.

We present a smartphone-based credential system for international travel in which a digital credential is created by an issuer (the immigration authority) and verified by an airport kiosk controlled by the border security authority.

© Springer Nature Switzerland AG 2019
N. Zincir-Heywood et al. (Eds.): FPS 2018, LNCS 11358, pp. 46–58, 2019.
https://doi.org/10.1007/978-3-030-18419-3_4

This paper has the following structure. Section 2 provides a brief discussion of the travel process today, along with some of the drawbacks that can be seen in this system. Section 3 presents the architecture of our proposed system. Section 4 describes the credential issuance process, and Sect. 5 describes the credential verification process. Section 6 discusses our prototype implementation, highlighting the benefits that are now available to the various stakeholders. The final section presents our conclusions and discusses some directions for ongoing and future work in this area.

2 The Current Travel Process

Today's travel process makes use of chip-augmented paper-based credentials, biometric verification, and e-border systems.

In the current travel and identity landscape, ICAO compliant chip-augmented passports (e-passports) are widely deployed. The e-Passport contains printed pages and data stored electronically on the chip. Of the 10 to 20 printed pages in the passport, there is one distinguished page (often referred to as the "bio-data" page) which is of particular interest. On this page are printed a passport photograph, subject attribute data, a machine readable zone *mrz*, and various security markings. The *mrz* contains various document identification information, of which some fields are used as a low-entropy secret allowing a two-step authentication protocol (c.f. ICAO Basic Access Control [1]) between passport and inspection station to protect wireless read-access to the e-passport chip. Our proposed system takes full advantage of today's e-passport and all the security and standards currently in place for its processing and use.

A strong binding is required between the e-passport and the individual to whom it is issued. Biometric technology has offered the strongest and most robust of such bindings. A number of biometric modalities are used in international travel systems including face, fingerprints, and iris [6]. The most prevalent and universal of modalities in travel is facial biometrics, which is the single mandatory biometric in ICAO-compliant e-passports [1]. Algorithms for facial matching in the portrait-styled images used in e-passports are well studied [7]. Our system builds on [8], offering formal definition and a prototype construction for mobile travel credentials (MTC). The algorithm is defined in terms of privacy-respecting biometrics [9–11]. The construction and prototype are defined to be compatible with ICAO Standards, corporate-standard cryptography, e-passport facial biometrics, and commercial biometric matchers.

Our algorithm also defines a QR-code [12] based protocol which is analogous to the e-passport protocol to allow authenticated read of the credential using NFC.

Finally, the e-border landscape is comprised of the interconnected systems of multiple authorities including foreign immigration agencies, airlines, and border security. Immigration systems include traditional and web-enabled systems and, increasingly, mobile systems to support the issuance of visas and electronic travel authorizations (eTA) [13–15]. Various airlines implement "Advanced Passenger Information" and "Passenger Name Record" (API/PNR) systems [5] which provide passenger information to border security systems before take-off, to allow risk-based board/no-board decisions to be made. Airlines and Border Security Authorities often provide a self-service system featuring airport kiosks that perform biometric and passport checks [3, 4]. The system proposed in this paper demonstrates how a mobile travel credential can integrate with an online travel authorization issuance system and a self-serve kiosk at the border, to demonstrate a possible architecture that can be used in today's environment to provide increased convenience, privacy, efficiency, reliability, security, and accountability.

2.1 Drawbacks in the Current Travel Process

The current travel process works reasonably well for most travelers, but it does have a number of limitations or drawbacks that can be improved. Several of these are listed below.

- In today's travel system, travelers may be required to be physically present at a travel authority in order to obtain a travel credential such as a visa or an eTA. Furthermore, manual processes at issuance time and at verification time (at the airport) can lead to delays and frustration for travelers.
- Travelers applying for a visa or eTA today may fill out an application by hand or may use an online form. In either case, data may be missing or incorrect (e.g., due to typographical errors), leading to delays in processing and, potentially, mistakes in allowing or disallowing travel.
- Finally, manual processing and electronic transaction logs stored in various systems with different levels of protection can lead to situations in which records of decisions are either not kept or are vulnerable to unauthorized modification.

The travel process proposed in the following sections was designed to mitigate the above drawbacks to improve the experience of both travelers and travel authorities.

3 Proposed System Architecture

Our proposed system (see Fig. 1 below) has a smart-phone application that captures a facial biometric (i.e., a "selfie" photo), reads an e-passport, collects some data from the user for the credential application form, and (collaboratively with an immigration server) creates a digital mobile travel credential (MTC) which is stored on the phone. This credential is later presented to a travel kiosk at the airport of arrival along with a fresh biometric and a scan of the e-passport. The kiosk is where privacy-respecting biometric verification is performed and permission to enter the country is determined.

An app on the mobile device is responsible for presenting the travel application questionnaire to the user (e.g., intended destination, dates of travel, etc.) and obtaining the user's responses. The app also retrieves "bio data" from the passport's *mrz* and chip, and uses the device camera to obtain a "selfie" photograph of the traveler. These are packaged together and sent to the travel authority (e.g., immigration server), which can do a passport integrity check, a biometric match of the selfie and the image from the e-passport chip, and other security checks as performed today. The server creates a credential (e.g., visa, eTA) that is digitally signed with the authority's private key and sent to the mobile device for storage.

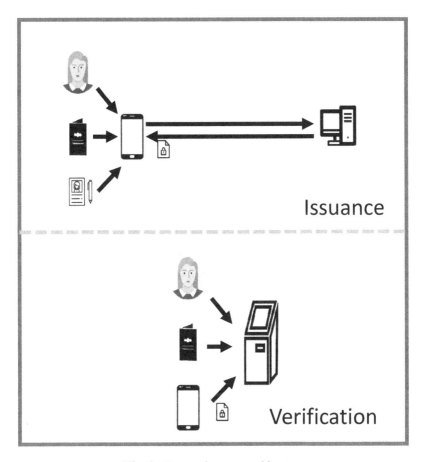

Fig. 1. Proposed system architecture

At the destination airport, the user will go to a self-serve kiosk. The kiosk will read the traveler's e-passport, take a photo of the traveler, and download the credential from the traveler's mobile device. Verification processes (including matching the new photo with the e-passport image, an integrity check of the passport, verification of the authority's digital signature on the travel credential, and revocation checks on the credential itself) will allow the kiosk to instruct the traveler to enter the country or to go to a secondary location (to meet with a human officer).

4   Credential Issuance Process

Issuance. As shown in Fig. 2, the credential issuance process is a request-response protocol between user U and issuer I. In the first step, using mobile device m, the traveler U assembles the request $q = \langle X', b_e, D \rangle$, submitting U's answers $X' = \{X_i\}$ to questionnaire Q, enrollment biometric b_e, and the e-passport data groups D.

User (U)	Issuer (I)

$X_I = m.kb(Q,U)$
 $mrz = m.c_1(P_{bd})$
 $b_e = m.c_1(U)$;
 $D = m.nfc\_bac(mrz,p)$ $\quad \xrightarrow{q=\langle b_e, X, D\rangle}$
	$< \dots, b_o, X_d, \dots > = D; X = [X_I, X_d]$
	 $a_1 = D_I(X)$;
	 $a_2 = M_I(b_o, b_e)$;
	 $a_3 = B_I(X)$;
	 $(\dots)$
	 $a_n = E_I(X_r)$;
	 $a = assess(A, t_i)$
	 if(a&b) :
	 $\quad\quad Y = \text{grant}(X)$
	 $\quad\quad rbr = \text{gen}(b_e)$
	 $\quad\quad c = issue(rbr, Y)$
	 else:
	 $\quad\quad exception(q,\ Y,\ b,\ r_1, r_2)$

$\quad\quad\quad\quad \xleftarrow{r=\langle c\rangle}$	
$m.store["p"] = r$	

Fig. 2. Mobile travel credential issuance protocol

When I receives q, the relevant data is parsed out of the passport into X, to support application data and conformance modules $\mathcal{R}_I = \{\mathcal{R}_{I_1}, \dots, \mathcal{R}_{I_n}\}$, as well as the action-labeling function *assess*() which assigns a label (e.g., "accept", "reject", escalate") to q. Based on the assigned label, I conducts the appropriate follow-up processing which could be to refuse the application or to escalate the case to supporting systems (which may include manual processes). If assessment yields acceptance, the response c is created. This credential is a cryptographic object, signed by the issuer and encrypted for the verifier.

Various techniques have been explored to mitigate the privacy concerns of biometric storage; one promising technique is a cryptographic primitive called a *fuzzy extractor* [11]. A fuzzy extractor is a scheme that takes input which is "fuzzy" (i.e., input that may vary over time, such as a biometric) and produces a highly random bit string and some additional data ("helper data") that can be publicly known. On subsequent use, a variation of the original data is input (e.g., another biometric reading) along with the helper data. If the variation is sufficiently close to the original data, the same bit string will be produced; otherwise, a completely different bit string will be produced. The bit string produced by the fuzzy extractor system is long enough and random enough that it can be used as a cryptographic key (e.g., an AES key).

In our proposed system, we use the fuzzy extractor as follows. The traveler's face biometric at issuance time (i.e., the selfie photo) is input to the fuzzy extractor to produce an AES key and the helper data. The AES key is used to encrypt the credential. The helper data can be stored on the phone along with the credential. The AES key is itself encrypted using the public key of the kiosk at the destination airport. In our system, this derived AES key is referred to as a "renewable biometric reference", or RBR.

Note that since the communication between the mobile device and the issuance server occurs over the Internet, a secure communication channel must be established between this client and server. The obvious choice would be to use SSL/TLS so that the server can be cryptographically authenticated and the mobile device can transfer the relevant travel application data with confidence.

5 Credential Verification Process

Figure 3 shows the workflow between the smartphone, the kiosk, and the server systems at the time of verification. The kiosk application guides the user through the sequence, instructing the traveler to put her passport on the document reader, and steering the traveller through the acquisition process for the verification-time facial image. Once the passport is read and the fresh image is captured, the mobile credential from the phone is transferred via NFC to the kiosk. At this point, the kiosk uses a commercial matcher $\mathcal{M}_V$ to perform biometric matching between the chip image and the fresh facial image. If the match is within the accepted threshold for the border security process, the kiosk verifies the credential obtained from the phone. If the credential is valid (note that this validation process may include an online revocation

User (U)		Verifier (V)
U	$\xrightarrow{<x_v,b_v>}$	X_v, b_v
	$\xrightarrow{p}$	$mrz = K.c_1(P_{bd})$
		$D = K.nfc(p)$
		$< \dots , b_o, X_d = \{x_1, x_2, \dots x_n\}, \dots > = D$
	$\xrightarrow{<c>}$	$a_0 = ver(c, I_{pk})$
$m.nfc(s_2)$		$< Y, rbr > = decrypt(c, V_{sk})$
		$(y_1, y_2, y_3) = Y$
		$a_1 = D_I(P_{bd}, X)$
		$\qquad a_2 = \mathcal{M}_I(b_o, b_v)$
		$a_{3,2} = (y_1 == x_1)$
		$a_{3,3} = expired(y_2, y_3)$
		$a_{3,4} = revoked(y_2, y_3)$
		$a = assess(A, t_i)$
		$if(a == "accept")$
		$\qquad grant\_access(X)$
		$else$
		$\qquad escalate(q, Y, b, r_1, r_2)$
	$\xleftarrow{instruct}$	

Fig. 3. Mobile travel credential verification protocol

check with the immigration server to confirm the current status of the eTA), the next screen shows that the application was successful; otherwise, it shows an error code and the traveler is referred to the border service officer to solve the problem.

Upon arrival, the traveler photo taken by the kiosk is used to re-derive the AES key (along with the helper data downloaded from the phone). This key is then compared with the AES key decrypted using the kiosk private key (alternatively, the re-derived key is used to attempt to decrypt the credential that has been downloaded from the phone). If the kiosk photo and helper data can generate the correct AES key, then this is highly likely to be the person that applied for the credential at issuance time. This RBR technology allows biometric verification without the use of a stored biometric template.

In this verification process, the kiosk is able to confirm the binding between the human user and the passport (using accurate face matching technology), between the human user and the mobile travel credential (using a privacy-respecting biometric approach), and between the passport and the mobile travel credential (using digital signature technology over the data from the passport that is also encoded in the credential). This conjunction of bindings enhances security over the processes in place today in which a human officer does a manual face match between the traveler standing in front of him/her and the image on the passport bio-data page.

6   Prototype Implementation

We developed an android application to obtain the application request data from the user, as well as to read the passport data and allow a selfie to be captured. This app also communicates with an issuance server to create a mobile travel credential and store it on the phone. We also developed software on the kiosk to take a traveler photo, read the passport, download the mobile travel credential from the traveler phone, and communicate with backend servers, as required, for the verification process. We further developed a biometric token approach for the RBR which uses a commercial face matcher and hashing to produce a biometric key. In addition, we pursued a parallel research project to apply the fuzzy extractors of [10] to the MTC scenario.

Credential Issuance
The mobile device m is responsible for data acquisition. The issuance server S creates a signed and encrypted mobile travel credential c, and sends it to the client. The MTC c contains the RBR, and the attributes $Y = \{passport\_no, passport\_exp\_dt, eta\_num, eta\_exp\_dt\}$. In order to achieve the best performance and scalability, the server side uses restful web service architecture, built on Apache Tomcat Server. The ECDSA, RSA, and AES encryption algorithms are implemented by standard java crypto libraries to achieve the highest reliability.

Request q is processed by a connected Server S hosted by I. Server S has access to a 1:1 biometric matcher $\mathcal{M}_I$, supporting corporate information systems DB_I, risk scoring modules $\mathcal{R}_I = \{\mathcal{R}_{I_1}, \ldots, \mathcal{R}_{I_n}\}$, and a labeling function $assess(\mathcal{R}, T)$ which applies a set of thresholds $T = \{\tau_1, \ldots, \tau_n\}$ to perceived risk to determine the required next steps in processing an application. We assume a simplistic "green", "yellow", "red" labeling scheme which signals the approval, escalation for manual intervention, or automated refusal of request q. On approval of q, I prepares credential c which is stored on m for presentation at the verification system at the border.

Credential Verification

Verifier V commissions self-service kiosk K which is responsible for presenting a questionnaire Q_v, processing answers, capturing the verification biometric, reading the passport, accessing risk, and labelling the outcome (which can include manual intervention, or automated approval).

Key Generation

Key generation algorithms are as per ECDSA [16], RSA [17] and AES [18]. Storage uses X.509 encoding for the public keys and PKCS-8 encoding for the private keys.

Communications

HTTPS is used to establish a secure communication channel for all communicating entities [19, 20]. HTTPS uses SSL/TLS to provide a secure channel for the exchange of data by implementing encryption and certificate-based authentication.

Issuance Data Acquisition

The answers to the questionnaire X_I were obtained from keyboard input. Facial biometric b_e was obtained using the smartphone front-facing camera. The application rendered an oval overlay to help guide the user through photo capture. Open source optical character recognition was used to extract the BAC keying fields from mrz. Reading D from m was achieved using JMRTD [21], which also provided facilities to parse D and complete ICAO Passive Authentication.

Issuance Risk Assessment and Conformance

Biometric risk was simplified to threshold match scores of commercial 1:1 face recognition engines. Thus, $\mathcal{R}_{I_b} = B_I(\mathcal{M}_I, t_I, b_o, b_e)$. Document risk was assessed in two manners. First, as a function of the BAC and ICAO integrity checks on D, and second, as a simulated call to the Interpol "Stolen and Lost Travel Document" database [2]. Attribute risk was illustrated using mock business rules to assign country-specific risk given the input data X_I.

Prototype-RBR Generation

Having passed risk and conformance assessment, the last step was to generate the credential itself. The biometrically derived AES key (RBR) was created using the procedure described in Sect. 4.

Credential Issuance

The credential was signed using the issuer's private ECDSA key, the signed credential was encrypted using RBR as an AES key, and RBR was encrypted using the RSA public key of the kiosk. This whole package was then stored on the traveler's phone.

Verification: Data Acquisition

As represented in Fig. 4, standard kiosk features are used to acquire X_v $mrz, P_{bd},$ and D. X_v is obtained by user input on the soft-keyboard of k. The biometric b_v of U is captured by the kiosk's image capture camera. The document reader of k captures an image of P_{bd}, obtains mrz and uses it to read D.

$$X_v = k.kb(Q_v)$$
$$b_v = k.c_1(U)$$
$$mrz = k.doc\,(P_{bd})$$
$$D = \text{m.nfc}(mrz)$$

Fig. 4. Data acquisition at the time of verification

In the prototype, k did not have facilities to read c. A custom prototype peripheral was constructed to do so. This module consisted of a cradle to hold the phone against an *nfc* reader [22], a camera [23], and an ODroid controller [24]. The traveler inserts m into the cradle, at which point the kiosk's NFC module is able to download c.

Credential Opening

Having obtained c from the NFC module, the kiosk first verifies the signed credential against the issuer verification key *Ipk* then applies a 2 step decryption process (see Fig. 5). First, *Vsk* is used with *rsa.dec$_{Vsk}$* to decrypt c_1. This yields symmetric key k_s which is then used to decrypt c_2 with *aes.dec* to produce $<Y>$.

$$\text{if } ecdsa.ver_{Ipk}(c, \sigma_I):$$
$$k_s = rsa.dec_{Vsk}(c_1)$$
$$<Y> = aes.dec_{k_s}(c_2)$$

Fig. 5. Credential opening

Conformance and Risk Assessment

The sequence of validations completing the verification protocol are as follows.

(1) The freshly obtained biometric is compared against the extracted passport photo $B_I(\mathcal{M}_V, t_V, b_o, b_V)$. A favorable match suggests that the individual at the kiosk is the rightful passport holder.

(2) The *rbr* derived from the kiosk photo (and the helper data from the phone) is used to decrypt the downloaded credential. Success indicates that the credential holder (physically present at the kiosk) is the same individual to whom the mobile travel credential was originally issued.

(3) The *mtc_exp_dt* must be greater than the current date. This ensures that travel is within the permitted MTC period.

(4) An online call to the Issuer is made to verify that the MTC is not revoked. This ensures that no recent problems exist in the current subject's case.

Together these checks ensure the entitlement-ownership relationship: the subject at the kiosk is the passport holder; the passport holder is the person to whom the MTC was issued; the MTC is still valid.

6.1   Benefits of the Proposed System

Section 2.1 discussed some of the drawbacks of the current travel process. In this section we recall those drawbacks and mention how they are mitigated by our proposed system.

- *In today's travel system, travelers may be required to be physically present at a travel authority in order to obtain a travel credential such as a visa or an eTA Furthermore, manual processes at issuance time and at verification time (at the airport) can lead to delays and frustration for travelers.*

Our proposed system automates these processes and incorporates self-serve airport kiosks so that the entire travel process may occur without queues and human intervention, greatly increasing convenience and efficiency.

- *Travelers applying for a visa or eTA today may fill out an application by hand or may use an online form. In either case, data may be missing or incorrect (e.g., due to typographical errors), leading to delays in processing and, potentially, mistakes in allowing or disallowing travel.*

In our system, passport data is read electronically, ensuring that it is complete and correct in the application request; this greatly enhances reliability during the issuance process.

- *Manual processing and electronic transaction logs stored in various systems with different levels of protection can lead to situations in which records of decisions are either not kept or are vulnerable to unauthorized modification.*

Our proposed system uses strong cryptographic protection (including encryption and digital signatures) throughout, ensuring that transaction logs cannot be altered, greatly enhancing the accountability of all actors in the travel process.

7   Conclusions and Future Work

The current travel process today relies on traveler identification that is largely paper-based (though augmented with an e-passport chip), along with traditional biometric verification systems and extensive manual processing of passenger queues. In this paper we have proposed novel credential issuance and verification processes that can bring multiple benefits to the travel process, including convenience, privacy, efficiency, security, reliability, and accountability. Our proof-of-concept implementation has been successfully completed and demonstrates secure credential issuance using a mobile app and a server, and secure credential verification using a mobile app and an airport kiosk. This implementation confirms the viability of our approach and provides a solid foundation for further work in this area.

Future Work. While this paper and the prototype focus on only two traveler touchpoints (issuance and verification), we believe our paradigm delivers most benefit when multiple checkpoints are placed throughout the travel continuum. Further work continues in this area to demonstrate how an intelligent system with risk-aware adaptive processes applied to the travel continuum can be built using our proposed approach [25, 26, 27].

This paper demonstrated the generation and verification of RBR using the e-passport chip image. While this is a workable approach that can be deployed on an international scale, we believe significant benefit to privacy can be delivered using a fuzzy extractor approach. Ongoing work examines the applicability of fuzzy extractors to the passport face biometric modality.

Self-enrollment using a smartphone certainly augments convenience and may streamline issuer costs. However, as we have discussed in this paper, self-serve enrollment with an uncontrolled enrollment environment and bring-your-own mobile devices brings a level of vulnerability. On-going work is being conducted in the area of levels-of-assurance for mobile enrolment and quantifying risks and counter-measures.

The area of 1:1 verification with mobile phone generated images is under study. Our project empirically experienced acceptable results. A follow-up paper reporting the biometric results is in development.

Finally, our study demonstrated immutability of processing logs for reliable accountability. The reader may discern the applicability of Distributed Ledger Technologies (DLT) to this area. While full ecosystem availability of traveler data may seem to offer large potential [28], legal concerns over privacy risks in the area of international travel are ongoing [29, 30]. Misapplied, DLT could exacerbate privacy concerns, resulting in immense exposure for citizens and Government data custodians [31]. As always, privacy and security must be considered together [32]. Future work will explore the applicability of DLT in this, and in other areas of social-service and cyber-physical, social systems [33].

References

1. ICAO 9303-Machine Readable Travel Documents. http://www.icao.int/publications/pages/publication.aspx?docnum=9303. Accessed 12 Sept 2018
2. Safjanski, T.: Prospects for the development of the international criminal police organisation interpol. Intern. Secur. 7(2), 267 (2015)
3. Frontex: Best practice technical guidelines for automated border control (ABC) systems, Research and Development Unit, Warsaw (2012)
4. Nuppeney, M., Breitenstein, M., Niesing, M.: EasyPASS-evaluation of face recognition performance in an operational automated border control system. In: International Biometric Performance Conference (2010)
5. U.S. Department of Homeland Security, Privacy Impact Assessment for the Advance Passenger Information System (APIS) (2007)
6. Schouten, B., Bart, J.: Biometrics and their use in e-passports. Image Vis. Comput. 27(3), 305–312 (2009)
7. Li, S.Z., Jain, A.: Handbook of Face Recognition, 2nd edn. Springer, London (2011). https://doi.org/10.1007/978-0-85729-932-1

8. Bissessar, D., Adams, C., Stoianov, A.: Privacy, security and convenience: biometric encryption for smartphone-based electronic travel documents. In: Abielmona, R., Falcon, R., Zincir-Heywood, N., Abbass, H.A. (eds.) Recent Advances in Computational Intelligence in Defense and Security. SCI, vol. 621, pp. 339–366. Springer, Cham (2016). https://doi.org/10.1007/978-3-319-26450-9_13

9. Rathgeb, C., Andreas U.: A survey on biometric cryptosystems and cancelable biometrics. EURASIP J. Inf. Secur. **2011**(3), (2011). https://doi.org/10.1186/1687-417X-2011-3

10. Sutcu, Y., Li, Q., Memon, N.: Protecting biometric templates with sketch: theory and practice. IEEE Trans. Inf. Forensics Secur. **2**(3), 503–512 (2007)

11. Dodis, Y., Reyzin, L., Smith, A.: Fuzzy extractors: how to generate strong keys from biometrics and other noisy data. In: Cachin, C., Camenisch, J.L. (eds.) EUROCRYPT 2004. LNCS, vol. 3027, pp. 523–540. Springer, Heidelberg (2004). https://doi.org/10.1007/978-3-540-24676-3_31

12. ISO/IEC 18004:2000(E). Information Technology Automatic identification and data capture techniques Bar code symbology QR Code. Standard, International Organization for Standardization, Geneva

13. Australian eTA. https://www.australiantraveling.com/?utm_source=google&utm_medium=cpc&gclid=EAIaIQobChMIm9-p5bO93QIVFHdeCh0rMw4nEAAYAiAAEgIcY_D_BwE. Accessed 12 Sept 2018

14. Canadian eTA. https://www.canadianevisa.com/?gclid=EAIaIQobChMI0vqMirS93QIVDDBpCh3P1wQVEAAYAiAAEgKTcPD_BwE. Accessed 12 Sept 2018

15. United States Customs and Border Protection Services Electronic System for Travel Authorizations. https://esta.cbp.dhs.gov/esta/. Accessed 12 Sept 2018

16. Johnson, D., Menezes, A., Vanstone, S.: The elliptic curve digital signature algorithm (ECDSA). Int. J. Inf. Secur. **1**(1), 36–63 (2001)

17. Rivest, R., Shamir, A., Adleman, L.: A method for obtaining digital signatures and public key cryptosystems. Commun. ACM **21**(2), 120–126 (1978)

18. Daemen, J., Rijmen, V.: The Design of Rijndael. Springer, Heidelberg (2002). https://doi.org/10.1007/978-3-662-04722-4

19. Rescorla, E.: SSL and TLS: Designing and Building Secure Systems. Addison-Wesley Longman Publishing Co., Inc., Boston (2001)

20. Sherif, M.: Protocols for Secure Electronic Commerce, 2nd edn. CRC Press, Boca Raton (2016)

21. JMRTD: An Open Source Java Implementation of Machine Readable Travel Documents. https://jmrtd.org/. Accessed 12 Sept 2018

22. ACR122U USB NFC Reader. http://www.acs.com.hk/en/products/3/acr122u-usb-nfc-reader/. Accessed 12 Sept 2018

23. ODroid USB camera product page. http://www.hardkernel.com/main/products/prdt_info.php?g_code=G146883099080. Accessed 12 Sept 2018

24. ODroid XU4 product page. http://www.hardkernel.com/main/products/prdt_info.php. Accessed 12 Sept 2018

25. Mostowski, W.I., Poll, E.: Electronic passports in a nutshell. ICIS, Nijmegen (2010)

26. Shaikh, R.A., Adi, K., Logrippo, L.: Dynamic risk-based decision methods for access control systems. Comput. Secur. **31**(4), 447–464 (2012)

27. Fall, D., Okuda, T., Kadobayashi, Y., Yamaguchi, S.: Risk adaptive authorization mechanism (RAdAM) for cloud computing. J. Inf. Process. **24**(2), 371–380 (2016)

28. World Economic Forum: Canada to Test Advancements in Biometrics and Blockchain to Welcome International Travellers. https://www.weforum.org/press/2018/01/canada-to-test-advancements-in-biometrics-and-blockchain-to-welcome-international-travellers/. Accessed 12 Sept 2018

29. Kaunert, C., Léonard, S., MacKenzie, A.: The social construction of an EU interest in counter-terrorism: US influence and internal struggles in the cases of PNR and SWIFT. Eur. Secur. **21**(4), 474–496 (2012)

30. Carpanelli, E., Lazzerini, N.: PNR: passenger name record, problems not resolved? The EU PNR conundrum after opinion 1/15 of the CJEU. Air Space Law **42**(4), 377–402 (2017)

31. Li, X., Jiang, P., Chen, T., Luo, X., Wen, Q.: A survey on the security of blockchain systems. Future Gener. Comput. Syst. pp. 1–25 (2017). https://arxiv.org/abs/1802.06993v2

32. Cavoukian, A., Chibba, M.: Cognitive cities, big data and citizen participation: the essentials of privacy and security. In: Portmann, E., Finger, M. (eds.) Towards Cognitive Cities. SSDC, vol. 63, pp. 61–82. Springer, Cham (2016). https://doi.org/10.1007/978-3-319-33798-2_4

33. Sheth, A., Anantharam, P., Henson, C.: Physical-cyber-social computing: an early 21st century approach. IEEE Intell. Syst. **1**, 78–82 (2013)

Cloud Security and Big Data

Cloud Security Auditing: Major Approaches and Existing Challenges

Suryadipta Majumdar[1]([⊠]), Taous Madi[2], Yosr Jarraya[3],
Makan Pourzandi[3], Lingyu Wang[2], and Mourad Debbabi[2]

[1] Information Security and Digital Forensics, University at Albany, Albany, NY, USA
smajumdar@albany.edu
[2] CIISE, Concordia University, Montreal, QC, Canada
{t_madi,wang,debbabi}@encs.concordia.ca
[3] Ericsson Security Research, Ericsson Canada, Montreal, QC, Canada
{yosr.jarraya,makan.pourzandi}@ericsson.com

Abstract. Cloud computing is emerging as a promising IT solution for enabling ubiquitous, convenient, and on-demand accesses to a shared pool of configurable computing resources. However, the widespread adoption of cloud is still being hindered by security and privacy concerns. Various cloud security and privacy issues have been addressed in the literature. However, the mere existence of such security mechanisms is usually insufficient to fully relieve cloud tenants from their security and privacy concerns. To increase tenants' trust in cloud, it is of paramount importance to provide adequate auditing mechanisms and tools to verify the security postures of their applications. However, there are currently many challenges in the area of cloud auditing and compliance validation. There exists a significant gap between the high-level recommendations provided in most cloud-specific standards and the low-level logging information currently available in existing cloud infrastructures. Furthermore, the unique characteristics of cloud computing may introduce additional complexity to the task, e.g., the use of heterogeneous solutions for deploying cloud systems may complicate data collection and processing and the sheer scale of cloud, together with its self-provisioning, elastic, and dynamic nature. In this paper, we conduct a survey on the existing cloud security auditing approaches. Additionally, we propose a taxonomy identifying the classifications based on auditing objectives and auditing techniques. We further devise a systematic process flow for cloud security auditing. Also, we conduct a comparative study on existing works to identify their strengths and weaknesses. Finally, we report existing challenges in cloud security auditing.

Keywords: Security auditing · Cloud security · Auditing challenges · Survey

© Springer Nature Switzerland AG 2019
N. Zincir-Heywood et al. (Eds.): FPS 2018, LNCS 11358, pp. 61–77, 2019.
https://doi.org/10.1007/978-3-030-18419-3_5

1   Introduction

Cloud computing has been gaining momentum as a promising IT solution for enabling cost-effective, ubiquitous, and on-demand access to a shared pool of configurable computing resources. Based on the provided services, cloud computing has been divided into three main models, namely, infrastructure as a service (IaaS), platform as a service (PaaS), and software as a service (SaaS). In those models, there exist at least three main stakeholders: cloud service providers, tenants and their users.

A cloud service provider owns a significant amount of computational, storage and networking resources, and offers different paid services (e.g., IaaS, PaaS, etc.) to its customers by utilizing this pool of resources. A cloud tenant, the direct customer of cloud providers, enjoys the ad-hoc and elastic (i.e., on demand provisioning and deprovisioning) nature of the cloud to use the shared pool of resources for conducting his operations. Usually, tenants are different companies or departments within a company, while users are customers availing services offered by cloud tenants.

While cloud computing has seen such increasing interests and adoption, the fear of loosing control and governance still persists due to the lack of transparency and trust [41]. Security auditing and compliance validation may increase cloud tenants' trust in the service providers by providing assurance on the compliance with the applicable laws, regulations, policies, and standards. However, there are currently many challenges in the area of cloud auditing and compliance verification. For instance, there exists a significant gap between the high-level recommendations provided in most cloud-specific standards (e.g., Cloud Control Matrix (CCM) [7] and ISO 27017 [22]) and the low-level logging information currently available in existing cloud infrastructures (e.g., OpenStack [38]). In practice, limited forms of auditing may be performed by cloud subscriber administrators [36], and there exist a few automated compliance tools (e.g., [12,47]) with several major limitations, which are discussed later in this section. Furthermore, the unique characteristics of cloud computing may introduce additional complexity to the task, e.g., the use of heterogeneous solutions for deploying cloud systems may complicate data collection and processing, and the sheer scale of the cloud together with its self-provisioning, elastic, and dynamic nature, may render the overhead of many verification techniques prohibitive. In particular, the multi-tenancy model and self-service nature of clouds usually imply significant operational complexity, which may prepare the floor for misconfigurations and vulnerabilities leading to violations of security compliance. Therefore, the security compliance verification with respect to security standards and policies is desirable to boost the trust relationship between the cloud stakeholders. Evidently, the Cloud Security Alliance (CSA) has recently introduced the Security, Trust & Assurance Registry (STAR) for security assurance in clouds, which defines three levels of certification, namely, self-auditing, third-party auditing, and continuous, near real-time verification of security compliance [8]. However, above-mentioned complexities coupled with the sheer size of clouds (e.g., a decent-size cloud is said to have around 1,000 tenants and 100,000 users [39]) implies one of the main challenges in cloud security auditing. In summary, the major challenges are to handle the unique nature of cloud and to deal with the sheer size of cloud in providing a scalable and efficient security auditing solution for clouds.

To this end, existing approaches can be roughly divided into three categories. First, the retroactive approaches (e.g., [3,11,12,23,29,32,47,48,50]) catch compliance violations after the fact by verifying different configurations and logs of the cloud. However, they cannot prevent security breaches from propagating or causing potentially irreversible damages (e.g., leaks of confidential information or denial of service). Second, the intercept-and-check approaches (e.g., [5,19,27,37,43]) verify the compliance of each user request before either granting or denying it, which can solve the limitation of the former approach. However, existing intercept-and-check methods cause a substantial delay in responding to each user request. Third, the proactive approaches, as in [5,30,31,37,51], address the limitations of previous approaches by starting the auditing process in advance and responding in a practical time at runtime. However, this approach is still suffering from certain practicality issues, such as how to decide about triggering the proactive step and how to reduce the manual process involved in the auditing process (a detailed discussion is provider in Sect. 4).

Contributions. The main contributions of our paper are as follows:

- As per our knowledge, this is the first effort to study the existing work on cloud security auditing and categorize the current techniques based on their adopted techniques and auditing objectives. To this end, we first study the landscape of cloud security auditing, then identify the existing categories and finally propose a taxonomy to present the whole landscape.
- In addition, we are the first to identify the structure of the automated security auditing process. For this purpose, we utilize our above-mentioned study to identify the mandatory steps of an automated security auditing system, and present the process flow of such auditing process.
- Furthermore, we are the first to conduct a qualitative comparison between existing works to highlight their coverage, strengths and weaknesses.
- Finally, we report the unaddressed challenges in cloud security auditing as the key observations of this survey. Our hope is that those challenges will draw the attention among security researchers to further improve the field of cloud security auditing.

The remainder of the paper is organized as follows. Section 2 discusses the structure of the automated security auditing process. Then, Sect. 3 describes the existing works, presents our proposed taxonomy and summarizes the findings of our comparative study. Afterwards, in Sect. 4, we report the existing challenges in cloud security auditing. Section 5 discussed different aspects of cloud security auditing. Finally, Sect. 6 concludes the paper discussing potential future work.

2 Structure of the Automated Security Auditing Process

Though security auditing is not a new process, automation of this process and complexity of targeted infrastructures introduce non-trivial challenges. Manual auditing is still in practice, where internal or third party auditors conduct the auditing process based on the collected data/evidence. Initial approaches of automating the auditing process are mostly to detect network intrusions. Later it has been adapted in other domains, such as data systems, access control and distributed systems. One of the most recent additions in the list is the cloud infrastructure. Based on the proposed solutions and best practices, we identify different phases (as in Fig. 1) of an automated security auditing process.

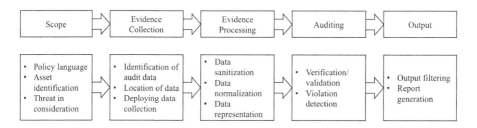

Fig. 1. Different steps of the cloud security auditing process

Defining the Scope and Threat Model. As a very first step, an organization should define the scope of its auditing. Part of it is to identify the critical and sensitive assets, operations and the modules in the system that deal with those assets and operations. The following step is to identify threats or nature of threats to be considered for the auditing process. Most of the time, threat model depends on the nature of the business and demand of customers. Part of this step is to describe security assumptions while considering each threat. To this end, last few years different studies have been conducted to identify risks and threats in the cloud computing ecosystem. Based on those threats, several security properties are proposed by CSA [6], ENISA [14], ISO [22], NIST [35], CUMULUS [9], etc.

Data/Evidence Collection. The next phase is to gather evidences/data to conduct the audit process. Based on the target system and threat model, audit data is enlisted. In some cases (e.g., cloud and distributed systems), locating those audit data is non-trivial.

The data collection phase has become more dynamic with the virtualization and multi-tenancy; which results in an increase in the amount of data to be collected. We also consider security aspects of data collection in addition to the different runtime and continuous data collection techniques of different data types. The trust model ensures that the audit data provided by a tenant is real and fresh. At the same time, there might exist the privacy concerns in a central auditing system, such as any tenant must not leak any sensitive information to the auditor, which can benefit any other tenants in case of colluding with the auditor.

In the cloud, most of the audit data is any events, logs and system configurations. Data collection techniques vary in terms of targeted environments and data, e.g., what data to collect based on the scope, threat model and objectives, and how to collect data (more challenging in a cloud-based system).

Data/Evidence Processing. The previous step collects raw data from the system. It requires further processing to be able to conduct auditing. In case of verifying compliance with a policy language, it depends on the language. Collected data needs to be sanitized, as data is collected from different sources. For better understanding and interpretation, different correlation methods are applied on sanitized data to categorize them. There are different techniques (e.g., call graph, information flow graph, reachability graph) to represent the audit data. Heterogeneous data is normalized by different methods, e.g., [10]. Storing this processed audit data is also an important phase specially when dynamic cloud auditing generates enormous amount of data over time.

Auditing. In the auditing phase, processed data is verified against the policies for any violation. The process either validates the system or detects if any anomaly exists. There are different auditing techniques proposed over time, though comparatively less automated techniques exist for the cloud. To understand better and to adapt other approaches, automated auditing methods in other analogous environments, such as intrusion detection systems and event correlation in multi-domain network/infrastructure, might be interesting. We consider different techniques of verifying policy compliance or detection of any policy violation including formal verification and validation (V&V) methods.

Audit Output. The proper representation of auditing output is the last and one of the important phases of security auditing. The audit report varies depending on the different demands and requirements of the customers (e.g., tenants). Hierarchy-based reporting helps to fulfill different levels of expectation. A major concern in outputting the result is not to leak any sensitive and unnecessary information to any tenant. Proper information isolation must be ensured.

3   Survey on Cloud Security Auditing

This section first categorizes the existing cloud security auditing, then elaborate each category mainly based on their coverage and adopted verification techniques and finally present a taxonomy based on these works.

There exist mainly three categories of cloud security auditing approaches. In the following, we discuss each of the approach with corresponding example works.

3.1 Retroactive Auditing

Retroactive auditing approach (e.g., [3,11,12,23,29,32,47,48,50]) in the cloud is a traditional way to verify the compliance of different components of a cloud. Works under this approach in the cloud targets a wide range of security properties that cover various cloud layers, such as data, user and virtual infrastructure.

There are several works that target auditing data location and storage in the cloud (e.g., [21,23,48,50]). Wang et al. [48] propose a cloud storage system which enables privacy-friendly public auditing to ensure data security in the proposed system. The work leverages public key based homomorphic linear authenticator (HLA) to significantly reduce the communication and computation overhead at the auditor side. Kai et al. [23] can handle multiple auditing requests to verify the data integrity in the multi-cloud environment. In addition, similar as the former this work preserves the privacy of the audit data. On the other hand, Ismail et al. [21] propose a game theory based auditing approach to verify the compliance of data backup requirements of users. Unlike previous ones, Wang et al. [50] offer auditing of data origin and consistence in addition to data integrity.

There exist other works, which target virtual infrastructure change auditing (e.g., [11,12,28,29,32,47]). These works cover different layers (e.g., user, virtual network, etc.) in the virtual infrastructure. Particularly, Ullah et al. [47] propose an architecture to build an automated security compliance tool for cloud computing platforms focusing on auditing clock synchronization and remote administrative & diagnostic port protection. Doelitzscher [11] proposes on-demand audit architecture for IaaS clouds and an implementation based on software agents to enable anomaly detection systems to identify anomalies in IaaS clouds for the purpose of auditing. The works in [11,47] have the same general objective, which is cloud auditing, but they use empirical techniques to perform auditing whereas we use formal techniques to model and solve the auditing problem. Madi et al. [28,29] verify a list of security properties to audit the cross-layer consistencies in the cloud.

In addition, several industrial efforts include solutions to support cloud auditing in specific cloud environments. For instance, Microsoft proposes SecGuru [3] to audit Azure datacenter network policy using the SMT solver Z3. IBM also provides a set of monitoring tool integrated with QRadar [20], which is their security information and event management system, to collect and analyze events in the cloud. Amazon is offering web API logs and metric data to their AWS clients by AWS CloudWatch & CloudTrail [2] that could be used for the auditing purpose. Although those efforts may potentially assist auditing tasks, none of them directly supports auditing a wide range of security properties covering authentication, authorization and virtual infrastructure on cloud standards.

Furthermore, there are several auditing solutions (e.g., [16–18,32,46]) targeting the user-level (e.g., authentication and authorization) of the cloud. Majumdar et al. [32] verify the role-based access control implementation in OpenStack, a popular cloud platform. This work also verifies a list of security properties to ensure proper implementation of authentication steps in the cloud.

To accommodate the need of secure collaborative environments such as cloud computing, there have been some efforts towards proposing multi-domain/multi-tenant access control models (e.g., [16,17,46]). Gouglidis and Mavridis [17] leverage graph theory algorithms to verify a subset of the access control security properties. Gouglidis et al. [18] utilize model-checking to verify custom extensions of RBAC with multi-domains [17] against security properties. Lu et al. [26] use set theory to formalize policy conflicts in the context of inter-operation in the multi-domain environment.

3.2   Intercept-and-Check Auditing

Existing intercept-and-check approaches (e.g., [5,19,27,33,37,43,45]) perform major verification tasks while holding the event instances blocked. Works under this category cover the virtual network, user-level and software defined network (SDN) layers of a cloud environment as discussed in the following.

The works (e.g., [5,37]) at the virtual network level are mainly verifying the security properties to safeguard multiple layers in a virtual network through an intercept-and-check approach. These works focus on operational network properties (e.g., black holes and forwarding loops) in virtual networks, whereas our effort is oriented toward preserving compliance with structural security properties that impact isolation in cloud virtualized infrastructures. Designing cloud monitoring services based on security service-level agreements have been discussed in [40].

The user-level runtime auditing is proposed in Patron [27] and Majumdar et al. [33]. More specifically, Patron [27] audits the access control rules defined by the cloud tenants. In addition, Patron enforces these rules on the cloud by leveraging the middleware supported in OpenStack, one of the major cloud platforms. Majumdar et al. [33] utilize similar interception approach in OpenStack and audit the proper deployment of various authentication and authorization plugins, such as single sign-on (SSO), role-based access control (RBAC) and attribute-based access control (ABAC) in the cloud.

There are also few works (e.g., TopoGuard [19] and TopoGuard+ [43]) which adopt the intercept-and-check approach in the software defined network (SDN) environment. TopoGuard [19] and TopoGuard+ [43] perform the interception and enforcement to prevent topology tempering attacks in SDN. Those works in SDN can be complements to the above-mentioned solutions for other layers in the cloud.

3.3   Proactive Auditing

The concept of proactive security auditing for clouds is different than the traditional security auditing concept. The first proactive auditing approach for clouds is proposed in [5]. Additionally, the Cloud Security Alliance (CSA) recommends continuous auditing as the highest level of auditing [8], from which latter works (e.g., [30,31]) are inspired. The current proactive and runtime auditing mechanisms are more of a combination of traditional auditing and incident management. For example, LeaPS [31] learns from incidents and intercepted events to process or detect in a similar manner as a traditional incident management system. At the same time, LeaPS verifies and enforces compliance against different security properties, which are mostly taken from different security standards, and provide detailed evidence for any violation through LeaPS dashboard. Therefore, the concept of proactive security auditing is a combination of incident management and security auditing.

Proactive security analysis has also been explored for software security enforcement through monitoring programs' behaviors and taking specific actions (e.g., warning) in case security policies are violated. Many state-based formal models are proposed for those program monitors over the last two decades. First, Schneider [42] modelled program monitors using an infinite-state-automata model to enforce safety properties. Those automata recognize invalid behaviors and halt the target application before the violation occurs. Ligatti [24] builds on Schneider's model and defines a more general program monitors model based on the so called edit/security automata. Rather than just recognizing executions, edit automata-based monitors are able to suppress bad and/or insert new actions, transforming hence invalid executions into valid ones. Mandatory Result Automata (MRA) is another model proposed by Ligatti et al. [13,25] that can transform both actions and results to valid ones. Narain [34] proactively generates correct network configurations using the model finder Alloy, which leverages a state of the art SAT solver. To this end, they specify a set of end-to-end requirements in First Order Logic and determine the set of existing network components. Alloy uses a state of the art SAT solver to provide the configurations that satisfy the input requirements for each network component. Considering the huge size of cloud environments and the tremendous space of possible events, adapting those solutions in the cloud is possibly very challenging.

Weatherman [5] is aiming at mitigating misconfigurations and enforcing security policies in a virtualized infrastructure. Weatherman has both online and offline approaches. Their online approach intercepts management operations for analysis, and relays them to the management hosts only if Weatherman confirms no security violation caused by those operations. Otherwise, they are rejected with an error signal to the requester. The work defines a realization model, that captures the virtualized infrastructure configuration and topology in a graph-based model. The latter is synchronized with the actual infrastructure using the approach in [4]. Two major limitations of this proposition are: (i) the model capturing the whole infrastructure causes a scalability issue for the solution, and (ii) the time consuming operation-checking that should be performed on the emergence of each event, makes security enforcement not feasible for large size data centers. Congress [37] is an OpenStack project offering both online and offline policy enforcement approaches. The offline approach requires submitting a future change plan to Congress, so that the changes can be simulated and the impacts of those changes can be verified against specific properties.

In the online approach, Congress first applies the operation to the cloud, then checks its impacts. In case of a violation, the operation is reverted. However, the time elapsed before reverting the operation can be critical to perform some illicit actions, for instance, transferring sensitive files before loosing the assigned role. Foley et al. [15] provide an algebra to assess the effect of security policies replacement and composition in OpenStack. Their solution can be considered as a proactive approach for checking operational property violations.

3.4   Taxonomy of Cloud Security Auditing

Based on the above-mentioned study on cloud security auditing, we devise a primary taxonomy for these works (as in Fig. 2). We consider the whole landscape from the perspective of their coverage and applied techniques. Therefore, we first categorize them based on their targeted cloud layers (e.g., data, user, virtual network and SDN), then further identify various high-level security properties that these works support, and finally show their adopted approaches. Thus, it is trivial to understand which approaches are already explored for certain security problems under a particular cloud layer. Furthermore, our taxonomy can be useful towards building a fine-grained classification of cloud security auditing approaches.

3.5   Comparative Study

We conduct a comparative study based on the taxonomy presented in the previous section. Table 1 summarizes the findings of this study. The first and second columns of the table enlist existing works and their verification methods. The next four columns present their covered layers in the cloud. We mainly include works on four cloud layers: data, user, virtual network and software defined network (SDN). In next three columns, we show the approaches (retroactive, intercept-and-check and proactive) that a work adopts. Afterwards, there are five features enlisted to demonstrate the special skills of these works. The caching feature is marked when a work enables caching of verification results to enhance the efficiency of the auditing process. We mark the dependency model when a work utilizes the dependency relationship in the cloud to improve the efficiency and accuracy of the auditing process. The pre-computation step is to identify the works which performs a significant part of the verification step in advance to reduce the response time of the runtime (usually in intercept-and-check and proactive) solutions. There exist few works which support auditing of multiple requests together. For them, we mark the batch auditing feature. The active auditing feature is an active-probing-based auditing solution which does not fully rely on the cloud provider for the audit data and instead actively participate in the targeted protocol to verify certain properties. The next four columns indicate the supporting cloud platforms for these auditing solutions. We mark the adaptable to others column when a work provide detailed discussion on the process of porting the solution to different platforms. In the last four columns, we evaluate existing works based on the commonly observed constraints in the

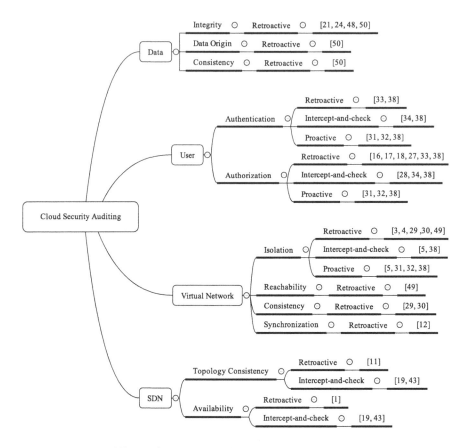

Fig. 2. A taxonomy of cloud security auditing

field of cloud security auditing. The after-the-fact constraint is marked if a work cannot prevent a security violation. The prohibitive delay is checked when a runtime work (i.e., intercept-and-check and proactive approaches) causes significant delay in responding to a user request. For retroactive solutions, we mark this column as not applicable (N/A). If a work involves significant manual effort (apart from the inputs from the users) in the auditing process, then we check the manual effort constraint. The limited coverage constraint is defined based on the expressiveness of a auditing solution. For instance, a work supporting first order logic to define security properties does not suffer from this constraint.

The key observations of this comparative study are as follows. First, there is no single auditing solution to verify multiple layers of the cloud. Therefore, today's cloud tenants require at least three different solutions to fulfill their auditing need; which might not be very usable for the tenants. Second, even though intercept-and-check approach is designed to prevent security violations, existing works under this category are not practical due to their prohibitive delay. Third, the proactive auditing approach is a promising solution to overcome the limitations of both retroactive and intercept-and-check approach. However, this approach still suffers from several practical issues, such as relying on manual efforts and limiting the expressiveness of security properties. Finally, there exist several features in the wild which significantly can improve the efficiency and accuracy of the auditing solution. However, there is a need of a unified solution with all these features at least to overcome major constraints.

4 Challenges in Cloud Security Auditing

In the following, we discuss the key challenges in cloud security auditing that we identified during our survey.

High-level Security Properties. There is a significant gap between the high-level standards (defining security requirements) and the low-level cloud configurations (providing the audit data). Even though several works (e.g., [28,29,32]) highlight this challenge and partially address the concern, the issue still persists in interpreting security guidelines and defining security properties ready to be used in auditing solutions. Current solutions rely on manual identification of security properties, which is infeasible and error-prone especially when we consider the multiple layers of cloud and intend to provide a unified security solution for the whole cloud.

Non-trivial Log Processing. One mandatory and non-trivial step of cloud security auditing is log processing. This step involves several challenging tasks. First, identifying the heterogeneous sources of audit data requires well realization of the deployed cloud system, which usually consists of several complex components, e.g., management platform and layer-2 plugins. Second, due to the different nature (e.g., database and text files) of storing the configurations and logs, the collection of audit data has to be performed by adopting multiple methods. Finally, the diverse format of the logs require extensive processing efforts to uniform the format before using them in auditing.

Reducing Manual Involvement. Automating the auditing process is a must in a dynamic environment like cloud to ensure the accuracy and efficiency. However, the current solutions still rely on manual efforts in several critical steps. Fully eliminating or at least reducing manual effort is not trivial mainly for the following two reasons. First, defining the security properties is a mandatory step for any auditing process and we fully rely on human inputs for this step. Existing rule mining techniques in access control might be useful in automating this step. Second, all intercept-and-check and proactive approaches (as reported in Sect. 4) rely on manual identification of critical operations (which potentially can violate a property). Applying machine learning or more specifically interactive machine learning techniques may reduce the manual efforts involved with this step.

Unified Auditing Solution for Multi-layer Clouds. Table 1 pinpoints that a tenant requires at least three auditing solutions if s/he wants to verify all four layers of her/his cloud, and there is a need of unified auditing solution supporting multi-layer of a cloud. However, to propose a unified solution is non-trivial

Table 1. Summary of existing cloud security auditing solutions highlighting their adopted methods, covered cloud layers, applied approaches, offered features, supported platforms and constraints. The symbols (•), (-) and N/A mean supported/required, not supported/required, and not applicable, respectively. Note that, for both Weatherman and Congress, V1 and V2 refer to their proactive and intercept-and-check variants, respectively.

Proposals	Methods	Data	User	Virtual Net.	SDN	Retroactive	Intercept-and-check	Proactive	Caching	Dependency model	Pre-computation	Batch auditing	Active auditing	Supporting OpenStack	Supporting Azure	Supporting VMware	Adaptable to others	After-the-fact	Prohibitive delay	Manual effort	Limited coverage
Wang et al. [48]	Cryptographic	•	-	-	-	•	-	-	-	-	-	•	-	-	-	-	•	•	N/A	-	-
Kai et al. [23]	Cryptographic	•	-	-	-	•	-	-	-	-	-	•	-	-	-	-	•	•	N/A	-	-
Doelitzscher et al. [12]	Custom algorithm	-	-	•	-	•	-	-	-	-	-	-	-	•	-	-	-	•	N/A	-	-
Ullah et al. [47]	Custom algorithm	-	-	•	-	•	-	-	-	-	-	-	-	•	-	-	-	•	N/A	-	-
Solanas et al. [44]	Classifiers	-	•	-	-	•	-	-	-	-	-	-	-	•	-	-	-	•	N/A	-	-
Majumdar et al. [32]	CSP	-	•	-	-	•	-	-	-	-	-	-	-	•	-	-	-	•	N/A	-	-
Madi et al. [28,29]	CSP	-	-	•	-	•	-	-	-	-	-	-	-	•	-	-	-	•	N/A	-	-
Cloud radar [4]	Graph theory	-	-	•	-	•	-	-	-	-	-	-	-	-	-	•	-	•	N/A	-	-
TenantGuard [49]	Graph theory	-	-	•	-	•	-	-	-	-	-	-	-	•	-	-	-	•	N/A	-	-
SecGuru [3]	SMT	-	-	•	-	•	-	-	-	-	-	-	-	-	•	-	-	•	N/A	-	-
QRadar [20]	Custom	-	-	•	-	•	-	-	-	-	-	-	-	-	-	•	-	•	N/A	-	-
SPV [1]	Custom	-	-	-	•	•	•	-	-	-	-	•	•	•	-	-	•	•	N/A	-	-
Patron [27]	Custom algorithm	-	•	-	-	-	-	•	-	•	-	-	-	•	-	-	-	-	•	•	-
Weatherman (V1) [5]	Graph theory	-	-	•	-	-	-	•	-	-	-	-	-	-	-	•	-	-	•	•	•
Congress (V1) [37]	Datalog	-	•	•	-	-	-	•	-	-	-	-	-	•	-	-	-	-	•	•	-
TopoGuard [19,43]	Custom	-	-	-	•	-	-	•	-	-	-	-	-	-	-	•	-	-	•	-	•
Majumdar et al. [33]	CSP + Custom	-	•	-	-	-	-	•	-	-	-	-	-	•	-	•	-	-	•	•	-
Weatherman (V2) [5]	Graph theory	-	-	•	-	-	-	•	-	•	-	-	-	-	-	•	-	-	-	•	•
Congress (V2) [37]	Datalog	-	•	•	-	-	-	•	-	•	-	-	-	•	-	-	-	-	-	•	•
PVSC [30]	Custom algorithm	-	•	•	-	-	-	•	•	•	•	-	-	•	-	-	•	-	-	•	•
LeaPS [31]	Custom + Bayesian	-	•	•	-	-	-	•	-	•	•	-	-	•	-	-	•	-	-	•	•

for the following fact. First, each layer of the cloud contains unique auditing requirements (e.g., audit data type and security properties). Second, there exist security threats involving multi-layer (as reported in [28]); which currently being ignored in the solutions dedicated for a single layer. Finally, it is very difficult to be comprehensive in covering security properties from various layers. However, we believe that this is a more generic problem in the field of auditing and require more attention from the researchers to overcome the concern.

Privacy Concerns in Audit Inputs and Outputs. Both third party and cross-tenant auditing raise privacy concerns resulting from both audit inputs and outputs. In addressing these privacy concerns, there exist at least two major challenges. First, how we can preserve tenants' privacy in the input data so that the utility (i.e., auditing capability) is not much affected. Second, how to hide cross-tenant sensitive information so that the usefulness of auditing output remains unchanged.

5 Discussion

In the following, we discuss several important aspects of cloud security auditing.

Why Traditional Auditing is not Enough for the Cloud. Based on the previously discussed cloud security issues, it is obvious that traditional security auditing techniques are not enough to be directly applied to the cloud. The two most existing on-premise IT models are IT housing and IT outsourcing [11]. In IT housing, it belongs to the customer to provide and manage his own hardware. The datacenter provider just provides the remaining facilities such as network components, cooling and power. Traditional IT outsourcing is generally a medium to long term contract. In the latter, the customer rents all the infrastructure components from the service provider. The rented infrastructure is exclusively used by one customer which is called the single-tenant model. A prior communication with the provider is required whenever any modification is to be applied to the rented infrastructures. In these two models, the IT organization has full governance over the different IT technology layers. In the cloud, however, as we move from IaaS to PaaS to SaaS, the level of control of cloud providers increases and the burden of access, control, management and the infrastructure's trust boundaries is considerably shifted to the cloud provider and responsibilities become more or less shared between the latter and its customers, which raises trust issues between the two parties.

How Cloud Auditing Helps Mitigating Security Issues. In a cloud environment, though asymmetric, trust needs to be boosted in both directions. Most importantly, the potential customer needs to trust the cloud provider in order to feel comfortable when outsourcing his assets. The other way around, the cloud provider needs as well to gain some assurance that the customer will benefit from the offered services in a honest way and does not use it for cybercrime, but at the same time, the provider is supposed to immune his services against malicious insiders. Although trust plays a vital role in the cloud ecosystems, it should be further boosted with other tools. With this regard auditing is a good fit to increase the confidence of different stakeholders. Continuous auditing allows to analyze the service conditions and the infrastructure health through detailed log records to access conformity between security measures and policies. Although it seems that cloud providers might not be willing to allow for auditing tasks, they actually should have their own incentives. In effect, auditing helps reducing the scope of search and identifying responsible parties in case of incidents or legal actions which, in some cases, can exonerate the provider and prevent him considerable money loss. For instance, the cloud security alliance recommends auditing different critical components of a cloud including privileged user access, regulatory compliance, isolation, tenant segregation, monitoring, and data storage and processing.

6   Conclusion

Cloud computing has seen a lot of interests and adoption lately. Nonetheless, the widespread adoption of cloud is still being hindered by the lack of transparency and accountability, which has traditionally been ensured through security compliance auditing techniques. In this paper, we conducted a survey on the existing cloud security auditing approaches. To this end, we first categorized the existing solutions and elaborate each category with example works. Second, we proposed a taxonomy identifying the classifications mainly based on auditing objectives and auditing techniques. Third, we conducted a comparative study on these works to identify the strengths and weaknesses of these works. Finally, we identified current challenges in cloud security auditing; which potentially may draw the attention of security researchers. However, there are few limitations of this work which we intend to overcome in our future work. For instance, we plan to increase the granularity of the proposed taxonomy to pinpoint more precisely the gaps in cloud security auditing. In addition to qualitative comparison presented in this paper, we intend to compare existing works quantitatively to understand better how to improve the efficiency and accuracy of these approaches.

Acknowledgement. The authors thank the anonymous reviewers for their valuable comments. This work is partially supported by the Natural Sciences and Engineering Research Council of Canada and Ericsson Canada under CRD Grant N01823 and by PROMPT Quebec.

References

1. Alimohammadifar, A., et al.: Stealthy probing-based verification (SPV): an active approach to defending software defined networks against topology poisoning attacks. In: Lopez, J., Zhou, J., Soriano, M. (eds.) ESORICS 2018. LNCS, vol. 11099, pp. 463–484. Springer, Cham (2018). https://doi.org/10.1007/978-3-319-98989-1_23
2. Amazon Web Services: Security at scale: logging in AWS. Technical report, Amazon (2013)
3. Bjørner, N., Jayaraman, K.: Checking cloud contracts in Microsoft Azure. In: Natarajan, R., Barua, G., Patra, M.R. (eds.) ICDCIT 2015. LNCS, vol. 8956, pp. 21–32. Springer, Cham (2015). https://doi.org/10.1007/978-3-319-14977-6_2
4. Bleikertz, S., Vogel, C., Groß, T.: Cloud radar: near real-time detection of security failures in dynamic virtualized infrastructures. In: Proceedings of the 30th Annual Computer Security Applications Conference (ACSAC), pp. 26–35. ACM (2014)
5. Bleikertz, S., Vogel, C., Groß, T., Mödersheim, S.: Proactive security analysis of changes in virtualized infrastructures. In: Proceedings of the 31st Annual Computer Security Applications Conference (ACSAC), pp. 51–60. ACM (2015)

6. Cloud Security Alliance: Security guidance for critical areas of focus in cloud computing v3.0 (2011)
7. Cloud Security Alliance: Cloud control matrix CCM v3.0.1 (2014). https://cloudsecurityalliance.org/research/ccm/. Accessed 14 Feb 2018
8. Cloud Security Alliance: CSA STAR program and open certification framework in 2016 and beyond (2016). https://downloads.cloudsecurityalliance.org/star/csa-star-program-cert-prep.pdf. Accessed 14 Feb 2018
9. CUMULUS: Certification infrastructure for multi-layer cloud services project (CUMULUS). EU project (2012)
10. Distributed Management Task Force, Inc.: Cloud auditing data federation (2016). https://www.dmtf.org/standards/cadf
11. Doelitzscher, F.: Security Audit Compliance for Cloud Computing. PhD thesis, Plymouth University (2014)
12. Doelitzscher, F., Fischer, C., Moskal, D., Reich, C., Knahl, M., Clarke, N.: Validating cloud infrastructure changes by cloud audits. In: Eighth World Congress on Services (SERVICES), pp. 377–384. IEEE (2012)
13. Dolzhenko, E., Ligatti, J., Reddy, S.: Modeling runtime enforcement with mandatory results automata. Int. J. Inf. Secur. **14**(1), 47–60 (2015)
14. ENISA: European union agency for network and information security (2016). https://www.enisa.europa.eu
15. Foley, S.N., Neville, U.: A firewall algebra for OpenStack. In: Conference on Communications and Network Security (CNS), pp. 541–549. IEEE (2015)
16. Ghosh, N., Chatterjee, D., Ghosh, S.K., Das, S.K.: Securing loosely-coupled collaboration in cloud environment through dynamic detection and removal of access conflicts. IEEE Trans. Cloud Comput. **4**, 1 (2014)
17. Gouglidis, A., Mavridis, I.: domRBAC: an access control model for modern collaborative systems. Comput. Secur. **31**, 540–556 (2012)
18. Gouglidis, A., Mavridis, I., Hu, V.C.: Security policy verification for multi-domains in cloud systems. Int. J. Inf. Secur. **13**(2), 97–111 (2014)
19. Hong, S., Xu, L., Wang, H., Gu, G.: Poisoning network visibility in software-defined networks: new attacks and countermeasures. In: Proceedings of 2015 Annual Network and Distributed System Security Symposium (NDSS 2015), February 2015
20. IBM: Safeguarding the cloud with IBM security solutions. Technical report, IBM Corporation (2013)
21. Ismail, Z., Kiennert, C., Leneutre, J., Chen, L.: Auditing a cloud provider's compliance with data backup requirements: a game theoretical analysis. IEEE Trans. Inf. Forensics Secur. **11**(8), 1685–1699 (2016)
22. ISO Std IEC. ISO 27017. Information technology- Security techniques- Code of practice for information security controls based on ISO/IEC 27002 for cloud services (DRAFT) (2012). http://www.iso27001security.com/html/27017.html. Accessed 14 Feb 2018
23. Kai, H., et al.: An efficient public batch auditing protocol for data security in multi-cloud storage. In: 8th ChinaGrid Annual Conference (ChinaGrid), pp. 51–56. IEEE (2013)
24. Ligatti, J., Bauer, L., Walker, D.: Run-time enforcement of nonsafety policies. ACM Trans. Inf. Syst. Secur. (TISSEC) **12**(3), 19 (2009)
25. Ligatti, J., Reddy, S.: A theory of runtime enforcement, with results. In: Gritzalis, D., Preneel, B., Theoharidou, M. (eds.) ESORICS 2010. LNCS, vol. 6345, pp. 87–100. Springer, Heidelberg (2010). https://doi.org/10.1007/978-3-642-15497-3_6
26. Lu, Z., Wen, Z., Tang, Z., Li, R.: Resolution for conflicts of inter-operation in multi-domain environment. Wuhan Univ. J. Nat. Sci. **12**(5), 955–960 (2007)

27. Luo, Y., Luo, W., Puyang, T., Shen, Q., Ruan, A., Wu, Z.: OpenStack security modules: a least-invasive access control framework for the cloud. In: IEEE 9th International Conference on Cloud Computing (CLOUD) (2016)
28. Madi, T., et al.: ISOTOP: auditing virtual networks isolation across cloud layers in OpenStack. ACM Trans. Priv. Secur. (TOPS) **22**, 1 (2018)
29. Madi, T., Majumdar, S., Wang, Y., Jarraya, Y., Pourzandi, M., Wang, L.: Auditing security compliance of the virtualized infrastructure in the cloud: application to OpenStack. In: Proceedings of the Sixth ACM Conference on Data and Application Security and Privacy (CODASPY), pp. 195–206. ACM (2016)
30. Majumdar, S., et al.: Proactive verification of security compliance for clouds through pre-computation: application to OpenStack. In: Askoxylakis, I., Ioannidis, S., Katsikas, S., Meadows, C. (eds.) ESORICS 2016. LNCS, vol. 9878, pp. 47–66. Springer, Cham (2016). https://doi.org/10.1007/978-3-319-45744-4_3
31. Majumdar, S., et al.: LeaPS: learning-based proactive security auditing for clouds. In: Foley, S.N., Gollmann, D., Snekkenes, E. (eds.) ESORICS 2017. LNCS, vol. 10493, pp. 265–285. Springer, Cham (2017). https://doi.org/10.1007/978-3-319-66399-9_15
32. Majumdar, S., et al.: Security compliance auditing of identity and access management in the cloud: application to OpenStack. In: 7th International Conference on Cloud Computing Technology and Science (CloudCom), pp. 58–65. IEEE (2015)
33. Majumdar, S., et al.: User-level runtime security auditing for the cloud. IEEE Trans. Inf. Forensics Secur. **13**(5), 1185–1199 (2018)
34. Narain, S.: Network configuration management via model finding. In: Proceedings of the 19th Conference on Large Installation System Administration Conference (LISA), pp. 15–15 (2005)
35. NIST. SP 800–53. Recommended Security Controls for Federal Information Systems (2003)
36. Open Data Center Alliance: Open data center alliance usage: Cloud based identity governance and auditing rev. 1.0. Technical report, Open Data Center Alliance (2012)
37. OpenStack: OpenStack Congress (2015). https://wiki.openstack.org/wiki/Congress. Accessed 14 Feb 2018
38. OpenStack: OpenStack open source cloud computing software (2015). http://www.openstack.org. Accessed 14 Feb 2018
39. OpenStack: OpenStack user survey (2016). https://www.openstack.org/assets/survey/October2016SurveyReport.pdf. Accessed 14 Feb 2018
40. Petcu, D., Craciun, C.: Towards a security SLA-based cloud monitoring service. In: Proceedings of the 4th International Conference on Cloud Computing and Services Science (CLOSER), pp. 598–603 (2014)
41. Ren, K., Wang, C., Wang, Q.: Security challenges for the public cloud. IEEE Internet Comput. **16**(1), 69–73 (2012)
42. Schneider, F.B.: Enforceable security policies. Trans. Inf. Syst. Secur. (TISSEC) **3**(1), 30–50 (2000)
43. Skowyra, R., et al.: Effective topology tampering attacks and defenses in software-defined networks. In: Proceedings of the 48th Annual IEEE/IFIP International Conference on Dependable Systems and Networks (DSN 2015), June 2018
44. Solanas, M., Hernandez-Castro, J., Dutta, D.: Detecting fraudulent activity in a cloud using privacy-friendly data aggregates. Technical report, arXiv preprint (2014)

45. Tabiban, A., Majumdar, S., Wang, L., Debbabi, M.: PERMON: an openstack middleware for runtime security policy enforcement in clouds. In: Proceedings of the 4th IEEE Workshop on Security and Privacy in the Cloud (SPC 2018), June 2018
46. Tang, B., Sandhu, R.: Extending OpenStack access control with domain trust. In: Au, M.H., Carminati, B., Kuo, C.-C.J. (eds.) NSS 2014. LNCS, vol. 8792, pp. 54–69. Springer, Cham (2014). https://doi.org/10.1007/978-3-319-11698-3_5
47. Ullah, K.W., Ahmed, A.S., Ylitalo, J.: Towards building an automated security compliance tool for the cloud. In: 12th International Conference on Trust, Security and Privacy in Computing and Communications (TrustCom), pp. 1587–1593. IEEE (2013)
48. Wang, C., Chow, S.S., Wang, Q., Ren, K., Lou, W.: Privacy-preserving public auditing for secure cloud storage. IEEE Trans. Comput. **62**(2), 362–375 (2013)
49. Wang, Y., et al.: TenantGuard: scalable runtime verification of cloud-wide VM-level network isolation. In: Proceedings of 2017 Annual Network and Distributed System Security Symposium (NDSS 2017), February 2017
50. Wang, Y., Wu, Q., Qin, B., Shi, W., Deng, R.H., Hu, J.: Identity-based data outsourcing with comprehensive auditing in clouds. IEEE Trans. Inf. Forensics Secur. **12**(4), 940–952 (2017)
51. Yau, S.S., Buduru, A.B., Nagaraja, V.: Protecting critical cloud infrastructures with predictive capability. In: 8th International Conference on Cloud Computing (CLOUD), pp. 1119–1124. IEEE (2015)

Secure Joins with MapReduce

Xavier Bultel[1], Radu Ciucanu[2], Matthieu Giraud[3(✉)],
Pascal Lafourcade[3], and Lihua Ye[4]

[1] IRISA, Université de Rennes 1, Rennes, France
`xavier.bultel@irisa.fr`
[2] INSA Centre Val de Loire, Univ. Orléans, LIFO EA 4022, Bourges, France
`radu.ciucanu@insa-cvl.fr`
[3] LIMOS, Université Clermont Auvergne, Clermont-Ferrand, France
{`matthieu.giraud,pascal.lafourcade`}`@uca.fr`
[4] Harbin Institute of Technology, Harbin, China
`16s003041@stu.hit.edu.cn`

Abstract. MapReduce is one of the most popular programming paradigms that allows a user to process Big data sets. Our goal is to add privacy guarantees to the two standard algorithms of join computation for MapReduce: the *cascade* algorithm and the *hypercube* algorithm. We assume that the data is externalized in an *honest-but-curious* server and a user is allowed to query the join result. We design, implement, and prove the security of two approaches: (i) *Secure-Private*, assuming that the public cloud and the user do not collude, (ii) *Collision-Resistant-Secure-Private*, which resists to collusions between the public cloud and the user i.e., when the public cloud knows the secret key of the user.

Keywords: Database query · MapReduce · Security · Natural joins

1 Introduction

With the advent of Big data, new techniques have been developed to process parallel computation on a large cluster. One of them is the MapReduce programming paradigm [11], which allows a user to keep data in public clouds and to perform computations on it. A MapReduce program uses two functions (*map* and *reduce*) that are executed on a large cluster of machines in parallel. The popularity of the MapReduce paradigm comes from the fact that the programmer does not need to handle aspects such as the partitioning of the data, scheduling the program's execution across the machines, handling machine failures, and managing the communication between different machines.

MapReduce users often rent storage and computing resources from a public cloud provider (e.g., Google Cloud Platform, Amazon Web Services, Microsoft Azure). External storage and computations with a public cloud make the Big data processing accessible to users that can not afford building their own clusters. Yet, outsourcing data and computations to a public cloud involves inherent

© Springer Nature Switzerland AG 2019
N. Zincir-Heywood et al. (Eds.): FPS 2018, LNCS 11358, pp. 78–94, 2019.
https://doi.org/10.1007/978-3-030-18419-3_6

security and privacy concerns. Since the data is externalized, it can be communicated over an untrustworthy network and processed on some untrustworthy machines, where malicious public cloud users may learn private data.

We address the fundamental problem of computing relational joins between an arbitrary number of relations in a privacy-preserving manner using MapReduce. We assume that the data is externalized in the cloud by the

Fig. 1. The system architecture.

data owner and there is a user that is allowed to query it as shown in Fig. 1. This standard model has been used recently by Dolev et al. [14].

We next present via a running example the concept of relational joins. Then, we present MapReduce computations, our problem statement, and illustrate the privacy issues related to joins computation with MapReduce.

Example 1. The data owner is a hospital storing relations R_1, R_2, R_3 cf. Fig. 2. The (natural) join of these relations, denoted $R_1 \bowtie R_2 \bowtie R_3$, is the relation whose tuples are composed of tuples of R_1, R_2 and R_3 that agree on shared attributes. In our case, the attribute *Name* is shared between R_1 and R_2. Moreover, the attribute *Disease* is shared between intermediate join result $(R_1 \bowtie R_2)$ and relation R_3. In Fig. 2, we give both the intermediate result $(R_1 \bowtie R_2)$ and the final result $(R_1 \bowtie R_2) \bowtie R_3$. We observe that tuple (Alice, NYC) from relation R_1, tuple (Bob, Diabetes) from relation R_2, and tuple (Bob, London, Diabetes) from relation $R_1 \bowtie R_2$ do not participate to the final result.

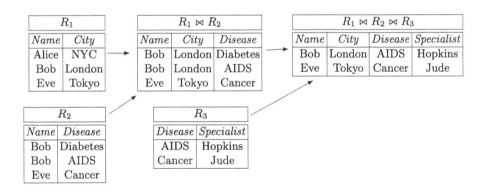

Fig. 2. Joins between relations R_1, R_2 and R_3.

1.1   Joins with MapReduce

Two algorithms for computing relational joins with MapReduce are presented in the literature: the *Cascade* algorithm (i.e., a generalization of the binary join from Chapter 2 of [18]) and the *Hypercube* algorithm [4,9]. In the following, a *reducer* refers to the application of the reduce function to a single key.

Cascade Algorithm. To compute an n-ary join ($n \geqslant 2$), the cascade algorithm uses $n-1$ MapReduce rounds i.e., a sequence of $n-1$ binary joins. A binary join works as follows: first, it applies the *map* function on the first two relations R_1 and R_2 that are spread over sets of nodes $\mathcal{R}_1$ and $\mathcal{R}_2$, respectively. The map function creates for each tuple of each relation a *key-value* pair where key is equal to values of shared attributes between the two relations, and value is equal to non-shared values of the tuple as well as the name of the relation. Then, the key-value pairs are grouped by key i.e., all key-value pairs output by the map phase which have the same key are sent to the same reducer. For each key and from the associated values coming from these two relations, the *reduce* function creates all possible tuples corresponding to the joins of these two relations. We obtain as intermediate result a new relation denoted Q_2 that is spread over a set of nodes $\mathcal{Q}_2$. This first step defines the first round of the cascade algorithm. We illustrate this process in Fig. 3.

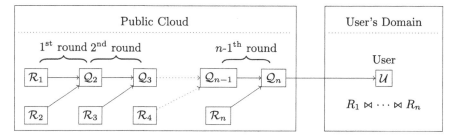

Fig. 3. Cascade of joins with MapReduce between n relations.

Example 1 Continued. To compute $(R_1 \bowtie R_2) \bowtie R_3$ with MapReduce following the cascade algorithm, we start by joining R_1 and R_2. Relations R_1 and R_2 share attribute *Name*. Hence from R_1, the map produces the following key-value pairs: (Alice, $(R_1,$ NYC)), (Bob, $(R_1,$ London)), and (Eve, $(R_1,$ Tokyo)). These key-value pairs are sent to three different reducers depending on the key value. From relation R_2, the map produces key-value pairs (Bob, $(R_2,$ Diabetes)), (Bob, $(R_2,$ AIDS)), and (Eve, $(R_2,$ Cancer)). We stress that values of pairs (Bob, $(R_2,$ Diabetes)) and (Bob, $(R_2,$ AIDS)) are sent to the same reducer as the pair (Bob, $(R_1,$ London)) since all these pairs have the same key. Similarly, (Eve, $(R_2,$ Cancer)) and (Eve, $(R_1,$ Tokyo)) are sent to the same reducer. The pair (Alice, $(R_1,$ NYC)) does not participate in the join result since no other pair shares the same key. Then, from values $(R_1,$ London), $(R_2,$ Diabetes), and $(R_2,$ AIDS) present on the reducer associated to the key Bob, the reduce creates all possible tuples with values coming from different relations i.e., (Bob, London, Diabetes) and (Bob, London, AIDS). Similarly, the reducer associated to the key Eve produces (Eve, Tokyo, Cancer). These tuples correspond to the relation $(R_1 \bowtie R_2)$ cf. Fig. 2. We apply the map and the reduce functions on relations $(R_1 \bowtie R_2)$ and R_3 sharing the attribute *Disease*. From $(R_1 \bowtie R_2)$, the map function produces key-value pairs: (Diabetes, $(R_1 \bowtie R_2,$ Bob, London)), (AIDS,

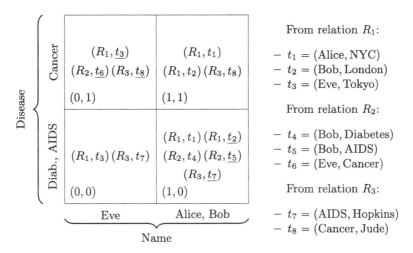

Fig. 4. Running example with hypercube algorithm. Underlined tuples correspond to tuples that participate to the final join result.

$(R_1 \bowtie R_2$, Bob, London)), and (Cancer, $(R_1 \bowtie R_2$, Eve, Tokyo)). From R_3, the map produces: (AIDS, $(R_3$, Hopkins)), and (Cancer, $(R_3$, Jude)). Finally, the reduce step produces tuples (Bob, London, AIDS, Hopkins) and (Eve, Tokyo, Cancer, Jude) corresponding to relation $(R_1 \bowtie R_2) \bowtie R_3$ cf. Fig. 2.

Hypercube Algorithm. Contrarily to cascade, the hypercube computes the join of all n relations in only one MapReduce round. The hypercube has dimension d (where d is the number of join attributes). There are $p = \prod_{1 \leqslant j \leqslant d} \alpha_j$ reducers denoted $\mathcal{H}_i$ (for $1 \leqslant i \leqslant p$), where α_j is the number of buckets associated with the jth attribute. Hence, each reducer $\mathcal{H}_i$ can be uniquely identified by a point in the hypercube. For each relation R_i spread over a set of nodes $\mathcal{R}_i$, the *map* function computes the image of all tuples on the d dimensions of the hypercube to decide to which reducers $\mathcal{H}_i$ the tuple should be sent. Then, each reducer computes all possible combinations of input tuples that agree on shared attributes, only if all n relations are represented on the same reducer. All these combinations correspond to the final result of the n-ary join.

Example 1 Continued. We have two join attributes (*Name* and *Disease*), hence two hash functions h_N and h_D for attributes *Name* and *Disease*, respectively. For instance, assume 4 reducers establishing a 2×2 square cf. Fig. 4, where $h_N(\text{Eve}) = 0$, $h_N(\text{Alice}) = h_N(\text{Bob}) = 1$, $h_D(\text{Diabetes}) = h_D(\text{AIDS}) = 0$, and $h_D(\text{Cancer}) = 1$. For each tuple of each relation, we compute the value of the *Name* component (if there exists) with the hash function h_N and the value of the *Disease* component (if there exists) with the hash function h_D. For instance, the tuple $t_6 = (\text{Eve}, \text{Cancer})$ of the relation R_2 is sent to the reducer of coordinates $(0, 1)$ since $h_N(\text{Eve}) = 0$ and $h_D(\text{Cancer}) = 1$ (cf. Fig. 4). If one of these two attributes is missing in a tuple, then the tuple is replicated over all reducers associated to the different values of the missing attributes of the tuple. For example, tuple $t_1 = (\text{Alice, NYC})$ of relation R_1 has no attribute *Disease*, and consequently, is sent to reducers $(1, 0)$ and $(1, 1)$. In such a situation we may write $(1, \star)$ to simplify presentation. Finally, each reducer performs all possible combinations over tuples that agree on join attributes of the three relations R_1, R_2, and R_3. We obviously obtain the same final result as for cascade algorithm.

1.2 Problem Statement

We assume three participants: the data owner, the public cloud, and the user (cf. Fig. 1). The data owner externalizes n relations $R_{1 \leqslant i \leqslant n}$ to the public cloud. We assume that the public cloud is *honest-but-curious* i.e., it executes dutifully the computation tasks but tries to learn the maximum of information on tuples of each relation. In order to preserve privacy of data owner and to allow the join computation between relations, we want that the cloud learns nothing about input data or join result. Moreover, we want that the user who queries the join result learns nothing else than the final join result i.e., she does not learn information on tuples of relations that do not participate to the final result.

Sets of nodes of type $\mathcal{R}$, $\mathcal{Q}$, and $\mathcal{H}$ are *honest-but-curious*. We denote by $\mathbb{R}_i$ the set of attributes of a relation R_i, for $1 \leqslant i \leqslant n$. In the case of the cascade algorithm, we denote by $\mathbb{Q}_i$ the set of attributes of relation Q_i for $1 \leqslant i \leqslant n$, where $R_1 = Q_1$. Finally we denote by $\mathbb{X}$ the set of shared attributes between the n relations i.e., $\mathbb{X} = |\cup_{1 \leqslant i \neq j \leqslant n} \mathbb{R}_i \cap \mathbb{R}_j|$.

We expect the following security properties:

1. Neither a set of nodes $\mathcal{R}_i$ nor data owner learn final result data.
2. A set of nodes $\mathcal{Q}_i$ (resp. $\mathcal{H}_i$) cannot learn owner's data and final result.
3. The user learns nothing else than result $R_1 \bowtie \ldots \bowtie R_n$ i.e., he does not learn tuples from the input relation that do not participate in the result.

Example 1 Continued. Looking at the three security properties of the problem statement, we see that the cascade and the hypercube algorithms do not respect properties (1), (2), and (3). In fact, both algorithms reveal to the public cloud all tuples of relations R_1, R_2 and R_3 since they are not encrypted. Moreover, if the user colludes with the intermediate set of nodes $\mathcal{R}_1 \bowtie \mathcal{R}_2$, then he learns tuples that he should not, in this case the tuple (Bob, London, Diabetes) (Fig. 2).

Contributions. We propose two approaches that extend the two aforementioned join algorithms while ensuring the desired security properties, and remaining efficient from both computational and communication points of view.

- The *Secure-Private* (SP) approach assumes that the public cloud and the user do not collude. We encrypt all values of each tuple using a public key encryption scheme with the user public key pk_u. To be able to perform the equality joins between relations we rely on pseudo-random functions.

- The *Collision-Resistant-Secure-Private* (CRSP) approach assumes that the public cloud and the user collude, that means the public cloud knows the private key sk_u of the user. In this case, we cannot encrypt all tuples using simply a public encryption scheme since the public cloud can decrypt all these encrypted tuples using the secret key of the user. To avoid this problem, we introduce a proxy such that the data owner also uses the public key of the proxy pk_t to encrypt ciphers of tuple values. Thus, we avoid that the public cloud decrypts tuples values received from the data owner even if the public cloud has the secret key sk_u of the user.
- We give experimental results of our SP and CRSP approaches for the cascade and the hypercube algorithms using Apache Hadoop [1] open-source MapReduce implementation and a real-world Twitter dataset [2].
- We prove that our SP and CRSP approaches satisfy the security properties using the random oracle model. We also notice a limitation regarding learning repetitions between pseudo-random values which seems to us inherent because we need to perform equi-joins.

Related Work. Since the seminal MapReduce paper [11], different protocols have been proposed to perform operations in a privacy-preserving manner [12] such as search [6,20], count [24], matrix multiplication [7] or joins [14].

Chapter 2 of [18] presents an introduction to the MapReduce paradigm. In particular, it includes the MapReduce algorithm for cascade joins that we enhance with privacy guarantees. Very few approaches address the privacy preserving execution of relational joins in MapReduce and have different assumptions than we do. For instance, Emekçi et al. [16] proposed protocols to perform joins in a privacy-preserving manner using the Shamir's secret sharing [23]. Contrary to us, they do not consider the MapReduce paradigm and their approach cannot be trivially adopted in MapReduce because values of shared attributes are encrypted in a non-deterministic way. Laur et al. [17] also proposed a protocol to compute joins using secret sharing but do not consider the MapReduce paradigm and their approach is limited to two relations. Chow et al. [8] introduced a generic model that uses two non-colluding servers to perform join computation between n relations in a privacy-preserving manner but do not consider the MapReduce paradigm. On the other hand, we assume a more general setting where the public cloud servers collude. Dolev et al. [14] proposed a technique for executing MapReduce computations in the public cloud while preserving privacy using the Shamir's secret sharing [23] and accumulating-automata [13]. Join computation is executed on secret-shares in the public cloud and at the end, the user performs the interpolation on the outputs. Contrary to us, authors assume that the different cloud nodes do not collude, otherwise they can construct the secret from shares. Moreover in our setting, we externalized entirely the computation in the cloud and the user has only to decrypt the join result, contrary to the need of doing interpolations in [14]. Finally, none of the aforementioned approaches propose a secure approach for the hypercube algorithm with MapReduce.

Finally, the system that is most closely related to our work is Popa et al.'s CryptDB [21,22]. CryptDB provides practical and provable confidentiality in the face of curious server for applications backed by SQL databases. It works by executing SQL queries over encrypted data using a collection of efficient SQL-aware encryption schemes. However, they do not consider the MapReduce paradigm.

To the best of our knowledge, we are the first to propose two secure approaches of join computation for the cascade and the hypercube MapReduce algorithms, where the user has only to decrypt the result received from the cloud.

Outline. We present the cascade and hypercube algorithms for the n-ary join computation with MapReduce in Sect. 2. We present our SP and CRSP approaches for both algorithms in Sect. 3. In Sect. 4, we compare experimentally the performance of our approaches vs the insecure algorithms. Then, we prove the security of the SP and CRSP approaches in Sect. 5. Finally, we outline conclusion and future work in Sect. 6.

2 n-ary Joins with MapReduce

We formally present the standard algorithms for computing n-ary joins $Q = R_1 \bowtie \ldots \bowtie R_n$ with MapReduce: *cascade* i.e., a sequence of $n-1$ rounds of binary joins [18] and *hypercube* [4] i.e., a single round doing all the $n-1$ joins. We have already presented examples for both algorithms in Sect. 1.1.

Algorithm: BinaryJoin(Q, R)

Map function
Input: $(key, value)$
// *key*: id of chunk of Q or R
// *value*: coll. of $t_q \in Q$ or $t_r \in R$
foreach $t_q \in Q$ **do**
    emit $(\pi_{\mathbb{Q} \cap \mathbb{R}}(t_q), (\mathbb{Q}, t_q))$;
foreach $t_r \in R$ **do**
    emit $(\pi_{\mathbb{Q} \cap \mathbb{R}}(t_r), (\mathbb{R}, t_r))$;

Algorithm: BinaryJoin(Q, R)

Reduce function
Input: $(key, value)$
// *key*: $\pi_{\mathbb{Q} \cap \mathbb{R}}(t)$ with $t \in Q$ or $t \in R$
// *values*: coll. of $(\mathbb{Q}, t_q)$ or $(\mathbb{R}, t_r)$
foreach $(\mathbb{Q}, t_q) \in values$ **do**
    foreach $(\mathbb{R}, t_r) \in values$ **do**
       emit $(t_q \bowtie t_r, t_q \bowtie t_r)$;

Fig. 5. BinaryJoin algorithm for natural join with MapReduce between Q and R.

2.1 Cascade Algorithm

We recall that the ith round of the cascade algorithm takes action between sets of nodes $\mathcal{Q}_i$ and $\mathcal{R}_{i+1}$, with $1 \leqslant i \leqslant n-1$ and that relation R_1 is denoted Q_1. The term chunk refers to a fragment of information. Moreover, $\mathbb{R}$ denotes the schema of the relation R i.e. the set of attributes of the relation R.

We present in Fig. 5 the binary join with MapReduce between two relations. To compute join between n relations $R_1, \ldots, R_n$, we apply $n-1$ times the binary join (Fig. 5) as presented in the cascade algorithm in Fig. 6. The final relation Q_n corresponds to $R_1 \bowtie \cdots \bowtie R_n$.

Algorithm: CascadeJoin$(R_1, \ldots, R_n)$

for $1 \leqslant i \leqslant n-1$ **do**
$\quad | \quad Q_{i+1} \leftarrow$ BinaryJoin(Q_i, R_{i+1});

Fig. 6. Cascade algorithm.

2.2 Hypercube Algorithm

We assume that we have an hypercube of dimension d, where $d = |\mathbb{X}| = |\{X_1, \ldots, X_d\}| = |\cup_{1 \leqslant i \neq j \leqslant n} \mathbb{R}_i \cap \mathbb{R}_j|$ i.e., d is the number of join attributes.

Moreover, we assume that we have d (non-cryptographic) hash functions h_ℓ (where $1 \leqslant \ell \leqslant d$) such that $h_\ell \colon X_\ell \to [\![0, \alpha_\ell]\!]$ where α_ℓ is the number of buckets for the attribute X_ℓ. Hence, the hypercube is composed of $\alpha_1 \cdots \alpha_\ell$ reducers where each reducer is uniquely identified by a d-tuple $(x_1, \ldots, x_d)$ with $x_\ell \in [\![0, \alpha_\ell]\!]$ for $1 \leqslant \ell \leqslant d$. In the following, we denote by A_j^i the j-th attribute of the relation R_i where $1 \leqslant i \leqslant n$ and $1 \leqslant j \leqslant |\mathbb{R}_i|$.

We present in Fig. 7 the hypercube algorithm for the join computation with MapReduce between n relations $R_1, \ldots, R_n$. The map function sends the pair to the corresponding reducer of the hypercube associated to the coordinates of the key-value pair's key where the star $\star$ in the ℓ-th coordinate means that we dupli-cate the tuple t on all the α_ℓ buckets of the ℓ-th dimension of the hypercube. Then, if the same reducer of the hypercube has at least one tuple coming from all the n relations and that these tuples agree on their shared attributes then the reduce function produces all possible key-values pairs of the form $(t_1 \bowtie \ldots \bowtie t_n, t_1 \bowtie \ldots \bowtie t_n)$ where $t_i \in R_i$ (with $1 \leqslant i \leqslant n$).

Algorithm:
  HypercubeJoin$(R_1, \ldots, R_n)$

Map function
Input: $(key, value)$
// *key*: id of chunk of $R_{1 \leqslant i \leqslant n}$
// *value*: collection of $t \in R_i$
foreach $t \in R_i$ **do**
$\quad$ **for** $1 \leqslant \ell \leqslant d$ **do**
$\quad\quad$ **if** $X_\ell \in \mathbb{R}_i$ **then**
$\quad\quad\quad$ $x_\ell \leftarrow h_\ell(\pi_{X_\ell}(t))$;
$\quad\quad$ **else** $x_\ell \leftarrow \star$;
$\quad$ emit $((x_1, \ldots, x_d), (\mathsf{R}_i, t))$.

Reduce function
Input: $(key, values)$
// *key*: $(x_1, \ldots, x_d)$, $x_\ell \in [\![0, \alpha_\ell]\!]$
// *values*: collection of (R_i, t)
for $1 \leqslant i \leqslant n$ **do**
$\quad | \quad R_i' \leftarrow \cup_{(\mathsf{R}_i, t) \in values}\{t\}$;
for $t \in R_1' \bowtie \cdots \bowtie R_n'$ **do**
$\quad | \quad$ emit (t, t).

Fig. 7. Hypercube algorithm.

3 Secure n-ary Joins with MapReduce

Before formally presenting our secure algorithms, we present the needed crypto-graphic tools. We illustrate the intuition of each of our algorithms while relying on our running example from the Introduction.

3.1 Cryptographic Tools

We define negligible function, pseudo-random function, and public key encryption cryptosystem.

Definition 1 (Negligible function). *A function $\epsilon : \mathbb{N} \to \mathbb{R}$ is negligible in η if for every positive polynomial $p(\cdot)$ and sufficiently large η, $\epsilon(\eta) < 1/p(\eta)$.*

Definition 2 (Pseudo-random function). *Let η be a security parameter. A function $f \colon \{0,1\}^{\ell(\eta)} \times \{0,1\}^{l_0} \to \{0,1\}^{l_1}$ is a pseudo-random function if it is computable in polynomial time in η and if for all polynomial-size $\mathcal{B}$,*

$$\left| \Pr\left[\mathcal{B}^{f(k,\cdot)} = 1\colon k \xleftarrow{\$} \{0,1\}^{\ell(\eta)}\right] - \Pr\left[\mathcal{B}^{g(\cdot)} = 1\colon g \xleftarrow{\$} \mathsf{Func}[l_0,l_1]\right]\right| \leqslant \epsilon(\eta)$$

where, $\ell(\cdot)$ is a polynomial function, $\mathsf{Func}[l_0,l_1]$ is the space of functions defined over domain $\{0,1\}^{l_0}$ and codomain $\{0,1\}^{l_1}$, $\epsilon(\cdot)$ is a negligible function in η and the probabilities are taken over the choice of k and g.

In the rest of the paper, the pseudo-random function $f(k,\cdot)$ is denoted $f_k(\cdot)$.

Definition 3 (Public Key Encryption). *Let η be a security parameter. A Public Key Encryption (PKE) scheme Π is defined by three algorithms $(\mathcal{G}, \mathcal{E}, \mathcal{D})$:*

$\mathcal{G}(\eta)$: *it takes the security parameter η and returns a key pair $(\mathsf{pk}, \mathsf{sk})$.*
$\mathcal{E}_{\mathsf{pk}}(m)$: *it takes a public key pk and a plaintext m and returns the ciphertext c.*
$\mathcal{D}_{\mathsf{sk}}(c)$: *it takes a private key sk and a ciphertext c and returns the plaintext m.*

3.2 Preprocessing and Outsourcing

To prevent the cloud from learning the content of relations, the data owner protects each relation $R_{1 \leqslant i \leqslant n}$ before outsourcing. The protected relation obtained from R_i is denoted $\hat{R}_i$ and is sent to the public cloud by the data owner.

The data owner protects relations in two ways. First, it uses a pseudo-random function $f_k(\cdot)$ where k is the data owner secret key. The data owner applies $f_k(\cdot)$ on values of shared attributes of each tuples of relations $R_{1 \leqslant i \leqslant n}$. Since a pseudo-random function is deterministic, it allows the cloud to perform equality tests between values of join attributes. On other hand, the data owner encrypts for each user each component of tuples with an *indistinguishable under chosen plaintext attack* (IND-CPA)

Algorithm: PreProc$(R_1, \ldots, R_n)$

$\mathsf{visited} \leftarrow \varnothing;$
for $1 \leqslant i \leqslant n$ **do**
  $\hat{R}_i \leftarrow \varnothing;$
  $\mathbb{R}_i^f \leftarrow \{A^f | A \in R_i \cap \mathbb{X}\};$
  $\mathbb{R}_i^{\mathcal{E}} \leftarrow \{A^{\mathcal{E}} | A \in R_i \backslash \mathsf{visited}\};$
  $\hat{R}_i \leftarrow \mathbb{R}_i^f \cup \mathbb{R}_i^{\mathcal{E}};$
  for $t \in R_i$ **do**
    $t_f \leftarrow \times_{A^f \in \mathbb{R}_i^f} f_k(\pi_A(t));$
    $t_{\mathcal{E}} \leftarrow \times_{A^{\mathcal{E}} \in \mathbb{R}_i^{\mathcal{E}}} (\mathcal{E}_{\mathsf{pk}_u}(\pi_A(t)));$
    $\hat{R}_i \leftarrow \hat{R}_i \cup \{t_f \times t_{\mathcal{E}}\};$
  $\mathsf{visited} \leftarrow \mathsf{visited} \cup \mathbb{R}_i;$

Fig. 8. Preprocessing of relations.

public key encryption scheme (e.g., ElGamal [15], RSA-OAEP [5]) using the public key pk_u of the user. Hence the encrypted values of non-shared attributes do not give any information to an adversary. Values of shared attributes are also encrypted using the public scheme encryption since we want the user can decrypt them.

We present the preprocessing algorithm in Fig. 8. The set visited prevents the data owner from (IND-CPA) encrypting several times the same values. We stress that A^f and $A^{\mathcal{E}}$ are just notations making explicit the correspondences between initial and outsourced data. For instance, if a relation R has one attribute "Name" that is shared with an other relation, then this attribute in the protected relation will be denoted "Name^{f}"; we apply the same way the notation $A^{\mathcal{E}}$. Moreover $\hat{\mathbb{R}}_i$ is the schema of the protected relation $\hat{R}_i$. We give an example for the cascade algorithm in Fig. 9 using the running example.

For both algorithms, we remark that the cloud knows when components of same attribute are equal since a pseudo-random function is deterministic. We see in Fig. 9 that the cloud knows that $\hat{R}_2$ and $\hat{R}_3$ share two same values of disease since values 18 and 99 are present in both relations. However, we notice that only the data owner knows the secret key k used by the pseudo-random function.

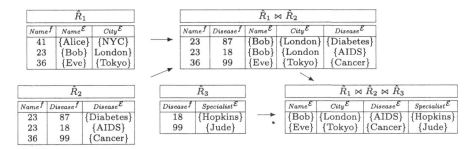

Fig. 9. Intuition of the SP approach. We denote an IND-CPA public encryption scheme by $\{\cdot\}$, and pseudo-random values by integers.

3.3   SP n-ary Joins with MapReduce

We present the Secure-Private (SP) approach for cascade and hypercube algorithms to compute joins between $n > 2$ relations with MapReduce. We recall that we assume in the SP approach that the user and the public cloud do not collude.

SP Cascade Algorithm. If a relation participating at the i-th round contains an attribute that will participate to the join in a following round, the algorithm must anticipate the pseudo-random values of the shared attribute to perform joins. In the original cascade algorithm presented in Sect. 2.1, tuples are not encrypted and the anticipation is not necessary since each tuple value is available. In the SP approach, we add in value of pairs the pseudo-random evaluations of all needed pseudo-random values allowing joins in other rounds. This is possible since the preprocessing done by the data owner outsources protected relations containing pseudo-random evaluations of values of join attributes.

The process of the SP-cascade algorithm is presented in Fig. 10. The SP approach between relations $\hat{Q}_i$ and $\hat{R}_{i+1}$ participating at the i-th round is presented in Fig. 11, where $\hat{Q}_i = \hat{Q}_{i-1} \bowtie \hat{R}_i$ and $\hat{Q}_1 = \hat{R}_1$.

Algorithm: SecCascade($\hat{R}_1, \ldots, \hat{R}_n$)

for $1 \leqslant i \leqslant n - 1$ **do**
$\quad \mid \quad \hat{Q}_{i+1} \leftarrow \mathsf{SecBinary}(\hat{Q}_i, \hat{R}_{i+1}, i);$

Fig. 10. SecCascade algorithm.

SP Hypercube Algorithm. We present the SP approach for the hypercube algorithm in Fig. 12. The main difference compared to the insecure approach is that the map function receives encrypted tuples from the data owner. As for the cascade algorithm, we add pseudo-random evaluations in value of each pair allowing the reduce function to check correspondences of tuples on join attributes.

Algorithm:
 SecBinary($\hat{Q}_i, \hat{R}_{i+1}, i$)

Map function
Input: $(key, value)$
// key: id of chunk of $\hat{Q}_i/\hat{R}_{i+1}$
// value: coll. $t \in \hat{Q}_i$ or $t \in \hat{R}_{i+1}$
if $i = 1$ **then**
$\quad \mid \quad$ **foreach** $t_q \in \hat{Q}_1$ **do**
$\quad \quad \mid \quad$ emit $(\pi_{\mathbb{Q}_1^f \cap \mathbb{R}_2^f}(t), (\mathbb{Q}_1, t_q));$
$\quad$ **foreach** $t_r \in \hat{R}_{i+1}$ **do**
$\quad \mid \quad$ emit $(\pi_{\mathbb{Q}_i^f \cap \mathbb{R}_{i+1}^f}(t), (\mathbb{R}_{i+1}, t_r)).$

Reduce function
Input: $(key, values)$
// key: $\pi_{\mathbb{Q}_i^f \cap \mathbb{R}_{i+1}^f}(t)$
// values: coll. of $(\mathbb{Q}_i, t_q)$ and
$(\mathbb{R}_{i+1}, t_r)$
for $(\mathbb{Q}, t_q) \in values$ **do**
$\quad \mid \quad$ **for** $(\mathbb{R}, t_r) \in values$ **do**
$\quad \quad \mid \quad t = t_q \times t_r;$
$\quad \quad \mid \quad$ **if** $i \neq n - 1$ **then**
$\quad \quad \quad \mid \quad$ emit
$\quad \quad \quad \quad (\pi_{\mathbb{Q}_{i+1}^f \cap \mathbb{R}_{i+2}^f}(t), t);$
$\quad \quad \mid \quad$ **else**
$\quad \quad \quad \mid \quad$ emit $(t, t).$

Fig. 11. SecBinary algorithm.

Algorithm:
 SecHypercube($\hat{R}_1, \ldots, \hat{R}_n$)

Map function
Input: $(key, value)$
// key: id of chunk of $\hat{R}_i$ for
$1 \leqslant i \leqslant n$
// value: collection of $t \in \hat{R}_i$
foreach $t \in \hat{R}_i$ **do**
$\quad \mid \quad$ **for** $1 \leqslant \ell \leqslant d$ **do**
$\quad \quad \mid \quad$ **if** $X_\ell^f \in \mathbb{R}_i^f$ **then**
$\quad \quad \quad \mid \quad x_\ell \leftarrow h_\ell(\pi_{X_\ell^f}(t));$
$\quad \quad \mid \quad$ **else** $x_\ell \leftarrow \star;$
$\quad \mid \quad$ emit
$\quad \quad ((x_1, \ldots, x_d), (\mathbb{R}_i, t)).$
Reduce function
Input: $(key, values)$
// key: $(x_1, \ldots, x_d)$
// values: coll. of $(\mathbb{R}_i, t)$
for $1 \leqslant i \leqslant n$ **do**
$\quad \mid \quad R_i' \leftarrow \bigcup_{(\mathbb{R}_i, t) \in values}\{t\};$
for $t \in R_1' \bowtie \cdots \bowtie R_n'$ **do**
$\quad \mid \quad$ emit $(t, t).$

Fig. 12. SecHypercube algorithm.

3.4   CRSP n-ary Joins with MapReduce

We present the Collision-Resistant-Secure-Private (CRSP) approach for cascade and hypercube algorithms to compute joins between $n > 2$ relations with MapReduce. We recall that we assume in the CRSP approach that the user and the public cloud collude i.e., the public cloud knows the secret key sk_u of the user. Even in this scenario, we want that the security properties are satisfied.

When the public cloud and the user collude, the SP approach does not satisfy anymore the security properties since the public cloud can decrypt all tuples using the user's private key sk_u. Hence, the user learns intermediate results that she should not know, and property security (3) is not satisfied.

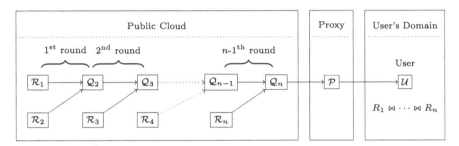

Fig. 13. CRSP n-ary joins with MapReduce.

To solve this issue, we introduce a trusted set of nodes as proxy (which do not collude with the public cloud and the user) denoted $\mathcal{P}$. This proxy has a key pair $(\mathsf{pk}_t, \mathsf{sk}_t)$. The public key pk_t is used by the data owner in the preprocessing phase. In this case the value of $t_\mathcal{E}$ is equal to $\times_{A^\mathcal{E} \in \mathbb{R}_i^\mathcal{E}} \mathcal{E}_{\mathsf{pk}_t}(\mathcal{E}_{\mathsf{pk}_u}(\pi_A(t)))$. In fact, the data owner encrypts (with the proxy public key) each encrypted values obtained with the user public key pk_u. This avoids the public cloud to decrypt the encrypted components outsourced in the cloud. Hence, the public cloud does the join computation as usually, and sends the result to the proxy. The proxy uses his secret key sk_t and sends the result only encrypted by the user's public key to the user. We illustrate the CRSP approach in Fig. 13.

CRSP Cascade Algorithm. The CRSP approach for the cascade algorithm between n relations uses the same algorithm than the SP approach and is presented in Fig. 10. The difference lies in the preprocessing where the data owner uses the proxy public key pk_t to encrypt the encrypted values obtained using the user public key. Hence, the public cloud cannot use the user's secret key sk_u to learn information about tuples. We stress that $\mathcal{P}$ is a trusted set of nodes i.e., the proxy colludes neither with the public cloud nor the user.

CRSP Hypercube Algorithm. The CRSP approach for the hypercube algorithm between n relations presented in Fig. 12 uses the same algorithm than the SP approach. As for the cascade algorithm in the CRSP approach, the difference lies in a second encryption of values done by the data owner using the proxy public key. This second encryption avoids the public cloud to learn information on relations sent by the data owner, even if the cloud and the user collude.

4   Experimental Results

We present the experimental results for the insecure, SP and CRSP approaches with the cascade and hypercube algorithms using the Hadoop [1] implementation of MapReduce. We have done all computations on a cluster running on Ubuntu Server 14.04 with Vanilla Hadoop 2.7.1 using Java 1.7.0. The cluster is composed of one master node and of three data nodes. The master node has four CPU cadenced to 2.4 GHz, 80 Gb of disk, and 8 Gb of RAM. The three data nodes have of two CPU cadenced to 2.4 GHz, 40 Gb of disk, and 4 Gb of RAM.

We use the real-world *Higgs Twitter Dataset* [2] that we denote by relation $R(A, B)$ where attributes A and B encode followee-follower relation on Twitter. The relation $R(A, B)$ has 15M tuples. To perform joins with this dataset, we generate two relations $S(B, C)$ and $T(C, A)$ that are copies of R. The join query used in our experiments is $R(A, B) \bowtie S(B, C) \bowtie T(C, A)$, consisting on all directed triangles of the *Higgs Twitter Dataset*. Using such a dataset and query is a standard practice in the database community literature to evaluate the performance of join query algorithms, as recently done e.g., in [9]. We use the AES encryption scheme [10] as the pseudo-random function, and the RSA-OAEP encryption scheme [5] as the public key encryption scheme.

Scalability. We present in Fig. 14a the running time for the cascade and hypercube algorithms, for each security approach. The different numbers of selected tuples come from the original dataset, where a sample is selected randomly. In the figures presented in Fig. 14, we consider size up to $2, 356, 225$ tuples because after such a size, our cluster gives out-of-memory errors hence we cannot compare meaningful results for all approaches. We report average times over five runs. For the hypercube algorithm, we use four buckets for each of the three dimensions defined by attributes A, B, and C, hence a total number of $4^3 = 64$ reducers. Without any security, the cascade and hypercube algorithms perform very similarly, although the hypercube seems a bit better for the largest input data sizes. For each of our secure approaches (SP and CRSP), the hypercube algorithm performs better than the cascade, hence the aforementioned trend is visible starting from small input data sizes. Intuitively, this happens because the hypercube avoids computing large intermediate results as may happen in practice when triangle queries are computed with a cascade approach.

Behind the Curtain. We look in details at the main parts behind the algorithm execution for SP Cascade (Fig. 14b), SP Hypercube (Fig. 14c), CRSP Cascade (Fig. 14d), and CRSP Hypercube (Fig. 14e). For each of the aforementioned cases, the cryptography is not the dominant cost, which confirms our intuition that the overhead needed to secure standard join algorithms is a constant factor. The communication and the computation dominate the total execution time.

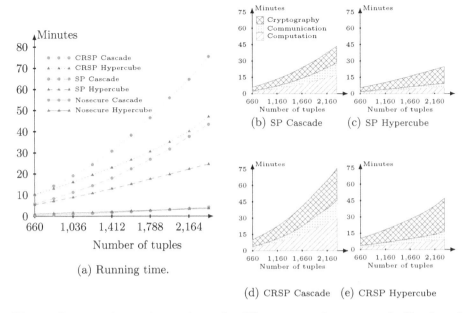

(a) Running time.

(b) SP Cascade   (c) SP Hypercube

(d) CRSP Cascade   (e) CRSP Hypercube

Fig. 14. Running time and zoom-in on the different steps of our protocols. Number of tuples are expressed in thousands.

5   Security Proofs

We present briefly the security proofs of the cascade and the hypercube algorithms in our two approaches considering the *Random Oracle Model* (ROM). Complete proofs are given in the technical report available online [3]. We use the standard multi-party computations definition of security against honest-but-curious adversaries. We refer the reader to [19] for further details.

Theorem 1. *Assume f is a secure pseudo random function and Π is an IND-CPA public key encryption scheme. Then, the SP cascade and the SP hypercube algorithms securely computes joins between n relations in ROM in the presence of honest-but-curious adversaries if the cloud and the user do not collude.*

Proof. We use the hybrid argument. For each protocol (SP cascade and SP hypercube), we first build a simulator Sim_1 where the pseudo random function is simulated by a random oracle. We show that it does not exist a polynomial-time algorithm such that it can distinguish the view of real protocols to the view of Sim_1 since we assume that f is a secure pseudo random function. Values of attributes are encrypted using a public key encryption scheme with the user's public key, hence we build a second simulator Sim_2 working as Sim_1 but where all encryptions are replaced by random values. We show that a distinguisher can distinguish an execution of Sim_1 to an execution of Sim_2 only with a negligible probability if the public key encryption scheme is semantically secure. By transitivity, we prove that it does not exist a polynomial-time algorithm that can distinguish the view generated by real protocols and the view generated by the simulator Sim_2. Hence, if f is a secure pseudo random function and Π is an IND-CPA public key encryption scheme, then the SP cascade and the SP hypercube algorithms securely computes joins between n relations in ROM in the presence of honest-but-curious adversaries if the cloud and the user do not collude.

Theorem 2. *Assume f is a secure pseudo random function and Π is an IND-CPA public key encryption scheme. Then, the CRSP cascade and the CRSP hypercube algorithms securely computes joins between n relations in ROM in the presence of honest-but-curious adversaries even if the public cloud and the user collude.*

Proof. First, we use the hybrid argument to show that it does not exist a polynomial-time algorithm that is able to distinguish the view of the cloud colluding with the user generated by the real protocols (CRSP cascade and CRSP hypercube) and the view generated by a simulator using inputs and outputs of the cloud and of the user. As in the previous proof, it relies on the secure pseudo random function f and on the IND-CPA public key encryption scheme. In the same way, we prove that we can perfectly simulate the view of the proxy using its input and output. Hence, if f is a secure pseudo random function and Π is an IND-CPA public key encryption scheme, the CRSP cascade and the CRSP hypercube algorithms securely computes joins between n relations in ROM in the presence of honest-but-curious adversaries even if the public cloud and the user collude.

6   Conclusion

We have presented two efficient approaches for computing joins with MapReduce. The SP approach assumes that the cloud and the user do not collude, whereas the CRSP approach resists to collusion, but needs more resources as it needs to communication with an honest proxy. We have thoroughly compared these two approaches with respect to their privacy guarantees and their practical performance using a standard real-world dataset.

As future work, we plan to integrate our secure join algorithms in a secure query optimizer system based on the MapReduce paradigm. We also aim at designing a protocol that is secure in the standard model and that not depends on a trusted third party.

Acknowledgements. This research was conducted with the support of the FEDER program of 2014–2020, the region council of Auvergne-Rhône-Alpes, the support of the "Digital Trust" Chair from the University of Auvergne Foundation, the Indo-French Centre for the Promotion of Advanced Research (IFCPAR) and the Center Franco-Indien Pour La Promotion De La Recherche Avancée (CEFIPRA) through the project DST/CNRS 2015-03 under DST-INRIA-CNRS Targeted Programme.

References

1. Apache Hadoop. https://hadoop.apache.org/
2. Higgs Twitter Dataset. http://snap.stanford.edu/data/higgs-twitter.html
3. Secure Joins with MapReduce - Technical report. https://hal.archives-ouvertes.fr/hal-01903098
4. Afrati, F.N., Ullman, J.D.: Optimizing joins in a MapReduce environment. In: EDBT (2010)
5. Bellare, M., Rogaway, P.: Optimal asymmetric encryption. In: De Santis, A. (ed.) EUROCRYPT 1994. LNCS, vol. 950, pp. 92–111. Springer, Heidelberg (1995). https://doi.org/10.1007/BFb0053428
6. Blass, E.-O., Di Pietro, R., Molva, R., Önen, M.: PRISM – privacy-preserving search in MapReduce. In: Fischer-Hübner, S., Wright, M. (eds.) PETS 2012. LNCS, vol. 7384, pp. 180–200. Springer, Heidelberg (2012). https://doi.org/10.1007/978-3-642-31680-7_10
7. Bultel, X., Ciucanu, R., Giraud, M., Lafourcade, P.: Secure matrix multiplication with MapReduce. In: ARES (2017)
8. Chow, S.S.M., Lee, J., Subramanian, L.: Two-party computation model for privacy-preserving queries over distributed databases. In: NDSS (2009)
9. Chu, S., Balazinska, M., Suciu, D.: From theory to practice: efficient join query evaluation in a parallel database system. In: SIGMOD Conference (2015)
10. Daemen, J., Rijmen, V.: The Design of Rijndael: AES - The Advanced Encryption Standard. ISC. Springer, Heidelberg (2002). https://doi.org/10.1007/978-3-662-04722-4
11. Dean, J., Ghemawat, S.: MapReduce: simplified data processing on large clusters. In: OSDI (2004)
12. Derbeko, P., Dolev, S., Gudes, E., Sharma, S.: Security and privacy aspects in MapReduce on clouds: a survey. Comput. Sci. Rev. **20**, 1–28 (2016)
13. Dolev, S., Gilboa, N., Li, X.: Accumulating automata and cascaded equations automata for communicationless information theoretically secure multi-party computation: extended abstract. In: ASIACCS (2015)
14. Dolev, S., Li, Y., Sharma, S.: Private and secure secret shared MapReduce. In: DBSec (2016)
15. ElGamal, T.: A public key cryptosystem and a signature scheme based on discrete logarithms. In: Blakley, G.R., Chaum, D. (eds.) CRYPTO 1984. LNCS, vol. 196, pp. 10–18. Springer, Heidelberg (1985). https://doi.org/10.1007/3-540-39568-7_2
16. Emekçi, F., Agrawal, D., El Abbadi, A., Gulbeden, A.: Privacy preserving query processing using third parties. In: ICDE (2006)
17. Laur, S., Talviste, R., Willemson, J.: From oblivious AES to efficient and secure database join in the multiparty setting. In: ACNS (2013)
18. Leskovec, J., Rajaraman, A., Ullman, J.D.: Mining of Massive Datasets, 2nd edn. Cambridge University Press, Cambridge (2014)
19. Lindell, Y. (ed.): Tutorials on the Foundations of Cryptography. Springer, Cham (2017). https://doi.org/10.1007/978-3-319-57048-8
20. Mayberry, T., Blass, E.-O., Chan, A.H.: PIRMAP: efficient private information retrieval for MapReduce. In: Sadeghi, A.-R. (ed.) FC 2013. LNCS, vol. 7859, pp. 371–385. Springer, Heidelberg (2013). https://doi.org/10.1007/978-3-642-39884-1_32
21. Popa, R.A., Redfield, C.M.S., Zeldovich, N., Balakrishnan, H.: CryptDB: protecting confidentiality with encrypted query processing. In: SOSP (2011)

22. Popa, R.A., Zeldovich, N.: Cryptographic treatment of CryptDB's adjustable join (2012)
23. Shamir, A.: How to share a secret. Commun. ACM **22**(11), 612–613 (1979)
24. Vo-Huu, T.D., Blass, E.-O., Noubir, G.: EPiC: efficient privacy-preserving counting for MapReduce. In: Bouajjani, A., Fauconnier, H. (eds.) NETYS 2015. LNCS, vol. 9466, pp. 426–443. Springer, Cham (2015). https://doi.org/10.1007/978-3-319-26850-7_29

Daedalus: Network Anomaly Detection on IDS Stream Logs

Aniss Chohra[✉], Mourad Debbabi[✉], and Paria Shirani[✉]

Security Research Centre, Gina Cody School of Engineering and Computer Science,
Concordia University, Montreal, Canada
{a_chohra,debbabi,p_shira}@encs.concordia.ca

Abstract. In this paper, we propose a scalable framework, called *Daedalus*, to analyze streams of NIDS (network-based intrusion detection system) logs in near real-time and to extract useful threat security intelligence. The proposed system pre-processes huge amounts of BRO NIDS logs received from different participating organizations and applies an elaborated anomaly detection technique in order to distinguish between normal and abnormal or anomalous network behaviors. As such, *Daedalus* detects network traffic anomalies by extracting a set of features of interest from the connection logs and then applying a time series-based technique in order to detect abnormal behavior in near real-time. Moreover, we correlate IP blocks extracted from the logs with some external security signature-based feeds that detect factual malicious activities (e.g., malware families and hashes, ransomware distribution, and command and control centers) in order to validate the proposed approach. Performed experiments demonstrate that *Daedalus* accurately identifies the malicious activities with an average F_1 score of 92.88%. We further compare our proposed approach with existing K-Means approaches and demonstrate the accuracy and efficiency of our system.

1 Introduction

During the last decade, a huge increase in the number of cyber threats and security attacks has been observed ranging from ransomware attacks to denial of service attacks and botnets, and from social engineering threats to data breach threats, which pose a serious threat to millions of users. Therefore, detection, prevention and mitigation of such attacks are essential, while this is a challenging task for the security analysts. As an example to such threats, *Wannacry Ransomware* [15] propagated worldwide during May 2017, had devastating consequences (e.g., major disruption to operations) in several countries affecting hundreds of thousands of machines and many organizations, such as Cambrian College in Canada and Saudi Telecom company. Another example is the *Mirai Botnet* [1], which had also a severe impact worldwide in late 2016 mostly in the U.S. by affecting vulnerable Internet of Things devices and turning them into a zombie army. These two examples alongside with many others make the detection, prevention, and mitigation of malicious activities of primordial importance

© Springer Nature Switzerland AG 2019
N. Zincir-Heywood et al. (Eds.): FPS 2018, LNCS 11358, pp. 95–111, 2019.
https://doi.org/10.1007/978-3-030-18419-3_7

and a paramount task for any security expert. Therefore, many techniques have been proposed and developed to monitor network traffics in real-time and provide insights and information on what is happening inside the network from a security perspective.

Intrusion detection systems (IDS) monitor and record network traffics in order to detect security threats and network violations in a fast and efficient manner. The main objective of any security expert is to find an approach that takes best advantage of the IDS logs and generates useful cyber threat intelligence. One of the most frequently used and efficient methods to leverage IDS logs is anomaly detection, which analyzes the traffic in order to detect network abnormalities and misbehaviours. On the other hand, *scalability* is a main concern that needs to be taken into account seriously, especially when the amount of traffic is tremendous (in the order of millions of connections). Thus, in order to address the *scalability* issue, various factors, such as time complexity of the proposed algorithms, and less memory and CPU consumption, should be one of the top priorities and considerations during the setup, development, implementation, and deployment of such solutions.

Different network anomaly detection techniques have been proposed in the literature. In [27], the authors compare three *standard or conventional SVMs*, *weighted SVMs*, and *one class SVMs (OC-SVM)* techniques to be used in their anomaly detection system, and then demonstrate that the latter achieves the highest accuracy rate of 78%. However, supervised techniques generally require several iterations for training to have an accurate model. In [8], the authors propose a deep learning-based anomaly detection approach for detecting cyberthreats in $5G$ networks in an efficient and fast manner. The authors demonstrate that their proposed technique can self-adapt itself depending on the volume of network flows collected. In [11], the authors propose a tool called *Kitsune* that detects anomalies on local networks by tracking the network behavior using an ensemble of *autoencoders* in a completely unsupervised manner. However, the last two aforesaid techniques [8,11] deal only with local and small networks, and indeed the *scalability* of their work on big data and large network traffics (e.g., hundreds of millions of connections similar to our case) has not been examined.

The goal of our research is to provide a *scalable* tool that can detect anomalies *accurately* in near-real time on any IDS stream logs (achieving *interoperability* [6]) and provide security analysts alarms and detailed information about the anomalous connections. To this end, we propose *Daedalus*, an anomaly detection time-series (statistical) based approach that addresses the aforementioned limitations and captures/summarizes the network profile and behavior from BRO NIDS connection logs [22,23]. Inspired by [4], we apply our proposed algorithm for predicting normal traffic behavior and removing noises and uncertainties [4] using *particle swarm optimization (PSO)* [2,9,26] combined with stationarity *augmented Dickey-Fuller* [12] test. Moreover, we compute the scores using *fuzzy logic* [4,10] to deal with imprecisions [4], and further decide whether obtained scores are anomalous by leveraging the *exponential weighted moving average*

(EWMA) [7] technique. Our work is inspired by the work presented in [4]; however, we consider more features which consists of source and destination bytes and packets separately, while in [4] the authors merge source and destination bytes into one value (the same applies to packets). Additionally, we have replaced the predictive step with an optimization algorithm, which provides a more scalable framework compared to genetic algorithms used by [4]. Finally, we examine the scalability of our technique, while such a test has not been performed in [4].

Contributions. The main contributions of this work are presented as follows.
- Elaboration of an anomaly detection technique on IDS stream data using time-series analysis to predict the normal behaviour and prevent anomalies. We further correlate the generated results with other security sources in order to validate the results of proposed anomaly detection approach.
- We propose a technique that regardless of IDS types, identifies the network anomalies. *Daedalus* extracts features that are common amongst most frequently used IDSs, and therefore achieves the interoperability goal.
- Our experimental results ascertain the accuracy of the proposed system, with an average F_1 score of 92.88%. In addition, we investigate the scalability of *Daedalus* by performing the experiments on a large amount of connections. We further compare our proposed approach with existing K-Means approaches and demonstrate the accuracy and efficiency of our system.
- We generate relevant and useful threat intelligence out of huge amounts of IDS streams that can be used in the detection, prevention, identification, mitigation, and attribution of cyber threats.

2   Approach Overview

An overview of our approach is represented in Fig. 1, which consists of four major steps: *feature extraction, adaptive thresholding, predictive analysis,* and *anomaly detection.* In the *feature extraction* step, the features that are considered as paramount to our anomaly detection system are extracted. More specifically, we extract a set of eight features that can be found in any IDS logs in order to achieve system *interoperability.* We further summarize the network behavior/profile for each of the chosen features within a time batch of five minutes. The obtained eight time series representations are considered as the first input and observed network behavior/profile to our anomaly detection system.

In the next phase, an adaptive threshold using the *exponential weighted moving average (EWMA)* [7] statistical metric is calculated for each of the precomputed network behavior profiling time-series. The reason of using such technique is that daily users' Internet connections are in some way *auto-correlated* over time; meaning that each user connection on the Internet is mostly affected by his/her past interactions and not completely random, and the interactions' influences (weights) on the current connection decreases back in time. Therefore, we utilize a metric that best captures and defines these weights.

In the *predictive analysis* step, we consider a time-window of one hour and try to predict the expected behavior of each of these network features within

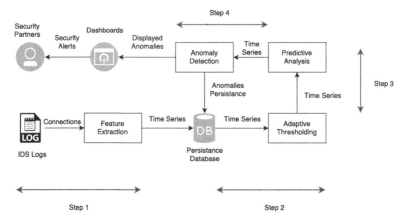

Fig. 1. Proposed anomaly detection approach

the same time frame without any noise or seasonal trends. Consequently, we utilize the *particle swarm optimization (PSO)* optimization algorithm, which is designed to mimic the social behavior of some animals (e.g., birds and fishes) [2]. We modify and adapt this algorithm to our objectives by defining the *fitness* function as the *augmented Dickey-Fuller (adfuller)* test [12], which examines the stationarity of a given time series as input.

Finally, in the last step, we take as input the three pre-computed time series for each feature and compute the corresponding anomaly scores. More specifically, a *fuzzy logic* inference system which has two main *Fuzzification* and *Defuzzification* phases is utilized. In *Fuzzification phase*, a membership function (Gaussian membership function) is applied on the time series, in which the anomaly scores are computed. Afterwards, in the *Defuzzification phase*, the adaptive thresholding is applied on these scores, and further according to obtained scores and their representative threshold, the associated features are flagged as either anomalous or non-anomalous.

3   Anomaly Detection Time-Series Approach

In this section, we describe our time-series based anomaly detection approach, which is combined with particle swarm optimization (PSO) algorithm.

3.1   Feature Extraction

Prior anomaly detection process, a set of features should be extracted. This task is primordial as it affects the final results of the approach tremendously. Many works have been achieved in the field of network anomaly detection in order to determine what are the features that give better insights of the network behavior [3,4,6]. In this work, we aim at not merely gather a set of attributes that best describe the network profile and behavior, but also obtain an anomaly detection system which works with any IDS logs, such as BRO, Snort and Suricata IDSs. Achieving the latter property provides the *interoperability* to our proposed system. Therefore, we target the possible features that are present in any IDS system. According to the aforesaid criteria and alongside with some literature review [6] regarding this objective, we extract the set of eight features of *Originator IP Address, Responder IP Address, Originator TCP/UDP Port, Responder TCP/UDP Port, number of bytes sent by the originator IP, number of bytes sent by the responder IP, number of packets sent by the originator IP,* and *number of packets sent by the originator IP.*

On the other hand, we receive the connection logs in the order of millions (sometimes hundreds of millions connection logs) per day, and therefore there would be a scalability issue to process all of these connection logs in a reasonable time. Therefore, to address the scalability issue we propose to use time-batches splitting [4] of five minutes to reduce the amount of processing time.

Our approach is a time-series based technique, which accepts numerical values in order to build the time-series representations. However, the type of the first four selected features (*Originator and Responder IP Addresses,* and *Originator and Responder TCP/UDP Ports*) is nominal. In order to convert nominal attributes to numerical representations, inspired by [6], we choose to use *Shannon Entropy* [4,6,13] as a summarization tool to represent the distribution of the features. Additionally, the authors prove that feature distributions enable the detection of a wide range of network anomalies, including unknown anomalies. The authors further demonstrate that studying these distributions can lead to an automatic unsupervised classification (clustering) represented in Table 1.

The intuition behind studying traffic features distributions is that the majority of network attacks affect the distributions of aforementioned attributes. For instance, consider a DDOS attack in which multiple source hosts (compromised machines) flood the targeted destination machine until the aimed goal is achieved (take down a specific service). By looking at the distributions of both source and destination IPs it could be inferred whether there is any spike/surge in the source IPs distribution and a drop-down in the destination IPs distributions, which leads to the detection of anomalies/attacks.

Shannon Entropy is a good metric to represent the degree of dispersal or concentration of any distribution and quantify these changes in a single numerical value. Given an attribute $X = \{x_1, x_2, \ldots, x_n\}$, where x_i is the frequency of the i_{th} attribute sample with the targeted time-batch (five minutes), the *Shannon Entropy,* $H(X)$, is computed as follows [4,13]:

$$H(X) = \sum_{i=1}^{n} \left(\frac{x_i}{\sum_{i=1}^{n} x_i} \right) \cdot \log_2 \left(\frac{x_i}{\sum_{i=1}^{n} x_i} \right) \tag{3.1}$$

Finally, we need to quantify the other four numerical values (sent bytes and packets from both originator and responder IPs) into a single value. For this purpose, inspired by [4] we simply consider the cumulative sum of each one of

Table 1. Effect of various anomalies on different feature distributions [6]

Anomaly type	Description	Affected distributions on			
		Src IP	Dest IP	Src Port	Dest Port
Denial of Service (DoS)	A single infected host is used to attack a victim and disable some services	Low	Low	-	-
Distributed Denial of Service (DDoS)	Multiple infected hosts and internet connections are used to target a single host	High	-	-	-
Port scanning	A large amount of traffic is sent to a small amount of destination IPs using large amount of destination ports	-	Low	-	High
Network scanning	A large amount of traffic is sent to a large amount of destination IPs using a small amount of destination ports	-	High	-	Low
Outage events	The traffic amount goes down due to the fact that a service went down, equipment failure, or maintenance operations	≈ 0	≈ 0	≈ 0	≈ 0
Flash crowd attacks	A huge surge in the amount of traffic going to one single destination IP		Low		Low

their values during the specific time-batch. By performing all the pre-processing steps, we end up with a full time-series representations (eight time-series, one for each feature) for the observed network behavior over the time.

3.1.1 Adaptive Thresholding

The next step of our approach consists of finding a metric to compute the thresholds of our pre-computed time-series representations. We deal with Internet connections, which are auto-correlated; meaning that the behaviors of users using a specific network are not random and thus they are affected mostly by their past interactions on the Internet. Therefore, we use the *exponential weighted moving average (EWMA)* as such metric. *EWMA* is a statistical metric that allows analysts to monitor the average of the data by giving more importance to the most recent data observations. This weighting system is computed in exponential fashion using all prior data observations. Considering that we have a time-series based representation of data observations in a specific time-window, *EWMA* is computed as follows [7]:

$$EWMA_t = \begin{cases} X_1, & \text{, if: } t = 1 \\ \alpha.X_t + (1 - \alpha).X_{t-1} & \text{, if: } t > 1 \end{cases} \tag{3.2}$$

where X_1 is the network observation at the time $t = 1$, X_t is the current network feature observation, X_{t-1} is the most recent (previous) network feature observation, and α is the weighting exponential factor which falls between 0 and 1 and is computed as $\alpha = e^{-\left(\frac{\epsilon}{\sigma}\right)}$ [18], where ϵ represents the time elapsed since the time-window started until the current observation, and σ represents the size of the time window (in our case it is set to one hour).

In addition, *EWMA* is a good statistical metric for measuring *historical volatility*, which represents the degree of dispersion for a given dataset over a defined period of time [24]. There are two main approaches to measure the volatility of data over time, namely *Implicit* and *Historical* [24]. *Historical* approaches assume that past data observations are essential for the prediction of future observations. *Implicit* approaches, on the other hand, ignore the past observations completely, and try to predict future observations based on the current observations. The fact that we are dealing with Internet connection logs implies that there are some auto-correlations (inter-connections) between the current and the past (most recent) internet connections of the users.

These summarization techniques have a major drawback in the way that all past observations during the time-window will have the same influence or weighting system [24]. This weakness would significantly influence and affect our results. Let's take an example where we have Internet connection logs over one month, and during let's say the 24th day of this month a DDOS attack occurred affecting all the source IPs in the logs that we receive. The next day (25th), this DDoS attack led the services to shut down or outage of most services on the targeted hosts (source) or IPs. If one applies the approach where the same weights are applied to all the observations of that month, this will terribly affect our system in the way that when computing the measure for the 25th day, and considering that the time window is of one month, the same importance will be given to the day when the attack occurred (previous day) but also to all previous days of the month. However by applying *EWMA* and computing the historical volatility measure for the day after the attack occurred (25th), the previous and most recent day (24th) will be given much more weight and importance over the previous days of the month, leading to capturing more patterns of the attack from the network flow attributes.

As an example of the resulting time series for these two steps (features extraction and adaptive thresholding), we collect around 400 million connections from one participating organization and apply these two steps on them. The obtained time-series representations are depicted in Figs. 2 and 3 respectively. The blue

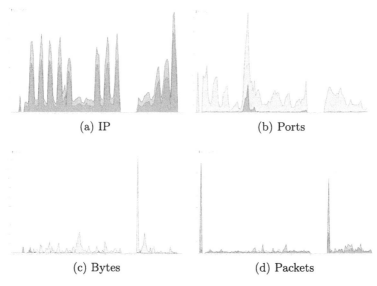

Fig. 2. Originators observed behaviours (in blue) and adaptive thresholds (in red) (Color figure online)

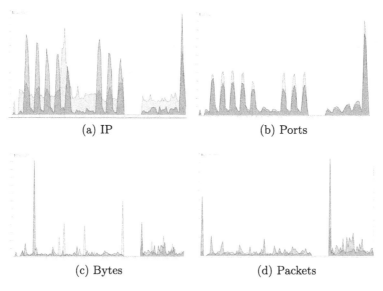

Fig. 3. Responders observed behaviours (in blue) and adaptive thresholds (in red) (Color figure online)

curves represent the observed feature behavior (from the features extraction step) and the red curves depict the computed adaptive thresholds (from the adaptive thresholding step).

3.1.2   Predictive Analysis

The next step of our anomaly detection system consists of predicting the normal network profile or behavior. One common and simple approach that is generally applied would be computing the differences between observed (real) network traffic and computed (fixed) thresholds and in the case of positive results, infer that the real traffic is anomalous (above thresholds), otherwise no anomaly is detected. However, we are dealing with Internet connection logs, which are not pre-filtered (or pre-cleaned) and are received on a daily basis, that result into a huge number of false positives. For instance, each day thousands or even hundreds of thousands of users and academics connect to Google website, if we consider only the two pre-computed steps (feature extraction and adaptive thresholding), we would end up with a lot of misleading attacks classifications and false positives (it could be classified as a DDOS attack). Therefore, we expand these two steps with another predictive step, which tries to delete most of the false positive incidences; in other words, given a real raw network traffic, we ask our system *how much clean the network traffic should look like?*

In order to do so, we opt for using an optimization algorithm, namely particle swarm optimization (PSO) [2,9,26] as shown in Algorithm 1, which achieves the desired goal of this step. PSO is a meta-heuristic global optimization technique that belongs to the family of *swarm intelligence* algorithms [2]. It is based in analogy with the social behavior of certain animals and most precisely *bird flocks* and *fish schools*. In PSO, the ensemble or set of possible solutions to the optimization task are called a *swarm* and each element of this swarm is called a *particle*. These particles move and change their positions in the search (parameter) space based on their own and neighbors' best performances. Therefore, this evolution process of the swarm is based on two main principles: *cooperation* and *competition* among these particles across multiple generations (several iterations).

Algorithm 1. Particle Swarm Optimization Algorithmic Description [2,9,26]

- **Initialization Process:** For each of the N particles:
1: Initilize the position $x_i(0) \forall i \in N$
2: Set the particle's best personal or local position as its initial position: $p_i(0) = x_i(0)$
3: Compute the fitness of the particle and if $f(x_j(0)) \geq f(x_i(0)) \forall i \neq j$ initialize the swarm global best as: $g = x_j(0)$
- **Repeat the following steps until the pre-defined criterias are met:**
4: Update the particle velocity according to the equation (3.6).
5: Update the particle position according to the equation (3.5).
6: Compute the fitness of the particle $f(x_i(t+1))$
7: if $f(x_i(t+1)) \geq f(p_i)$, update the particle's personal or local best as: $p_i = x_i(t+1)$
8: if $f(x_i(t+1)) \geq f(g)$, update the swarm's global best as: $g = x_i(t+1)$
- **Once the stopping criterias are met and the iterations are stopped, the best solution to the problem is represented by g.**

Accordingly, in PSO, each particle is defined in the D-dimensional search space, where D represents the set of parameters to be optimized. The position of the i_{th} particle is defined by the following vector $x_i = [x_{i1}, x_{i2}, x_{i3}, \ldots, x_{iD}]$, and the population (swarm) of N candidate solutions is $X = \{x_1, x_2, x_3, \ldots, x_N\}$. In their journey of finding the optimal solution, each particle updates its own position using $x_i(t+1) = x_i(t) + v_i(t+1)$, where t and $t+1$ represent two successive iterations of the algorithm and v_i represents a vector called the *velocity*, which governs the way the particle changes its position across the search space. The velocity parameter is defined according to three factors: (i) *Inertia or Momentum:* represents the previous velocity of the same partcile (previous iteration of the algorithm) and helps prevent from drastic position changes. (ii) *Cognitive Component:* represents the possibility of the partcile to return to the previous position. (iii) *Social Component:* identifies the ability of the particle to move forward the best solution of the whole swarm.

Based on these definitions, the velocity of the i_{th} particle is defined as $v_i(t + 1) = v_i(t) + c_1 (p_i - x_i(t)) R_1 + c_2 (g - x_i(t)) R_2$, where p_i represents the particle's best solution (local or personal best), while g represents the global best (the overall best solution found by the whole swarm). The two real-values of c_1 and c_2 are called *acceleration constants* that define the way by which the particle moves toward the global best solution. On the other hand, R_1 and R_2 represent respectively two diagonal matrices of randomly generated numbers from a uniform distribution in the interval $[0, 1]$. For both *cognitive* and *social* components to influence the particle's velocity in a stochastic way, the acceleration constants are generally set to 2 so that they meet the $0 \leq c_1.c_2 \leq 4$ criteria [9].

In order to get the PSO work correctly, the *fitness* or *objective* function, which defines the stopping criteria of the optimization task needs to be defined. In this work, we aim our predicted time-series to achieve stationary. The reason behind this logic is the fact that time-series statistical summarization techniques (such as the mean, variance, and standard deviation) do not give consistent results due to the presence of trends and seasonal effects (presence of periodic fluctuations). While time-series are stationary, they are not bounded by the time and summary statistics are more consistent. In addition, they can easily be modelled by statistical modelling approaches (e.g., forecasting techniques). Thus, it is always recommended to check if a time-series representation is stationary, and if not, make it stationary by the removal of any trends and seasonal effects before moving to analysing the *residual effects* [20].

One of the most frequently used stationary tests techniques is the *Augmented Dickey-Fuller Test (adfuller)* [12], which is a type of statistical test and autoregressive model for stationary that belongs to the *unit root* tests family. In *adfuller* algorithm, a time-series is considered as non-stationary if one of its monomials is equal to 1; this is equivalent to say that it can be defined in function of some specific trend (case of null hypothesis satisfied). On the other hand, if this test is rejected (alternate hypothesis satisfied), none of its monomials would be equal to 1, therefore it is considered as stationary [20].

In our work, once we build our representation of the network traffic behavior or profile (feature extraction phase), we then call *adfuller* test on each of the features' time-series. If at least one of the eight time-series is found as non-stationary (null hypothesis satisfied), then we trigger our PSO implementation in order to remove the presence of any trends and seasonal effects on that specific time-series. Otherwise (in the case of alternate hypothesis satisfaction and thus the null hypothesis rejection), if all the time-series are stationary, we do not trigger our PSO implementation and consider for our anomaly detection module only the observed behavior and the computed adaptive thresholds. Algorithm 2 best describes this statement.

3.1.3   Anomaly Detection

The final step of our anomaly detection system consists of using all the pre-computed time-series for detecting anomalies on each feature. For that purpose we employ *Fuzzy-Logic* [4,10] or fuzzy inference system for computing anomaly scores for each feature. In the fuzzification step, we compute anomaly scores ranging between 0 and 1 on the pre-computed time-series (observed, thresholds, and predicted behaviors) using the *Gaussian Membership Function* as defined in Eq. 3.7. If the prediction step was not triggered, we compute these scores using the Eq. 3.8. After the fuzzification process is terminated, we move on to the defuzzification process, where we define adaptive thresholds on these anomaly scores using the same technique presented for adaptive thresholding step (*EWMA*), and then flag each feature as anomalous (flag it as 1 if the anomaly score is above the threshold) or not (flag it as 0 if the anomaly score is below the threshold). The Gaussian membership function is defined as follows [4,10]:

$$score_k = 1 - e^{\frac{-(x_k - y_k)^2}{2 \cdot \epsilon_k^2}} \tag{3.7}$$

where k ranges from 0 to 8 and represents the corresponding feature, x_k represents the observed or expected behavior, y_k represents the predicted feature behavior in the case our predictive step is triggered, and ϵ_k represents the computed adaptive threshold for that feature. However, if the prediction step is not triggered, the Gaussian membership function is defined as follows:

$$score_k = e^{-(x_k - \epsilon_k)^2} \tag{3.8}$$

Algorithm 2. Predictive Algorithm.

```
 1: InputVector ← ObservedSeries
 2: for each FeatureTS ∈ InputVector do
 3:    InputData ← Feature − Time − Series
 4:    Stop ← False
 5:    ResultingTimeSeries ← InputData
 6:    iCounter ← 0
 7:    while Stop = False and iCounter ≤ 20
       do
 8:       p_value ← ADFULLER(InputData)
 9:       if p_value > 0.5 then
10:          InputData ← PSO(InputData)
11:       else
12:          ResultingTimeSeries ← InputData
13:          Stop ← True
14:       end if
15:    end while
16: end for
17: end
```

Algorithm 3. Proposed Fuzzy Inference Algorithm.

```
 1: InputVector ← ObservedSeries
 2: for each FeatureTS ∈ InputVector do
 3:    for each Obse, Threshl, Pred ∈ FeatureTS
       do
 4:       S ← GUASSIANFUN(Obs, Threshl, Pred)
 5:       TH ← ANOMALY-THRESHL(S)
 6:       for each score, threshold ∈ S, TH do
 7:          if score ≥ threshold then
 8:             anomaly_flag ← 1
 9:          else
10:             anomaly_flag ← 0
11:          end if
12:       end for
13:    end for
14: end for
15: end
```

Algorithm 3 describes how anomalies are detected on each feature. At the end of this process, we end up with each connection extended with eight anomaly scores and flags (one for each feature), as depicted in Table 2. Each connection is considered as anomalous if at least one of these eight flags is set to 1.

Table 2. Anomaly scores and flags

Anomaly	Features
Scores (between 0 and 1)	id_orig_h_anomaly_score, id_resp_h_anomaly_score, id_orig_p_anomaly_score, id_resp_p_anomaly_score, orig_bytes_anomaly_score, resp_bytes_anomaly_score, orig_pkts_anomaly_score, resp_pkts_anomaly_score
Flags (either 0 or 1)	id_orig_h_anomaly_flag, id_resp_h_anomaly_flag, id_orig_p_anomaly_flag, id_resp_p_anomaly_flag, orig_bytes_anomaly_flag, resp_bytes_anomaly_flag, orig_pkts_anomaly_flag, resp_pkts_anomaly_flag

4   Evaluation

This section gives more details about our experimental dataset and the evaluation metrics used to validate our proposed technique.

4.1   Experimental Setup

All of our experiments are conducted on a dedicated processing server running CentOS Linux version 7 with Intel Xeon E5-2630 2.30 GHz CPU and 126 GB of RAM. Our framework is developed by using Python programming language and by leveraging *Elasticsearch* as an indexing and search database for data analytics. *Apache Spark* alongside with *pandas* Python library are used to improve the scalability and to exploit the full capacity of our server (CPU and RAM resources). *Kibana* is used as a visualization tool on top of *Elasticsearch* in order to create the required dashboards. *X-Pack* security tool, which is a plugin that can be integrated on top of both *Elasticsearch* and *Kibana* is employed to provide additional functionalities of *user management, user authentication*, and *indices access roles*. All the data are stored in a storage server of 500TB capacity.

Experimental Dataset. In order to perform the experiments, a number of organizations participated to collect and share their IDS logs. Almost 90% of the participants installed BRO IDS, with some exceptions that employed other types of IDS. Moreover, the locations of the sensors were different. Some organizations choose to install their BRO sensors outside their firewalls, and therefore collect all the connections incoming and outgoing to/from their network. This results into sharing more consistent sizes of logs per day (sometimes hundreds of millions of connections each day). Whilst others capture only the traffic outgoing from their network, and thus less connection logs are received. In total, we receive millions of connection logs from the participants on a daily basis, which are stored on the dedicated storage server as compressed files.

Evaluation Metrics. In order to evaluate the performance and validate our approach, *Accuracy* ($\frac{TP+TN}{TP+FP+TN+FN}$), and F_1 *score* ($\frac{2\times TP}{2\times TP+FP+FN}$) metrics are computed.

4.2 Ground Truth Correlation

In this section, we validate the results of our anomaly detection technique by correlating them with some existing resources. We test our technique on a set of connection logs and identify the anomalies. Then, all the detected anomalous connections are correlated with external security feeds, such as malware sandboxing reports. The IP blocks are extracted from each connection (originator and responder IPs) and are correlated with the extracted malicious IPs from existing security sources within the same time interval that the connection occurred. We consider only three days of lag. Therefore, we first perform malware correlation within the same day that the connection occurred. If there is no match, we continue the correlation with the data of previous day. This process is repeated until the last three days. The reason of considering the three days of lag is due to the fact that most of the malware tend to change their IP addresses in order to evade detection. We further perform the correlation with an open-source ransomware database, *Ransomware Tracker* [21], which will be updated in the case of the detection of a new worldwide ransomware. Therefore, we download the *Ransomware Tracker* database, and on a weekly basis we check for any changes to keep our database updated.

From the correlation results, we consider the number of connections that were detected both by our system as anomalies and by the correlation as malicious as *true positives (TP)*, the ones that we flagged as anomalous but did not return correlation results as *false positives (FP)*, the benign connection that were not flagged as anomalies as *true negatives (TN)*, and the malicious connection that were not flagged as anomalous as *false negatives (FN)*. As an example, we examine $2,438,294$ connections detected as anomalous (from approximately 400 million connections) from one of the randomly chosen participating organization collected from August 20, 2018 to 4th of September 2018. We correlate our results with both malware and ransomware databases and then measure the aforementioned security metrics. Our experiments show that *Daedalus* achieves 83.68% of accuracy and 91.11% of F_1 score.

4.3 Validation on Benchmark Dataset

We further examine our proposed technique with benchmark datasets. We choose *UNBCIC 2017 IDS Dataset* [14, 25], which contains the BRO connection logs as well as two csv files that label the connections as Benign, DDoS or PortScan.

We run our proposed technique on $350,137$ randomly selected connection logs in order to detect anomalies, among which $256,540$ were detected as true positives (flagged as anomalous and labeled either as DDoS attacks or Port Scan attacks), $16,775$ connections were detected as false positives (flagged as anomalous but there were no correlation results with DDoS and Port Scanning datasets), $64,575$ were detected as true negatives (neither detected as anomalous nor DDoS nor Port Scanning), and $12,247$ were detected as false negatives (were not flagged as anomalous but there were correlation matches with DDoS and Port Scanning). The obtained results demonstrate 91.71% of accuracy and 94.64% of F_1 score.

4.4 Comparison with Other Anomaly Detection Approaches

In this section, we compare our proposed technique with an exiting anomaly detection approach. To this end, we choose the *K-Means* clustering method [17] written in *Python* to detect anomalies on time series data. In this approach, the anomalies are detected based on the *reconstruction error curve*. We modify the provided implementation in order to fit it with the format of our datasets by using only four features (originator bytes and packets, and responder bytes and packets), and we also reduce the default number of clusters to 3. The implementation is applied on the same dataset of *UNBCIC 2017 IDS*, and then the results are correlated with the labelled dataset (DDoS and PortScan attacks). The obtained results show that we achieve 44.38% of accuracy and 56.28% of F_1 score.

4.5 Scalability Study

We compare the execution time and resources consumption of our last two evaluations (Subsects. 4.3 and 4.4 using $350,137$ connections from *UNBCIC 2017 IDS*) with the K-Means algorithm and report the results as illustrated in Table 3. The *htop Linux* command [19] is used to monitor the percentage of each CPU core usage.

Table 3. Scalability comparison

	Our approach	K-Means
Execution time	19 (m) and 25 (s)	1 h and 16 (m)
CPU cores used	24 cores dedicated; less than 50% usage for each core	24 Cores Dedicated; 3 cores were used critically (more than 70% usage)
Memory (RAM) used	4 GB	5.22 GB

5   Related Work

In this section, we present briefly the most recent and prominent works that have been achieved and proposed in the field of network anomaly detection. In [5], the authors proposed a new SVM system called *robuts support vector machines (RSVMs)* and compared its performance with classical SVM systems and nearest neighbours classifiers using the DARPA BSM dataset of 1998. The authors have proved that their proposed technique achieves 81.8% accuracy results and less then 1% false positives rates. In addition, the suggested method can considerably reduce the execution time, as it generates less support vectors compared to conventional SVMs. In [27], the authors have compared three SVM techniques for their anomaly detection system, namely: *standard or conventional SVMs, weighted SVMs*, and *one class SVMs (OC-SVM)*. They observed that the latter one achieves the highest accuracy detection rates with almost 78%. In [8], the authors proposed a deep learning based anomaly detection approach for detecting cyberthreats in $5G$ networks in an efficient and fast manner. They showed that their proposed technique can self-adapt itself depending on the volume of network flows collected. In [4], on which the logic of our paper is mainly based, the authors have used a network behavior profiling technique that is based mainly on *genetic algorithms* and *fuzzy logic*. The authors have compared their suggested method with other techniques of *SVM approach, Rigid thresholds, ACODS approach*, and *outlier detection* one, and demonstrated that their technique achieves a higher *area under the curve (AUC)*. In [11], the authors have proposed a tool called *Kitsune* that detects anomalies on local networks by tracking the network behavior using an ensemble of *autoencoders* in a completely unsupervised manner. Last but not least, in [16], the authors have studied the detection of intrusions in web services using *Auto-Regressive Integrated Moving Average (ARIMA)* technique.

6   Conclusion and Future Discussions

In this paper, we presented *Daedalus*, a highly scalable time-series and unsupervised anomaly detection approach on network IDS logs. Our main contribution resides in the predictive analysis step which has been improved significantly in terms of scalability. This technique was validated during a three-steps process: *ground truth correlation, validation on a benchmark dataset*, and *comparison with other techniques*. The results show that our approach achieves higher accuracy results and better resources consumption (execution time, CPU cores usage and memory). Investigating other anomaly detection techniques, such as long-short terms memory networks (LSTMs), gated recurrent units (GRUs), and autoencoders, and further comparing them with our proposed technique is the subject of our future work.

References

1. Antonakakis, M., et al.: Understanding the mirai botnet. In: Proceedings of the 26th USENIX Security Symposium (2017)
2. Eberhart, R., Kennedy, J.: A new optimizer using particle swarm theory. In: Proceedings of the Sixth International Symposium on Micro Machine and Human Science. MHS 1995, pp. 39–43. IEEE (1995)
3. Goldberg, D., Shan, Y.: The importance of features for statistical anomaly detection. In: HotCloud (2015)
4. Hamamoto, A.H., Carvalho, L.F., Sampaio, L.D.H., Abrão, T., Proença Jr., M.L.: Network anomaly detection system using genetic algorithm and fuzzy logic. Expert Syst. Appl. **92**, 390–402 (2018)
5. Hu, W., Liao, Y., Vemuri, V.R.: Robust anomaly detection using support vector machines. In: Proceedings of the International Conference on Machine Learning, pp. 282–289 (2003)
6. Lakhina, A., Crovella, M., Diot, C.: Mining anomalies using traffic feature distributions. In: ACM SIGCOMM Computer Communication Review, vol. 35, pp. 217–228. ACM (2005)
7. Machaka, P., Bagula, A., Nelwamondo, F.: Using exponentially weighted moving average algorithm to defend against ddos attacks. In: 2016 Pattern Recognition Association of South Africa and Robotics and Mechatronics International Conference (PRASA-RobMech), pp. 1–6. IEEE (2016)
8. Maimo, L.F., Gomez, A.L.P., Clemente, F.J.G., Pérez, M.G., Pérez, G.M.: A self-adaptive deep learning-based system for anomaly detection in 5g networks. IEEE Access **6**, 7700–7712 (2018)
9. Marini, F., Walczak, B.: Particle swarm optimization (PSO). A tutorial. Chemom. Intell. Lab. Syst. **149**, 153–165 (2015)
10. Mendel, J.M.: Fuzzy logic systems for engineering: a tutorial. Proc. IEEE **83**(3), 345–377 (1995)
11. Mirsky, Y., Doitshman, T., Elovici, Y., Shabtai, A.: Kitsune: an ensemble of autoencoders for online network intrusion detection. In: 25th Annual Network and Distributed System Security Symposium, NDSS 2018, San Diego, California, USA, February 18–21, 2018 (2018)
12. Mushtaq, R.: Augmented dickey fuller test
13. Sbert, M., Shen, H.-W., Viola, I., Chen, M., Bardera, A., Feixas, M.: Tutorial on information theory in visualization. In: SIGGRAPH Asia 2017 Courses, p. 17. ACM (2017)
14. Sharafaldin, I., Lashkari, A.H., Ghorbani, A.A.: Toward generating a new intrusion detection dataset and intrusion traffic characterization. In: ICISSP, pp. 108–116 (2018)
15. Shinde, R., et al.: Survey on ransomware: a new era of cyber attack
16. Shirani, P., Azgomi, M.A., Alrabaee, S.: A method for intrusion detection in web services based on time series. In: 2015 IEEE 28th Canadian Conference on Electrical and Computer Engineering (CCECE), pp. 836–841. IEEE (2015)
17. Anomaly detection with k-means clustering (2015). http://amid.fish/anomaly-detection-with-k-means-clustering
18. An exponentially weighted moving average implementation that decays based on the elapsed time since the last update, approximating a time windowed moving average (2017). https://gist.github.com/jhalterman/f7b18b30160ae7817bb93894056eb380

19. htop(1) - linux man page https://linux.die.net/man/1/htop
20. How to check if time series data is stationary with python (2016). https://machinelearningmastery.com/time-series-data-stationary-python/
21. Ransomware tracker website (2018). https://ransomwaretracker.abuse.ch/tracker/
22. The bro network security monitor. https://www.bro.org/
23. Bro log files. https://www.bro.org/sphinx/script-reference/log-files.html
24. Exploring the exponentially weighted moving average (2018). https://www.investopedia.com/articles/07/ewma.asp
25. UNBCIC 2017 IDS Dataset (2017). http://www.unb.ca/cic/datasets/ids-2017.html
26. Wang, X., Zhang, H., Zhang, C., Cai, X., Wang, J., Ye, M.: Time series prediction using LS-SVM with particle swarm optimization. In: Wang, J., Yi, Z., Zurada, J.M., Lu, B.-L., Yin, H. (eds.) ISNN 2006. LNCS, vol. 3972, pp. 747–752. Springer, Heidelberg (2006). https://doi.org/10.1007/11760023_110
27. Zhang, X., Gu, C., Lin, J.: Support vector machines for anomaly detection. In: The Sixth World Congress on Intelligent Control and Automation. WCICA 2006, vol. 1, pp. 2594–2598. IEEE (2006)

IoT Security

Configuring Data Flows in the Internet of Things for Security and Privacy Requirements

Luigi Logrippo$^{(\boxtimes)}$ and Abdelouadoud Stambouli

Department of Computer Science and Engineering Gatineau,
Université du Québec en Outaouais, Gatineau, Québec, Canada
`{luigi,staal6}@uqo.ca`

Abstract. The Internet of Things is a highly distributed, highly dynamic environment where data can flow among entities (the 'things') in complex data flow configurations. For data secrecy, it is important that only certain data flows be allowed. Research in this area is often based on the use of the well-known lattice model. However, as shown in previous papers, by using a basic result of directed graph theory (or of order theory) it is possible to use a less constrained model based on partial orders, for which a formal notion of secrecy can be defined. We define a notion of 'allowed contents' for each 'thing' and then the data flows follow by inclusion relationships. By taking advantage of transitivity of data flows and of strongly connected component algorithms, these data flow relationships can then be simplified. It is shown that several data flow relationships can coexist in a network. Two small examples are presented, one on hospital applications and another on e-commerce. Implementation issues are discussed.

Keywords: Internet of Things · Data secrecy · Data confidentiality · Privacy · Data flow control · Partial orders

1 Introduction and Motivation

Given that we have a network of *entities* representing an abstract view of an Internet of things (IoT) network, how can we set up the data communications channels between entities so that data originating in one entity can or cannot reach another entity? Being able to answer this question is important to answer questions of:

- *Secrecy* (also called *confidentiality*): can data stored in an entity reach another entity? This question has clear consequences for the question of *privacy*, which will be implied henceforth.
- *Integrity*: can data originating from an entity at some level of integrity reach an entity at higher level of integrity, thus potentially polluting it?
- *Availability*: can an entity always access the data it needs?

It is of course a basic requirement for the IoT that "data should be able to flow as needed" with as little confinement as possible, but also "data should not flow to unauthorized parties" [22]. With respect to privacy, we agree that "the fundamental

© Springer Nature Switzerland AG 2019
N. Zincir-Heywood et al. (Eds.): FPS 2018, LNCS 11358, pp. 115–130, 2019.
https://doi.org/10.1007/978-3-030-18419-3_8

nature of a privacy violation is an improper information flow" [13]. Paper [23] takes a broad view of the importance of information flow control to achieve legal obligations in the IoT. Many IoT diagrams in the literature show bidirectional channels among entities, however clearly for secrecy and privacy some channels may have to be unidirectional or absent altogether. These problems are common between the IoT and Cloud, since IoT is often implemented on Cloud platforms [9, 11, 12].

We propose in this paper a new method to design networks with data flow topologies (i.e. configurations of entities and channels) that can satisfy secrecy requirements as specified in terms of logic expressions. We will also mention why we believe that integrity requirements are also addressed by the same method. Related important questions that we discuss in this paper are the following: given certain data flow relationships in an IoT system, and the fact that we know that certain data originate in certain entities, which are the entities that will be privy to these data? Which are the most secret or least secret entities, in the sense that data that are in them cannot or can propagate to others?

As already discussed in [14] and [24], it turns out that a simple result of directed graph theory, associated with well-known efficient algorithms, can be used to provide solutions for this problem, which are generic, i.e. independent of the application, or of the devices used to implement the entities, or of the physical network. These papers did not explicitly consider the IoT, which will be the focus of this paper.

2   Literature Review

Although the concept of Internet of Things is not much older than our century, the literature on the general subject of 'security in the IoT' is already extensive, and several survey papers exist. However most of this literature is about attacks, vulnerabilities, access control, and is not particularly related to the problem of data flow control for security. We are interested in globally controlling all the possible 'things' where the data of certain other 'things' can end through sequences of data transfers, while access control controls data transfers between pairs of 'things'. In this brief literature review, we cite only papers that are closely related to our problem and proposed solution.

An extremely influential pioneering paper on the general subject of data flow in programs and networks is the one by Denning [4]. It showed that by using principles of lattice structuring, data flow security properties can be guaranteed in programs or networks. Almost all papers cited here refer to the lattice model by proposing applications, variants and enhancements of it. Our model has in common with the lattice model the fact that it is relational, rather than state-transition based. It generalizes Denning's model because it uses partial orders instead of lattices. In [14] it is shown that partial orders are necessary and sufficient for data flow secrecy and that they always exist. In [24] it is shown that they can be efficiently found.

It should be noted that the subjects of flow control in the IoT and in the Cloud are closely intertwined and on the way to integration [2]. Many papers in this general research area propose the use of authentication, encryption and access control methods, including variations of RBAC [6], in the IoT. Many of these papers are reviewed in [16]. Although authentication, encryption and access control are mechanism for realizing flow control, we will limit our consideration here to methods for designing the overall flow control.

Much classical literature, such as the paper of Samarati et al. [19] deals with the problem of preventing or blocking illegal flows. Our purpose is dual, i.e. to identify (in a current configuration) or permit (in a configuration to be established) all legal flows.

Blackstock and Lea [3] address the need for IoT data flow platforms to create "systems suitable for executing on a range of real-time environments, toward supporting distributed IoT programs that can be partitioned between servers, gateways and devices". They describe their experiences with two existing data flow platforms towards designing their own.

Narendra Kumar and Shyamasundar [15] use a formalism based on identifying separate *subjects* and *objects* (rather than *entities* only) and separate reading and writing authorizations, rather than on a single *CanFlow* relationship as we do. They define a Readers and Writers Flow Model based on Denning's lattice model. Each entity is provided with a label defining the entities that can read from it and the entities that can write on it. This paper is in the context of Cloud computing. In a very recent follow-up paper [12], Khobragade and the two authors just cited extend their method to the IoT. We will come back to these papers in the Conclusions.

Bacon et al. [1, 12, 18] have developed data flow control methods and software for the Cloud and the IoT using data tagging. We agree that data tagging seems to be necessary for configuring data flows. as we will see later in our paper.

Schütte and Brost [21] present a policy language, LUCON, designed to control the routing of messages across services. Message routes can be model-checked to see whether they violate policies. The method uses message labels to which policies refer in order to decide what happens to the messages during routing. Again, this kind of labelling will play a role in our model.

These papers agree on the fact that generic solutions for IoT data flow control exist, and should be used before application-specific ones. We share this opinion.

Although IoT networks are usually represented as directed graphs (digraphs), we could not find a single paper that references or uses the basic result of digraph theory that is presented in the following section, and which is the basis of our method. The use of this result, instead of the classical lattice model, is the salient distinguishing characteristic of our approach.

3   Basic Concepts

This section is mainly an adaptation to the IoT context of results presented in [14, 24]. We consider sets of abstract *entities* that can communicate among themselves by unidirectional abstract *channels* (bidirectional arrows in our diagrams mean that there are two channels in opposite directions). Entities represent 'things' or objects such as sensors, databases, etc. Each entity has computing and storage power, can also have sensing capabilities. We call *network topology* a given set of entities with channels between them, which is fixed at any network *state*. We use the letter e with primes and subscripts to denote variables for entities. We write $CF_1(e, e')$ (*can flow*) to say that there is a channel that can carry data from e to e'. In practice, CF_1 can be implemented in several ways, this will be discussed later. We write $CF(e, e')$ if there is a communication path, consisting of one or several channels, from e to e'. If the data of e is encrypted so that e' cannot decrypt it, then the relation is false.

Definition 1: $CF(e, e')$ is true if:

(a) $CF_1(e, e')$ or
(b) there is a e'' such that $CF_1(e, e'')$ and $CF(e'', e')$.

So CF is a *transitive* relationship. This is a pessimistic view, which can make networks over-protected; it ignores the fact that some entities may decide to block some data. Our (perhaps simplistic) view is that if Alice talks to Bob and Carl talks to Alice, Carl can expect whatever he says to end up with Bob. We also assume that CF is *reflexive*, since we can assume the existence of a channel from any entity to itself, although for simplicity such channels will be left implicit. It is important to note that, by its transitivity and reflexivity, CF is a *quasi-order* [7]. The relation CF will be shown in the form of directed graphs (or *digraphs*). To enhance this generic view, in Sect. 6 we shall informally introduce the notion of several separate data flows.

We say that an entity e *can hold* data x, written $CH(e, x)$, iff data item x can be present in e. $CH(e, x)$ can be a fact known a priori, an axiom. For example, a sensor in a refrigerator can hold a temperature reading. In other cases, $CH(e, x)$ can be a derived fact, if there exists a e' such that $CH(e', x)$ and $CF(e', e)$. So, if there is a channel from the sensor to a HomeComputer (HC), then the HC can also hold the temperature reading.

It would be possible to continue in the same way, considering the level of granularity of single data items; however in this paper we won't need to reason at this fine level of granularity. Henceforth we use the notation $CH(e, e')$ to say that entity e can hold the data in e'. In the example above, if there is a channel that can carry data from a sensor in the refrigerator to the HC, we say that both the sensor and the HC *can hold* all data in the sensor. In our examples below we will construct networks by using a reverse principle, i.e. starting from the fact that HC can hold all data in the sensor, we conclude that there is a flow, or a channel, from the sensor to the HC.

Formally, we write:

Definition 2:

(a) $CH(e, e)$ is our axiom
(b) $CH(e, e')$ iff $CF(e', e)$ is our inference rule

The following definition will allow us to refer to all the data that can be contained in an entity, given a data flow configuration:

Definition 3:

$CHS(e) = \{e'$ such that $CH(e, e')\}$

CHS stands for *CanHoldSet*. For example, if there is a path from a fridge to a HC, and from a thermostat to the same HC, then the entity HC can hold temperatures from both the fridge and the thermostat.

Clearly, we have:

Property 1:

(a) *CF(e, e')* iff *CHS(e)* ⊆ *CHS(e')*
(b) *CF(e, e')* and *CF(e', e)* iff *CHS(e)* = *CHS(e')*

These definitions could appear to be counterintuitive at first because it might be thought that two different entities could be able to acquire the same data directly and independently, consider for example two independent sensors that sense the same conditions. When this is possible, it is still safe to assume, from the security point of view, that there is a bidirectional channel between the two entities.

We now describe the basic result of digraph theory that is at the basis of our method. This result also appears, in simpler form, in the theory of relations and in the theory of orders [7], but in our research area the graph-theoretical view may be the most useful, and so we adapt here the theory presented in [10]. We define *components* of our digraphs to be sets of entities such that for any two entities *e* and *e'* in the set, *CF (e, e')* and *CF(e', e)*. By Property 1, *CHS(e)* = *CHS(e')*. We are interested only in components that are *maximal*, i.e. they are not contained in larger components, so henceforth the adjective maximal will be implicit when we will mention components. Let us *condense* each component in a single node in the digraph. Since the original *CF* digraph represented a quasi-ordering, the resulting condensed digraph represents a *partial order* [7]: this is because all symmetric relationships have disappeared, having been encapsulated in nodes. Let us call *[e]* the node corresponding to the component containing entity *e* (clearly, the mapping *e* → *[e]* is a function). It is easily seen that there is a path (a *CF* relationship) from *e* to *e'* in the original digraph iff there is a path from *[e]* to *[e']* in the condensed digraph [10].

There are well-known and efficient (linear-time) algorithms to find condensed digraphs, and their use will be demonstrated in this paper. It is important to note that such condensed digraph will be acyclic. We will call such algorithms *strongly connected components algorithms*. We use Tarjan's algorithm [25] as implemented in MATLAB [8].

As a generalization of the above notation, we allow specifying flow relationships between sets of entities. For *S* and *S'* finite sets of entities, *CF(S, S')* means that *CF(e, e')* holds between *each e ∈ S* and *all e' ∈ S'*. The sets can be specified either by enumeration, or by set-theoretical expressions, based on the attributes of entities as we will see. For example, if *S* is a set of patients having a specific illness and *S'* is a set of doctors that specialize in that illness, then *CF(S, S')* means that data can flow from each patient in *S* to all doctors in *S'*.

So entities *e* have named attributes, in variable numbers and according to application needs. We assume that each entity has attributes according to application needs. Hence the constraint above can be specified as follows:

CH(e, e') **if** *patient(e)* **and** *illness e = stroke* **and** *doctor(e')* **and** *specialty (e')* = *stroke*

By Property 1, this implies *CF(S, S')*, where *S* is the set of all such patients and *S'* is the set of all such doctors.

We refine this view by allowing *CF* relationships to be specialized by the type of data involved. We shall see later an e-commerce example where there are two different *CF* relationships, one for ordering and one for billing. Many different *CF* relationships can coexist in a network. In real life, Alice might talk to Bob on work matters, but not on private matters. Knowing this, Carl can talk to Alice on private matters, assuming that this will not end up with Bob.

Note finally that we use the term *component* in the described graph theoretical meaning. This is quite different from the term's use in some IoT literature, where it can denote hardware entities with specific physical characteristics. In our sense, an entity that belongs to a singleton equivalence class is also a component. On the other hand, entities that are physically identical can belong to different components in our sense. We use the term *device* to refer to components in this other sense.

4   The Method

Our method is based on the idea that *if an entity* e *can hold all the data that an entity* e' *can hold (plus possibly other data) then* CF(e', e) *should be true*. So each entity will have attributes and will be associated with a logical expression, based on the available attributes, defining the set of data that it can hold. The channels will be placed by calculating the inclusion relationships between these sets. This can be done dynamically, in the sense that every time a new entity is defined, the channels it should have can be calculated, by checking the data set inclusion relationships between the new entity and the existing ones (this step is not trivial from the point of view of computational complexity, and will be discussed in future papers).

The method described so far may be impractical, since it might generate 'too many channels'. In terms of digraphs, its result can be visualized as a transitively closed digraph, see Fig. 1(a) for an example. According to the properties presented in the previous section, a streamlined digraph can be obtained in the following way:

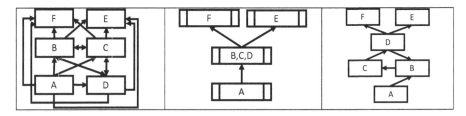

Fig. 1. (a): A data flow graph; (b) its partial order of components; (c) an equivlent data flow graph

(1) Using a strongly connected components algorithm, calculate the compressed digraph for the *CF* relation (recall that it will be acyclic).

(2) Calculate the transitive reduction of the compressed digraph, see Fig. 1(b) where each box represents a component (often a single algorithm will do both (1) and (2)).

(3) For each component in this last digraph, connect the entities (if they are more than one) in any way that maintains the mutual reachability relation;

(4) For any two components *S* and *S'* such that $S \subseteq S'$, connect one or more element (s) in *S* to one or more element(s) in *S'* (Fig. 1(c)). By transitivity, *CF(S, S')*.

In practice data flow graphs may be large and complex, with component nesting difficult to unravel, but each of the algorithms involved is (at most) polynomial, thus 'efficient' in complexity theory terms. Therefore, it might be conceivable to re-execute the procedure every time there is a change in a network, or periodically, whenever a network reconfiguration is desired.

Note that several communication paths that are direct in Fig. 1(a) are indirect by transitivity in Fig. 1(c). Our method may produce communication patterns inappropriate for the intended application, but it won't produce any that violate secrecy constraints. Step (3) can be done in different ways: in Fig. 1 we implemented the goal of reducing the number of edges by using transitivity, but other goals can be implemented. Therefore, we propose the use of this method as a basic method only, that may be adapted to the needs of specific networks.

The use of this method will be assumed in the rest of the paper. The theory above will be used implicitly.

5   Network Creation: A Hospital Example

We use here small examples to demonstrate our method, but as mentioned this is scalable because of the existence of efficient algorithms.

As a first example, we consider a toy hospital system. In its final configuration, the system will be as in Fig. 2, however we will show how it can be built step by step.

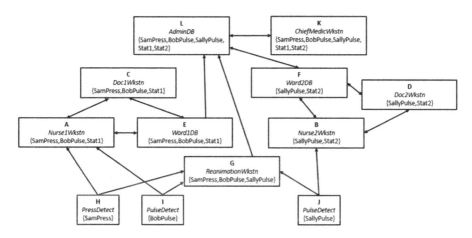

Fig. 2. A hospital example

The types of the entities are: *PressDetect, PulseDetect, NurseWkstn, DocWkstn, ReanimationWkstn, WardDB, ChiefMedicWkstn, AdminDB* (in Fig. 2, numerals are added to the type names in order to distinguish different instances). We have three patients, *Sam, Bob* and *Sally*, which however do not appear as entities but as parts of the labels of the entities. In other words, we have labels: *SamPress, BobPulse, Sally-Press* etc. We also have some statistical data that are created in some entities. When an entity of one of the mentioned types is created, it is associated with a label, which indicates the data that it can hold. We use a command *New* to create a new entity with a label. A channel, which is a *CF* relationship, is automatically created between the new entity and all the previously created entities such as the label of the new entity is included in the label of the previously existing entity. Then the method of Sect. 4 can be executed to reduce the edges if possible. For example,

New(A) = Nurse1Wkstn{SamPress, BobPulse, Stats1}.
New(B) = Nurse2Wkstn{SallyPulse, Stats2}.
New(C) = Doc1Wkstn{SamPress, BobPulse, Stats1}.
New(D) = Doc2Wkstn{SallyPulse, Stats2}.
New(E) = Ward1DB{SamPress, BobPulse, Stats1}.
New(F) = Ward2DB{SallyPulse, Stats2}.
New(G) = ReanimationWkstn{SamPress, BobPulse, SallyPulse}.
Etc.

After C is created, we have $CF(A, C)$ and $CF(C, A)$ since $CH(A) = CH(C)$. Similarly for D and B. After H is created, we have $CF(H, A)$, $CF(H, C)$ etc. So channels are created between entities as the entities are created. In the graph of Fig. 2, we have placed the entities in ascending order of inclusion, starting from those that have the smallest *CHSs* at the bottom. Certain things of interest can be seen: for example, we say that *BobPulse* is a *secret of* the set of entities {I, G, A, E, C, L, K} which are the only entities that *CanHold* this data (in terms of [14, 24] this is the *Area of BobPulse*). It can also be said that entities that appear towards the bottom of the partial order are the least secretive, because they allow their data to flow up to other entities. On the contrary, entities appearing at the top {L, K} are the most secretive, because their data cannot flow further. They are also the entities that can hold the most data, in fact they can hold all data available in the network in this example.

Note that there are some non-singleton components in this digraph, they are {A, C, E},{B, F, D},{L, K}. In each such component, the entities are mutually reachable and so they can all hold the same data. The partial order of equivalence classes for this digraph is shown in Fig. 3.

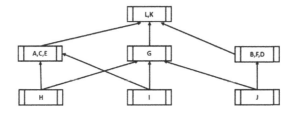

Fig. 3. Partial order of components for the hospital example

Note also the following important point. Suppose that for some reason, the entities are created in the following order: first H, then L, then C. In practice this might lead to a mis-configuration and there might be application-specific protocols to prevent this from happening. Without this, our method will produce the following results. After L is created, data can flow from H to L, and after C is created, data can flow from H to C, also from C to L. At this point, transitive reduction will eliminate the direct flow from H to L. Secrecy constraints will never be violated and whatever order is followed in the creation of entities, we will always end up with the network depicted in Fig. 2.

6 Separate Data Flows: An E-Commerce Example

We introduce now a second example, where for readability we have done some simplifications of notation with respect to the previous one (for example, we don't explicitly show that each entity contains its own data). This is an e-commerce network with four clients, two retailers and four suppliers. Client 3 and 4 collaborate and so they share data. We have two retailers. Finally, we have four suppliers, of which the first three collaborate and so share client data. After having created all the entities, the network is as shown in Fig. 4.

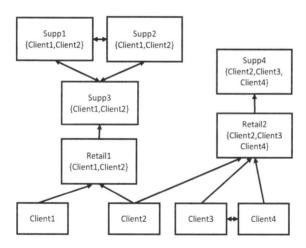

Fig. 4. An e-commerce example

The partial order of equivalence classes for this example is shown in Fig. 5.

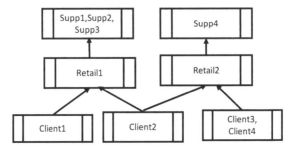

Fig. 5. Partial order of components for the e-commerce example

Again, this example can be analyzed to see what data are secret of which entities.

This example is useful to show the (usual) necessity of having several coexistent but separate data flows in the same network. The previous diagrams dealt with ordering information. Billing information travels in the opposite direction, and has different secrecy requirements. Since each client should get only its own bills (except perhaps for Clients 3 and 4 who share bills), then this requires defining as many separate data flows as there are clients. Figure 6 shows the data flow for the bills of *Client 1* (in this case we show a downward flow for consistency with the previous figure). To keep the two flows separate, we can identify the label sets that are relevant for each flow. For example, the labels for *Supp1* could be as follows: *Supp1:Order{Client1,Client2};Bill1 {Bill1-1};Bill2{Bill1-2}*. This means that *Supp1* participates in three data flows, one for ordering and two for billing, for each of its two possible clients. This starts to be complex, but seems to be necessary for the secrecy of bills.

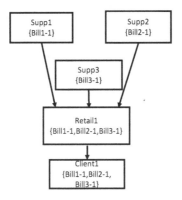

Fig. 6. Partial billing flow in the e-commerce example

7 Network Re-configurations

We must allow for data flow changes that can be requested by end users or administrators, entities which we see as external to our networks. These changes must be in some way approved by authorities in charge of protecting security and privacy in the system. Often one such change will motivate others in order to maintain useful dataflows. In Fig. 1, suppose that there is a request by which *Client1* should be allowed to subscribe to *Retail 2*, and the request is granted. Then *Retail2{Client2,Client3,Client4}* becomes *Retail2{Client1,Client2,Client3,Client4}*. *Retail2* can no longer flow to *Supp4*. So another authorization seems to be necessary for *Supp4{Client2,Client3,Client4}* to become *Supp4{Client1,Client2,Client3,Client4}* and *Supp4* or some conflict of interests among clients may refuse this second change. Therefore, the requesting and granting of authorizations cannot be purely local, it must be done with a global plan to do all the other changes that may be necessary to return to a desired global flow. A method to avoid such problems would be to deny authorizations unless it is possible to grant at the same time all others that are necessary to maintain the required flow structure. All such authorizations would have to be granted at the same time. The mechanisms for these label changes will vary according to the nature of the system. In almost every system there will be incompatibilities that cannot be violated, e.g. if two clients are in conflict of interest, it must be impossible for each of them to hold secret data from the other, or even for a third party to jointly hold their secret data. Label changes that lead to such combinations must be refused.

From the point of view of access control theory, it is interesting to note that such transformations are essentially the same that are implicit in classical mechanisms such as 'High water mark' and 'Chinese wall'. The former is the attribution of new authorizations and the latter is the preclusion of certain combinations of authorizations [20].

We leave entity disappappearance, removal of authorizations, declassification of data, etc. to further research [12, 18]. In some cases, local repairs may be possible, and at worst a global reorganization according to our method might be necessary.

8 Towards a Language for IoT Secrecy Requirements

Clearly, it is necessary to have a language for defining abstract entity types and allow the creation of different topologies of instantiated entities, with different allowed contents. We will in this section give an idea of how such a language could be constructed, although it has the potential of becoming quite complex. For ease of use, this language might have to provide for the definition of entities that are not devices or 'things' but can be instrumental in defining attributes of 'things', such as wards, nurses, doctors, patients and clients, etc.

Essentially, the language must provide:

- primitives to define entity *types* with attributes, such as entity Ward, entity Supplier etc. We will distinguish two types: types for real 'things' in the network, and they will prefixed by capital T, and types for logical concepts used to define the attributes of the 'things'. These will be prefixed by a capital L.

- an operator to define *New* entities with given attributes, and one to *Dismiss* them
- operators to *Add* or *Remove* attributes from entities
- primitives to define constraints for data flows; below we have simply a *CH* relationship as we will see.

In our hospital example, we could have the following types:

LType Patient(PatientId)   (to define logical type Patient)
TType PressDetect(DetectId)   (to define a device PressDetect with a DetectId)
TType PulseDetect(DetectId)   (to define a PulseDetect)
LType Ward(WardId).
LType Nurse(NurseId)
TType NurseWkstn(WkstnId)

etc., and the following operators:

Assign (DetectId,Patientid)   (to assign a detector to a patient)
Assign (PatientId, WardId)   (to assign a patient to a ward)
Assign (NurseId,WardId)   (to assign a nurse to a ward)
Assign (WkstnId,WardId)   (to assign a workstation to a ward)
Etc.

We need also a number of *CanHold* definitions, which generalize the previously introduced labels, such as the following one:

CH(*WkstnId,DetectId*) if *Assign(PatientId,WardId(WkstnId))* **and** *Assign(DetectId, PatientId)*

The network construction can start as follows:

New Ward (Emerg).   New Patient (Sam).
New NurseWkstn(EmergWkstn)   Assign (Sam,Emerg)
New Nurse (Alice)   New PressDetect(PRD0001)
Assign (Alice,Emerg).   Assign (PRD0001, Sam)
Assign (EmergWkstn,Emerg)   Etc.

Now, by the *CH* definition we know that *EmergWkstn* can hold the data in Sam's pulse detector *PRD0001* and so data can flow from the latter to the former. This establishes a *CF* relationship, hence a channel. So we have created a network with two physical devices and a channel, and the procedure presented in Sect. 4 can be executed, although of course it won't find anything to improve.

In some systems there can be many more *CanFlow* requirements than *NoFlow* requirements, or many more *CanNotHold* requirements than *CanHold*. in fact the negative requirements could be more obvious for the designer than the positive. One could allow the designer to specify the negative requirements, and then the positive ones could be found by complementing the negatives. Another possibility would be to allow the designer to specify both positive and negative requirements, but this would require a system to detect and correct inconsistencies. We leave these issues for future research.

9 Implementation Issues

The conventional way to enforce data flows is by enforcing access controls on the individual channels. The literature on techniques available for this is extensive, and one recent comprehensive paper with a good literature review is [16].

Tags allow deciding whether certain data can cross certain channels; they must follow the data as they move in the network. Data tagging for access control and flow control has been studied in the literature [1, 5, 18], as well as provenance tagging [17] but they are not part of widely implemented access control methods, because these consider tags only for subjects and data objects (such as databases). In order to implement our method, data must be tagged in two ways: to determine what flow the data belongs to (ordering, billing) and to determine the data's provenance (Pressure detector, Client1 ...).

It is likely that implementations of our method will require a combination of routing and encryption. Routing will be based on the tags and then the question that comes up is how to combine our method with IoT routing methods.

The Routing Protocol for Low-Power and Lossy Networks (RPL) is a protocol defined by the Internet Engineering Task Force (IETF). It is one of the best-known protocols for routing in the IoT [26], and it supports ad hoc configuration. RPL uses for routing DODAGs (Destination-Oriented Directed Acyclic Graphs). DODAGs describe efficient routes between the sink and other nodes for both collecting and distributing data traffic. DODAGs are usually constructed on the basis of criteria of transmission efficiency called OF (Objective Functions). New entities will autonomously find their place in the network by using OFs. The ideas presented in this paper may lead to research on methods for combining our own acyclic data flow digraphs with the DODAGs, thus including data flow constraints in RPL routing, hence possibly in Objective Functions.

Encryption appears to be necessary to establish channels that go through nodes that should not be able to read the data.

Clearly, implementation issues require further research.

10 Discussion

Although one of the basic requirements IoT is that the system topology should be very dynamic and varied, at present and for the foreseeable future, the IoT is a vast collection of customized subsystems, each with its own set of users, data sets and functionalities, as well as data security requirements: e.g. hospital networks for hospitals, home networks for homes, warehouse systems for companies, fleets for truck companies, etc. Each subsystem will have its own specific organization and data flows. In specific networks, entities are organized according to these structures, and new entities that enter a network must join pre-extisting structures. These structures of course can be changed, but each change must be prepared by the re-evaluation of several aspects, in our case of the data security aspects.

We have limited ourselves to a high-level view, based on entities that have a functional meaning for the end-user. In reality, the IoT includes types of entities that we have not considered, such as routers, gateways, etc. Our view could be extended to such other entities: routers and gateways are also limited by the kinds of data that they can hold. However if encrypted data is transmitted through an entity that cannot decrypt it, then we cannot say that data cant flow to this second entity by effect of this transmission. This transmission belongs to a lower logical layer.

Although we have concentrated ourselves on secrecy, we argue that our method takes care simultaneously of the main aspects of the two data security properties of secrecy and integrity. This is because each of these properties specifies what should be the origin of the data each entity can hold, and this is what our labels specify. Concerning availability, our method can only allow to conclude that certain data 'can be available' to certain entities, but for them to be actually available the 'possible' data transfers must be executed. In other words, our model does not guarantee that a system will actually function, it can only guarantee conformity to data security requirements, essentially that certain data can or cannot reach certain 'things'.

11   Conclusions and Future Work

We have presented a method for configuring IoT networks in such a way as to comply to logically specified security data flow constraints. The method is exact, in the sense that it allows all and only specified data flows. It is also scalable, since it uses efficient algorithms. It could be seen as a generalization of well-known Mandatory Access Control methods. We have also proposed a language for specifying the constraints.

With respect to previous work, the approach that is most similar to ours is the one of [12]. As mentioned, in this paper a distinction is made between subjects and objects and labels are assigned to subjects and objects to define which objects subjects can read or write. However in the IoT it may be impossible to distinguish between subjects and objects, or between reading and writing (these distinctions are common in access control, less common in the IoT). In addition, the labels in our method determine directly what the data contents of each entity can be. Perhaps the approaches of our two methods can be mutually transformed, but ours uses a more direct notation, based on the possible data contents of the 'things', as specified by our logical expressions.

Surely, the solutions we have given for our two examples are not different from those that could have been obtained by intuition, without using our method. We take this fact as a confirmation that our method finds acceptable solutions, and would continue to find them for examples of thousands of entities, possibly generated by requirement languages such as the one we have sketched.

Based on our concepts, one can imagine graphic interfaces that would make it possible to design IoT systems with secrecy requirements by manipulating on the screen graphic representations such as the ones we have used. For scalability however, abstraction mechanisms such as encapsulation will have to be devised. It is interesting to consider that the problem of removing unwanted communication paths in existing networks is much more difficult than the problem of allowing only certain paths at the design stage, in fact we have not been able to find any solution for the first problem. This is because unwanted paths can be part of other paths that are wanted.

Acknowledgment. This research was funded in part by the Natural Sciences and Engineering Research Council of Canada. We are grateful to N.V. Narendra Kumar for having carefully reviewed the paper.

References

1. Bacon, J., et al.: Enforcing end-to-end application security in the cloud. In: Gupta, I., Mascolo, C. (eds.) Middleware 2010. LNCS, vol. 6452, pp. 293–312. Springer, Heidelberg (2010). https://doi.org/10.1007/978-3-642-16955-7_15
2. Botta, A., de Donato, W., Persico, V., Pescapé, A.: Integration of cloud computing and internet of things: a survey. Future Gener. Comput. Syst. **56**, 684–700 (2016)
3. Blackstock, M., Lea, R.: Towards a distributed data flow paradigm for the Web of Things. In: Proceedings 5th ACM International Workshop on the Web of Things (WoT 2014), pp. 34–39 (2014)
4. Denning, D.E.: A lattice model of secure information flow. Commun. ACM **19**(5), 236–243 (1976)
5. Etalle, S., Hinrichs, T.L., Lee, A.J., Trivellato, D., Zannone, N.: Policy administration in tag-based authorization. In: Garcia-Alfaro, J., Cuppens, F., Cuppens-Boulahia, N., Miri, A., Tawbi, N. (eds.) FPS 2012. LNCS, vol. 7743, pp. 162–179. Springer, Heidelberg (2013). https://doi.org/10.1007/978-3-642-37119-6_11
6. Ferraiolo, D.F., Kuhn, D.R., Chandramouli, R.: Role-Based Access Control, 2nd edn. Artech House, Boston (2007)
7. Fraïssé, R.: Theory of Relations. North-Holland, Amsterdam (1986)
8. Gilat, A.: MATLAB: An Introduction with Applications, 2nd edn. Wiley, Hoboken (2004)
9. Gubbi, J., Buyya, R., Marusic, S., Palaniswami, M.: Internet of Things (IoT): a vision, architectural elements, and future directions. Future Gener. Comput. Syst. **29**(7), 1645–1660 (2013)
10. Harary, F., Norman, R.Z., Cartwright, D.: Structural MODELs: An Introduction to the Theory of Directed Graphs. Wiley, New York (1965)
11. Jiang, L., Xu, L.D., Cai, H., Jiang, Z., Bu, F., Xu, B.: An IoT-oriented data storage framework in cloud computing platform. IEEE Trans. Ind. Inf. **10**(2), 1443–1451 (2014)
12. Khobragade, S., Narendra Kumar, N.V., Shyamasundar, R.K.: Secure synthesis of IoT via readers-writers flow model. In: Negi, A., Bhatnagar, R., Parida, L. (eds.) ICDCIT 2018. LNCS, vol. 10722, pp. 86–104. Springer, Cham (2018). https://doi.org/10.1007/978-3-319-72344-0_5
13. Landwehr, C.E.: Privacy research directions. Commun. ACM **59**(2), 29–31 (2016)
14. Logrippo, L.: Multi-level access control, directed graphs and partial orders in flow control for data secrecy and privacy. In: Imine, A., Fernandez, José M., Marion, J.-Y., Logrippo, L., Garcia-Alfaro, J. (eds.) FPS 2017. LNCS, vol. 10723, pp. 111–123. Springer, Cham (2018). https://doi.org/10.1007/978-3-319-75650-9_8
15. Narendra Kumar, N.V., Shyamasundar, R.: Realizing purpose-based privacy policies succinctly via information-flow labels. In: Big Data and Cloud Computing (BDCloud 2014), pp. 753–760 (2014)

16. Ouaddah, A., Mousannif, H., Abou Elkalam, A., Ait Ouahman, A.: Access control in the internet of things: big challenges and new opportunities. Comput. Netw. **112**, 237–262 (2017)
17. Park, J., Nguyen, D., Sandhu, R.: A provenance-based access control model. In: 2012 10th Annual International Conference on Privacy, Security and Trust, pp. 137–144 (2012)
18. Pasquier, T., Bacon, J., Singh, J., Eyers, D.: 2016. Data-centric access control for cloud computing. In: Proceedings of 21st ACM Symposium on Access Control Models and Technologies (SACMAT 2016), pp. 81–88 (2016)
19. Samarati, P., Bertino, E., Ciampichetti, A., Jajodia, S.: Information flow control in object-oriented systems. IEEE Trans. Knowl. Data Eng. **9**(14), 524–538 (1997)
20. Sandhu, R.S.: Lattice-based enforcement of Chinese Walls. Comput. Secur. **11**(8), 753–763 (1992)
21. Schütte, J., Brost, G.S.: LUCON: data flow control for message-based IoT systems. arXiv preprint arXiv:1805.05887, 2018 - arxiv.org
22. Singh, J., Pasquier, T., Bacon, J., Ko, H., Eyers, D.: Twenty security considerations for cloud-supported Internet of Things. IEEE Internet Things J. **3**(3), 269–284 (2016)
23. Singh, J., Pasquier, T., Bacon, J., Powles, J., Diaconu, R., Eyres, D.: Big ideas paper: policy-driven middleware for a legally-compliant Internet of Things. In: Proceeding Middleware 2016 Proceedings of the 17th International Middleware Conference, Art. No. 13 (2016)
24. Stambouli, A., Logrippo, L.: Data flow analysis from capability lists, with application to RBAC. Inf. Process. Lett. **141**, 30–40 (2019)
25. Tarjan, R.E.: Depth-first search and linear graph algorithms. SIAM J. Comput. **1**(2), 146–160 (1972)
26. Winter, T., Thubert, P. (eds.): RPL: IPv6 routing protocol for low-power and lossy networks. Internet Engineering Task Force IETF RFC 6550, March 2012

Validating Requirements of Access Control for Cloud-Edge IoT Solutions (Short Paper)

Tahir Ahmad[1,2(✉)] and Silvio Ranise[1]

[1] Security & Trust Unit, FBK-ICT, Trento, Italy
{ahmad,ranise}@fbk.eu
[2] DIBRIS, University of Genova, Genoa, Italy
tahir.ahmad@dibris.unige.it

Abstract. The pervasiveness of Internet of Things (IoT) solutions have stimulated research on the basic security mechanisms needed in the wide range of IoT use case scenarios, ranging from home automation to industrial control systems. We focus on access control for cloud-edge based IoT solutions for which—in previous work—we have proposed a lazy approach to Access Control as a Service for the specification, administration, and enforcement of policies. The validity of the approach was evaluated in a realistic smart-lock scenario. In this paper, we argue that the approach is adaptable to a wide range of IoT use case scenarios by validating the requirements elicited when analyzing the smart lock scenario.

Keywords: Access control · IoT · Requirements validation

1 Introduction

While the Internet of Things (IoT) is already making an impact on the global economy, market forecasts note that both IoT and the business models associated with it are immature at this point [2]. It is believed (see, e.g., [1]) that the true potential of the IoT will be achieved only if the problems of today IoT solutions are solved or, at least, alleviated. The most important issues of IoT implementations include interoperability, latency, safety, security, trust, and privacy. If the problems related to guarantee these properties are not adequately addressed, Gartner predicts that by 2020, 80% of all IoT projects will fail at the implementation stage [2].

One of the most important approaches to ensure suitable levels of service to fulfill the properties above stems from cloud computing and its combination with edge computing. This approach seems to be promising in tackling several of the challenges identified by Gartner in [2] with particular attention to latency and security by exploiting the following two observations. First, both network latency and the amount of computation to be done in the cloud (e.g., data analytic) are

© Springer Nature Switzerland AG 2019
N. Zincir-Heywood et al. (Eds.): FPS 2018, LNCS 11358, pp. 131–139, 2019.
https://doi.org/10.1007/978-3-030-18419-3_9

decreased by playing out some computationally lightweight assignments (e.g., pre-processing or aggregation of data) near the end points generating the information. Second, Cloud Service Providers (CSPs)—such as Amazon, Google, and Microsoft—offer a cornucopia of well-engineered and widely tested security mechanisms (e.g., Identity and Access management) that might be valuable addition to cloud-edge solutions, when incorporated with security measures for endpoints, i.e. edge and smart devices.

The main roadblock to the wider adoption of cloud-edge IoT solutions is their complexity, arising from the combination of heterogeneous techniques, including virtual machines, server-less and mobile computing together with communication protocols for resource constrained devices. This prevents the possibility of confining the core functionality of security mechanisms to a trusted base as it is the case with more traditional systems. To illustrate, consider security policy evaluation; it becomes unreliable when updates to the latest version of the policies are prevented by some features of mobile devices such as the so called air mode that aims to guarantee availability. It is thus no more possible to separate the concerns of validating and enforcing policies as typically done in a long line of works in the literature (see, e.g., [10]). For these reasons, [3] proposes a new approach to design and implement access control—which is one of the most important security mechanisms—for cloud-edge IoT solutions. The idea is to offer Access Control as a Service (ACaaS) for the specification and management of policies independently of the CSP while leveraging its enforcement mechanisms.

In [3], the lazy approach to ACaaS for cloud-edge IoT solutions is justified by a thorough analysis of a realistic smart-lock use case scenario. This has lead to the identification of a minimum set of requirements that any ACaaS should satisfy for its effective use with cloud-edge IoT solutions. However, the smart-lock scenario is one of the many possible IoT use cases. The obvious question of the validity of the requirements in [3] naturally arises, in particular their completeness, when considering the heterogeneity of the possible use cases including transportation, health and well-being, home and building automation, smart metering, and industrial control systems. To answer the question, we consider the IoT use case scenarios in [11] whose main goal is to list the relevant authorization problems of heterogeneous IoT deployments. We argue that the set of requirements in [3] is complete in the sense that covers all the requirements elicited in the scenarios of [11]. This implies that the implementation of the lazy approach to ACaaS described in [3]—which is shown to verify all the requirements—can be effectively deployed across a wide spectrum of IoT uses cases.

The paper is organized as follows. Sect. 2 summarizes the lazy approach to ACaaS for cloud-edge IoT solutions. Sect. 3 discusses the access control requirements of the use cases in [11]. Sect. 4 validates the requirements of the lazy approach to ACaaS against those in [11] and draws some conclusions.

2   A Lazy Approach to ACaaS in Cloud-Edge Solutions

ACaaS allows for outsourcing the administration and enforcement of access control policies to a trusted third party. The advantages of ACaaS are several and include a comprehensive and uniform support for policy administration and an expressive and high-level (independent of a particular CSP) policy specification language. These allow for mitigating the problems of access control mechanisms that are available in current cloud-edge solutions by Amazon, Google, and Microsoft, such as limited support for policy administration, vendor lock-in (because of proprietary policy languages), and limited expressiveness in specifying complex authorization conditions that depend on a several resource and context attributes.

The main difference between the lazy approach in [3] and most existing ACaaS solutions [4–6,8] is that the former outsources the management but not the enforcement of policies. Following and extending [9], the lazy approach to ACaaS translates a high-level policy language based on Attribute Based Access Control (ABAC) [7] to the policy language adopted by a given CSP. This allows, on the one hand, to reuse well-engineered, robust, and tested enforcement mechanisms and, one the other hand, reduce the overhead due to the invocation of an external evaluation point for every authorization request (as it is the case in other ACaaS solutions). Two additional advantages are the possibility to avoid vendor lock-in by translating to the various policy specification languages of the available CSPs and to improve on latency by speeding up the authorization request evaluation with the help of edge computing that is available in most cloud-edge IoT solutions.

Based on the thorough analysis of a smart-lock use case scenario, [3] identifies seven main requirements for access control systems for IoT. The requirements are shown in Table 1 and are briefly discussed in the following. (AC1) An access control system for IoT should be applicable in all security contexts by allowing the specification of authorization conditions that are depend on several attributes of users, resources, and the environment. (AC2) The access control system should provide stakeholders with a single administration point for easy translation of multiple (possibly conflicting) security requirements into enforceable access control policies and the configuration of security mechanisms that better fit other functional requirements (e.g., enforcement of policies in the edge to avoid latency problems). (AC3) The inherent difficulties in defining authorization conditions are exacerbated by a plethora of access control mechanisms offered by the various CSPs; this makes the porting of policies across different platforms a daunting task, thereby resulting in vendor lock-in. (AC4) An access control system should provide hooks to customize policy evaluation with respect to the needs of the application domain; for IoT, it is crucial to augment the access control system with event driven functions for the evaluation of custom constraints in access control policies. (AC5) Several IoT applications have stringent latency requirements, it is thus crucial for access control systems to optimize the process of evaluating authorization requests by choosing the most appropriate configuration that combines cloud and edge computing. (AC6) Cloud computing supports the use of several different technologies (e.g., mobile devices) that may significantly enlarge the attack surface; for instance, connectivity problems or features of mobile devices (such as air mode) may cause coherence problems with the distribution of policies that have been modified in the cloud. (AC7) Many predict the exponential growth of the number of smart devices; this implies a substantial scalability problems for the management and administration of access control systems.

Table 1. Requirements of access control systems for IoT

ID	Requirement	Description
AC1	Expressibility	The access control system must allow users to specify fine-grained access control policies
AC2	Administration	The access control system must provide an administration point to easily configure policies for connected devices and available resources
AC3	Portability	The access control system needs to be platform independent
AC4	Extensibility	The access control system must support the enforcement of arbitrary security constraints
AC5	Latency	The access control system must be designed according to the latency requirements of the IoT application
AC6	Reliability	The access control system must provide a reliable access decision in every system state
AC7	Scalability	The access control system must be able to handle a growing number of devices and amount of data generated and processed by those devices

While we have already argued that the implementation of the lazy approach described in [3] verifies requirements (AC1)–(AC7), in the following we validate the requirements by showing that the authorization problems identified in [11] arising in a variety of heterogeneous IoT use cases are all instances of the requirements in Table 1.

3   Authorization Problems from IoT Use Cases

For the sake of brevity, we consider only two of the seven use cases from [11] (however, our findings hold also for the other five use cases). Each use case description contains a table summarizing the authorization problems by using the labels used in [11] for ease of reference, a high level description, and the relationship with the requirements in Table 1. The latter will be discussed in Sect. 4.

3.1   Container Monitoring for Food Transportation

Containers are used for storage and transportation of goods that need various type of climate control such as cooling and freezing. Container monitoring is a challenging task and IoT provides an opportunity for its simplification. The process involves various stakeholders such as food vendor, transporters and the super market chain, each with different monitoring requirements. The vendor packs food in sensor fitted boxes that communicate with a climate-control system. Each container carry boxes of same owner however adjacent containers might contains boxes of different owners. Keeping in view, the environmental constraints on the way, the sensors might need to communicate to the endpoints over the Internet via relay stations owned by the transport company. The ownership of goods also changes on the way while they are handed over from one stakeholder to the other. The main authorization problems are the following.

- U1.1: Each stakeholder have different authorization needs of resources and endpoints.
- U1.2: Each stakeholder requires integrity and authenticity of relevant sensor data.
- U1.3: Each stakeholder requires the confidentiality of relevant sensor data.
- U1.4: Stakeholders require authorization enact without manual intervention.
- U1.5: The capability of stakeholders to grant and revoke authorization permission.
- U1.6: Ensure the reliability of authorization in presence of relay stations.
- U1.7: Ensure the reliability of authorization without access to remote authorization server.

3.2   Smart Metering

Smart meters provide a reliable and secure source for real-time insight on energy consumption. Consider an Advance Metering Infrastructure (AMI) as a use case scenario of smart metering that measures, collects, analyzes usage, and interacts with metering devices either on request or on predefined schedule. It allows consumers to control their utility consumption and aids utility providers in accurate and timely billing. Smart meters deal with sensitive user related data and are often installed in hostile locations that makes security assurance as a concerns for users as well as service providers. The main authorization problems are the following.

- U5.1 The utility providers want to make sure that an attacker can not use data from a compromised meter to attack
- U5.2 The utility providers want to control the flow of data in their smart metering network.
- U5.3 The utility providers want to ensure the integrity and confidentiality of data.

Table 2. Container monitoring use case

Authorization problems	Description	Requirements
U1.1, U1.2, U1.3	The language used to express access control policies must ensure the integrity/confidentiality of sensor data and also allow specification of fine-grained access control polices by different stakeholders	AC1: Expressibility
U1.4, U1.5	Pre-configured access control that require minimal or no configuration at access time. The administration point must allow user to grant and revoke authorization permissions	AC2: Administration
U1.2	The access control must be extensible to ensure authenticity of sensor data	AC4: Extensibility
U1.6, U1.7	Reliability of authorization mechanism in every system state	AC6: Reliability

Table 3. Smart metering

Authorization problems	Description	Requirements
U5.1, U5.2, U5.3, U5.4, U5.5, U5.9	The language used to express access control policies must be able to completely capture the security requirements of an organization. The access control mechanism must ensure integrity and confidentiality of user related data	AC1: Expressibility
U5.4, U5.7	The access control system provide a single point of administration. It must allow management of user related data	AC2: Administration
U5.5, U5.6, U5.8	Correct enforcement of authorization policies. The access control mechanism must be reliable in every system state	AC6: Reliability
U5.7	The coherence of the access control system must be guaranteed as the network scales	AC7: Scalability

– U5.4 Consumers want to access own usage data and also prevention of unauthorized access to such data.
– U5.5 The utility providers want the authorization policies enact even if the meters uses intermediaries for Internet connectivity.
– U5.6 Authorization mechanism must be enforced during all times without human intervention.
– U5.7 Keeping in view the scale of the network, direct update of authorization policies on each and every node is almost impossible.
– U5.8 Authentication and authorization must work even if messages are stored and forward over multiple nodes.
– U5.9 Consumers want to preserve privacy by providing access to fine-grained level of consumption data to the utility providers.

4 Discussion and Conclusion

We argue why the authorization problems listed in Sects. 3.2 and 3.1 are covered by the requirements in Table 1 as shown in Tables 2 and 3. This validates the requirements for the container monitoring and the smart metering scenarios. We make two observations. First, similar results can be obtained for the other five use cases in [11]. Second, the only reason for which (AC3) does not show up in the analysis is that the use cases do not consider the problem of porting a solution to a different IoT platform.

(AC1): Expressibility. The language used to express access control policies must ensure the integrity and confidentiality of data and allow specification of access rules for single entity as well as group of entities. These requirements are easily satisfied by the use of a language based on ABAC which is well-known (see, e.g., [7]) to support the specification of complex confidentiality and integrity goals by permitting the definition and combination of several policy idioms for defining fine-grained and context dependent authorization conditions.

(AC2): Administration and (AC5): Latency. The single point of administration is important mainly in two respects. First, it simplifies the specification of enforceable policies that result from the reconciliation of possibly conflicting security goals by different stakeholders. Support for this task comes from the precise semantics of the high-level specification language. Second, by allowing the configuration of how the enforcement of policies is performed (e.g., authorization requests are evaluated on the edge), the single point of administration permits to fine tune the system to satisfy other crucial requirements, such as Latency.

(AC4): Extensibility. To guarantee the authenticity, integrity, and confidentiality of the widely heterogeneous types of data acquired and processed by IoT devices, it is crucial to provide the ACaaS with points of extension that allow for the integration of the most appropriate, with respect to to the type of device and use case scenario—code for data acquisition and processing. This is fundamental in the presence of constrained environments in which devices and protocols are limited and can support neither heavy computation (e.g., standard cryptography) nor communication (e.g., TLS).

(AC6): Reliability. The distributed nature of cloud-edge IoT solutions give rise to synchronization and coherence problems that may adversely affect security; e.g., updates of access control policies should be propagated as quickly as possible to avoid taking the wrong decision when the evaluation of authorization requests is distributed. To complicate the situation further is the presence of some functionality of, for example, mobile computing (such as air mode), that can be exploited to retain rights that have been revoked by presenting invalid access token to edge devices.

(AC7): Scalability. When considering very large deployments, the number of IoT devices may become so large and the topology of the network so complex to make the enforcement of evolving policies very difficult, if possible at all. An ACaaS should be able to blend with the elasticity of cloud-based IoT solutions to cope with a possibly exponential growth of IoT devices and the associated communication overhead.

4.1   Conclusion

We have validated the requirements on access control (c.f. Table 1) for IoT solutions that we have elicited in [3] from the analysis of a realistic smart-lock use case scenario. We have done this by considering the variety of use case scenarios (such as container monitoring and smart metering) presented in [11], a document whose main goal is to identify authorization problems. We have successfully shown that each authorization problem is covered by one (or more) of the previously identified requirements. This entitles us to conclude that the implementation of the lazy approach to ACaaS for cloud-edge IoT solutions of [3] can be effectively re-used in several other IoT uses cases. Indeed, qualitative and quantitative evidence that such an implementation verifies the requirements have been already provided in [3].

References

1. IEC Role in the Internet of Things (2016). www.iec.ch/about/brochures/pdf/technology/iec_role_IoT.pdf. Accessed 10 Sept 2018
2. IoT 2020: Smart and Secure IoT Platform (2016). www.iec.ch/whitepaper/pdf/iecWP-IoT2020-LR.pdf. Accessed 10 Sept 2018
3. Ahmad, T., Morelli, U., Ranise, S., Zannone, N.: A lazy approach to access control as a service (ACaaS) for IoT: an AWS case study. In: Proceedings of the 23nd ACM on Symposium on Access Control Models and Technologies, pp. 235–246. ACM (2018)
4. Alonso, Á., Fernández, F., Marco, L., Salvachúa, J.: IAACaaS: IoT application-scoped access control as a service. Futur. Internet **9**(4), 64 (2017)

5. Fotiou, N., Machas, A., Polyzos, G.C., Xylomenos, G.: Access control as a service for the cloud. J. Internet Serv. Appl. **6**(1), 11 (2015)

6. Fremantle, P., Aziz, B., Kopecký, J., Scott, P.: Federated identity and access management for the Internet of Things. In: International Workshop on Secure Internet of Things, pp. 10–17. IEEE (2014)

7. Hu, V.C., et al.: Guide to ABAC Definition and Considerations. No. 800–162 in NIST (2013)

8. Kaluvuri, S.P., Egner, A.I., den Hartog, J., Zannone, N.: SAFAX–an extensible authorization service for cloud environments. Front. ICT **2**, 9 (2015)

9. Morelli, U., Ranise, S.: Assisted authoring, analysis and enforcement of access control policies in the cloud. In: De Capitani di Vimercati, S., Martinelli, F. (eds.) SEC 2017. IAICT, vol. 502, pp. 296–309. Springer, Cham (2017). https://doi.org/10.1007/978-3-319-58469-0_20

10. Samarati, P., de Vimercati, S.C.: Access control: policies, models, and mechanisms. In: Focardi, R., Gorrieri, R. (eds.) FOSAD 2000. LNCS, vol. 2171, pp. 137–196. Springer, Heidelberg (2001). https://doi.org/10.1007/3-540-45608-2_3

11. Seitz, L., Gerdes, S., Selander, G., Mani, M., Kumar, S.: Use cases for authentication and authorization in constrained environments. Technical report (2016)

Software Security, Malware Analysis, and Vulnerability Detection

Evading Deep Neural Network and Random Forest Classifiers by Generating Adversarial Samples

Erick Eduardo Bernal Martinez[1], Bella Oh[2], Feng Li[3], and Xiao Luo[3(✉)]

[1] Department of CS, IUPUI, Indianapolis, IN, USA
ebernalm@iu.edu
[2] Department of CSE, Michigan State University, East Lansing, MI, USA
oheunjeo@msu.edu
[3] Department of CIT, IUPUI, Indianapolis, IN, USA
{fengli,luo25}@iupui.edu

Abstract. With recent advancements in computing technology, machine learning and neural networks are becoming more wide-spread in different applications or software, such as intrusion detection applications, antivirus software and so on. Therefore, data safety and privacy protection are increasingly reliant on these models. Deep Neural Networks (DNN) and Random Forests (RF) are two of the most widely-used, accurate classifiers which have been applied to malware detection. Although their effectiveness has been promising, the recent adversarial machine learning research raises the concerns on their robustness and resilience against being attacked or poisoned by adversarial samples. In this particular research, we evaluate the performance of two adversarial sample generation algorithms - Jacobian-based Saliency Map Attack (JSMA) and Fast Gradient Sign Method (FGSM) on poisoning the deep neural networks and random forests models for function call graph based malware detection. The returned results show that FGSM and JSMA gained high success rates by modifying the samples to pass through the trained DNN and RF models.

Keywords: Adversarial Machine Learning · Neural Network · Random Forest · Graphlet

1 Introduction

With recent advancements in machine hardware and computing technology, researchers have been focusing on expanding the usage of machine learning. Machine learning refers to inputting large amounts of data to an algorithm during a training phase. This, in turn, causes the algorithm (or model) to learn particular patterns of the training data, and then react on new data depending on those learned patterns. With this technique, machines gain the ability to self-improve and adapt to new data. This technology can be used in several different

© Springer Nature Switzerland AG 2019
N. Zincir-Heywood et al. (Eds.): FPS 2018, LNCS 11358, pp. 143–155, 2019.
https://doi.org/10.1007/978-3-030-18419-3_10

aspects, including related searches on Google or self-driven cars. Because of the automation gained from it, machine learning can increase the comfort and efficiency of our daily lives. Hence, this topic is currently under intensive studies. However, on the other side, hackers attempt to attack or poison the machine learning algorithms. Hacking into the machine learning algorithm leads to great security threats on data privacy and security; therefore, adversarial machine learning, a new research field intending to investigate how to detect adversarial activities of the machine learning algorithms, is needed.

In this paper, we investigate and compare two adversarial example generation algorithms that attempt to mislead the trained machine classifiers for malware detection. The first algorithm is known as Jacobian-based Saliency Map Attack (JSMA), proposed by Papernot et al. [8]. It exploits the forward derivative of a deep neural network (DNN) to find perturbations, then creates adversarial modifications to some components of normal malware data using the perturbations. The second algorithm is known as Fast Gradient Sign Method (FGSM) [12]. This method aims to generate malicious samples by using gradient computations. Both methods attempt to generate adversarial malware samples so that a trained machine learning model would classify the adversarial malware samples as benign. In this research, we explore and compare these two adversarial example generation algorithms on two well-known learning algorithms: deep neural network (DNN) and random forest (RF). Deep neural networks are a series of interconnected nodes. Each connection between nodes has a weight associated with it, and the nodes are structured in layers: an input layer, a series of hidden layers, and an output layer. The random forest, another machine learning algorithm, is composed of several decision trees. It classifies data by growing binary branches from splitting variables, and it is known to be useful for several classification and regression tasks. The malware dataset used in this research is a graphlet dataset which include 2394 function call graphs extracted from Android malware and benign applications. Each malware or benign instance in this dataset is described as a set of graphlets. This dataset is built by a previous research [3]. The returned results of this research show that FGSM can generate instances to evade both DNN and RF algorithms with 100% success rate when degree of perturbation is high. On the other hand, JSMA can gain high success rate with DNN but not with RF algorithm. We hypothesize that is because JSMA is based on selecting the features first before generating perturbation values; therefore, the selected features might be different from those selected by RF to build the tree structure. The FGSM can be further evaluated on generate instances to evade other machine learning algorithms in the near future.

The rest of paper is organized as following: related work is presented in Sect. 2, the details of the FGSM and JSMA algorithms for generating adversarial samples are given in Sect. 3, two classification algorithms - DNN and RF are described in Sects. 4 and 5 demonstrates the experimental settings and discusses the results, Sect. 6 explains how we validate the generated adversarial samples, the conclusion and future work is concluded in Sect. 7.

2   Related Work

Adversarial Machine Learning is a relatively new field of study. Attacks on Deep Neural Networks and Random Forests, in particular, are emerging. There are related techniques and concepts described in the literature.

Some literatures provide tactics of adversarial data manipulation given that the target classifier is minimally exposed to the adversary, such as having only the information of its final classification decision. Given these conditions, Dang et al. [13] performed an evasion attack on non-image datasets. They targeted two generic PDF malware classifiers - PDF_{RATE} and Hidost - then generated malicious samples using only a blackbox morpher and a sandbox in order to find the most optimal path of modifications needed for a file to missclassify from malware to benignware. This met the challenge of evading the two PDF classifiers by morphing malicious samples "in the dark". The method, although effective and capable of wider application, was limited by the amount of queries that can be made to a classifier while also avoiding detection. Another method of evasion is generating malicious samples and testing them on phishing website classifiers. Hu and Tan [13] proposed a generative adversarial network (GAN) based algorithm named MalGAN to generate adversarial malware examples. These examples were able to bypass machine learning based detection models, not knowing what type of model it is. This was made possible due to a substitute detector that MalGAN uses to fit the black-box malware detection system. Then, a generative network was trained to minimize the malicious probabilities predicted by the substitute detector. Although relatively difficult in application, MalGAN proves to be effective, decreasing adversarial malware detection rates to almost zero.

More recently, Elsayed, et al. [15] devised a technique to re-purpose a target model by means of an adversarial program. The adversarial program was added to a network's input in order to force it to perform a different task. This kind of attack was ideal for an adversary that has gained access to a neural network's parameters. Grosse et. al. [16] also constructed an adversarial attack on machine learning malware detectors. They take into account the existing adversarial-crafting algorithms, but expand on it to use discrete, often binary, input domains as opposed to continuous ones. In addition, they proved that their manipulated program would perform malware functions. This work provided a more discrete, yet promising method to generate adversarial samples. Jia et. al. [17], on the other hand, focused on the prevention of adversarial attribute inference attacks, specifically on machine learning algorithms. An attribute inference attack leverages a machine learning classifier to infer a target user's private attributes. To counteract this, Jia et. al. [17] created a method that evades users' original information from the attacker's classifiers by adding noise to the user information. This study showed a way of using evasion as security instead of attack. Another recent work looked into classifier evasion via altering malware binary payloads [18], which is the most similar to ours. It also aimed to evade neural network malware/benignware classifiers. However, it differs in that we also evaluate evasion success in RF classifiers and that our approach does not modify binary payloads. Rather, we propose that an adversary can simply modify the function calls of their malware to attain the results we seek.

Although all of the mentioned works inspired our work, the strongest motivation behind this literature was to utilize the methods developed by Goodfellow et al. [12] and Papernot et al. [5]. Both of these works develop methods aimed to perturbing MNIST images in order to cause misclassification. Goodfellow et al. addresses a method known as *Fast Gradient Sign Method* (FGSM). Given a model with an associated cost function, the FGSM crafts an adversarial sample for an original sample by computing perturbations. Perturbations are made to every value of the whole sample vector. Increasing the perturbations increases the likelihood of the adversarial sample being mis-classified, but also decreases the discreteness of the adversarial change.

Papernot et al. [5] propose the *Jacobian-based Saliency Map Attack* (JSMA) respectively. Given a model, an adversarial sample is created by adding a perturbation to only a subset of the values in the given sample vector. The two attacks will be elaborated further in Sect. 5 of our paper. The JSMA attack is known to be strong with targeted misclassification and creates less perturbations than the FGSM, making it less detectable, but with greater cost. FGSM is more applicable in any misclassification attack and can quickly create many adversarial samples, but makes larger perturbations, creating danger of detection. After the proposal of these two attacks, Papernot et al. [9] then makes use of both methods to study the evading success of the attacks among different machine learning classifiers.

Our work differs from the above in that we attempt to use the FGSM and JSMA methods developed by Goodfellow et al. and Papernot et al. respectively in order to attack the trained DNN and RF classifiers using the malware Graphlet Frequency Distribution (GFD) vectors. We have also studied the perturbation degree required to attain satisfactory results as well as the evading success to Deep Neural Network and Random Forest classifiers.

3   Adversarial Sample Generation

Consider a malicious adversary that wants to deploy a malicious android application in a setting where their target uses a malware detection engine. The adversary has knowledge about the classifier used by their target, but does not have access to the model used by their target. Further, the adversary is aware that the target uses either a DNN or RF model to classify via graphlet frequency distributions of function call graphs. The adversary also has access to a modest set of malicious and benign android applications, and uses them to create a simple DNN or RF malware classifier.

In this study, we compare two algorithms to execute evasion attacks on classifiers that have completed their training phase. The goal of these algorithms is to modify malware instances so that the changes are unnoticeable, but they are enough to mislead the classifier into classifying the modified malware as benign. This section explains the two different attack methodologies used to maliciously modify the regular malware samples.

3.1 Fast Sign Gradient Method (FGSM)

The Fast Sign Gradient Method is developed by Goodfellow, et al. [12], which can be summarized follows. Given a classification model F with an associated cost function $J(\theta, x, y)$, the adversary generates an adversarial sample using Eq. 1:

$$x^* = x + \eta \tag{1}$$

where η is defined as Eq. 2:

$$\eta = \epsilon \; sign(\nabla_x J(\theta, x, y)) \tag{2}$$

where ϵ refers to a perturbation, which can be any arbitrary number between 0 and 1. This perturbation value influences the significance of the modification as well as the effectiveness of the algorithm. Higher ϵ values yield better results, however they also result in less subtle differences between x and x^*. Nevertheless, the objective is to generate sample x^* to be mis-classified from class x to class y without modifying the model F. In our study, the objective is to generate x^* to be mis-classified from malware to benign without modifying the Deep Neuron Networks and Random Forest.

3.2 Jacobian-Based Saliency Map Attack (JSMA)

The Jacobian-based Saliency Map Attack (JSMA), proposed by Papernot et al. [8], exploits the forward derivative of a deep neural network (DNN) and finds perturbation. To decide which features to change, the algorithm orders each feature by its importance in creating the adversarial sample. Then, the input components are added to the perturbation value in the importance order. This is continued until the sample becomes mis-classified as the target. This is accomplished using the adversarial saliency map, defined as Eq. 3.

$$S(X, t)[i] = \begin{cases} 0, if \; \frac{\partial F_i(X)}{\partial X_i}) < 0 \; or \; \sum_{j \neq t} \frac{\partial F_i(X)}{\partial X_i}) > 0 \\ (\frac{\partial F_i(X)}{\partial X_i})| \sum_{j \neq t} \frac{\partial F_i(X)}{\partial X_i})|, otherwise \end{cases} \tag{3}$$

Given target t, exploiting this map allows $F_t(X)$, the target class output, to increase while probabilities $F_j(X)$ of other classes $j \neq t$ decrease, until target $t = arg \; max \; F_j(X)$. With this method, modifications can be made to malware data that will lead the model to mis-classify it as normal. The advantage of this algorithm is that it requires very small changes to be made to minimum number of features from the original malware data. Hence, it makes the attack more discrete. However, the computational cost is higher than the FGSM method.

4 Learning Algorithms

In this study, we evaluated the two adversarial sample generation algorithm on two well-known and widely used learning algorithms: Deep Neural Network and Random Forest. These two algorithms are described as following.

4.1 Deep Neural Network (DNN)

Deep Neural Network (DNN) is a machine learning technique consisting of inter-connected nodes. An example of a DNN classifier is given in Fig. 1. There are several implementations of this technique. However, they all have three key features: one layer of input nodes, a set number of hidden layers, and a final layer of output nodes. Each connection from one node to another has a weight value; this value is used to determine the activation of the node it is connected to. The number of nodes and connections in each layer are ideally set to represent some linear or non-linear problem; the network as a whole is called the model. In this study, we implement a fully connected neural net as a classifier for detecting malware in the dataset.

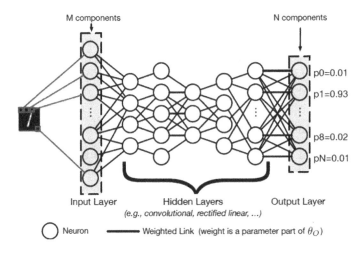

Fig. 1. Example of a DNN classifier. M components are the number of neurons at the input layer. Normally, they equal to the number of features in the dataset. N components at the output layers correspond to the number of classes to predict. Given an input, there is a associated probability of each class at the output layer. The probability to a class is between 0 and 1.

The Deep Neural Network is similar to other machine learning algorithms. In order to build the model, a training phase and a testing phase are involved. During the training phase, the network accepts inputs and feed forward mathematical operations that ultimately set off an activation function on each node of the network. The activation of the node relies on the weights associated with itself. Normally, higher weight results in greater activation. The activation of the final layer is then compared to the inputs, and a cost or a loss is computed. The weights of the final layer and the preceding layers are adjusted based on the cost function in order to minimize the cost of the next prediction. Once the training phase is done, the trained model can be loaded into a system for testing. The testing phase simply refers to inputting test data that was not used in the train phase and then predicting their class labels - malware or benign in the study, and calculating the accuracy.

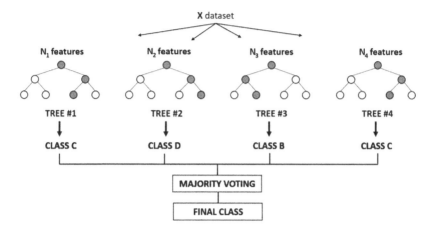

Fig. 2. RF classifier and its basic structure.

4.2   Random Forest (RF)

A random forest (RF) is a classifier composed of several decision trees [4]. Figure 2 demonstrates a visual explanation of the random forest skeleton [14]. If a dataset D is the input of the classifier, the algorithm creates several sets of randomly selected samples of D. Each decision tree randomly takes one set of the samples as its input. Then, each tree grows binary branches from splitting variables. For this study, the trees use the entropy algorithm to determine splitting variables. Entropy measures the uncertainty of the class in a subset of examples, and the goal is to maximize the purity of the groups for every split. Therefore, the algorithm will always choose a splitting variable that will decrease the entropy. Each tree stops growing either after reaching maximum depth or purity. After all decision trees classification finish, the most frequent output (majority vote) of all the trees becomes the output of the random forest. Comparing to decision tree, the random forest may be visually difficult to interpret. However, it's supposed to avoid the problem of over-fitting due to the "majority vote" output. Also, it increases independence among trees, making it robust when dealing with a large number of features in data.

5   Experiments and Results

5.1   Data Set

The dataset used in this study is a graphlet dataset for function call graphs of Android applications [3]. It is comprised of 2394 samples. The training set consists of 597 malware and 600 benign samples, while the testing set consists of 600 malware and 597 benign samples. These malware and benign samples present function call graphs of programs that are extracted from the Android applications [10]. A function call graph contains nodes and edges, each node represents a function while each edge represents a function call. Each function call may be one way or bi-directed. A graphlet is a sub-graph which consists of n nodes from a function call graph. Figure 3 shows the number of combinations obtained from a graphlet of $n = 3$. A function call graph can contain different combinations of these graphlets. Gao et al. [10] extracts graphlet frequency distribution (GFD) vectors from $n = 3$ up to $n = 5$. A GFD vector presents a function call graph. Each entry of the vector presents the frequency of a type of a graphlet i ($i \in \{1, \ldots, N\}$). In this dataset, there are $N = 125$ different types of graphlets. They are attributes of the input data to train and test the DNN and RF classifiers.

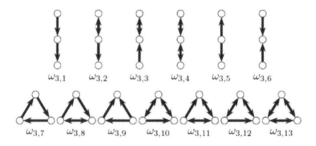

Fig. 3. The 13 graphlet types when $n = 3$

5.2   Classification Performance on Normal Samples

Before the learning algorithms are tested by the generated adversarial samples, they are evaluated and compared against the traditional evaluation metric for classification. Since only malware and benign samples are included in our experimental dataset, this turns to a binary classification task.

Deep Neural Network. The deep neural network implemented in this research consists of 125 input nodes which corresponds to the types of graphlet, 3 hidden layers consisting of 100, 50 and 10 nodes respectively, and 2 output nodes which corresponds to the output classes: malware and benign. The training set described in Sect. 5.1 is used to train the model, then the model is tested by the test set. After the network is trained for 15 epochs utilizing an Adam optimizer and a learning rate of 0.0001, it gains an accuracy 85.38% training set and 83.62% on test set.

Random Forest. The "Random Forest" package in WEKA machine learning tool [11] is used to implement the algorithm. The network has 125 input nodes, one node for each graphlet type. Same training and test data setting is used for training the RF model. The RF algorithm achieves 99.9% on the training set and 87.80% accuracy on test set. Although the accuracy rates of RF algorithm are higher than those gained by DNN algorithm, the accuracy differences between training and testing is significantly higher than that of the DNN algorithm. This implies that the RF algorithm might overfit to the training data.

Table 1 provides an overview of the accuracy of both algorithms.

Table 1. Classification accuracy on the original data

	DNN	RF
Training	85.38%	99.9%
Test	83.62%	87.80%

5.3 Performances of Adversarial Sample Generation Algorithms

In this section, we analyze and output the overall effectiveness and efficiency of the adversarial sample generational methods - FGSM and JSMA.

The two methods are evaluated from two aspects: (1) the average difference between original malware and generated adversarial malware with the increasing of the perturbation (a parameter that controls the subtlety of modifications made) (2) the relationship between perturbation and the success rate of evading the detection of the trained machine learning models. In order to evaluate two methods from the first aspect, 200 malware samples from the testing dataset were modified through using FGSM and JSMA respectively. Figure 4 shows the

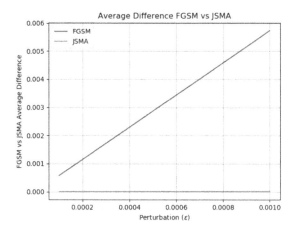

Fig. 4. Average difference among adversarial vs. original GFD vectors

averaged difference of the 200 samples with the increase of perturbation. The averaged difference is calculated as the sum of element-wise difference between the original malware GFD vector and the generated adversarial malware GFD vector. It is found that as the perturbation increases, the difference between the original malware and generated adversarial malware by FGSM increases, whereas the difference between the original malware and the generated adversarial malware by JSMA is not noticeable and stays almost the same. Through looking into the detailed adversarial malware, it is found that JSMA only makes very negligible changes to most of the original malware graph. It increases a few values from 0 to whatever the perturbation was. For example, if the perturbation value is .001, then it typically changes about 2 elements of the GFD from 0 to the perturbation and leaves the rest nearly identical.

After analyzing the degree of perturbations and their effects, we generate 5 groups, a total of 1000 adversarial generated malware using perturbation value of $\epsilon = 1e-7, 5e-7, 1e-5, 5e-5$, and $1e-3$ respectively. Then, these groups of 200 adversarial malware are inputted into the trained DNN and RF classifiers. The success rate is used to evaluate how success the generated adversarial malware can evade the trained DNN and RF. Success rate is calculated as Eq. 4. The total number of adversarial malware is 200 in this case.

$$Success\ Rate = \frac{Number\ of\ adversarial\ malware\ classified\ as\ benign}{Total\ number\ of\ adversarial\ malware} * 100.$$

(4)

The success rates for all 5 groups are shown in Table 2 and Fig. 5. From the results, we can tell the FGSM attack creates successful adversarial examples for both classifiers with good success rates when the perturbation is about 1e-5. In order to gain a high success rate, JSMA needs a higher perturbation value than the FGSM. We also notice that the FGSM-generated adversarial malware can evade the detection of both DNN and RF. Meanwhile, the JSMA-generated adversarial malware cannot evade the detection of RF. Only 13–14% of the adversarial malware generated by JSMA are classified as benign. We hypothesize that this is due to the nature of the algorithms of the RF and JSMA. The JSMA only modifies around 10 to 20 most important attributes of the input. Given that its attribute importance ranks are similar to that of the RF, slightly changing important attributes might only change some of the top few splitting variable attributes of the RF. If the change is not significant, this may not change the RF's decision. To improve the success rate of the JSMA could be increasing the number of features to modify. However, it might be computationally costly.

Overall, both adversarial malware generation methods successfully generate malware that evade the detection of DNN. Based on Table 2, given that the success rate of JSMA on RF is relatively low, we could draw the conclusion that RF may be a more robust model for classifying malware presented as GFD vectors. However, this might also be because the JSMA method creates adversarial malware using neural network features (number of inputs, prediction outputs, etc.), and are therefore more specifically geared to target neural networks like DNN.

Table 2. Different Model Performance Results

Attack method	Performance on attack (%)		
	Perturbation	RF	DNN
FGSM	1.e-7	13.0	16.5
JSMA	1.e-7	13.0	12.5
FGSM	5.e-7	14.5	24.0
JSMA	5.e-7	13.0	12.5
FGSM	1.e-5	81.0	92.5
JSMA	1.e-5	13.0	13.5
FGSM	5.e-5	100.0	100.0
JSMA	5.e-5	14.0	89.5
FGSM	1.e-3	100.0	100.0
JSMA	1.e-3	14.0	100.0

6   Conceptual Validation of the Generated Adversarial Malware

In this section, we demonstrate how a function call graph can be modified conceptually to reflect generated adversarial malware - graphlet frequency distribution (GFD) vector. A function call graph can be sub-divided into graphlets which consists of n nodes. Figure 3 demonstrates 13 directed graphlets of 3 nodes that could be found in a FCG. The GFD vector is a vector of length m which is the total number of different graphlets in the whole dataset. Each unit of the vector

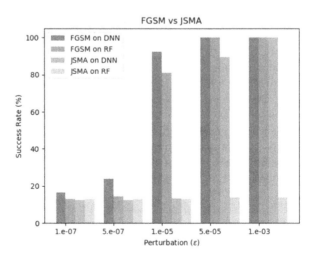

Fig. 5. Comparison between FGSM and JSMA performance on DNN and RF classifiers

is the relative frequency of the corresponding graphlet in the function call graph [10]. The relative frequency of each type of graphlet is calculated as Eq. 5:

$$\frac{f_{n,i}}{\sum_{i=1}^{n} f_{n,i}} \tag{5}$$

where $f_{n,i}$ is type i graphlet of n nodes,

Hence, one relative frequency of a graphlet increases, it affects the relative frequencies of every other graphlet. So, a desired adversarial GFD vector is minimized change to the units of the original GFD vector. As shown in Fig. 5, both FGSM and JSMA make small changes to the GFD vectors. In particular, JSMA maintains the changes needed in order to attain desired results to only modifying but a few units of the original GFD vector. In our test, JSMA simply increases the frequency of a unit from zero to the value of the assigned perturbation (ϵ) while making negligible changes to other units. We have investigated how many units increased in this manner by using ϵ values of $1e-5, 1e-4, 1e-3, 1e-2, 1e-1$. It is found that 10, 4, 2, 2 and 2 units changed with these ϵ values respectively. This indicates that the less number of units affected the more ϵ grows. So, in order to change the original malware to adversarial one, a very small amount of graphlets to original function call graph is needed. More specifically, $\epsilon \sum_{i=1}^{n} f_{n,i}$ need to be added to the original function call graph of the malware. The changes are small enough that the generated adversarial GFD vector remains nearly identical to the original.

7   Conclusion and Future Work

In this research, we explore two algorithms: FGSM and JSMA for generating of adversarial graphlet frequency distribution (GFD) vectors. The Deep Neural Network and Random Forest classifiers are used to test adversarial graphlet frequency distribution (GFD) vectors to see whether they can evade the detection. It is found that the FGSM gains 100% success rate on both DNN and RF classifiers by using any perturbation $\epsilon \geq 1e-5$, while the JSMA samples yields high success rates (close to 100%) when using $\epsilon \geq 1e-4$ on classifier DNN. The JSMA method on the RF classifier merely succeeds in misclassifying 14% of samples with perturbations as high as $\epsilon = 1e-3$. Nevertheless, we conclude that both methods are a viable way to generate adversarial graphlet frequency distribution vectors. In the future, we plan to evaluate FGSM and JSMA on other machine learning algorithms and other types of data. Integration of FGSM and JSMA algorithms can also be investigated in the future.

Acknowledgment. This research was made possible with the support of the Indiana University-Purdue University Indianapolis Department of Computer Information and Information Science, with funding from National Science Foundation and United States Department of Defense. The author(s) would like to thank to Dr. Mohammad Al Hasan, Tianchong Gao and Sheila Walter for their support.

References

1. Hu, W., Tan, Y.: Generating Adversarial Malware Examples for Black-Box Attacks Based on GAN (2017)
2. Subasi, A., Molah, E., Almkallawi, F., Chaudhery, T.J.: Intelligent phishing website detection using random forest classifier. In: 2017 International Conference on Electrical and Computing Technologies and Applications (ICECTA), Ras Al Khaimah, pp. 1–5 (2017)
3. Peng, W., Gao, T., Sisodia, D., Saha, T.K., Li, F., Al Hasan, M.: ACTS: extracting android app topological signature through graphlet sampling. In: 2016 IEEE Conference on Communications and Network Security (CNS), pp. 37–45 (2016)
4. Bosch, A., Zisserman, A., Munoz, X.: Image classification using random forests and ferns. In: 2007 IEEE 11th International Conference on Computer Vision, Rio de Janeiro, pp. 1–8 (2007)
5. Papernot, N., McDaniel, P., Jha, S., Fredrikson, M., Celik, Z.B., and Swami, A.: The limitations of deep learning in adversarial settings. In: Proceedings of the 1st IEEE European Symposium on Security and Privacy, pp. 372–387 (2016)
6. Feinman, R., Curtin, R.R., Shintre, S., Gardner, A.B.: Detecting Adversarial Samples from Artifacts. arXiv preprint arXiv:1703.00410 (2017)
7. Papernot, N., Carlini, N., Goodfellow, I., Feinman, R.: Cleverhans v2. 0.0: an adversarial machine learning library. arXiv preprint arXiv:1610.00768 (2016)
8. Papernot, N., McDaniel, P., Jha, S., Fredrikson, M., Celik, Z.B., Swami, A.: The limitations of deep learning in adversarial settings. IEEE European Symposium on Security and Privacy (EuroS, P), Saarbrucken, pp. 372–387 (2016)
9. Papernot, N., McDaniel, P., Goodfellow, I., Jha, S., Celik, Z.B., Swami, A.: Practical black-box attacks against machine learning. In: Proceedings of the 2017 ACM on Asia Conference on Computer and Communications Security (ASIA CCS 2017), pp. 506–519. ACM, New York, (2017), https://doi.org/10.1145/3052973.3053009
10. Gao, T. et al.: Android Malware Detection via Graphlet Sampling, pp. 1–14 (2018). Unpublished
11. The WEKA Workbench: Online Appendix for "Data Mining: Practical Machine Learning Tools and Techniques", 4th edn. Morgan Kaufmann (2016)
12. Goodfellow, I.J., et al.: Explaining and harnessing adversarial examples. In: Proceedings of the International Conference on Learning Representations (2015)
13. Dang, H., Huang, Y., Chang, E.: Evading classifiers by morphing in the dark. In: ACM CCS, pp. 119–133. ACM (2017)
14. Holczer, B.: Random Forest Classifier - Machine Learning. Global Software Support, 7 March 2018. www.globalsoftwaresupport.com/random-forest-classifier-bagging-machine-learning/
15. Elsayed, G., Goodfellow, I., Sohl-Dickstein, J.: Adversarial Reprogramming of Neural Networks (2018). https://arxiv.org/pdf/1806.11146.pdf. Accessed 22 Oct 2018
16. Grosse, K., Papernot, N., Manoharan, P., Backes, M., McDaniel, P.: Adversarial examples for malware detection. In: Foley, S.N., Gollmann, D., Snekkenes, E. (eds.) ESORICS 2017. LNCS, vol. 10493, pp. 62–79. Springer, Cham (2017). https://doi.org/10.1007/978-3-319-66399-9_4
17. Jia, J., Gong, N.Z.: AttriGuard: A Practical Defense Against Attribute Inference Attacks via Adversarial Machine Learning. https://arxiv.org/pdf/1805.04810.pdf. Accessed 22 Oct 2018
18. Kreuk, F., et al.: Deceiving End-to-End Deep Learning Malware Detectors using Adversarial Examples (2018). https://arxiv.org/pdf/1802.04528.pdf. Accessed 22 Oct 2018

Protection of Systems Against Fuzzing Attacks

Léopold Ouairy[1]([⊠]), Hélène Le-Bouder[2], and Jean-Louis Lanet[1]

[1] INRIA, Rennes, France
{leopold.ouairy,jean-louis.lanet}@inria.fr
[2] IMT-Atlantique, Rennes, France
helene.le-bouder@imt-atlantique.fr

Abstract. A fuzzing attack enables an attacker to gain access to restricted resources by exploiting a wrong specification implementation. Fuzzing attack consists in sending commands with parameters out of their specification range. This study aims at protecting *Java Card* applets against such attacks. To do this, we detect prior to deployment an unexpected behavior of the application without any knowledge of its specification. Our approach is not based on a fuzzing technique. It relies on a static analysis method and uses an unsupervised machine-learning algorithm on source codes. For this purpose, we have designed a front end tool *fetchVuln* that helps the developer to detect wrong implementations. It relies on a back end tool *Chucky-ng* which we have adapted for *Java*. In order to validate the approach, we have designed a mutant applet generator based on *LittleDarwin*. The tool chain has successfully detected the expected missing checks in the mutant applets. We evaluate then the tool chain by analyzing five applets which implement the *OpenPGP* specification. Our tool has discovered both vulnerabilities and optimization problems. These points are then explained and corrected.

Keywords: Unsupervised machine-learning · k-Nearest-Neighbors · Vulnerability detection · Fuzzing attacks · Java Card · Chucky

1 Introduction

A fuzzing attack aims at sending crafted messages to a running program in order to test all the possible paths of its control flow. With this method and according to the system response, an attacker can detect a deviation of the program's expected behavior, in response to his message. This same crafted message can perturb the program's state machine and change its current state. By modifying the state of the program, an attacker can illegally gain access to resources stored onto the *Java Card*. One of the reasons for this illegal transition in the state machine can be related to the absence of input validation tests. Such a forgotten condition is called a *missing-check*. With this work, we aim at detecting those *missing-checks* before a fuzzing attack.

© Springer Nature Switzerland AG 2019
N. Zincir-Heywood et al. (Eds.): FPS 2018, LNCS 11358, pp. 156–172, 2019.
https://doi.org/10.1007/978-3-030-18419-3_11

Our approach is not based on a fuzzing attack, but on a static analysis of the source codes. To achieve this task, we have created three tools. The first one, *ChuckyJava* is an adaptation of *Chucky-ng* [8,17] for *Java*. The second tool we have designed is *fetchVuln*. It is a front-end layer above *ChuckyJava* which aims at automating tests of *ChuckyJava*. Moreover, it gathers all the outputs that *ChuckyJava* generates and it processes them to produce a report about vulnerable methods of the applet under analysis. The last tool is *LittleDarwinJC* which is based on *LittleDarwin* [10]. Its objective is to generate *Java* mutant applets and it enables us to characterize and evaluate the ability of *fetchVuln* to detect those mutants. We have tested *fetchVuln* on an applet set implementing *OpenPGP*. This evaluation has brought to the fore two optimization problems while we have discovered two vulnerabilities in the implementations.

The context is presented in Sect. 2. The state of the art is exposed in Sect. 3. Section 4 explains the functioning of *Chucky-ng*. The adaptation phase is shown in Sect. 5. We expose our methodology in Sect. 6. Then, we describe our results and discuss the evaluation of the performances in Sect. 7. The limitations of our tool are exposed in Sect. 8. To finish, we present our conclusion in Sect. 9.

2   Context

A program with a state machine accepts only a set of commands from a specific state. Such commands enable the program to change its state from one to another. A specification clarifies both states and transition links that shall be implemented for a program. *OpenPGP* is an open version of the Pretty Good privacy (*PGP*) standard defining encryption formats. Figure 1 shows a fragment of the *OpenPGP* state machine specification with the command COMPUTE_DIGITAL_SIGNATURE. It allows or denies the data to be signed before being written to the card. The *S* node (state *Selected*) is where the program accepts messages. During the process, the state checks the value of the

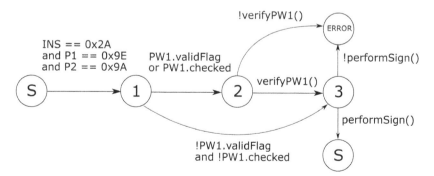

Fig. 1. Partial state machine of the *COMPUTE_DIGITAL_SIGNATURE*. There are conditions to transition from a state to another. States are represented by the nodes. The *S* node is the *Selected* state. Source from the *OpenPGP* specification [11]

incoming message in order to determine which command to execute. This is represented by the test on transition from state *S* to the state *1*. The state machine then checks the parameter *PW1* (*Password 1*) if necessary. If *verifyPW1()* fails, then the state machine enters the *ERROR* state. If the test succeeds, the applet can perform the signature operations. By entering in the state *S*, the program waits for another command. To illustrate a *missing-check*, suppose that the condition *verifyPW1()* from node *2* to node *3* is missing does not exist. It is possible for an attacker to enter state *3* with a wrong *PW1*.

3   State of the Art

Dynamic and Hybrid Protection. Dynamic and hybrid protection techniques consist in filtering user controlled inputs. We have found this kind of input cleaning on web application domains. As an example, the XSS attack mitigation which uses (*UrlEncoder* or *HtmlEncoder* [9] for example) to filter user controlled inputs. This step has to ensure that the message format and its application domain are correct. One drawback of this mitigation method is the possibility of missing cases against a new attack and it needs to be updated to improve the filtering accuracy. If an attacker has access to the source code of the library, then he can adapt its inputs to bypass the secure filter. In her PhD [5], Kamel proposes to implement a filtering library *API JCXSSFilter*. She chooses to adapt it to fit in the *OWASP*'s *ESAPI* [1] open-source web application. Added to this, the use of such secure libraries add an extra overhead in the system.

Formal Methods. The tools *Z* [14], *VDM* [3] rely on formal methods. They aim to mathematically specify the expected behavior of a sequential system by using sets, relations and functions. Burdy *et al.* [2] present an experiment on formal validation of *Java Card* applets. To specify a behavior, the user has to annotate his *Java* classes with the *Java Modeling Language*. One of the drawbacks of this method is the necessity to specify the right behavior for all classes. Depending on the size of the project, this step can be difficult. Added to this, if the specification of the applet changes, the developer has to adapt his code in order to fit it to the new expected behavior.

Static Analysis. A concolic analysis performs both concrete and symbolic analysis for a given source code. This is the case for the tool *JDart* [7] which relies on this kind of static analysis. For instance, the symbolic execution aims at discovering the paths a program can follow, while the concrete one proposes valid inputs to use in order to follow a specific path.

In the static analysis field, taint analysis techniques aims at following the evolution of an input through a program. To illustrate this method, suppose that one wants to follow a parameter. To do this, the tool has to taint this variable. Then, every variable which uses this tainted parameter gains the same taint color. *Pixy* [4] uses taint analysis. It aims at propagating limited string value information in order to handle some of *PHP*'s most dynamic features.

One drawback of a concolic analysis is that if there is a lot of paths, then the analysis could never finish its execution.

Text Mining. Text mining is a technique which consists in extracting the terms (words) present in software components (files) and their frequencies. Then, the term frequencies are correlated in order to build a model which predicts if a given software component is vulnerable. This method is implemented in the tool of Scandariato *et al.* [13].

Machine Learning. The tool entitled *Chucky-ng* [8], based on *Chucky* [17], relies on machine-learning to discover vulnerabilities in a source code. It extracts and compares functions with a unsupervised machine-learning algorithm in order to flag the vulnerable ones. *Chucky-ng* relies on the *k-Nearest-Neighbors* [12] algorithm. An important advantage for this tool is that *Chucky-ng* does not require to calibrate the tool with any sort of training step.

3.1   Our Contribution

At the best of our knowledge, no tool for mitigation against fuzzing attacks on *smart cards* is publicly available. We do not want to create a *smart card* fuzzer to extract vulnerabilities for two reasons. The first one is the required time to send a command from a terminal to a *smart card* is time expensive. We want our tool to perform an analysis in the best delays. The second reason is that *smart cards* contains Non Volatile Memory (*NVM*). Such memory has a short life expectation. Therefore, sending too many commands to the card would trigger many write functions and then prematurely aging the card.

We have created both *fetchVuln* and *ChuckyJava*. The former is the front-end of *ChuckyJava*. The latter allows the parsing of *Java* source codes and perform on them the unsupervised machine-learning technique of *Chucky-ng*.

4   Description of *Chucky-ng*

Chucky-ng takes three inputs:

- the folder of applet's source codes to analyze,
- one or more *API* symbols, such as variable names, parameter names or method names,
- the number of neighbors to select k.

The *API* symbols are the element that *Chucky-ng* searches in every method of the source code. An analyst can add several *API* symbols in the analyze queue. Therefore, in order to be added to the methods to analyze, this same method must manipulate all of these *API* symbols. The necessity of the k parameter is explained in the *Neighborhood discovery* step. Once *Chucky-ng* succeeds its execution, it returns an anomaly score for each function containing at least one of the *API* symbol. The tool processes the anomaly score in four distinct steps: The parsing, the neighborhood discovery, the reduction of the vector's dimensions and the anomaly detection.

4.1 Parsing

The tool named *Joern* [16], first parses *Java* files in the applet's folder source code to analyze. Based on this, it creates a *Code Property Graph* [17]. This graph gathers all nodes and links of the abstract syntax tree, the control flow graph and the data flow graph into one single graph. This same graph focuses mainly on the representation of functions from the source code.

4.2 Neighborhood Discovery

During this step, *Chucky-ng* creates a set of functions which contain at least one *API* symbol under analysis. This is done by running through the *Code Property Graph*. From this set, *Chucky-ng* picks one function. Then, it represents every function of the set as vectors of dimension |*API symbols*|. It uses the machine-learning algorithm *k-Nearest-Neighbors* [12] on these vectors in an unsupervised way, in order to gather the most k similar neighbors to the picked one. This value of k is required as input and it determines the number of similar functions to gather. The *k-Nearest-Neighbors* algorithm is split into two steps.

The first step aims at increasing the selection of neighbor's accuracy. To do so, *Chucky-ng* uses an approach based on *Inverse Document Frequency (IDF)* in order to discriminate rares *API* symbols. It insists on the fact that rare symbols are meaningful compared to others used by the vast majority of the function set. Two functions using the same rare *API* symbols should be more similar than two functions using only regular *API* symbols. *Chucky-ng*'s set of vectors now contains these new values based on the *IDF*.

The second step consists in gathering the k most similar functions from the one picked at the beginning of the *Neighborhood discovery*. To do so, *Chucky-ng* processes the vectors using the cosine distance metric where x and y are vectors *API* symbols values restricted by the *IDF* filtering:

$$cos(\boldsymbol{x}, \boldsymbol{y}) = 1 - \frac{\boldsymbol{x} \cdot \boldsymbol{y}}{||\boldsymbol{x}|| \cdot ||\boldsymbol{y}||}. \tag{1}$$

The use of this distance metric is twofold. Since *Chucky-ng* needs to consider rare *API* symbols, this metric takes into account both the orientation and the *Euclidean* distance of vectors.

Since *Chucky-ng* has the similar methods set to the one picked, it does not need the vectors anymore. Instead, *Chucky-ng* uses new vectors whose dimensions are the number of the total number of expressions used in every method of the set. Mind that the *Neighborhood discovery*, the *Reduction of vector's dimension* and the *Anomaly detection* steps are repeated as many times as there are methods in the set.

4.3 Reduction of the Vector's Dimension

This step objective is to reduce the dimension of the method set. It achieves this by removing tests of the program which does not manipulate any of the

API symbols. For example, if a control structure does not uses this *API* symbol either in its condition or body, *Chucky-ng* discards this control structure for the rest of the algorithm. It reduces the total number of expressions and therefore the dimension of vectors. To do so, *Chucky-ng* relies on the *Code Property Graph* in order to taint the *API* symbol evolution through the source code.

Added to this, *Chucky-ng* manages to reduce the dimensions of the vectors by normalizating the remaining expressions. It suppresses minor syntactical differences. As an example, the binary relational operators ($\leqslant$, $<$, $\geqslant$, $>$) are now replaced by $CMP expression. It affects the arguments, the return value of callees (*callees*) and the conditions of control structures. For example, the expression $if(ident \leqslant 1)$ is normalized as $if(ident\ \$CMP\ \$NUM)$. It reduces the impact of small syntactical differences.

4.4   Anomaly Detection

During this step, *Chucky-ng* creates a model of normality. This object is a vector whose dimensions are each of the remaining expressions. For each dimension, the value is the average presence for this expression in all the functions of our set as shown in Eq. (3). Let E be the normalized expression set and X the set of neighbor functions. $\varphi(x)$ is the mapping function that transforms neighbors in a vector space. The function $I(x, e)$ is equal to 1 if neighbor x contains the expression e. Otherwise I is equal to 0.

$$\varphi : X \rightarrow \mathbb{R}^{|E|}, \varphi(x) \mapsto (I(x, e))_{e \in E}. \tag{2}$$

Let μ be the vector of normality and N the neighbor set.

$$\mu = \frac{1}{|N|} \sum_{n \in N} \varphi(n), \mu \in \mathbb{R}^{|E|}. \tag{3}$$

Chucky-ng then creates a distance vector d as in Eq. (4) which corresponds to the values of the normality model minus the values of our function vector under test. The distance vector is in fact the list of the anomaly scores for each expression.

$$d = \mu - \varphi(x), d \in \mathbb{R}^{|E|}. \tag{4}$$

To finish, the anomaly score for the function under analysis is the maximum value of the distance vector as shown in Eq. (5). Its range is from $[-1.00, 1.00]$. If the anomaly score is closer to 1.00, our function is more likely to omit an expression, compared to the other functions. On the contrary, if it is closer to -1.00, our function has an expression that none of the others perform.

$$Score = max(d). \tag{5}$$

Even if *Chucky-ng* precises the anomaly score for a whole function, in practice, we observe all of its expression's anomaly scores. For example, if a function's anomaly score is set to 1.00 for an expression, all scores ranked under 1.00 are hidden by the result of *Chucky-ng*. To be efficient, an analyst has to read the whole distance vector including the -1.00 expressions. As we have discovered in the methodology (Sect. 6), an anomaly score of -1.00 is meaningful in our case: it corresponds to an *extra-check*. In other words, the applet may accept an unwanted additional command in the state machine.

5 Adaptation

5.1 From *C/C++* to *Java*

Java shares notions that are similar to those in *C++*. For instance, the *class abstraction* and *virtual methods* are similar. While such notions are shared with *C++*, we have syntactically adapted them in order to fit to the *Joern* [16], the parser. To achieve this task, we have modified *Joern* and *Chucky-ng* in order to link them together to the functionalities we have implemented. We now explain how we handle those specificities.

Abstract Classes. Methods which are declared in an abstract class in *Java* do not have definition. Since such methods are defined in another *Java* source file, *ChuckyJava* discards methods only declared. This prevent the use of duplicates methods.

Virtual Methods. If a class inherits of methods defined in the *Java API*, than *ChuckyJava* cannot parse them. To prevent this, we have created a tool that gathers both used and defined classes in the source code, and then it warns the user if a class is used but is never declared. This can happen if the user calls an object constructor from the *Java's API*.

New Expressions. We have to take into account new expressions or control flow structures. As an example, in *C++*, the *try/catch* clause does not have the *finally* block. Since this last one is executed either if the *catch* is triggered or not, we have decided to treat it as code block, outside of the control flow of the *try/catch*. Other ways to iterate exists in *Java* and not in *C++* such as the iteration over a list. For example, *for(Element e: elements) { [...] }*.

New Operators. We have implemented two binary operators which exist in *Java* but not in *C/C++*. Those operators are the structure comparison operator of strict equality $===$ and the bit shift to the right, which includes the sign byte $>>>$.

Switch/Cases. *Chucky-ng* does not handle and detect missing *cases* in a *switch/-case* structure. *ChuckyJava* takes into account the missing *cases* in order to detect this kind of *missing-check*. It means that *ChuckyJava* can now return an anomaly score for such tests. Every applet has to declare a *process* method in order to handle the reception of a message from an external source. In many cases, they use a *switch/case* to handle the instruction byte and launch the expected operations. In *Java Cards*, *switches* are important since they inform us about the allowed or denied commands of an applet.

5.2   ChuckyJava

We modify the *ChuckyJava*'s algorithm in order to improve its accuracy during the *Neighborhood discovery* step.

Object Type. For the Neighborhood Discovery step, we now take into account two new *API symbols.* An object's cast type and the type of an object if it is created as a parameter of a method call. To illustrate the cast, from the expression *(byte) 0x0F*, we now extract the *byte* type and we include it in the vector's dimension. For the second new *API* symbol, the expression *call(new OwnerPin(0x03, 0x04))* corresponds to the object creation inside a method call. From now on, the type *OwnerPin* would be included in the vector's dimension too. These modifications improve *ChuckyJava*'s ability to gather similar functions with a better accuracy.

6   The Methodology

This section presents the test framework we have created. It includes the three tools *fetchVuln, LittleDarwinJC, ChuckyJava.* Figure 2 shows the relation between those tools.

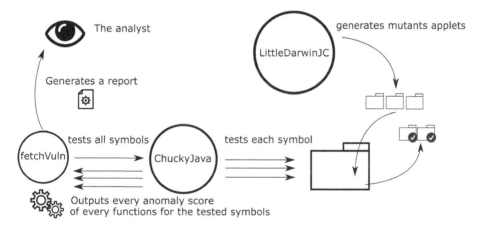

Fig. 2. *fetchVuln* requests *ChuckyJava* to test every *API* symbols. For each analyzed symbols, the output from *ChuckyJava* is stored and processed by *fetchVuln. LittleDarwinJC* produces different sets from the original ones, each of them containing one single mutation

6.1   FetchVuln

We have created the tool *fetchVuln.* This front-end's objective is to help an analyst to discover vulnerabilities easier. This tool operates in two distinct steps. It can be seen as a top layer over *ChuckyJava.*

Firstly, it lists all *API* symbols used within all the applets and their usage. Based on this, the tool is able to perform an analysis with *ChuckyJava* for each of these symbols. This is useful since *ChuckyJava* requires to specify one or multiple *API* symbols. Once *ChuckyJava* returns its output containing the anomaly score for each selected methods, *fetchVuln* stores it. It is stored as a list of triplets: method, *missing-check* (or feature) and anomaly score.

Secondly, when the execution of *ChuckyJava* for each *API* symbol is done, it outputs a report. Based on a configurable output filter value, this report contains the anomaly scores, the method names, the locations in the source code and the *missing-check* associated. This is readable by an analyst and it sorts the result from the highest anomaly score 1.00 to the defined output filter value. Moreover, our tool feedbacks statistics. For instance, it is able to output the number of *API* symbols for which we do not have enough similar neighbors. This can happen if a precise parameter name is used in too few functions. Another example of statistics that *fetchVuln* outputs is the number of functions with anomalies compared to total number of functions.

6.2   LittleDarwinJC

Thanks to *fetchVuln*, we are now able to output automatically a vulnerability report for an applet folder. We validate the adaption of *Chucky-ng* to *Java*. Secondly, we want to verify *fetchVuln* capacity to detect single variation of conditions in a source code. It enables us to characterize our tool. To do this, we have chosen to adapt the tool *LittleDarwin* [10]. We base our tool *LittleDarwinJC* on it since it generates mutations on the source code instead of the bytecode of a *Java* file. Then, we create a folder of one applet[1]. This same applet is duplicated five times inside the folder. *LittleDarwinJC* creates many copies of the original applets folder as there are existing conditions in the applet. On each folder, it removes one different single condition. Therefore, each applet folder is now a mutant and none of these mutants is duplicated. Then, a temporary tool we have created requests *fetchVuln* to perform an analysis on every mutant applet folders. If its final report shows an abnormal method with an anomaly score set to 1.00, then the mutant has been found by *fetchVuln*. We conclude from our tests that *fetchVuln* is able to detect *missing-checks*.

An *extra-check* is the anomaly where only one applet of the set performs a tests, but none of the others. A *missing/extra-assignment* is similar to *missing/extra-checks*, but on variable assignments. After this first step, we have tested the tool ability to discover other varieties of anomaly. From our results, *fetchVuln* is able to detect *extra-checks* and *missing/extra-assignments* too. Moreover, since we implemented the *switch-case* as conditions in *Chucky-Java*, *fetchVuln* is able to detect *missing-checks* within the *cases*.

---

[1] https://github.com/FluffyKaon/OpenPGP-Card.

7   Evaluation

7.1   Vulnerability Results

Description of the Dataset. Our dataset is made of five different *Java Card* applets, all implementing the *OpenPGP* [11] specification. Among these applets, we can find two different versions of *OpenPGP*: the 2.0.1 one, and the 3.3.1 one. These applets and their *OpenPGP* versions are listed in Table 1.

Table 1. *OpenPGP* applets and their implementation versions

Applet name	OpenPGP version
FluffyPGP	2.0.1
JCOpenPGP	2.0.1
MyPGPid	2.0.1
OpenPGPCard	2.0.1
SmartPGP	3.3.1

To communicate from a card terminal to the *Java Card*, one has to send an *APDU* object which contains the communication information. Among the bytes sent during this process, we present three *APDU*'s header bytes: the CLA byte, the INS byte and the P1 byte. The CLA (Class) byte is used to define the interindustry class. The second one is the INS (Instruction) which enables the applet to determine which command the user wants to perform. The last one, the P1 (Parameter 1) byte, is a parameter for the instruction command. We analyze the results of *fetchVuln* and therefore *ChuckyJava*.

A   Useless   Check.   We   have   executed   an   analysis   on   the   callee *JCSystem.makeTransient-ByteArray*. We set the value of the number of neighbors to select (parameter k) to 4. Since all applets implement a *process* method, this value of k enables us to gather all the *process* functions in order to compare them with *ChuckyJava*. Listing 1.1 shows the output we obtain with *ChuckyJava* for the *PGPKey* constructor in the *PGPKey.java* file.

Listing 1.1. The anomaly score, the expression, the function and file concerned

```
-1.00    "( null $CMP $RET )" PGPKey PGPKey.java:38
```

Since the anomaly score is evaluated to -1.00, it means that the test is performed in this method while it is not in other similar methods. We can verify this assumption with this code snippet available in the Appendix A. At this point in the applet, *tmpBuf* has been declared but no memory has been allocated, this it points on null. The evaluation is always *true*. *ChuckyJava* detects here a useless test which can be eliminated.

Dead Code Detection. We are able to detect dead code with *ChuckyJava*. Listing 1.2 shows the output we obtain for analysis of the *process* method of the *MyPGPid* applet.

Listing 1.2. *ChuckyJava* output for *MyPGPid*

```
-1.00    "case ISO7816.INS_SELECT"    process MyPGPid.java
```

ChuckyJava returns an anomaly score of −1.00. It means that the *process* function performs a *case ISO7816.INS_SELECT* which is not in other *process* functions. By analyzing the code of Appendix B, we can see a test performed at the beginning: *selectingApplet()*. Both this test and the *case ISO7816.OFFSET_INS* check the value of the *APDU*'s INS byte. Moreover, both of them returns immediately if this byte's value is *0xA4*. This explains why the second test in the *switch* can not be reached and is therefore not necessary.

A Misuse of the CLA Byte. By analysing the *ChuckyJava* output for the *process* method, we are able to detect a misuse of the CLA byte. This same byte has to be checked before usage, as requested in the *OpenPGP* specification [11]. In the *MyPGPid* applet, this byte is tested by a bitwise *AND* and the value 0xFC, but not in the other applets.

Listing 1.3. misuse of the CLA byte

```
-1.00    "buffer[ISO7816.OFFSET_CLA] = (byte)(buffer[ISO7816.OFFSET_CLA
    ↪ ] & (byte) 0xFC)    process MyPGPid.java:347
```

We have discovered that this assignation performed, but the value of *buffer[ISO7816.-OFFSET_CLA]* is practically never checked in the source code. The value is verified once in a method. Nearly every values for the CLA byte are possible for this applet. An attacker could be able to exploit it to make the program unexpectedly enter in a new state. The *OpenPGP* specification stipulates that this CLA byte shall be verified in order to allow only specific values (most of the time: 0x00, 0x0C, 0x10 or 0x1C according to the current state).

A Missing-Check for the P1 Byte. We have discovered an anomaly for the P1 byte. We have investigated the *verify* functions of our applet set. The output of *ChuckyJava* in Listing 1.4 warns us about an anomaly existing in the *OpenPGPApplet.java* file. This anomaly shows the *verify* function which does not use nor check the P1 byte while the others do it.

Listing 1.4. Missing-check of P1 byte

```
0.67    "buffer[ISO7816.OFFSET_P1] $CMP (byte)($NUM)"    verify
    ↪ OpenPGPApplet.java:413
```

According to the specification for the *verify* method, the P1 byte shall be set to 0x00 for this precise command. This is a *missing-check* because it is performed in the *verify* functions of the other applets of the set. The code snippet for *OpenPGPApplet* is available in Appendix C. The anomaly score of 0.67 instead of 1.00 is due to a limitation which we discuss in Sect. 8.

7.2   Performance Evaluation

A quality assurance tool (*QA*) in *smart cards* aims at verifying if all the specified commands are implemented (conformance testing). Our tool *fetchVuln* is not a *QA* tool. It detects if the applet has more functionalities than expected. To illustrate this purpose, imagine an applet which is perfectly implementing the *OpenPGP* specification. Each command a user send to the applet returns the expected output. We now suppose that a back-door exists in the applet. A *QA* tool is not able to detect it, because the applet performs perfectly according to its specification. However, since *fetchVuln* detects *extra-checks*, it is able to discover such an anomaly in an applet.

7.3   Time Overheads

This performance evaluation focuses on the advantages of using *fetchVuln* instead of a physical verification.

To test a *Java* applet, an analyst can first generate several different messages. Then, he sends them individually to the *smart card* to obtain the output. Finally, he verifies that the combination input/output is conform to the specification. The drawback of physically testing the inputs is the communication cost between a *smart card* and the terminal. It is time expensive. We have tested the method and the process has last roughly one second to transmit a single command to the applet *FluffyPGPApplet*. The time required with such an analysis, increases with the number of states which the specification plans. As a comparison, *fetchVuln* requires about 3 min to analyze a set of five applets implementing the *OpenPGP* specification, including *FluffyPGPApplet*. This analyzes was performed on a *Intel i7-7600U* 2.8 GHz CPU, using two of the four threads available in a virtual environment.

8   Limitations

8.1   Number of Missing-Checks

During the fourth step, *ChuckyJava* creates vectors which contain information about the presence or not of a normalized expression only. For example, the condition *if (k == 3)* is normalized as *(k $CMP $NUM)*. If there are multiple conditions comparing k with a number, the tool normalizes them with the same expression. Then, the value for the dimension *(k $CMP $NUM)* is equal to one regardless of the number of comparison. We can see in Listing 1.5 that two tests are executed. However, only one is performed in Listing 1.6. After the normalization step, both vectors representing the code snippet have the dimension *(k $CMP $NUM)*. Its value is equal to one in both vectors. This leads to a non-detection of some *missing-checks*.

Listing 1.5. Two comparisons of number with k

```
public void test(int k)
{
  if(k <= 1)
    callee(1);
  else if(k <= 2)
    callee(2);
}
```

Listing 1.6. Vulnerable code

```
public void test(int k)
{
  if(k <= 1)
    callee(1);
  //Missing check...
  callee(2);
}
```

8.2 Missing Distinction Between Variables and Constants

We are able to observe that in some cases it is not possible for *ChuckyJava* to distinguish a variable from a constant. Listing 1.7 shows an initialization with a variable. This same variable could be uninitialized at this point but there is no test to verify it. In Listing 1.8, the same function call uses a constant as a parameter. Since it is a constant, it is more likely to be defined in one of the project classes. In this example, its value is set to *10*. It is not necessary to test its value before using it. However, if the other applets use a variable as like in Listing 1.7, then *ChuckyJava* detects a wrong *missing-check* here for code snippet in Listing 1.8.

Listing 1.7. Local variable

```
if(my_variable > 0)
    myInitMethod(my_variable);
```

Listing 1.8. Constant

```
private static final int MY_CONSTANT = 10;
myInitMethod(MY_CONSTANT);
```

Added to this, *ChuckyJava* is not able to handle differences between identifiers. For example, we want *ChuckyJava* to analyze the identifier *buffer*. Then, all similar identifiers (*tmpBuff*, *buf*, etc.) are discarded. To perform an accurate analyze with our tool, we first have to normalize the used identifiers, which is one of our current research directions.

9   Conclusion

We have designed a tool chain which includes *ChuckyJava*, *fetchVuln* and *LittleDarwinJC*. It aims at detecting incorrect implementations of specification within *Java Card* applets. We have improved the original tool by adding various features. *fetchVuln* has successfully detected mutant applets generated with *LittleDarwinJC*. Added to this, we have discovered that our tool is able to detect *extra-checks* and *missing-assignments* too. In real conditions, *fetchVuln* is able to detect wrong implementations specification. However, the tool has two limitations. We are currently working on the identifier problem since it is the most restrictive one. Because it is a known problem, we have found different methods to start with. We are heading to source code de-obfuscation and source codes merging techniques [6,15] to solve this limitation.

A   PGPKey Constructor

```
private static byte[] tmpBuf;
[...]
public PGPKey() {
  key = new KeyPair(KeyPair.ALG_RSA_CRT, KEY_SIZE);
  fp = new byte[FP_SIZE];
  Util.arrayFillNonAtomic(fp, (short) 0, (short) fp.length, (byte) 0);
  Util.setShort(attributes, (short) 1, KEY_SIZE);
  Util.setShort(attributes, (short) 3, EXPONENT_SIZE);
  //The useless check
  if(tmpBuf == null) {
   tmpBuf = JCSystem.makeTransientByteArray((short) (KEY_SIZE_BYTES /
       ↪ 2), JCSystem.CLEAR_ON_DESELECT);
  }
 }
```

B   Process Function of MyPGPid Applet

```
public void process(APDU apdu) {
    byte[] buffer = apdu.getBuffer();
    short lc;
    boolean status = false;

    // ignore the applet select command dispached to the process
    if (selectingApplet()) {
        return;
    }

    buffer[ISO7816.OFFSET_CLA] = (byte)(buffer[ISO7816.OFFSET_CLA] & (
        ↪ byte)0xFC);

    if (buffer[ISO7816.OFFSET_INS] == GET_RESPONSE) {
        if (remainingDataLength <= 0) {
            ISOException.throwIt(ISO7816.SW_CONDITIONS_NOT_SATISFIED);
        }
        else { sendData(apdu, tmpData, remainingDataLength);}
        return;
    } else {
        remainingDataLength = 0;
        remainingDataOffset = 0;
    }

    switch (buffer[ISO7816.OFFSET_INS]) {
        case ISO7816.INS_SELECT:
            return;
```

```
case GET_DATA:
    getData(apdu);
    return;
case PUT_DATA:
    putData(apdu);
    return;
case PUT_DATA_CHAINING:
    putDataChaining(apdu);
    return;
case VERIFY:
    if (buffer[ISO7816.OFFSET_P1] != 0) { ISOException.throwIt
        ↪ (ISO7816.SW_WRONG_P1P2); }
    lc = apdu.setIncomingAndReceive();
    if (lc == 0) {
        ISOException.throwIt(ISO7816.
            ↪ SW_SECURITY_STATUS_NOT_SATISFIED);
    }
    switch (buffer[ISO7816.OFFSET_P2]) {
        case (byte)0x81:
            if (chv1.getTriesRemaining() == (byte)0) {
                ISOException.throwIt(SW_PIN_BLOCKED);
            }
            status = chv1.check(buffer, (short)ISO7816.
                ↪ OFFSET_CDATA, (byte)lc);
            break;
        case (byte)0x82:
            if (chv2.getTriesRemaining() == (byte)0) {
                ISOException.throwIt(SW_PIN_BLOCKED);
            }
            status = chv2.check(buffer, (short)ISO7816.
                ↪ OFFSET_CDATA, (byte)lc);
            break;
        case (byte)0x83:
            if (chv3.getTriesRemaining() == (byte)0) {
                ISOException.throwIt(SW_PIN_BLOCKED);
            }
            status = chv3.check(buffer, (short)ISO7816.
                ↪ OFFSET_CDATA, (byte)lc);
            break;
        default:
            ISOException.throwIt(ISO7816.SW_WRONG_P1P2);
    }
    if (!status) { ISOException.throwIt(ISO7816.
        ↪ SW_SECURITY_STATUS_NOT_SATISFIED);}
    return;
case GENERATE_ASYMMETRIC_KEY_PAIR:
    generateAssymetricKeyPair(apdu);
    return;
case PERFORM_SECURITY_OPERATION:
    performSecurityOperation(apdu);
    return;
case CHANGE_REFERENCE_DATA:
    /* Fall through */
case RESET_RETRY_COUNTER:
    changeResetChv(apdu);
    return;
case INTERNAL_AUTHENTICATE:
    if (buffer[ISO7816.OFFSET_P1] != 0 || buffer[ISO7816.
        ↪ OFFSET_P2]
        != 0) {
        ISOException.throwIt(ISO7816.SW_WRONG_P1P2);
    }
    if (!chv2.isValidated()) {
        ISOException.throwIt(ISO7816.
            ↪ SW_SECURITY_STATUS_NOT_SATISFIED);
    }
    lc = receiveData(apdu, tmpData);
    sig.init(keyAuth.getPrivate(), Cipher.MODE_ENCRYPT);
```

```
                lc = sig.doFinal(tmpData, (short)0, lc, tmpData, (short)0)
                    ↪ ;
                sendData(apdu, tmpData, lc);
                return;
            case GET_CHALLENGE:
                if (buffer[ISO7816.OFFSET_P1] != 0 || buffer[ISO7816.
                    ↪ OFFSET_P2]
                    != 0) {
                    ISOException.throwIt(ISO7816.SW_WRONG_P1P2);
                }
                lc = apdu.setOutgoing();
                random.generateData(tmpData, (short) 0, lc);
                apdu.setOutgoingLength(lc);
                apdu.sendBytesLong(tmpData, (short) 0, lc);
                return;
            //case EXPORT_KEY_PAIR:
                //exportKeyPair(apdu);
                //return;

            case INS_CARD_READ_POLICY:
                ReadPolicy(apdu);
                return;
            case INS_CARD_KEY_PUSH:
                KeyPush(apdu);
                return;

            default:
                ISOException.throwIt(ISO7816.SW_INS_NOT_SUPPORTED);
        }
    }
}
```

C   Verify Function of OpenPGPApplet

```
private void verify(APDU apdu, byte mode) {
  if (mode == (byte) 0x81 || mode == (byte) 0x82) {
   // Check length of input
   if (in_received < PW1_MIN_LENGTH || in_received > PW1_MAX_LENGTH)
    ISOException.throwIt(ISO7816.SW_WRONG_LENGTH);

   // Check given PW1 and set requested mode if verified succesfully
   if (pw1.check(buffer, _0, (byte) in_received)) {
    if (mode == (byte) 0x81)
     pw1_modes[PW1_MODE_NO81] = true;
    else
     pw1_modes[PW1_MODE_NO82] = true;
   } else {
    ISOException
    .throwIt((short) (0x63C0 | pw1.getTriesRemaining()));
   }
  } else if (mode == (byte) 0x83) {
   // Check length of input
   if (in_received < PW3_MIN_LENGTH || in_received > PW3_MAX_LENGTH)
    ISOException.throwIt(ISO7816.SW_WRONG_LENGTH);

   // Check PW3
   if (!pw3.check(buffer, _0, (byte) in_received)) {
    ISOException
    .throwIt((short) (0x63C0 | pw3.getTriesRemaining()));
   }
  } else {
   ISOException.throwIt(ISO7816.SW_INCORRECT_P1P2);
  }
}
```

References

1. OWASP enterprise security API (2009)
2. Burdy, L., Requet, A., Lanet, J.-L.: Java applet correctness: a developer-oriented approach. In: Araki, K., Gnesi, S., Mandrioli, D. (eds.) FME 2003. LNCS, vol. 2805, pp. 422–439. Springer, Heidelberg (2003). https://doi.org/10.1007/978-3-540-45236-2_24
3. Jones, C.: Systematic Software Development Using VDM, vol. 2. Prentice-Hall, Englewood Cliffs (1986)
4. Jovanovic, N., Kruegel, C., Kirda, E.: Pixy: a static analysis tool for detecting web application vulnerabilities. In: IEEE Symposium on Security and Privacy (2006)
5. Kamel, N.: Sécurité des cartes à puce à serveur web embarqué. Ph.D. thesis, Université of Limoges (2012)
6. Kuhn, A., Ducasse, S., Girba, T.: Semantic clustering: identifying topics in source code
7. Luckow, K., et al.: JDart: a dynamic symbolic analysis framework
8. Maier, A.: Assisted discovery of vulnerabilities in source code by analyzing program slices
9. OWASP: Xss (cross site scripting) prevention cheat sheet. https://www.owasp.org/index.php/XSS_(Cross_Site_Scripting)_Prevention_Cheat_Sheet
10. Parsai, A., Demeyer, S., Murgia, A.: LittleDarwin: a feature-rich and extensible mutation testing framework for large and complex Java systems
11. Pietig, A.: Functional specification of the OpenPGP application on ISO smart card operating systems
12. Sayad, S.: K nearest neighbors. http://chem-eng.utoronto.ca/~datamining/Presentations/KNN.pdf
13. Scandariato, R., Walden, J., Hovsepyan, A., Joosen, W.: Predicting vulnerable software components via text mining
14. Spivey, J.: Understanding Z: A Specification Language and Its Semantics, vol. 3. Cambridge University Press, Cambridge (1988)
15. Tairas, R., Gray, J.: Phoenix-based clons detection using suffix trees
16. Yamaguchi, F.: Joern. http://mlsec.org/joern/
17. Yamaguchi, F., Wressnegger, C., Gascon, H., Rieck, K.: Chucky: exposing missing checks in source code for vulnerability discovery

A Comparative Study Across Static and Dynamic Side-Channel Countermeasures

Yuri Gil Dantas$^{(\boxtimes)}$, Tobias Hamann, and Heiko Mantel

Department of Computer Science, TU Darmstadt, Darmstadt, Germany
{dantas,hamann,mantel}@mais.informatik.tu-darmstadt.de

Abstract. Timing side-channel attacks remain a major challenge for software security, in particular for cryptographic implementations. Multiple countermeasures against such attacks have been proposed over the last decades, including static and dynamic approaches. Although such countermeasures have been extensively studied in the literature, previous evaluations have mostly relied on simplified system settings. In this article, we provide a comparative evaluation of the effectiveness of both static and dynamic countermeasures in a realistic setting for Java programs. Our experimental setup considers the effects of the non-deterministic timing behavior introduced by the Java VM, in particular involving just-in-time compilation (JIT). Our empirical results indicate that such countermeasures vary heavily on how much they can reduce information leakage, and show that negative effects of non-deterministic timing behavior on their effectiveness are substantial.

1 Introduction

One particular class of timing side-channel vulnerabilities that is frequently exploited by adversaries is caused by conditionals that are dependent on secret data [9]. In this case, a timing side channel is introduced when the if branch of a secret-dependent conditional takes a different time to be executed then the else branch. An adversary can exploit this to deduce information about the secret. For cryptographic implementations, for instance, it has been shown that attacks can, in the worst case, leak the entire secret key [8].

In order to mitigate timing side channels caused by such conditionals, one can modify program behavior to reduce information leakage via the channel. For this article, we consider two classes of such program modifications, which we refer to as static and dynamic transformations. Conceptually, *static transformations*, like cross-copying [1] or conditional assignment [16], aim to completely remove timing side-channel vulnerabilities by modifying the source code of the target program. *Dynamic transformations*, like bucketing [10] or predictive timing mitigation [19], in contrast, delay program events at runtime up to well-defined points in time to reduce the amount of information leaked by the target program.

Previous evaluations of both static and dynamic transformations have been mostly carried out in simplified settings. One of the most prevalent simplifications is the assumption of deterministic timing behavior (e.g., [2,10]). In a system

© Springer Nature Switzerland AG 2019
N. Zincir-Heywood et al. (Eds.): FPS 2018, LNCS 11358, pp. 173–189, 2019.
https://doi.org/10.1007/978-3-030-18419-3_12

with deterministic timing behavior, each input always results in the same timing observation. The impact of non-deterministic timing behavior on bucketing has been investigated in [4]. In that study, two implementations of bucketing that reside at the application and kernel level were developed for reducing timing side channels in Java programs. Empirical results indicated that indeed both implementations performed comparably worse than previous evaluations in settings with deterministic timing behavior. To the best of our knowledge, such an evaluation has not been carried out for predictive timing mitigation. A previous study on different static transformations [14] has compared four well-known static transformations for Java in a simplified setting with just-in-time compilation (JIT) disabled. To date, the impact of non-deterministic timing behavior on different static transformation techniques has not been investigated as rigorously.

The goal of this article is to provide a comparative study on the effectiveness of static and dynamic transformations in a more practical setting that considers the non-deterministic timing behavior introduced by JIT. In particular, we provide an answer to the following research question: *'How do static and dynamic transformations compare to each other in terms of reduction of side-channel leakage?'*. To this end, we evaluate implementations of two static transformations (cross-copying and conditional assignment), and two dynamic transformations (bucketing and predictive timing mitigation). For the static transformations, we evaluate the implementations presented in [14] in a setting with JIT enabled. For the dynamic transformations, the results of [4] indicated that application-level implementations are more effective in reducing information leakage than kernel-level implementations. In order to better understand the effects of different implementation strategies on the application level for such transformations, we present an implementation that manually modifies the target program to enforce bucketing. We compare this implementation to the bucketing implementation presented in [4] that is using a generic enforcement mechanism. In addition, we present and evaluate two implementations of predictive timing mitigation on the application-level, using the same implementation strategies as for bucketing.

Our results indicate that the impact of non-deterministic timing behavior on side-channel countermeasures can be substantial. This impact reduces the effectiveness of both static and dynamic techniques when compared to simplified settings, e.g., assuming deterministic timing behavior. The reduction of effectiveness seems to be more severe for static techniques, and cross-copying seems to be especially affected. While evaluations of cross-copying in simplified settings indicated a reduction of information leakage by roughly 96% [14], the reduction is substantially smaller for our experiments – achieving, on average, a reduction of only 4.48%. The impact on conditional assignment, in contrast, is also clearly negatively affected, but still ensures an average reduction of roughly 87% (in contrast to over 99% in simplified settings [14]). Dynamic transformations seem to be more promising in settings with non-deterministic timing behavior, achieving an average reduction of over 90% in our experiments[1].

2   Timing Side Channels

In a timing side-channel attack, an adversary exploits the timing behavior of a program to deduce secret information. Timing side channels have been a long-standing problem for software security, going back to the work of Kocher [9]. A classical example of a timing-side channel vulnerability can be found in the square-and-multiply implementation of modular exponentiation. Modular exponentiation (modExp for short) is an operation that can be used to compute $p = c^d \pmod{n}$. This is especially relevant in RSA implementations, where c is the ciphertext, d the secret key, and n the modulus. In a nutshell, the running time of the square-and-multiply implementation of modExp is dependent on the Hamming weight of the secret key, thus leaking private information to an adversary.

The algorithm of the square-and-multiply implementation of modExp is illustrated in Fig. 1. The timing behavior of modExp depends on the secret d since Line 5 is executed more often when more bits of d are set (condition of Line 4). This enables adversaries to learn the Hamming weight of d by measuring the running time of modExp. If an adversary knows the Hamming weight of the secret key, the brute force search space is reduced, opening the possibility of deducing the entire secret key.

```
1  input: c, d, n;
2  r ← 1;
3  for i = 1 to length(d) do
4      if d % 2 == 1 then
5          |   r ← (r * c) % n;
6      end
7      c ← (c * c) % n;
8      d ← d ≫ 1;
9  end
10 return r % n;
```

Fig. 1. Algorithm of modExp

Statistical Estimation of Information Leakage. A side channel can be modeled as an information-theoretical channel with input alphabet X and output alphabet Y, where X and Y are random variables [15]. Intuitively, X models the possible secret inputs that a program can process, while Y models the possible (timing) observations an adversary can gather through the side channel. The leakage that occurs via the side channel can be measured by the notion of mutual information of X and Y. Mutual information describes the amount of information that Y contains about X, and is calculated as the difference between the (Shannon) entropy [17] and the conditional (Shannon) entropy.

The channel capacity $C(X;Y)$ [17] is defined as the worst-case (i.e., maximal) mutual information across all prior distributions. We use the notion of channel capacity to evaluate the effectiveness of the static and dynamic transformations

---

[1] We provide all implementations and experimental results online: https://drive. google.com/file/d/1CHfHD6Huo2Wp2y_ZQb7OgsKeNxiuhxB3/view?usp=sharing.

considered in this article. To this end, we use the leakiEst tool [3] that provides statistical estimations of the channel capacity based on provided sample runs of a program for different inputs.

3   Static Transformations

Static transformation techniques for mitigating timing side channels like, e.g., cross-copying [1] and conditional assignment [16] aim at mitigating side channel vulnerabilities introduced by secret-dependent conditionals. In such settings, a timing side channel can occur when the if branch of a conditional takes a different execution time than the else branch. A special instance of this problem are secret-dependent conditionals that only consist of an if branch, and an empty else branch. Static transformation techniques modify the program code of a target program such that the executions of all branches in secret-dependent conditionals take the same time. In this section, we discuss two static transformation techniques, namely cross-copying and conditional assignment.

3.1   Cross-Copying

The approach of the cross-copying [1] technique is to add dummy statements resembling the complete corresponding other branch at the end of each branch of secret-dependent conditionals. The goal of this technique is to ensure that each branch takes the same execution time, because the statements of both branches will be executed. Cross-copying can be seen as a special case of unification [11], a similar technique that can add dummy statements at arbitrary points in each branch, and can thus lead to less dummy statements being added. In this article, we consider modExp that contains a secret-dependent conditional without an else branch. Hence, we investigate the simpler cross-copying rather than unification.

Previous work on the evaluation of different static transformation techniques [14] has shown how it is possible to implement cross-copying in Java programs. We leverage this implementation for our comparative experiments.

For the example presented in Fig. 1, cross-copying modifies the conditional starting in Line 4 as depicted in Fig. 2. The cross-copying technique adds a dummy variable (r_d) to the program, performing the same computation in both branches of the conditional. Note that only in the if branch the result is applied to the local variable that is used to calculate

```
1  input: c, d, n;
2  r ← 1;
3  for i = 1 to i = length(d) do
4      if d % 2 == 1 then
5      |   r ← (r * c) % n;
6      else
7      |   r_d ← (r * c) % n;
8      end
9      c ← (c * c) % n;
10     d ← d ≫ 1;
11 end
12 return r % n;
```

Fig. 2. modExp after cross-copying

the return value. In the else branch, the result of the computation is assigned to the dummy variable, which is expected to take the same execution time, but will not affect the return value of the algorithm. Hence, this implementation strategy for cross-copying is transparent.

3.2 Conditional Assignment

Conditional assignment [16] aims to mitigate timing side channels caused by an assignment to a local variable that affects the program state, and is dependent on secret information. The conditional assignment technique ensures that all computations that might occur based on the secret-dependent conditional are executed, and assign the desired value of these computed values to the variable afterwards using a bitmask that chooses the desired value of the computation. This approach eliminates secret-dependent conditionals, as the conditional is completely encoded by the masking process.

```
1 input: c, d, n;
2 r ← 1;
3 for i = 1 to i = length(d) do
4    r' ← (r * c) % n;
5    m = Mask(d % 2 == 1);
6    r ← (m & r') | (~m & r);
7    c ← (c * c) % n;
8    d ← d ≫ 1;
9 end
10 return r % n;
```

Fig. 3. modExp after conditional assignment

For the example presented in Fig. 1, conditional assignment modifies the conditional starting in Line 4 as depicted in Fig. 3. Instead of adding dummy assignments as for cross-copying, conditional assignment ensures that both the updated value r' (Line 4) from the if branch and the unchanged r are used for computing the new value of r (Line 6). The assignment to r is performed by masking the updated result and the non-updated result based on the original condition. The Mask function used in Line 5 is supposed to return $2^l - 1$ in the case that $d \% 2 == 1$ holds (the condition for the if branch to be taken), where l is the bitlength of the variable r. Correspondingly, the Mask function is supposed to return 0 in the case that $d \% 2 \mathbin{!} = 1$ holds (the condition for the else branch to be taken). Hence, the computation result that should not affect the return value of the algorithm is masked out, making conditional assignment transparent.

4 Dynamic Transformations

Dynamic transformation techniques for mitigating timing side channels monitor program behavior during runtime and react to the monitored behavior dynamically in order to reduce or prevent information leakage via a timing channel. In this section, we discuss implementations of two such dynamic transformation techniques, namely bucketing [10] and predictive timing mitigation [19].

4.1   Bucketing and Predictive Timing Mitigation in an Nutshell

The goal of both bucketing and predictive timing mitigation is to reduce the amount of information leakage via timing side channels at runtime. In contrast to the static transformations presented in Sect. 3, the goal of both techniques is not to completely remove timing side channels. They rather aim at reducing the amount of information that is leaked via the side channel, thus limiting the information about the secret that an adversary can learn. From a high-level perspective, both approaches delay sensitive program events to well-defined points in time, thus reducing the amount of possible distinct timing observations. It has been shown that reducing the number of possible distinct observations directly reduces the upper bound of possible information leakage via a timing channel (see, e.g., [12]). By adjusting this delay, both approaches allow a navigation in the tradeoff between security and performance.

To achieve the reduction of possible timing observations that an adversary can get, the two approaches follow different strategies. The bucketing technique discretizes the timing behavior of a protected program by delaying events to a set of predefined points in time, the so called bucket boundaries. Each event that occurs within the interval of a certain bucket is delayed up to the corresponding bucket boundary of that bucket. The approach of predictive timing mitigation, in turn, is to provide a certain prediction schedule that observed events shall adhere to. In case an event is observed before the next point in time that is scheduled – the so called quantum –, the event is delayed up to that quantum. In case the program violates the schedule, the schedule is adapted dynamically, penalizing the program for not adhering to the schedule. The time frame in which a given schedule is adhered to by the program is called an epoch. Penalizing the target program by updating the schedule thus starts a new epoch.

4.2   Implementations

Previous work on bucketing has investigated the effects of different implementation techniques for the bucketing mechanism on the security guarantees provided by these implementations [4]. That work provided first evidence that the choice of system layer where the implementation is placed can have a direct effect on the provided security by the implementation. In this article, we investigate two implementation strategies at the application layer for both bucketing and predictive timing mitigation: instantiations of the generic enforcement framework CLISEAU [6] for the two approaches, and manual implementations that are inlined into the protected program. We assume that program operations that cause a timing leak are located in specific methods. Hence, our implementations monitor invocations to these methods and delay program execution after each such method invocation. Our goal is to evaluate the effects of these different implementation strategies on the same system level.

Implementations of Dynamic Transformations Using CliSeAu.
CLISEAU is a generic framework for enforcing security requirements for Java
programs on the application level at runtime. Conceptually, CLISEAU encapsulates a target program into a so called enforcement capsule that consists of
four additional components responsible for the enforcement: the interceptor, the
coordinator, the local policy, and the enforcer. In this work, we follow the approach of [4], and focus on the interceptor component and the enforcer component
in our implementation. The interceptor is responsible for intercepting security-
relevant program events from the target program. Based on these intercepted
events, a decision how to handle the events is made. This decision is then enforced
by the enforcer component. For implementing dynamic side-channel mitigation
techniques, the interceptor component is used to determine the start time of
timing-sensitive computations, while the enforcer component is used to delay
events based on the delay strategy by a given mitigation technique.

This implementation strategy for dynamic side-channel mitigation has been
used to implement the bucketing mechanism in CLISEAU [4]. As a point of
comparison with predictive timing mitigation and static transformations, we
reuse the CLISEAU implementation of bucketing in this article. In a nutshell, the
implementation provides the CLISEAU components for enforcing bucketing for
Java programs, making it sufficient to declare the method signatures of timing-
sensitive computations and to provide the amount and placement of buckets to
instantiate it for a given target program. For more details, we refer the interested
reader to the original work [4].

We present an implementation of predictive timing mitigation in CLISEAU
that builds on the implementation of bucketing in CLISEAU. The overall work-

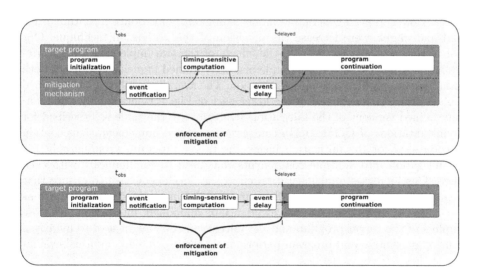

Fig. 4. Visualization of implementation strategy using a generic framework (upper
part), and inlining the mitigation (lower part)

flow of any dynamic transformation technique that delays program events at runtime can be seen in Fig. 4. In particular, the upper part of Fig. 4 shows the workflow when using a generic mechanism like CLISEAU. Just before a timing-sensitive computation is about to start (at time t_{obs}), the mechanism is notified, and program execution continues with the computation. After the computation, the mechanism is notified that the computation has been finished. Based on the delay strategy, the mechanism then delays further program execution to reduce the amount of distinct possible timing observations (up to time $t_{delayed}$). For predictive timing mitigation, there are two cases how the mechanism can delay program events based on the current schedule. In case the timing-sensitive computation finished before the next scheduled quantum, the mechanism delays further program execution up to that quantum and the program continues regularly. In case the computation does not finish before the next scheduled quantum, the mechanism adapts the schedule based on a predefined penalty function, i.e., a new epoch is started. The mechanism delays further program execution until the newly scheduled quantum, and keeps the new schedule afterwards. In order to instantiate the predictive timing mitigation implementation, users of the mechanism provide the method signatures of the methods containing timing-sensitive computations, and provide the initial schedule as well as the penalty function.

Manually Inlined Implementations. Instantiating a generic mechanism for mitigation techniques offers an increased level of reusability of the security solutions, as the instantiation can be specialized to a variety of target programs with relatively few implementation overhead. The clear separation of the target program and the enforcement mechanism also decouples the development of the mitigation mechanism, making it possible to treat security as an orthogonal aspect. However, such generic mechanisms inherently introduce a runtime overhead and might even decrease the precision of the mitigation technique. Our goal in this article is to evaluate the effects of the two implementation strategies empirically. We therefore provide manually inlined implementations of both bucketing and predictive timing mitigation. The overall workflow of such inlined implementations is depicted in the lower part of Fig. 4. Conceptually, the manually inlined versions of the mitigation strategies are the same as described for the instantiations of CLISEAU. In contrast, the inlined implementations contain all code used for the mitigation inside the target program, avoiding splitting the mitigation into multiple components that need to communicate with each other. This increases implementation effort, as developers have to ensure that the mitigation code is located at all occurrences of timing-sensitive computations manually. On the other hand, the avoidance of component interaction and close coupling of the target program and the mitigation code might lead to increased security guarantees and program performance. We provide an empirical evaluation of these effects in the next section.

5   A Comparative Security Evaluation

The goal of this section is to report and discuss the findings of our evaluation regarding the static and dynamic transformations presented in Sects. 3 and 4.

We provide all implementations of the transformation techniques, and all experimental results online.[2]

5.1   Experimental Setup, Metric, and Design

Setup. We conduct all experiments on a 3.7 GHz Intel Xeon E3-1240 server with 16 GB of RAM running Ubuntu 16.04 LTS with kernel 4.4.0, and OpenJDK 8. Furthermore, all experiments are conducted with JIT enabled using the so-called tiered optimization mode. We apply the static and dynamic transformations investigated in this article to an implementation of modExp in Java[3].

We consider a passive adversary who locally measures the running time of modExp using System.nanoTime(). Each measurement consists of a timing observation value collected by this adversary. We consider an adversary who can observe the execution time of the target program, but not the program's internal state. In particular, he cannot observe internal communication events used in the implementations of bucketing and predictive timing mitigation.

We conduct 100 samples for each mitigation technique to evaluate the practical impact of our results. For each sample, we start with a warm-up phase of 2^{19} measurements that is discarded in the results. We chose this number in order to reach the steady-state of JIT before collecting measurements for our experiments. This approach follows the best practices proposed in [7] for Java performance evaluations. Subsequently, we start with an experimental-phase of 2^{19} measurements that is kept in the results as these measurements relate to the steady-state of modExp. To evaluate the effectiveness of static and dynamic transformations in reducing timing side channels, we consider the mean and worst-case values of our sample distributions. From all collected samples, we reject outliers that lie further than 1 absolute standard deviation from the mean.

Metric. Following the methodology used in [4,14], we consider channel capacity as our metric to determine the effectiveness of static and dynamic transformations. That is, we measure the correlation between secret inputs and their timing distributions in order to estimate the amount of information (in bits) that might be leaked via a timing side channel.

Design. We conduct the so-called distinguishing experiments (as in [13,14]) for two distinct secret input values, namely key_1 and key_2. Both keys have 32 bits

---

[2] https://drive.google.com/file/d/1CHfHD6Huo2Wp2y_ZQb7OgsKeNxiuhxB3/view?usp=sharing.

[3] The modExp implementation considered in this article is the same used in [14].

(with Hamming weights 5 and 25, respectively[4]). Using distinguishing experiments, we can identify a side-channel vulnerability that enables adversaries to distinguish whether either key_1 or key_2 is used by modExp. In our experiments, we generated such distinct keys and conducted experiments with and without any transformation. As a result, we can quantify the channel capacity with the help of an off-the-shelf information leakage estimation tool named leakiEst [3].

5.2   Static Transformations

Static transformations have been evaluated in a simplified setting with JIT disabled in previous work [14]. Our goal in this article is to investigate the impact of non-deterministic timing behavior on static transformations. To this end, we quantify the effectiveness of cross-copying and conditional assignment in terms of channel capacity.

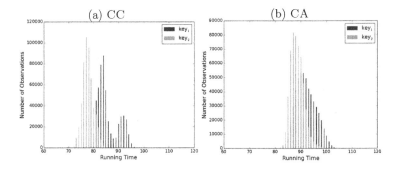

Fig. 5. Timing distributions of modExp after applying static transformations

Figures 5 and 6 illustrate our experimental results. Figure 6 shows the histogram of the scenario where no transformation (BASELINE) is applied to modExp. Figures 5a and b show the histograms of the scenarios where modExp is using cross-copying (CC) and conditional assignment (CA), respectively. The overall results regarding the effectiveness of cross-copying and conditional assignment are presented in Fig. 7.

We observe that when modExp is not using any transformation (Fig. 6) the timing distributions of key_1 and key_2 can be clearly distinguished. That is, the histograms indicate that an adversary can distinguish whether modExp is using key_1 or key_2 via a timing side channel. When modExp is using cross-copying, we can observe that the distributions are scarcely overlapping each other. On the other

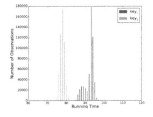

Fig. 6. BASELINE

---

[4] We also considered keys with other Hamming weights than 5 and 25, but this is outside the scope of this article.

hand, when modExp is using conditional assignment, the distributions are nearly overlapping. These results give us a first hint that cross-copying is not as effective as conditional assignment in a setting with JIT enabled.

Our results are quantified in terms of the channel capacity for the baseline, and both static transformations. For the transformations, we also consider the capacity reduction achieved by the techniques. We quantify both the mean channel capacity across our experimental samples (with 95% confidence intervals), and the worst-case capacity we have observed in the samples. We can observe that cross-copying and conditional assignment clearly differ on how much they can reduce the side-channel vulnerability in modExp. While cross-copying can only reduce the channel capacity by roughly 4.5% for the mean case, conditional assignment achieves a reduction of almost 90%. For the worst-case we observed in our experimental samples, cross-copying can only reduce the capacity by 2.35%, while conditional assignment achieves roughly 73% of reduction. These results substantiate those illustrated in Fig. 5, where e.g. the timing distributions of key_1 and key_2 are scarcely overlapping when cross-copying is applied to modExp.

scenario	channel capacity		reduction	
	mean	worst-case	mean	worst-case
baseline	0.9546±0.0042	0.9997	-	-
CC	0.9119±0.0042	0.9762	4.48%	2.35%
CA	0.1209±0.0065	0.2698	87.33%	73.01%

Fig. 7. Estimated capacity of timing side channels after static transformations

Our results indicate that the impact of the non-deterministic timing behavior introduced by JIT is substantial on cross-copying. In a setting with JIT disabled, as shown in [14], cross-copying is able to reduce the side-channel vulnerability in modExp by 96%. On the other hand, the impact of non-deterministic timing behavior on conditional assignment is clearly observable (the results of [14] have shown a reduction of 99.88% in a setting without JIT), but conditional assignment still seems to be quite effective in systems with non-deterministic timing behavior. While some impact of non-deterministic timing behavior on the effectiveness of static transformations are to be expected, we were surprised by the extent of the impact on cross-copying. Our investigations on the implementation of cross-copying have shown that indeed the mitigated branches look the same, also on the bytecode level. Possible explanations for the poor reduction achieved by cross-copying include factors like branch prediction, garbage collection, or system load. However, most of these factors apply also to conditional assignment, making it hard to find possible reasons for the difference in the achieved reductions. The conditional assignment technique completely eliminates conditionals by relying on bitmasks. Cross-copying, on the other hand, still includes conditionals in the mitigation – but they are designed to take the same execution time for each branch. We believe that this difference might be a key factor for the difference between both techniques.

5.3 Dynamic Transformations

With regard to dynamic transformations, our goal is to investigate the impact of non-deterministic timing behavior on different implementations of bucketing and predictive timing mitigation at the application level. To this end, we quantify the effectiveness of such transformations in terms of channel capacity.

Instantiation of Transformations. Following [4], we conduct experiments using bucketing in isolation. By isolation, we refer to an instantiation of a 1-bucketing. We set the same bucket size for both $keys_1$ and key_2. Note that this bucket size is greater than the expected worst case running time for either key. Events with running time greater than this bucket size are classified as outliers and, thus, they are released directly by the mechanism. The nature of the implementations of bucketing and predictive timing mitigation is different (as explained in Sect. 4.2), but in order to enable a comparison between such implementations, we instantiated predictive timing mitigation as follows. We set the initial quantum to the same value as the bucket size. In order to avoid effects of penalization, we choose the penalty function that directly releases events that are not arriving on time (classified as outliers), and stay within the same epoch without adapting the schedule.

We consider scenarios where modExp is using bucketing and predictive timing mitigation. We use subscripts to refer to when e.g., bucketing is manually

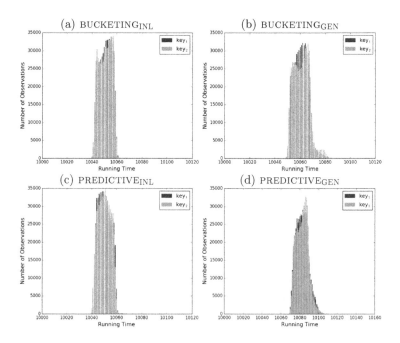

Fig. 8. Timing distributions of modExp after applying dynamic transformations

inlined into modExp (BUCKETING$_{INL}$) and implemented using a generic framework (BUCKETING$_{GEN}$). The histograms of such scenarios are depicted in Fig. 8. The histogram of the BASELINE is the same illustrated in Fig. 6. The overall results regarding the effectiveness of bucketing and predictive timing mitigation are described in Fig. 9.

The histograms of bucketing (Figs. 8a and b) and predictive timing mitigation (Figs. 8c and d) indicate there are no substantial difference between the timing distributions of key$_1$ and key$_2$. That is, their distributions are mostly overlapping. These results suggest successful mitigation of the timing side-channel vulnerability observed in Fig. 6.

Our experimental results are quantified in terms of channel capacity in Fig. 9. We quantify both the mean channel capacity across our experimental samples (with 95% confidence intervals), and the worst-case capacity we have observed in the samples. Our results show that both bucketing and predictive timing mitigation achieve a very high reduction regarding the side-channel vulnerability in modExp, regardless of the mean or worst-case results. One important observation is that there is a slight difference in the effectiveness of bucketing and predictive timing mitigation when implemented inlined and using a generic mechanism. For instance, considering the worst-case reduction, BUCKETING$_{INL}$ and PREDICTIVE$_{INL}$ can, respectively, reduce the channel capacity by roughly 95% and 94%, while BUCKETING$_{GEN}$ and PREDICTIVE$_{GEN}$ can, respectively, reduce the channel capacity by 91% and 92%.

scenario	channel capacity		reduction	
	mean	worst-case	mean	worst-case
baseline	0.9546±0.0042	0.9997	-	-
bucketing$_{INL}$	0.0137±0.0010	0.0484	98.56%	95.16%
bucketing$_{GEN}$	0.0354±0.0022	0.0891	96.29%	91.09%
predictive$_{INL}$	0.0117±0.0010	0.0626	98.77%	93.74%
predictive$_{GEN}$	0.0260±0.0017	0.0798	97.28%	92.02%

Fig. 9. Estimated capacity of timing side channels after dynamic transformations

Our experimental results reflect the fact that generic mechanisms can (although slightly) reduce the effectiveness of mitigation techniques. However, it is not clear to us whether BUCKETING$_{GEN}$ or PREDICTIVE$_{GEN}$ leak any additional information related to the secret key. This difference can happen due to additional overhead (e.g., communication between internal components) caused by generic mechanisms. Clarifying whether such information is related to the secret key appears to be an interesting direction for future work.

Regarding the results achieved by bucketing and predictive timing mitigation, we are not surprised by their similarities. Both transformations delay sensitive program events up to well-defined points in time. Furthermore, we instantiated predictive timing mitigation in a comparable fashion with bucketing.

Overall, our results show that both predictive timing mitigation and bucketing are effective in systems with non-deterministic timing behavior. On the other hand, our results also show that neither predictive timing mitigation nor bucketing (confirming the results from [4]) are able to completely close the timing side channel. Possible explanations for these results are activities in the CPU, e.g., system load, that can cause a latency in the response time of programs [4].

5.4   Comparison Between Static and Dynamic Transformations

This section summarizes our answer to the following research question: *'How do static and dynamic transformations compare to each other in terms of reduction of side-channel leakage?'*. In this section, we consider the worst-case reduction observed in our experiments. The summary of our results are given in Fig. 10. The blue bars illustrate cross-copying and conditional assignment as static transformations, and the green bars illustrate both implementation strategies for bucketing and predictive timing mitigation as dynamic transformations.

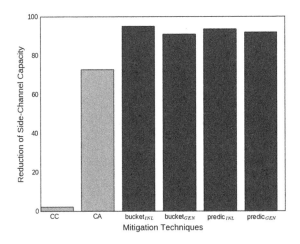

Fig. 10. Overall comparison between static and dynamic transformations

The first important observation is that all transformations are affected by our setting with non-deterministic timing behavior. In a system with deterministic timing behavior, each given input would always lead to the same timing observation. In such systems, all transformations investigated in this article are able to reduce the side-channel capacity by 100%. Our experimental results indicate that this is not true for systems with non-deterministic timing behavior, since neither transformation is able to reduce the side-channel capacity by that factor.

The second important observation is that the impact of non-deterministic timing is much more substantial on static than dynamic transformations. The dynamic transformations – bucketing and predictive timing mitigation – performed well in reducing the side-channel vulnerability in modExp. Regardless of the implementation strategy, both transformations performed well comparably by achieving reductions higher than 90%. In contrast, the static transformations – conditional assignment and cross-copying – performed worse in comparison.

Regarding cross-copying, the impact is substantial. Our experiments suggest that cross-copying can poorly reduce the channel capacity by 2.35%. This result is a huge drawback in comparison to the other transformations. Furthermore, in comparison to [14], which investigated cross-copying in a scenario with JIT disabled, the effectiveness of cross-copying falls from 96% to 2.35%. The impact is lower on conditional assignment, but still observable. Our experiments suggest that conditional assignment can reduce the channel capacity by 73%. This result is, however, a drawback in comparison to the results from [14]. That is, with JIT enabled, the effectiveness of conditional assignment falls from 99.88% to 73%.

In summary, our experimental results suggest that dynamic transformations are more effective than static transformations in our setting with JIT enabled.

6   Related Work

Mantel and Starostin [14] have investigated the trade-off between security and overhead of four well-known static transformations, namely cross-copying, conditional assignment, transactional branching, and unification. Their experimental results showed that such transformations differ w.r.t how much security and overhead they add to the program. Our work differs from [14] in how we evaluate static transformations. In [14], all experiments were conducted in a simplified Java environment (with JIT disabled). In contrast, we evaluate the impact of the non-deterministic timing behavior introduced by JIT on conditional assignment and cross-copying, showing that this impact is indeed substantial. Evaluating other techniques (like e.g., unification) in this setting are left for future work.

The effectiveness of dynamic transformation techniques has been evaluated from different perspectives. Bucketing has been originally presented for systems with deterministic timing behavior [10]. Subsequent studies of bucketing have established an algorithm for optimal bucket placement strategies in the tradeoff between security and performance [5]. The original work on bucketing included an information-theoretical upper bound on the leakage of the mitigation that is based on the number of distinct timing observations that an adversary can get, and the number of experiments the adversary obtains. Tighter bounds for this leakage have been presented (e.g., [12,18]). All of these bounds, however, assume that events can be released sharply at the bucketing boundaries.

Dantas et al. [4] have investigated the impact of non-deterministic timing behavior on bucketing. To this end, they provided two implementations of bucketing that reside at the application level and kernel level. Experimental results indicated that their implementations are not able to release events sharply at the bucket boundary. This led to a large number of observations that an adversary can gather via a timing side channel, and thus to a very high amount of information leakage predicted by the theoretical leakage bounds. Their experimental results also provided the first evidence that the choice of system layer where bucketing is placed can have a direct effect on the provided security by bucketing. That is, their experimental results indicated that bucketing implemented at the application level provides more security (w.r.t. leakage bounds and channel capacity) to Java programs than bucketing implemented at the kernel level. Our work builds on top of [4], providing an empirical investigation of two implementation strategies for bucketing at the application level.

The technique of predictive timing mitigation has been presented in [19] as a generalization of predictive black-box mitigation [2]. In [19], Zhang et al. leverage the black-box mitigation model to web applications. More concretely, they developed a server-side wrapper to mitigate timing leaks from web applications. The predictive black-box model assumes that it can precisely control when events are released by the model. As for bucketing, this assumption does not necessarily hold in systems with non-deterministic timing behavior. Our work empirically investigates predictive timing mitigation for non-deterministic timing behavior to enable a empirical evaluation with bucketing and static transformations.

7   Conclusion

We presented a comparative study on the effectiveness of static and dynamic transformations in a realistic setting with non-deterministic timing behavior. Our results are particularly interesting in three aspects: (1) We show that such transformations differ on how much they can reduce the timing side-channel capacity. (2) We show that the impact of non-deterministic timing behavior is substantial on static transformations, especially on cross-copying. (3) We show that dynamic transformations manually inlined into the target program are more effective (although slightly) than implementations using generic mechanisms.

An interesting direction for future work is a comparative study on the performance overhead caused by static and dynamic transformations. In particular, it could be interested to investigate the applicability of such transformations in resources-constrained settings like e.g., IoT devices.

Acknowledgments. This work was supported by the German Federal Ministry of Education and Research (BMBF) as well as by the Hessen State Ministry for Higher Education, Research and the Arts (HMWK) within CRISP. This work has been co-funded by the DFG as part of the project Secure Refinement of Cryptographic Algorithms (E3) within the CRC 1119 CROSSING.

References

1. Agat, J.: Transforming out timing leaks. In: POPL 2000, pp. 40–53 (2000)
2. Askarov, A., Zhang, D., Myers, A.C.: Predictive black-box mitigation of timing channels. In: CCS 2010, pp. 297–307 (2010)
3. Chothia, T., Kawamoto, Y., Novakovic, C.: A tool for estimating information leakage. In: Sharygina, N., Veith, H. (eds.) CAV 2013. LNCS, vol. 8044, pp. 690–695. Springer, Heidelberg (2013). https://doi.org/10.1007/978-3-642-39799-8_47

4. Dantas, Y.G., Gay, R., Hamann, T., Mantel, H., Schickel, J.: An evaluation of bucketing in systems with non-deterministic timing behavior. In: Janczewski, L.J., Kutyłowski, M. (eds.) SEC 2018. IAICT, vol. 529, pp. 323–338. Springer, Cham (2018). https://doi.org/10.1007/978-3-319-99828-2_23

5. Doychev, G., Köpf, B.: Rational protection against timing attacks. In: CSF 2015, pp. 526–536 (2015)

6. Gay, R., Hu, J., Mantel, H.: CliSeAu: securing distributed java programs by cooperative dynamic enforcement. In: Prakash, A., Shyamasundar, R. (eds.) ICISS 2014. LNCS, vol. 8880, pp. 378–398. Springer, Cham (2014). https://doi.org/10.1007/978-3-319-13841-1_21

7. Georges, A., Buytaert, D., Eeckhout, L.: Statistically rigorous java performance evaluation. In: OOPSLA 2007, pp. 57–76 (2007)

8. İnci, M.S., Gulmezoglu, B., Irazoqui, G., Eisenbarth, T., Sunar, B.: Cache attacks enable bulk key recovery on the cloud. In: Gierlichs, B., Poschmann, A.Y. (eds.) CHES 2016. LNCS, vol. 9813, pp. 368–388. Springer, Heidelberg (2016). https://doi.org/10.1007/978-3-662-53140-2_18

9. Kocher, P.C.: Timing attacks on implementations of Diffie-Hellman, RSA, DSS, and other systems. In: Koblitz, N. (ed.) CRYPTO 1996. LNCS, vol. 1109, pp. 104–113. Springer, Heidelberg (1996). https://doi.org/10.1007/3-540-68697-5_9

10. Köpf, B., Dürmuth, M.: A provably secure and efficient countermeasure against timing attacks. In: CSF 2009, pp. 324–335 (2009)

11. Köpf, B., Mantel, H.: Transformational typing and unification for automatically correcting insecure programs. Int. J. Inf. Secur. 6(2–3), 107–131 (2007)

12. Köpf, B., Smith, G.: Vulnerability bounds and leakage resilience of blinded cryptography under timing attacks. In: CSF 2010, pp. 44–56. IEEE (2010)

13. Mantel, H., Schickel, J., Weber, A., Weber, F.: How secure is green IT? The case of software-based energy side channels. In: Lopez, J., Zhou, J., Soriano, M. (eds.) ESORICS 2018. LNCS, vol. 11098, pp. 218–239. Springer, Cham (2018). https://doi.org/10.1007/978-3-319-99073-6_11

14. Mantel, H., Starostin, A.: Transforming out timing leaks, more or less. In: Pernul, G., Ryan, P.Y.A., Weippl, E. (eds.) ESORICS 2015. LNCS, vol. 9326, pp. 447–467. Springer, Cham (2015). https://doi.org/10.1007/978-3-319-24174-6_23

15. Millen, J.K.: Covert channel capacity. In: S&P 1987, pp. 60–66 (1987)

16. Molnar, D., Piotrowski, M., Schultz, D., Wagner, D.: The program counter security model: automatic detection and removal of control-flow side channel attacks. In: Won, D.H., Kim, S. (eds.) ICISC 2005. LNCS, vol. 3935, pp. 156–168. Springer, Heidelberg (2006). https://doi.org/10.1007/11734727_14

17. Shannon, C.E.: A mathematical theory of communication. In: ACM SIGMOBILE MC2R 2001, vol. 5 (1), pp. 3–55 (2001)

18. Smith, D.M., Smith, G.: Tight bounds on information leakage from repeated independent runs. In: CSF 2017, pp. 318–327 (2017)

19. Zhang, D., Askarov, A., Myers, A.C.: Predictive mitigation of timing channels in interactive systems. In: CCS 2011, pp. 563–574 (2011)

Cryptography

Card-Based Cryptographic Protocols with the Minimum Number of Cards Using Private Operations

Hibiki Ono and Yoshifumi Manabe[(✉)]

Kogakuin University, Shinjuku, Tokyo 163-8677, Japan
manabe@cc.kogakuin.ac.jp

Abstract. This paper proposes new card-based cryptographic protocols with the minimum number of cards using private operations under the semi-honest model. Though various card-based cryptographic protocols were shown, the minimum number of cards used in the protocol has not been achieved yet for many problems. Operations executed by a player where the other players cannot see are called private operations. Private operations have been introduced in some protocols to solve a particular problem or to input private values. However, the effectiveness of introducing private operations to the calculation of general logic functions has not been considered. This paper introduces three new private operations: private random bisection cuts, private reverse cuts, and private reveals. With these three new operations, we show that all of logical and, logical xor, and copy protocols are achieved with the minimum number of cards by simple three round protocols. This paper, then shows a protocol to calculate any logical functions using these private operations.

Keywords: Multi-party secure computation ·
Card-based cryptographic protocols · Private operations ·
Logical computations · Copy

1 Introduction

Card-based cryptographic protocols [9,17] have been proposed in which physical cards are used instead of computers to securely calculate values. den Boer [2] first showed a five card protocol to securely calculate logical AND of two inputs. Since then, many protocols have been proposed to calculate logical functions [3,4,14,16,18,21,27,29] and specific computations such as computations on three inputs [23,24], millionaires' problem [20,26], voting [15,19], random permutation [6,7], grouping [5], matching [13] and so on.

Private randomization is the most important primitive in these card-based protocols. Many recent protocols use random bisection cuts [18], which randomly execute swapping two decks of cards or not swapping. If the random value used in the randomization is disclosed, the secret input value is known to the players.

© Springer Nature Switzerland AG 2019
N. Zincir-Heywood et al. (Eds.): FPS 2018, LNCS 11358, pp. 193–207, 2019.
https://doi.org/10.1007/978-3-030-18419-3_13

There are two types of randomization: single player randomization and multiple player randomization. For the single player randomization, the player must not know the random value he selected. Ueda et al. [30] proposed several methods that can be done in front of people, but no one can know the random value. However, if a person privately brings a high-speed video camera, he might able to know the random value by analyzing the image. Currently, the size of high-speed video cameras is too large to privately bring without getting caught, but the size might become smaller in a near future. In the case, the randomization in a public place becomes difficult. By introducing additional cards, a random bisection cut can be executed using a random cut [30]. Koch and Walzer [10] proposed a protocol for a player to execute a private permutation that is unknown to the other players, but the player can prove that he really executed an allowed permutation. The protocol can be executed in a public place, but it needs additional special cards.

A simple solution to execute a private randomization is a multiple player randomization, in which some operations are executed in a hidden place. In order to execute a private random bisection cut, Alice executes a random bisection cut in a place where Bob cannot see (under the table, or in the back, etc.). Then, Bob executes a random bisection cut in a place where Alice cannot see. The result is unknown to either player. Note that the number of players can be arbitrarily increased. In order to know the random value, a person needs to know all of the values the players used. Such an operation that is done where the other players cannot see is called a private operation. So we have a natural question: if we introduce some private operations other than the random bisection cut, can we have effective card-based cryptographic protocols to calculate logical functions?

Private operations have been first introduced to solve millionaires' problem [20, 26]. The private operations used in the papers are similar to the primitives proposed in this paper, but the operations were embedded into the millionaires' protocol, thus it is not clear that the primitives can be used to the other protocols. Then private operations were used to calculate logical functions [12, 28]. These papers discussed a private operation that sets each player's private inputs. Though the number of cards used in these protocols is less than the ones in the conventional protocols, these protocols cannot be used for general cases when the players do not know the inputs, that is, the inputs are given as committed values. Protocols with committed inputs can also be used for the cases when each player knows his input values by setting his private inputs as committed values. Thus protocols that accept committed inputs are desirable. Another desirable property is committed output. If the output is given as a committed value, further private calculation can be done using the output value.

This paper considers card-based protocols with committed inputs and committed outputs using private operations under the semi-honest model. This paper introduces three private operations: private random bisection cuts, private reverse cuts, and private reveals. This paper shows protocols which execute logical and, logical xor, and copy with four cards, which is the minimum. We also show protocols that calculate any logical functions.

As for the number of cards used for copy protocols, 6 was the minimum for finite-runtime copy [18], as shown in Table 1. The protocol in [25] uses 5 cards, but the number of steps of the protocol is unbounded. It is proved to be impossible to achieve copy with 4 cards by the conventional model without private operations [8]. In their model, each card sequence has a probability to occur. Using the probabilities, players are prohibited to open a card that reveals secret information. Such arguments lead to the impossibility results. On the other hand, if private operations are executed, one card sequence can have two different probabilities: the one Alice knows and the other one Bob knows. Bob is allowed to privately open a card that does not reveal secret information to Bob.

The numbers of cards in committed-input, committed-output AND protocols are shown in Table 2. The protocol in [18] uses 6 cards. Though the protocol in [11] uses 4 cards, the protocol uses a non-uniform shuffle, which obtains one result by the probability of $1/3$ and the other result by the probability of $2/3$. Such a non-uniform shuffle is difficult to achieve without some special tools. Another four-card protocol with uniform shuffles [27] does not terminate within a finite time. It is proved to be impossible to achieve finite-runtime AND with 4 cards by the conventional model without private operations [8]. Our protocol uses 4 cards, which is the minimum, and it is easy to execute.

The number of cards in XOR protocols is shown in Table 3. Though the number of cards is the same in our protocol and [18], an input preserving (shown in Sect. 4.7) can be realized by our protocol without additional cards.

2   Preliminaries

This section gives the notation and basic definitions of card-based protocols. This paper is based on two type card model. In the model, there are two kinds of marks, ♣ and ♥. Cards of the same marks cannot be distinguished. In addition, the back of both types of cards is ?. It is impossible to determine the mark in the back of a given card with ?. One bit of data is represented by two cards as follows: ♣♥ $=0$ and ♥♣ $=1$. One pair of cards that represents one bit $x \in \{0,1\}$, whose face is down, is called a commitment of x, and denoted as $commit(x)$. It is written as $\underbrace{\boxed{?}\,\boxed{?}}_{x}$. Note that when these two cards are swapped, $commit(\bar{x})$ can be obtained. Thus, NOT can be calculated without private operations.

A linearly ordered cards are called a sequence of cards. A sequence of cards S whose length is n is denoted as $S = s_1, s_2, \ldots, s_n$, where s_i is the i-th card of the sequence. $S = \underbrace{\boxed{?}}_{s_1}\underbrace{\boxed{?}}_{s_2}\underbrace{\boxed{?}}_{s_3}\ldots,\underbrace{\boxed{?}}_{s_n}$. A sequence whose length is even is called an even sequence. $S_1 || S_2$ is a concatenation of sequence S_1 and S_2.

All protocols are executed by multiple players. Throughout of this paper, all players are semi-honest, that is, they obey the rule of the protocols, but try to obtain information x of $commit(x)$. There is no collusion among players executing one protocol together. No player wants any other player to obtain information of committed values.

3 Private Operations

We introduce three private operations: private random bisection cuts, private reverse cuts, and private reveals.

Primitive 1 *(Private random bisection cut). A private random bisection cut is the following operation on an even sequence $S_0 = s_1, s_2, \ldots, s_{2m}$. Alice selects a random bit $b \in \{0, 1\}$ and outputs*

$$S_1 = \begin{cases} S_0 & \text{if } b = 0 \\ s_{m+1}, s_{m+2}, \ldots, s_{2m}, s_1, s_2, \ldots, s_m & \text{if } b = 1 \end{cases}$$

Alice executes this operation in a place where Bob cannot see. Alice does not disclose the bit b.   □

Note that the protocols in this paper use the operation only when $m = 1$ and $S_0 = commit(x)$. Given $S_0 = \underbrace{\boxed{?}\boxed{?}}_{x}$, Alice's output $S_1 = \underbrace{\boxed{?}\boxed{?}}_{x \oplus b}$, which is $\underbrace{\boxed{?}\boxed{?}}_{x}$

or $\underbrace{\boxed{?}\boxed{?}}_{\bar{x}}$.

Note that a private random bisection cut is exactly the same as the random bisection cut [18], but the operation is done in a hidden place.

Primitive 2 *(Private reverse cut, Private reverse selection). A private reverse cut is the following operation on an even sequence $S_2 = s_1, s_2, \ldots, s_{2m}$ and the bit $b \in \{0, 1\}$, which is selected by Alice during a private random bisection cut. Alice outputs*

$$S_3 = \begin{cases} S_2 & \text{if } b = 0 \\ s_{m+1}, s_{m+2}, \ldots, s_{2m}, s_1, s_2, \ldots, s_m & \text{if } b = 1 \end{cases}$$

Alice executes this operation in a place where Bob cannot see. b is the secret value that only Alice knows. Alice does not disclose b.

Note that in many protocols below, the left m cards are selected after a private reverse cut. The sequence of these two operations is called a private reverse selection. A private reverse selection is the following procedure on an even sequence $S_2 = s_1, s_2, \ldots, s_{2m}$ and the bit $b \in \{0, 1\}$, which is selected by Alice during the private random bisection cut. Alice's output

$$S_3 = \begin{cases} s_1, s_2, \ldots s_m & \text{if } b = 0 \\ s_{m+1}, s_{m+2}, \ldots, s_{2m} & \text{if } b = 1 \end{cases} \qquad \qquad □$$

Next, we define a private reveal. Consider the case Alice executes a private random bisection cut on $commit(x)$. A private reveal, executed by Bob, is as follows.

Primitive 3 *(Private reveal). Bob privately opens a given committed bit. Since the committed bit is randomized by the bit b selected by Alice, the opened bit is $x \oplus b$.* □

Using the obtained value, Bob privately sets a sequence of cards.

Even if Bob privately opens the cards, Bob obtains no information about x if b is randomly selected and not disclosed by Alice. Bob must not disclose the obtained value. If Bob discloses the obtained value to Alice, Alice knows the value of the committed bit.

Card-based protocols are evaluated by the following criteria.

- The number of cards used in the protocol.
- The number of operations executed in the protocol.
- The number of communications: the number of times when cards are handed between players.

4 New Copy, Logical AND, and Logical XOR Protocols

Using the private random bisection cuts, private reveals, and private reverse cuts, COPY protocol, AND protocol, and XOR protocol with committed inputs and committed outputs can be realized with the minimum number of cards. All of these protocols are executed between two players, Alice and Bob. In Sect. 5, the number of players is increased in order to improve security.

4.1 COPY Protocol

Protocol 1 *(COPY protocol).*
Input: $commit(x)$. Output: m copies of $commit(x)$.

1. *Alice executes a private random bisection cut on $commit(x)$. Let the output be $commit(x')$. Note that $x' = x \oplus b$. Alice hands $commit(x')$ to Bob.*
2. *Bob executes a private reveal on $commit(x')$ and obtains x'. Bob makes m copies of x'. Bob faces down these cards. Bob hands these cards, m copies of $commit(x')$, to Alice.*
3. *Alice executes a private reverse cut to each copy of $commit(x')$ using the bit b Alice generated in the private random bisection cut. Alice outputs these copies.* □

The protocol is three rounds. The number of communications between players is two.

Theorem 1. *The COPY protocol is correct and secure. It uses the minimum number of cards.*

(Proof) Correctness: If $b = 0$, Bob sees x and makes m copies of x. Alice does nothing at the private reverse cut, thus m copies of x are obtained. If $b = 1$, Bob sees $\bar{x}$ and makes m copies of $\bar{x}$. Alice swaps each copy of $\bar{x}$, thus m copies of x are obtained.

Alice's security: Alice sees no opened cards, thus Alice obtains no information about x.

Bob's security: When Bob privately opens $commit(x')$, $x' = x \oplus b$, thus Bob obtains no information about x if b is randomly selected and not disclosed.

The number of cards: In order to obtain m copies of a commitment, at least $2m$ cards are necessary. The protocol is executed with $2m$ cards, thus the number of cards is the minimum.   □

Comparison of COPY protocols (when $m = 2$) is shown in Table 1. This protocol is the first protocol that achieves the minimum number of cards.

Table 1. Comparison of COPY protocols

Article	# of cards	Note
[3]	8	
[18]	6	
[25]	5	Number of steps is not bounded
This paper	4	Use private operations

4.2   AND Protocol

Logical AND can also be executed with the minimum number of cards.

Protocol 2 *(AND protocol).*
Input: commit(x) and commit(y). Output: commit(x ∧ y).

1. *Alice executes a private random bisection cut on commit(x). Let the output be commit(x'). Alice hands commit(x') and commit(y) to Bob.*
2. *Bob executes a private reveal on commit(x'). Bob sets*

$$S_2 = \begin{cases} commit(y)||commit(0) \text{ if } x' = 1 \\ commit(0)||commit(y) \text{ if } x' = 0 \end{cases}$$

   and hands S_2 to Alice.
3. *Alice executes a private reverse selection on S_2 using the bit b generated in the private random bisection cut. Let the obtained sequence be S_3. Alice outputs S_3.*   □

Note that the two cards that were not selected by Alice at the last step of the protocol, must be discarded. Since the unused cards have some information on x and y, information about input values are leaked if the cards are opened. The protocol is three rounds. The number of communications between players is two.

Theorem 2. *The AND protocol is correct and secure. It uses the minimum number of cards.*

(Proof) Correctness: The desired output can be represented as follows.

$$x \wedge y = \begin{cases} y \text{ if } x = 1 \\ 0 \text{ if } x = 0 \end{cases}$$

When Bob obtains $x' = 1$, $commit(y)||commit(0)$ is given to Alice. When Bob obtains $x' = 0$, $commit(0)||commit(y)$ is given to Alice. Thus Alice's output is $commit(y)$ if $(x', b) = (1, 0)$ or $(0, 1)$. Since $x' = x \oplus b$, these cases equal to $x = 1$.

Alice's output is $commit(0)$ if $(x', b) = (1, 1)$ or $(0, 0)$. Since $x' = x \oplus b$, these cases equal to $x = 0$. Therefore, the output is correct.

Alice and Bob's security: The same as the COPY protocol.

The number of cards: Any committed-input protocol needs at least four cards to input $commit(x)$ and $commit(y)$. When Bob sets S_2, the cards used for $commit(x')$ can be used to set $commit(0)$. Thus, the total number of cards is four and the minimum. □

A careful discussion is necessary when a player knows the value x of given $commit(x)$, for example, x is the player's private input value.

First, consider the case when Bob knows x. When Bob executes a private reveal on $commit(x \oplus b)$, Bob knows the bit b Alice selected. This scenario is not a security problem. Bob knows b, thus he knows whether the final output is $commit(0)$ or $commit(y)$ in advance. However, since

$$x \wedge y = \begin{cases} y \text{ if } x = 1 \\ 0 \text{ if } x = 0 \end{cases}$$

it is not new information for Bob who already knows x.

Note that if $x = 0$ and Bob wants to know y, Bob can replace $commit(y)$ with two new cards (that Bob hidden in his pocket), and sends $commit(0)||commit(0)$ to Alice. The result is still correct and Bob can privately open $commit(y)$ afterwards. In order to prevent this type of attack, marking currently using cards or a watch person (discussed in Sect. 5) is necessary.

Next, consider the case when Alice knows x. Alice knows $x' = x \oplus b$. Thus Alice knows whether the final output is $commit(0)$ or $commit(y)$ in advance, but it is not new information for Alice. Note that if $x = 0$ and Alice wants to know y, Alice can replace $commit(y)$ with two new cards during the execution. Prevention of this type of attack is just the same as the one for the case of Bob.

A similar discussion can be done for the other protocols shown in this paper.

A comparison of AND protocols is shown in Table 2. Though Koch et al. [11] showed a finite step protocol with the minimum number of cards, their protocol must use a non-uniform shuffle, which is not easy to realize.

Table 2. Comparison of AND protocols

Article	# of cards	Input	Output	Note
[2]	5	commit	non-commit	
[3]	10	commit	commit	Four color cards
[21]	12	commit	commit	
[29]	8	commit	commit	
[18]	6	commit	commit	
[1]	5	commit	commit	Number of steps is not bounded
[11]	4	commit	commit	Non-uniform shuffle
[27]	4	commit	commit	Number of steps is not bounded
[16]	4	commit	non-commit	
[28]	3	non-commit	non-commit	Use private operations
[12]	4	non-commit	commit	Use private operations
This paper	4	commit	commit	Use private operations

4.3 XOR Protocol

Protocol 3 *(XOR protocol).*
Input: commit(x) and commit(y). Output: commit(x ⊕ y).

1. *Alice executes a private random bisection cut on commit(x). Let the output be commit(x′). Alice hands commit(x′) and commit(y) to Bob.*
2. *Bob executes a private reveal on commit(x′). Bob sets*

$$S_2 = \begin{cases} commit(\bar{y}) \text{ if } x' = 1 \\ commit(y) \text{ if } x' = 0 \end{cases}$$

   and hands S_2 to Alice. Note that commit($\bar{y}$) can be obtained by swapping the two cards of commit(y).
3. *Alice executes a private reverse cut on S_2 using the bit b generated in the private random bisection cut. Let the obtained sequence be S_3. Alice outputs S_3.*   □

The protocol is three rounds. The number of communications between players is two.

Theorem 3. *The XOR protocol is correct and secure. It uses the minimum number of cards.*

(Proof) Correctness: The desired output can be represented as follows.

$$x \oplus y = \begin{cases} \bar{y} \text{ if } x = 1 \\ y \text{ if } x = 0 \end{cases}$$

When $x' = 1$, $commit(\bar{y})$ is given to Alice. When $x' = 0$, $commit(y)$ is given to Alice. Thus, Alice's output is $commit(\bar{y})$ if $(x', b) = (1, 0)$ or $(0, 1)$. Since $x' = x \oplus b$, these cases equal to $x = 1$.

Alice's output is $commit(y)$ if $(x', b) = (1, 1)$ or $(0, 0)$. Since $x' = x \oplus b$, these cases equal to $x = 0$. Therefore, the output is correct.

Alice and Bob's security: The same as the COPY protocol.

The number of cards: At least four cards are necessary for any protocol to input $commit(x)$ and $commit(y)$. This protocol uses no additional cards other than the input cards. □

A comparison of XOR protocols is shown in Table 3. Though the minimum number of cards is already realized by [18]. an input preserving (shown in Sect. 4.7) can be realized without additional cards.

Table 3. Comparison of XOR protocols

Article	# of cards	Input	Output	Note
[3]	14	commit	commit	Four color cards
[18]	4	commit	commit	
[28]	2	non-commit	commit	
[12]	2	non-commit	commit	
This paper	4	commit	commit	Use private operation
				Preserving an input is possible

4.4 Any Logical Functions

Though this paper shows AND and XOR, any two-variable logical functions can also be calculated by a similar protocol.

Theorem 4. *Any two-variable logical function can be securely calculated in three rounds and four cards.*

(Proof) Any two-variable logical function $f(x, y)$ can be written as

$$f(x, y) = \begin{cases} f(1, y) \text{ if } x = 1 \\ f(0, y) \text{ if } x = 0 \end{cases}$$

where $f(1, y)$ and $f(0, y)$ are y, $\bar{y}$, 0, or 1.

First, consider the case when both of $f(1, y)$ and $f(0, y)$ are 0 or 1. $(f(1, y), f(0, y)) = (0, 0)$ (or $(1, 1)$) means that $f(x, y) = 0$ (or $f(x, y) = 1$), thus we do not need to calculate f. $(f(1, y), f(0, y)) = (1, 0)$ (or $(0, 1)$) means the $f(x, y) = x$ (or $f(x, y) = \bar{x}$), thus we do not need to calculate f by a two player protocol.

Next, consider the case when both of $(f(1, y), f(0, y))$ are y (or $\bar{y}$). This case is when $f(x, y) = y$ (or $f(x, y) = \bar{y}$), thus we do not need to calculate f by a two player protocol.

The next case is when $(f(1, y), f(0, y))$ is $(y, \bar{y})$ or $(\bar{y}, y)$. $(f(1, y), f(0, y))$ $= (\bar{y}, y)$ is $x \oplus y$ (XOR). $(f(1, y), f(0, y)) = (y, \bar{y})$ is $\overline{x \oplus y}$, thus this function can be calculated as follows: execute the XOR protocol and NOT is taken to the output. Thus, this function can also be calculated.

The remaining case is when one of $(f(1, y), f(0, y))$ is y or $\bar{y}$ and the other is 0 or 1. We modify the second step of AND protocol, so that Bob sets

$$S_2 = \begin{cases} commit(f(1, y)) || commit(f(0, y)) \text{ if } x' = 1 \\ commit(f(0, y)) || commit(f(1, y)) \text{ if } x' = 0 \end{cases}$$

using one $commit(y)$ and the two cards used for $commit(x')$. Then, Alice obtains $commit(f(1, y))$ if $x = 1$ and $commit(f(0, y))$ if $x = 0$ by the private reverse selection.

Thus, any two-variable logical function can be calculated.   □

In [18] without private operations, two additional cards are required to calculate any two-variable logical function.

4.5   Parallel Computations

The above two-variable logical function calculations can be executed in parallel. Consider the case when $commit(x)$ and $commit(y_i)(i = 1, 2, \ldots, n)$ are given and $commit(f_i(x, y_i))(i = 1, 2, \ldots, n)$ need to be calculated. They can be executed in parallel. Alice executes a private random bisection cut on $commit(x)$ and hands $commit(x')$ and $commit(y_i)(i = 1, 2, \ldots, n)$ to Bob. Bob sets $S_2^i(i = 1, 2, \ldots, n)$ using x', $commit(y_i)$, and f_i. Alice executes a private reverse cut or a private reverse selection on each of $S_2^i(i = 1, 2, \ldots, n)$ using the bit b selected at the private random bisection cut. By the procedure, $commit(f_i(x, y_i))(i = 1, 2, \ldots, n)$ are simultaneously obtained.

4.6   Side Effects

When we execute the AND protocol, two cards are selected by Alice at the final step. The remaining two cards are not used, but they also output some values. The unused two cards' value is

$$\begin{cases} 0 \text{ if } x = 1 \\ y \text{ if } x = 0 \end{cases}$$

thus the output is $commit(\bar{x} \wedge y)$. The cards can be used as a side effect just like the six-card AND protocol in [18].

Generally, for a function f that is calculated by AND type protocol shown in Theorem 4, the side-effect output is $commit(\bar{x} \wedge f(1, y) \oplus x \wedge f(0, y))$.

4.7   Preserving Input

In the above protocols to calculate logical functions, the input commitment values are lost. If the input is not lost, the input commitment can be used as an input to another calculation. Thus, the input preserving calculation is discussed [22].

In the XOR protocol, $commit(x')$ is no more necessary after Bob sets S_2. Thus, Bob can send back $commit(x')$ to Alice when Bob sends S_2. Then, Alice can recover $commit(x)$ using the private reverse cut. In this modified protocol, the output is $commit(x \oplus y)$ and $commit(x)$ without additional cards or rounds.

As for the AND type protocol, $commit(x')$ can be sent back to Alice and Alice can recover $commit(x)$. This modified protocol needs 6 cards in total.

An input preserving calculation without increasing the number of cards can be executed for AND type protocols just like [22]. Note that the function f satisfies that one of $(f(0, y), f(1, y))$ is y or $\bar{y}$ and the other is 0 or 1. Otherwise, we do not need to calculate f by the AND type two player protocol. At the end of the protocol, the side-effect output is $\bar{x} \wedge f(1, y) \oplus x \wedge f(0, y)$. The output $f(x, y)$ can be represented as $x \wedge f(1, y) \oplus \bar{x} \wedge f(0, y)$. Execute the above input preserving XOR protocol for these two output values so that $f(x, y)$ is recovered. The output of XOR protocol is $\bar{x} \wedge f(1, y) \oplus x \wedge f(0, y) \oplus x \wedge f(1, y) \oplus \bar{x} \wedge f(0, y) = f(1, y) \oplus f(0, y)$. Since one of $(f(0, y), f(1, y))$ is y or $\bar{y}$ and the other is 0 or 1, the output is y or $\bar{y}$ (depending on f). Thus, input y can be recovered without additional cards. Thus, input preserving can be realized by 4 cards, which is the minimum. Comparison of input preserving AND type protocols is shown in Table 4.

Table 4. Comparison of input preserving AND protocols

Article	# of cards	Input	Output	Note
[22]	6	commit	commit	
This paper	4	commit	commit	Use private operations

4.8 n-Variable Logical Functions

Since any 2-variable logical function, $\bar{x}$, and COPY can be executed, any n-variable logical function can be calculated by the combination of the above protocols.

Using the technique in [22] and above input preserving logical function calculations, any n-variable logical function can be calculated with $2n + 4$ cards as follows.

Any logical function $f(x_1, x_2, \ldots, x_n)$ can be represented as follows: $f(x_1, x_2, \ldots, x_n) = \bar{x}_1 \wedge \bar{x}_2 \wedge \cdots \bar{x}_n \wedge f(0, 0, \ldots, 0) \oplus x_1 \wedge \bar{x}_2 \wedge \cdots \bar{x}_n \wedge f(1, 0, \ldots, 0) \oplus \bar{x}_1 \wedge x_2 \wedge \cdots \bar{x}_n \wedge f(0, 1, \ldots, 0) \oplus \cdots \oplus x_1 \wedge x_2 \wedge \cdots x_n \wedge f(1, 1, \ldots, 1)$.

Since the terms with $f(i_1, i_2, \ldots, i_n) = 0$ can be removed, this function f can be written as $f = \bigoplus_{i=1}^{k} v_1^i \wedge v_2^i \wedge \cdots \wedge v_n^i$, where $v_j^i = x_j$ or $\bar{x}_j$. Let us write $T_i = v_1^i \wedge v_2^i \wedge \cdots \wedge v_n^i$. The number of terms $k(< 2^n)$ depends on f.

Protocol 4 *(Protocol for any logical function (1)).*
Input: $commit(x_i)(i = 1, 2, \ldots, n)$. Output: $commit(f(x_1, x_2, \ldots, x_n))$.
   The additional four cards (two pairs of cards) p_1 and p_2 are used as follows.
   p_1: the intermediate value to calculate f is stored.
   p_2: the intermediate value to calculate T_i is stored.
Execute the following steps for $i = 1, \ldots, k$.

1. *Copy v_1^i from the input x_1 to p_2.*
2. *For $j = 2, \ldots, n$, execute the following procedure: Apply the input-preserving AND protocol to p_2 and input x_j (If AND is taken between $\bar{x}_j$, first execute NOT to the input, then apply the AND protocol, and return the input to x_j again).*
   At the end of this step, T_i is obtained at p_2.
3. *If $i = 1$, move p_2 to p_1. If $i > 1$, apply the XOR protocol between p_1 and p_2. The result is stored to p_1.*

At the end of the protocol, $f(x_1, x_2, \ldots x_n)$ is obtained at p_1.   □

The number of additional cards in [22] is 6. Thus our protocol reduces the number of cards. The number of rounds is $O(2^n)$.

   As another implementation with a larger number of cards, we show that any n-variable logical function can be calculated by the following protocol, whose technique is similar to the one in [12]. Let f be any n-variable logical function.

Protocol 5 *(Protocol for any logical function (2)).*
Input: $commit(x_i)(i = 1, 2, \ldots, n)$. Output: $commit(f(x_1, x_2, \ldots, x_n))$.

1. *Alice executes a private random bisection cut on $commit(x_i)(i = 1, 2, \ldots, n)$. Let the output be $commit(x_i')(i = 1, 2, \ldots, n)$ Note that one random bit b_i is selected for each $x_i(i = 1, 2, \ldots, n)$. Alice hands $commit(x_i')(i = 1, 2, \ldots, n)$ to Bob.*
2. *Bob executes a private reveal on $commit(x_i')(i = 1, 2, \ldots, n)$. Bob generates 2^n commitment $S_{a_1, a_2, \ldots, a_n}(a_i \in \{0, 1\}, i = 1, 2, \ldots, n)$ as $S_{a_1, a_2, \ldots, a_n} = commit(f(a_1 \oplus x_1', a_2 \oplus x_2', \ldots, a_n \oplus x_n'))$. Bob hands these commitments to Alice.*
3. *Alice outputs $S_{b_1, b_2, \ldots, b_n}$.*   □

   Since $S_{b_1, b_2, \ldots, b_n} = commit(f(b_1 \oplus x_1', b_2 \oplus x_2', \ldots, b_n \oplus x_n')) = commit(f(x_1, x_2, \ldots, x_n))$, the output is correct. The security is the same as the COPY protocol. The protocol is three rounds. The number of communication between players is two. The number of cards is 2^{n+1}.

5   Improving Security

Although this paper assumes all players are semi-honest, some players might be malicious in real cases. It is very hard to prevent malicious actions when a player executes a private operation. One countermeasure to deal with a malicious player is setting one watch person to each player.

The watch person for Alice watches the execution by Alice and verifies that (1) Alice does not open the cards, (2) Alice really uses a random number generator (for example, coin-flipping) to select her random bit, (3) Alice honestly executes a private random bisection cut using the random bit, and (4) Alice honestly executes a private reverse cut or private reverse selection using the bit generated in (2).

The watch person for Bob watches the execution by Bob and verifies that (1) Bob does not open the cards that are not allowed and (2) Bob honestly generates the committed cards using the value Bob privately opened.

Note that the watch persons must not disclose the values they watch.

When the number of players is more than two, each player can simultaneously act as a player and a watch person. Suppose that player $P_0, P_1, \ldots, P_{n-1}(n > 2)$ execute the AND protocol together and no collusion exists. Select some random number $i(0 < i < n)$. One player is out of the room when each player executes a round of the protocol. All the other players in the room watch the execution by the current player and verifies the correctness of the current player. $P_j(j = 0, \ldots, n-2)$ executes a private random bisection cut on $commit(x)$ using random bit b_j when $P_{j+i \mod n}$ is out of the room, thus $commit(x \oplus_{j=0}^{n-2} b_j)$ is obtained. P_{n-1} executes a private reveal and sets S_2 when $P_{n-1+i \mod n}$ is out of the room. Then, $P_j(j = 0, \ldots, n-2)$ executes a private reverse cut using b_j when $P_{j+i \mod n}$ is out of the room. When all the private reverse cuts are finished, the left pair is selected as the output. In this execution, any player cannot obtain the value of the committed value because he does not have all information if no collusion exists. Note that the number of watch persons can be arbitrary changed.

6   Conclusion

This paper proposed new card-based cryptographic protocols with the minimum number of cards using private operations. Though the private operations are effective, the protocols cannot be used when a malicious player exists. How to prevent active attacks using some protocol techniques just like the zero-knowledge proofs is an open problem.

References

1. Abe, Y., Hayashi, Y., Mizuki, T., Sone, H.: Five-card and protocol in committed format using only practical shuffles. In: Proceedings of 5th ACM International Workshop on Asia Public-Key Cryptography (APKC 2018), pp. 3–8 (2018)
2. den Boer, B.: More efficient match-making and satisfiability *the five card trick*. In: Quisquater, J.-J., Vandewalle, J. (eds.) EUROCRYPT 1989. LNCS, vol. 434, pp. 208–217. Springer, Heidelberg (1990). https://doi.org/10.1007/3-540-46885-4_23
3. Crépeau, C., Kilian, J.: Discreet solitary games. In: Stinson, D.R. (ed.) CRYPTO 1993. LNCS, vol. 773, pp. 319–330. Springer, Heidelberg (1994). https://doi.org/10.1007/3-540-48329-2_27

4. Francis, D., Aljunid, S.R., Nishida, T., Hayashi, Y., Mizuki, T., Sone, H.: Necessary and sufficient numbers of cards for securely computing two-bit output functions. In: Phan, R.C.-W., Yung, M. (eds.) Mycrypt 2016. LNCS, vol. 10311, pp. 193–211. Springer, Cham (2017). https://doi.org/10.1007/978-3-319-61273-7_10

5. Hashimoto, Y., Shinagawa, K., Nuida, K., Inamura, M., Hanaoka, G.: Secure grouping protocol using a deck of cards. In: Shikata, J. (ed.) ICITS 2017. LNCS, vol. 10681, pp. 135–152. Springer, Cham (2017). https://doi.org/10.1007/978-3-319-72089-0_8

6. Ibaraki, T., Manabe, Y.: A more efficient card-based protocol for generating a random permutation without fixed points. In: Proceedings of 3rd International Conference on Mathematics and Computers in Sciences and in Industry (MCSI 2016), pp. 252–257 (2016)

7. Ishikawa, R., Chida, E., Mizuki, T.: Efficient card-based protocols for generating a hidden random permutation without fixed points. In: Calude, C.S., Dinneen, M.J. (eds.) UCNC 2015. LNCS, vol. 9252, pp. 215–226. Springer, Cham (2015). https://doi.org/10.1007/978-3-319-21819-9_16

8. Kastner, J., et al.: The Minimum number of cards in practical card-based protocols. In: Takagi, T., Peyrin, T. (eds.) ASIACRYPT 2017, Part III. LNCS, vol. 10626, pp. 126–155. Springer, Cham (2017). https://doi.org/10.1007/978-3-319-70700-6_5

9. Koch, A.: The landscape of optimal card-based protocols. IACR Cryptology ePrint Archive, Report 2018/951 (2018)

10. Koch, A., Walzer, S.: Foundations for actively secure card-based cryptography. Cryptology ePrint Archive, Report 2017/423 (2017)

11. Koch, A., Walzer, S., Härtel, K.: Card-based cryptographic protocols using a minimal number of cards. In: Iwata, T., Cheon, J.H. (eds.) ASIACRYPT 2015. LNCS, vol. 9452, pp. 783–807. Springer, Heidelberg (2015). https://doi.org/10.1007/978-3-662-48797-6_32

12. Kurosawa, K., Shinozaki, T.: Compact card protocol. In: Proceedings of SCIS 2017. pp. 1A2–6 (2017). (in Japanese)

13. Marcedone, A., Wen, Z., Shi, E.: Secure dating with four or fewer cards. IACR Cryptology ePrint Archive, Report 2015/1031 (2015)

14. Mizuki, T.: Card-based protocols for securely computing the conjunction of multiple variables. Theor. Comput. Sci. **622**, 34–44 (2016)

15. Mizuki, T., Asiedu, I.K., Sone, H.: Voting with a logarithmic number of cards. In: Mauri, G., Dennunzio, A., Manzoni, L., Porreca, A.E. (eds.) UCNC 2013. LNCS, vol. 7956, pp. 162–173. Springer, Heidelberg (2013). https://doi.org/10.1007/978-3-642-39074-6_16

16. Mizuki, T., Kumamoto, M., Sone, H.: The five-card trick can be done with four cards. In: Wang, X., Sako, K. (eds.) ASIACRYPT 2012. LNCS, vol. 7658, pp. 598–606. Springer, Heidelberg (2012). https://doi.org/10.1007/978-3-642-34961-4_36

17. Mizuki, T., Shizuya, H.: Computational model of card-based cryptographic protocols and its applications. IEICE Trans. Fundam. Electron. Commun. Comput. Sci. **100**(1), 3–11 (2017)

18. Mizuki, T., Sone, H.: Six-card secure AND and four-card secure XOR. In: Deng, X., Hopcroft, J.E., Xue, J. (eds.) FAW 2009. LNCS, vol. 5598, pp. 358–369. Springer, Heidelberg (2009). https://doi.org/10.1007/978-3-642-02270-8_36

19. Nakai, T., Shirouchi, S., Iwamoto, M., Ohta, K.: Four cards are sufficient for a card-based three-input voting protocol utilizing private permutations. In: Shikata, J. (ed.) ICITS 2017. LNCS, vol. 10681, pp. 153–165. Springer, Cham (2017). https://doi.org/10.1007/978-3-319-72089-0_9

20. Nakai, T., Tokushige, Y., Misawa, Y., Iwamoto, M., Ohta, K.: Efficient card-based cryptographic protocols for millionaires' problem utilizing private permutations. In: Foresti, S., Persiano, G. (eds.) CANS 2016. LNCS, vol. 10052, pp. 500–517. Springer, Cham (2016). https://doi.org/10.1007/978-3-319-48965-0_30

21. Niemi, V., Renvall, A.: Secure multiparty computations without computers. Theor. Comput. Sci. **191**(1), 173–183 (1998)

22. Nishida, T., Hayashi, Y., Mizuki, T., Sone, H.: Card-based protocols for any boolean function. In: Jain, R., Jain, S., Stephan, F. (eds.) TAMC 2015. LNCS, vol. 9076, pp. 110–121. Springer, Cham (2015). https://doi.org/10.1007/978-3-319-17142-5_11

23. Nishida, T., Hayashi, Y., Mizuki, T., Sone, H.: Securely computing three-input functions with eight cards. IEICE Trans. Fundam. Electron. Commun. Comput. Sci. **98**(6), 1145–1152 (2015)

24. Nishida, T., Mizuki, T., Sone, H.: Securely computing the three-input majority function with eight cards. In: Dediu, A.-H., Martín-Vide, C., Truthe, B., Vega-Rodríguez, M.A. (eds.) TPNC 2013. LNCS, vol. 8273, pp. 193–204. Springer, Heidelberg (2013). https://doi.org/10.1007/978-3-642-45008-2_16

25. Nishimura, A., Nishida, T., Hayashi, Y., Mizuki, T., Sone, H.: Card-based protocols using unequal division shuffles. Soft Comput. **22**(2), 361–371 (2018)

26. Ono, H., Manabe, Y.: Efficient card-based cryptographic protocols for the millionaires' problem using private input operations. In: Proceedings of 13th Asia Joint Conference on Information Security (AsiaJCIS 2018), pp. 23–28 (2018)

27. Ruangwises, S., Itoh, T.: And protocols using only uniform shuffles. arXiv preprint arXiv:1810.00769 (2018)

28. Shirouchi, S., Nakai, T., Iwamoto, M., Ohta, K.: Efficient card-based cryptographic protocols for logic gates utilizing private permutations. In: Proceedings of SCIS 2017, pp. 1A2–2 (2017). (in Japanese)

29. Stiglic, A.: Computations with a deck of cards. Theor. Comput. Sci. **259**(1), 671–678 (2001)

30. Ueda, I., Nishimura, A., Hayashi, Y., Mizuki, T., Sone, H.: How to implement a random bisection cut. In: Martín-Vide, C., Mizuki, T., Vega-Rodríguez, M.A. (eds.) TPNC 2016. LNCS, vol. 10071, pp. 58–69. Springer, Cham (2016). https://doi.org/10.1007/978-3-319-49001-4_5

Cryptographic Formula Obfuscation

Giovanni Di Crescenzo[(⊠)]

Perspecta Labs, Basking Ridge, NJ, USA
`gdicrescenzo@perspectalabs.com`

Abstract. Under intractability assumptions commonly used in cryptography, we show an efficient program obfuscator for large classes of programs, including any arbitrary monotone formula over statements expressed as equalities to a secret. Previously, only a handful set of individual functions were known to have such program obfuscators. This result has both theoretical and practical relevance. On the theoretical side, it significantly increases the class of functions that are known to have a cryptographically secure program obfuscator, and it shows that general-purpose program obfuscation results do exist with at least some level of generality, despite the likely impossibility, proved in [2], to achieve a related notion of obfuscation for any arbitrary polynomial-time program. On the practical side, there are many computational programs that can be expressed as monotone formulae over equality statements, and can now be securely obfuscated. Our most foundational contribution is a new type of obfuscation: protecting the privacy of the formula gates, and thus of much of the computation carried out by the program, in addition to the privacy of secrets used by the program. Previous program obfuscators only targeted the privacy of secrets used by the program.

1 Introduction

The problem of program obfuscation (i.e., turning an input program into an intelligible one) is recently attracting a significant amount of attention in the cryptography literature. While previous studies on program obfuscation did not target rigorous obfuscation guarantees, in cryptographic program obfuscation a researcher's goal is to design an obfuscator following the standard of modern cryptography; i.e., by proving that any successful de-obfuscation attack can be used to efficiently solve a seemingly hard mathematical problem.

Interestingly enough, general solutions to the cryptographic program obfuscation problem seem to have far-reaching application potential. Examples of

Supported by the Defense Advanced Research Projects Agency (DARPA) SafeWare program via U.S. Army Research Office (ARO), contract number W911NF-15-C-0233. The U.S. Government is authorized to reproduce and distribute reprints for Governmental purposes notwithstanding any copyright annotation hereon. Disclaimer: The views and conclusions contained herein are those of the authors and should not be interpreted as necessarily representing the official policies or endorsements, either expressed or implied, of DARPA, ARO or the U.S. Government.

© Springer Nature Switzerland AG 2019
N. Zincir-Heywood et al. (Eds.): FPS 2018, LNCS 11358, pp. 208–224, 2019.
https://doi.org/10.1007/978-3-030-18419-3_14

surprising theoretical implications that would be made possible from a general solution to the cryptographic program obfuscation problem include: transforming any private-key encryption scheme into a public-key encryption one, and transforming any public-key encryption scheme into a fully-homomorphic one. Moreover, there is a host of real-life applications for cryptographic program obfuscation, including digital right management, protection against intellectual property theft, protection of secrets and policies embedded in software, etc.

Unfortunately, early results in the area [2] showed a likely impossibility of constructing a general-purpose obfuscator (i.e., an obfuscator whose input program is taken within the class of all polynomial-time programs), satisfying the virtual-black-box obfuscation notion. Thus, starting with [23], researchers have focused on constructing a special-purpose obfuscator (i.e., an obfuscator whose input program is taken within a small class of polynomial-time programs, often semantically interpreted as a 'single function'), although efficient constructions for obfuscators provable under widely accepted assumptions were given only for few functions. Obfuscators for point functions with fixed secret length [1,3,8,13,23], and point functions with variable secret length [12] were shown to be efficient in [1,12,13]. Other efficient obfuscators provable under widely accepted assumptions include short-distance matching [15], proxy re-encryption [20], and encrypted signatures [19]. Other special-purpose obfuscator proved under a widely accepted assumption were shown for wildcard-based matching [6], and compute-and-compare programs [24], or under heuristic assumptions, including the random oracle assumption (see, e.g., [21]), the generic group assumption (see, e.g., [11]), and assumptions related to approximated versions of multilinear forms (see, e.g., [17]).

1.1 Our Contribution and Comparison with Previous Work

In this paper we propose two efficient special-purpose obfuscators with obfuscation provable under widely accepted assumptions, and improving the state of the art in two important directions: expressibility and obfuscation quality.

As for expressibility, we show the first paradigm for efficient program obfuscation that works for a large family of functions (although smaller than the family of all polynomial-time programs), which is encouraging in light of the impossibility results in [2]. Our obfuscators efficiently combine obfuscators of point functions into obfuscators for monotone/boolean formulae over point functions, by running only a linear (in the number of formula inputs) number of point function obfuscators.

As for obfuscation quality, our techniques additionally provide a new type of obfuscation, protecting the privacy of some computation carried out by the program rather than just the privacy of secrets used by the program. For instance, our main obfuscator hides to an attacker whether gates in the monotone or boolean formula are, say, OR gates or AND gates, while potentially leaking the formula structure, in addition to protect the secrets involved in equality statements at the bottom of the formula. Previously to our results, obfuscators only protected the privacy of one particular secret string embedded in the program.

Our obfuscators satisfy an obfuscation notion from [3], which was proved to be incomparable with the original virtual-black-box notion. Informally speaking, this notion says that an obfuscation of a specific function in its class is not efficiently distinguishable from an obfuscation of a random function in the same class. Both notions offer useful guarantees, applicable to a large class of real-life scenario, including software theft, where the attacker steals a program but cannot guess (much of the) embedded secrets or computation.

Other contributions include: (1) defining two new obfuscation properties: formula indistinguishability obfuscation, for any functions expressible as formulae over equality statements, and output indistinguishability obfuscation, for any functions expressible as multi-bit-output equality functions; and (2) analyzing the resiliency to secret leakage or exhaustive search, and targeting the design of obfuscators that increase such security. This latter property is especially relevant in practical applications, where the amount of entropy in the secrets may vary across all secrets.

1.2 Basic Definitions, Approach and Statement of Main Results

Our goal is to design an obfuscator for a class of (secret-based) point functions, parameterized by secret strings $s_1, \ldots, s_m$, that output 1 if the input strings $x_1, \ldots, x_m$ satisfy $\phi((x_1 = s_1), \ldots, (x_m = s_m))$, where ϕ is a monotone formula, and 0 otherwise. (Wlog, we consider monotone formulae ϕ parameterized by strings $s_1, \ldots, s_m$, which have a 1-1 correspondence with fan-out-1, fan-in-2, monotone circuits denoted as $C_{\phi, s_1, \ldots, s_m}$.) The obfuscator we propose for this type of functions returns an obfuscated program which computes the same function, while protecting both the privacy of strings $s_1, \ldots, s_m$, and privacy of the formula within a class. In the simplest meaningful example, where $m = 2$ and ϕ is a 1-gate formula; the family has only 2 functions: $(x_1 = s_1) \vee (x_2 = s_2)$, and $(x_1 = s_1) \wedge (x_2 = s_2)$ and our second obfuscator hides s_1, s_2, and whether the gate is an AND or an OR. With our newly defined *formula indistinguishability obfuscation* property, we generalize this to any two adversarially chosen formulae within a known class. For instance, in our second obfuscator we consider the class of m-input monotone formulae with the same structure (i.e., the wire connections between the gates); note that in this case, we do not attempt to obfuscate the circuit structure.

A natural starting point to design new constructions would be to take the obfuscator for the equality function with secret s_i, for $i = 1, \ldots, m$. In fact, we use a variant of this obfuscator with multi-bit outputs, so that at obfuscation time, a label can be associated to each equality statement in a way that it can be recovered at evaluation time if and only if, except with negligible probability, the equality statement is satisfied by the current input. Our constructions follow the same paradigm, which can be abstractly described as follows.

INPUT TO Obf: a circuit whose description contains m-input formula f and secrets $s_1 \ldots s_m \in \{0, 1\}^n$; and security parameter 1^ℓ

INSTRUCTIONS FOR Obf:

1. Randomly choose *generation labeling* λ_g for ϕ
   let $u \in \{0,1\}^\ell$ be the label associated to ϕ's output by λ_g
   let $u_1, \ldots, u_m \in \{0,1\}^\ell$ be labels associated to the m input wires by λ_g
2. For $i = 1, \ldots, m$,
   generate obfuscation D_i of i-th equality statement,
   with secret s_i, and multi-bit output u_i
3. Let $oC_{D_1,\ldots,D_m,\lambda_g}$ be the circuit that, on input $(x_1, \ldots, x_m)$, goes as follows:
   based on $\lambda_g, D_1, \ldots, D_m$, randomly choose *evaluation labeling* λ_e for ϕ
   let $v \in \{0,1\}^\ell$ be the label associated by λ_e to ϕ's output wire
   if an *output test* T, based on λ_g, λ_e (including u, v), is true then return: 1
   else return: 0.
4. Return: obfuscated program $oC_{D_1,\ldots,D_m,\lambda_g}$

The generation labeling λ_g, the evaluation labeling λ_e and the output test T are instantiated differently for each of the 2 obfuscators proposed in the rest of the paper. Syntactically, labelings λ_g, λ_e for ϕ consist of an assignment of strings in $\{0,1\}^\ell$ to wires in the circuit associated with monotone formula ϕ, and the output test T is a predicate evaluated on these strings. In our main construction, these are instantiated as follows. Labeling λ_g is a known function labeling, previously used in other cryptography areas, such as secret sharing [4] and zero-knowledge proofs [22]. The obfuscator for an mbo equality function can be the scheme from [9], which is based on any obfuscator for point functions. These two ingredients are combined by setting the obfuscator's output string equal to the label associated with the equality statement. The labeling λ_e is new and is built based on λ_g so that the code for both λ_e and T does *not* depend on ϕ's gates, but only on its formula structure (i.e., how gates are connected to each other). Then, a wire label in λ_e can be computed if and only if the subformula having that wire as output is satisfied by the program input. Finally, in our main construction, the output test T consists of checking if the label u in λ_g associated with the output wire of ϕ is equal to the label v in λ_e associated with the same output wire.

Our first obfuscator works for the class of boolean formulae ϕ over point functions satisfying $\phi(0, \ldots, 0) = 0$ and having binary descriptions upper bounded by a known polynomial. The formula indistinguishability property of this obfuscator does not satisfy any resiliency to secret exposure. Our second obfuscator works for all monotone formulae over point functions and its formula indistinguishability satisfies resiliency to a linear number of exposed secrets on some subclass of formulae. Both obfuscators assume the existence of an obfuscator for point functions satisfying the rrIND-obfuscation notion. These were shown in [3] based on any deterministic encryption scheme, and thus happen to have several instantiations under widely accepted hardness assumptions (e.g., lattice problems [25] or lossy trapdoor functions [5], which in turn exist under group-theoretic assumptions, including the hardness of computing discrete logarithms, quadratic/decisional residuosity, etc.; see, e.g., [13,16]).

Finally, we remark that the class of monotone formulae over point functions has interesting *applicability properties* since it includes several variations of formulae related to well-known computational problems, on search, matching, set theory, access control, etc.

2   Definitions and Preliminaries

Basic Notations. The expression $\{0,1\}^n$ denotes the set of n-bit strings, where n is a positive integer. If S is a set, the expression $x \leftarrow S$ denotes the probabilistic process of uniformly and independently choosing x from set S. If A is an algorithm, the expression $y \leftarrow A(x_1, x_2, \dots)$ denotes the probabilistic process of running algorithm A on input $x_1, x_2, \dots$ and any necessary random coins, and obtaining y as output. A function ϵ over the set of natural numbers $\mathbb{N}$ is negligible if for every polynomial p, there exists an n_0 such that $\epsilon(n) < 1/p(n)$, for all integers $n \geq n_0$.

Formulae Over Point Functions. A *(secret-based) point function* $f_s : \{0,1\}^n \rightarrow \{0,1\}$ is a function, parameterized by a secret string s, that outputs 1 if input string x is $= s$ and 0 otherwise. The boolean circuit computing f_s is also denoted $C_{eq,s}$. A *multi-bit-output point function* (briefly, *mbo point function*) $f_{s,y} : \{0,1\}^n \rightarrow \{0,1\}$ is a function, parameterized by a secret string s and an output string y, that outputs $y \in \{0,1\}^\ell$ if input string x is $= s$ and 0^ℓ otherwise. The boolean circuit computing $f_{s,y}$ is also denoted $C_{eq,s,y}$.

Let ϕ be a boolean formula over m bits. A *boolean formula over point functions* $f_{\phi,s_1,\dots,s_m} : (\{0,1\}^n)^m \rightarrow \{0,1\}$ is a function, parameterized by secret strings $s_1, \dots, s_m$, that outputs $\phi(b_1, \dots, b_m)$, where $b_i = 1$ if $x_i = s_i$ and 0 otherwise, and $x_1, \dots, x_m$ are its input strings. The boolean circuit computing $f_{\phi,s_1,\dots,s_m}$ is also denoted $C_{\phi,s_1,\dots,s_m}$. A *monotone formula over point functions* is a boolean formula over point functions where ϕ is monotone (i.e., expressible only using AND and OR operations).

Obfuscators: Formal Definitions. Let Obf be an efficient probabilistic algorithm that, on input an n-bit circuit C, returns a circuit oC in time polynomial in n. We say that Obf *is an obfuscator* for the class of functions F, if, for any function $f \in F$, and any circuit C_f computing f:

1. *(Correctness)*: $\text{Prob}\left[oC_f \leftarrow \text{Obf}(C_f) : oC_f(x) = C_f(x)\right] \geq 1 - \delta$, for δ negligible in n.
2. *(Efficiency)*: The size of the *obfuscated circuit* oC_f is polynomial in the size of circuit C_f.

Several different obfuscation notions have been proposed in the literature. The original notion from [2], denoted here as *VBB-obfuscation*, was based on simulation through access to a virtual black box for the function. Here, we use the IND notion from [3], relabeled as real-vs-random indistinguishability obfuscation, and our new notion of formula indistinguishability obfuscation, and adapt definitions of both notions to the obfuscation of formulae over equality statements. As in

[3], we also use the notion of a *secret generator*: a (probabilistic) polynomial-time algorithm, denoted as sGen, that returns a secret string $y \in \{0,1\}^n$ (i.e., a string that is a parameter of the program to be obfuscated and that we would like to keep secret after running the obfuscator on the program).

Real-vs-Random Indistinguishability Obfuscation. Informally, this obfuscation notion says that no efficient adversary can distinguish an obfuscation of a circuit parameterized with random secret points from an obfuscation of a circuit with (real) secret points generated from algorithm sGen. More formally, let C_m be a class of m-input circuits. We say that the obfuscator Obf for class C_m *satisfies the real vs random indistinguishability notion* called *rrIND-obfuscation* from now on, relative to secret generator sGen if for all polynomial-time (adversary) algorithms $A = (A_1, A_2)$ such that A_1 returns a function in C_m, if it holds that

$$\left| \mathrm{Prob}\left[\mathrm{RealExp}_{\mathrm{Cm},A,\mathrm{sGen}}(1^n) = 1 \right] - \mathrm{Prob}\left[\mathrm{RandExp}_{\mathrm{Cm},A,\mathrm{sGen}}(1^n) = 1 \right] \right|$$

is negligible in n, where experiments RealExp, RandExp are detailed below.

$\mathrm{RealExp}_{\mathrm{Cm},A,\mathrm{sGen}}(1^n)$

1. $(s_1, \ldots, s_m, aux) \leftarrow \mathrm{sGen}(1^n)$,
2. $s = (s_1, \ldots, s_m)$
3. $(f, aux) \leftarrow A_1(1^n, aux)$
4. $oC_{f,s} \leftarrow \mathrm{Obf}(C_{f,s})$
5. **return:** $b \leftarrow A_2(1^n, oC_{f,s}, aux)$

$\mathrm{RandExp}_{\mathrm{Cm},A}(1^n)$

1. $(s_1, \ldots, s_m, aux) \leftarrow \mathrm{sGen}(1^n)$,
2. $u_i \leftarrow \{0,1\}^n$, for $i = 1, \ldots, m$
3. $u = (u_1, \ldots, u_m)$
4. $(f, aux) \leftarrow A_1(1^n, aux)$
5. $oC_{f,u} \leftarrow \mathrm{Obf}(C_{f,u})$
6. **return:** $b \leftarrow A_2(1^n, oC_{f,u}, aux)$

A composable version of this definition, called *composable rrIND-obfuscation* from now on, can be derived, similarly as in [3,9], by slightly modifying the above definition, as follows: in experiment RealExp, A_2 has access to a polynomial number of independently computed obfuscations based on the same formula f and the same secrets $s_1, \ldots, s_m$; in experiment RandExp, A_2 has access to a polynomial number of independently computed obfuscations based on the same formula f and random and independent (even across all obfuscations) secrets $s_1, \ldots, s_m$. The rrIND-obfuscation notion for the case of trivial formulae with a single input was first studied in [3], where it has been used mainly to demonstrate feasibility results of special-purpose obfuscators. In particular, under the existence of deterministic encryption schemes, the family of equality or point functions admits an obfuscator that satisfies this composable notion [3]. The existence of deterministic encryption schemes can be, in turn, established from lossy trapdoor functions [5], and the latter have been constructed from various standard number-theoretic hardness assumptions. We also note that the triviality theorems from [3] in the case of uniform secrets apply here as well. The relationship between VBB-obfuscation and rrIND-obfuscation was studied in [3] for the case of point functions, where it was proved that the two notions are incomparable, in that there is an obfuscator satisfying one notion that does not satisfy the other, and viceversa. This relationship carries over to our notion used here, since our generalized notion includes the one in [3] in the base case of one-input formulae. Moreover, [7] studies variants of the above rrIND-obfuscation notion, by further characterizing the predictability of algorithm sGen, and shows relationships of these variants with other literature notions.

Formula Obfuscation. Informally, the formula obfuscation notion says that no efficient adversary can distinguish among the obfuscations of two same-structure, but distinct, formulae from a given class, when evaluated over uniformly and independently chosen secrets. (Here, we simplify the definition by only considering uniformly distributed secrets, since all schemes in the paper will also satisfy rrIND-obfuscation, but note that the definition with respect to a secret generator sGen is easily derived.) Formally, we say that the obfuscator Obf for the class of formulae Φ *satisfies formula indistinguishability obfuscation* relative to secret generator sGen, if for all polynomial-time (adversary) algorithms $A = (A_1, A_2)$, such that A_1 returns same-structure formulae $\phi_0, \phi_1 \in \Phi$, it holds that

$$\left| \text{Prob} \left[\text{ObfExp}_{C,A,0}(1^n) = 1 \right] - \text{Prob} \left[\text{ObfExp}_{C,A,1}(1^n) = 1 \right] \right|$$

is negligible in n, where experiments $\text{ObfExp}_{C,A,0}, \text{ObfExp}_{C,A,1}$ are detailed below.

$\text{ObfExp}_{C,A,0}(1^n)$
1. $s_i \leftarrow \{0,1\}^n$, for $i = 1, \ldots, m$
2. $s = (s_1, \ldots, s_m)$
3. $(\phi_0, \phi_1, aux) \leftarrow A_1(1^n)$
4. $oC_{\phi_0,s} \leftarrow \text{mObf}(C_{\phi_0,s})$
5. **Return:** $b \leftarrow A_2(1^n, oC_{\phi_0,s}, aux)$

$\text{ObfExp}_{C,A,1}(1^n)$
1. $s_i \leftarrow \{0,1\}^n$, for $i = 1, \ldots, m$
2. $s = (s_1, \ldots, s_m)$
3. $(\phi_0, \phi_1, aux) \leftarrow A_1(1^n)$
4. $oC_{\phi_1,s} \leftarrow \text{mObf}(C_{\phi_1,s})$
5. **Return:** $b \leftarrow A_2(1^n, oC_{\phi_1,s}, aux)$

We also extend forIND-obfuscation to a notion capturing resilience to some secret exposure or search attacks. We say that an obfuscator for a class C of formulae over point functions satisfies *t-resilient (to exhaustive search attacks) forIND-obfuscation with respect to a subclass C_0 of formulae in C* if forIND-obfuscation holds even if the adversary is leaked or can compute via exhaustive search t secrets of its choice. More formally, this notion is obtained by modifying the above formal definition of the forIND-obfuscation notion, as follows:

1. step 3 in the above ObfExp experiments becomes: $(\phi_0, \phi_1, i_1, \ldots, i_t, aux) \leftarrow A_1(1^n, 1^\ell)$,
2. in step 5 of the same two experiments, A_2 takes $s_{i_1}, \ldots, s_{i_t}$ as additional inputs.
3. the condition in the definition holds for all adversaries A such that A_1 returns same-structure formulae ϕ_0, ϕ_1 that belong to $C_0 \subseteq \Phi$".

This property captures resiliency to leakage or exhaustive search attacks, which is especially relevant in applications where there are multiple secrets, and these may naturally have varying length or entropy. Accordingly, in the rest of the paper we also discuss this property for the two different solutions satisfying forIND-obfuscation.

3   Output Indistinguishability of Mbo Point Function Obfuscators

In this section we define a new obfuscation notion for mbo point functions, called output indistinguishability, and show that a previous technique from [9] can be used to transform any rrIND-secure obfuscator for point functions into an obfuscator for mbo point functions satisfying this new notion (in addition to rrIND-security). This result will be used later in the security proof for our formula obfuscators. We note that relationships between VBB-secure mbo point function obfuscators and symmetric encryption schemes, as studied in [10,14], do not imply this result as we consider rrIND-secure obfuscation.

Output Indistinguishability Obfuscation. Informally, an obfuscator for mbo point functions satisfies the output indistinguishability notion if no efficient adversary can distinguish an obfuscated program when the function's output is y_0 from an obfuscated program when the function's output is y_1, for any two output (same-length) strings y_0, y_1 returned by the adversary. (Here, we simplify the definition by only considering the uniform distribution for the program's secret, since all schemes in the paper will also satisfy rrIND-obfuscation, but note that the definition with respect to a secret generator sGen is easily derived.) More formally, let MboEqFC be a class of mbo point functions. We say that obfuscator MboEqObf for the class of functions MboEqFC satisfies *output indistinguishability obfuscation* (briefly, outIND-obfuscation) if for all polynomial-time (adversary) algorithms $A = (A_1, A_2)$ such that A_1 returns $(y_0, y_1) \in \{0,1\}^\ell$, it holds that

$$\left| \mathrm{Prob}\left[\mathrm{OutIndExp}_{\mathrm{MboEq},A,0}(1^n) = 1 \right] - \mathrm{Prob}\left[\mathrm{OutIndExp}_{\mathrm{MboEq},A,1}(1^n) = 1 \right] \right|$$

is negligible in n, where experiments $\mathrm{OutIndExp}_{\mathrm{MboEq},A,0}, \mathrm{OutIndExp}_{\mathrm{MboEq},A,1}$ are detailed below.

$\mathrm{OutIndExp}_{\mathrm{MboEq},A,0}(1^n)$

1. $s \leftarrow \{0,1\}^n$,
2. $(y_0, y_1, aux) \leftarrow A_1(1^n, 1^\ell)$
3. $oC_{s,y_0} \leftarrow \mathrm{MboEqObf}(C_{eq,s,y_0})$
4. **Return:** $b \leftarrow A_2(1^n, 1^\ell, oC_{s,y_0}, aux)$

$\mathrm{OutIndExp}_{\mathrm{MboEq},A,1}(1^n)$

1. $s \leftarrow \{0,1\}^n$,
2. $(y_0, y_1, aux) \leftarrow A_1(1^n, 1^\ell)$
3. $oC_{s,y_1} \leftarrow \mathrm{MboEqObf}(C_{eq,s,y_1})$
4. **Return:** $b \leftarrow A_2(1^n, 1^\ell, oC_{s,y_1}, aux)$

An Output-Indistinguishable Obfuscator. We now use a technique from [9] to prove that any rrIND-obfuscator for a point function can be transformed into an rrIND-obfuscator for an mbo point function. (We can actually establish this result using techniques from almost all other obfuscators in the literature for mbo point functions.) Let uGen denote the secret generator that returns uniformly and independently distributed secrets $s_1, \ldots, s_m \in \{0,1\}^\ell$. Formally, we show the following

Theorem 1. Let EqObf be an obfuscator for the class EqFC of (secret-based) point functions. There exists (constructively) an obfuscator MboEqObf for the class MboEqFC of (secret-based) mbo point functions such that:

1. if EqObf satisfies composable rrIND-obfuscation with respect to a secret generator sGen then MboEqObf satisfies rrIND-obfuscation with respect to sGen; and
2. if EqObf satisfies composable rrIND-obfuscation with respect to secret generator uGen then MboEqObf satisfies outIND-obfuscation.

We prove Theorem 1, by first defining an mbo point function obfuscator and then showing its properties. The obfuscator is almost identical to the construction in [9], the main difference being that it uses an rrIND-obfuscator for point functions instead of a VBB-obfuscator. Let $y = y_1 \cdots y_m$ be the desired output for an mbo point function, parameterized with secret s, from class MboEqFC. The obfuscator MboEqFC is defined by computing a concatenation of $m + 1$ outputs of the obfuscator EqObf for the (single-bit-output) point function, parameterized with secret s, and with the following values used as a secret: the first execution uses secret s; the next m executions use secret s when $y_i = 1$ or a random and independent n-bit string s_i when $y_i = 0$. Then, the obfuscated program is defined to compute all bits of the output string y by running all these obfuscated programs for the point function with secret s. If the input x is different from s, the first obfuscated version of EqObf will reveal that fact and the obfuscated program returns: 0^ℓ. Note that EqObf, satisfying the composable rrIND-obfuscation notion, is *not* a deterministic function and can be safely applied multiple times within MboEqObf without leaking the equality pattern of value y. A formal description follows.

INPUT TO MboEqObf: a circuit whose description contains secret string $s \in \{0,1\}^n$, output string $y \in \{0,1\}^\ell$

INSTRUCTIONS FOR MboEqObf:

1. Let $D_0 = \text{EqObf}(f_s)$ and $y = y_1 \cdots y_m$
2. For $i = 1, \ldots, m$,
    if $y_i = 1$ then set $s_i = s$
        else randomly and independently choose $s_i \in \{0,1\}^n$
    let $D_{y,i} = \text{EqObf}(f_{s_i})$
3. Let $oC_{D_0,D_{y,1},\ldots,D_{y,m},y}$ be the circuit that, on input x, does the following:
    if $D_0(x) = 0$ then output: 0 and halt
    for $i = 1, \ldots, m$,
        if $D_{y,i}(x) = 1$ then set $y_i = 1$ else set $y_i = 0$
    output: $y = y_1 \cdots y_m$.
4. Return: $(oC_{D_0,D_{y,1},\ldots,D_{y,m},y})$

To prove the rrIND-obfuscation property of MboEqObf, it suffices to prove that the following two distributions are computationally indistinguishable: (a) the circuit $oC_{D_0,D_{y,1},\ldots,D_{y,m},y}$ output by MboEqObf and computed on input a secret

s randomly sampled according to $sGen$; and (b) a circuit $oC_{rD_0,rD_{y,1},...,rD_{y,m},y}$ computed as in MboEqObf, but on input a uniformly distributed secret s'. We prove this by using a hybrid argument [18], and applying the composable rrIND-obfuscation of EqObf.

To prove the outIND-obfuscation property of MboEqObf, it suffices to show, for any outputs y_1, y_2 chosen by the adversary, that the following two distributions are computationally indistinguishable: (a) the circuit $oC_{D_0,D_{y_1,1},...,D_{y_1,m},y_1}$ output by MboEqObf and computed on input a uniformly distributed secret s; and (b) the circuit $oC_{D_0,D_{y_2,1},...,D_{y_2,m},y_2}$ output by MboEqObf and computed on input a uniformly distributed secret s. We note that $D_{y_1,i}$ and $D_{y_2,i}$ are equally distributed for all i such that $y_{1i} = y_{2i}$. On the other hand, for all i such that $y_{1i} \neq y_{2i}$, the obfuscated programs $D_{y_1,i}$ are outputs of EqObf on input the same uniformly distributed secret s, while the obfuscated programs $D_{y_2,i}$ are outputs of EqObf on input the uniformly and independently distributed secrets s_i. However, these are computationally indistinguishable by the assumed composable rrIND-obfuscation of EqObf with respect to secret generator uGen.

4   Our First Formula Obfuscator

In this section we show an obfuscator bObf for a class zBoolFC of boolean formulae over point functions $f_{\phi,s_1,...,s_m}$ such that ϕ is a boolean formula satisfying $\phi(0,...,0) = 0$ and has binary descriptions upper bounded by a known polynomial (note that this class includes all monotone formulae ϕ with this size upper bound as well as some non-monotone ones). This obfuscator satisfies both rrIND-obfuscation and forIND-obfuscation, although with no resiliency (indeed, knowledge of a single secret is sufficient to an attacker to learn the description of the entire formula). Therefore, this obfuscator is only useful in applications where secret leakage is unlikely and each secret is large enough to withstand exhaustive search attacks. Formally, we obtain the following

Theorem 2. Let EqObf be an obfuscator for the class EqFC of (secret-based) point functions. There exists (constructively) an obfuscator bObf for the class zBoolFC of boolean formulae over point functions such that

1. if EqObf satisfies composable rrIND-obfuscation with respect to a secret generator sGen then bObf satisfies rrIND-obfuscation with respect to sGen;
2. if EqObf satisfies composable rrIND-obfuscation with respect to uniform secret generator uGen then bObf satisfies forIND-obfuscation.

However, bObf does not satisfy 1-resilient forIND-obfuscation with respect to any formula in zBoolFC.

The obfuscator claimed in Theorem 2 is a simple instantiation of the paradigm described in Sect. 1. Thus, to explain it informally, it suffices to describe an obfuscator for mbo point functions, a generation labeling λ_g, an evaluation labeling λ_e, and an output test T. As obfuscator for mbo point functions, we use the scheme in Sect. 3 and its properties from Theorem 1. The generation labeling λ_g consists of labels $u_1, \ldots, u_m$, all set equal to a random string k, and a label u, which is set as the obfuscation of an mbo point function with k as secret string and with the binary description $desc(\phi)$ of formula ϕ as output string. The obfuscated program is defined, on input n-bit strings $x_1, \ldots, x_m$, to compute evaluation labeling λ_e, as follows. First, for $i = 1, \ldots, m$, it computes label v_i as the output of the obfuscated program for equality function with secret s_i, when evaluated on input x_i. If there is a $v_i \neq 0^\ell$, for some $i \in \{1, \ldots, m\}$, a string k' is set as equal to this v_i. Then, label v is computed as the output of the obfuscated program for equality function with secret k, when evaluated on input k', and the output test T, is simply set as "$v((u_1 = v_1), \ldots, (u_m = v_m))$". If all $v_i = 0^\ell$ then T is set to an unsatisfiable test. The output of the obfuscated program is then set as 1 if the test T is satisfied or as 0 otherwise. A formal description follows.

INPUT TO bObf: security parameter 1^σ and a circuit $C_{\phi, s_1, \ldots, s_m}$ whose description contains strings $s_1, \ldots, s_m \in \{0, 1\}^n$ and $desc(\phi)$, where ϕ is boolean formula satisfying $\phi(0, \ldots, 0) = 0$ and $|desc(\phi)| \leq p(m)$, for some public polynomial p.

INSTRUCTIONS FOR bObf:

1. Randomly choose $k \in \{0, 1\}^\sigma$ and set $u_1 = \cdots = u_m = k$
2. let $D_i = mboC_{s_i, u_i} = \mathrm{MboEqObf}(C_{eq, s_i, u_i})$, for $i = 1, \ldots, m$
3. set $u = D = mboC_{k, desc(\phi)} = \mathrm{MboEqObf}(C_{eq, k, desc(\phi)})$
4. let $oC_{D_1, \ldots, D_m, D, u}$ be the circuit that, on input $(x_1, \ldots, x_m)$, does the following:
       let $v_i = D_i(x_i)$, for $i = 1, \ldots, m$
       if $v_i \neq 0^\ell$ for some $i \in \{1, \ldots, m\}$ then set $k' = v_i$
           else output: 0 and halt
       let $desc(\phi) = v = D(k')$
       if $\phi((u_1 = v_1), \ldots, (u_m = v_m)) = 1$ then output: 1 else output: 0.
5. return: $(oC_{D_1, \ldots, D_m, u})$

The efficiency property of bObf follows from direct code inspection.

The correctness property of bObf follows from the following observation: if at least one of the x_i's is equal to at least one of the secrets s_i's, then $k' = k$, v is a description of formula ϕ, and test T is exactly the evaluation of ϕ on input $(u_1 = v_1), \ldots, (u_m = v_m)$.

To prove the rrIND-obfuscation property of MboEqObf, it suffices to prove that for any formula ϕ in zBoolFC, the following two distributions are computationally indistinguishable: (a) the circuit $oC_{D_1, \ldots, D_m, D}$ output by bObf and computed on input secrets $s_1, \ldots, s_m$ randomly sampled according to $sGen$ and formula ϕ; and (b) a circuit $oC_{rD_1, \ldots, rD_m, rD}$ computed as in MboEqObf, but on input random secrets $s'_1, \ldots, s'_m$ and formula ϕ. We prove this by using a hybrid argument [18], and applying the composable rrIND-obfuscation of EqObf.

To prove the forIND-obfuscation property, we first observe that secret string k is obfuscated as the output string of the mbo point function obfuscator MboEqObf using secret strings $s_1, \ldots, s_m$, and then observe that $desc(\phi)$ is obfuscated as the output string of the mbo point function obfuscator MboEqObf using k. Then the forIND-obfuscation property follows by a hybrid argument where we apply twice the outIND-obfuscation property of MboEqObf, established in Theorem 1 implying the obfuscation of k and $desc(\phi)$.

Finally, note that an adversary knowing any one of secrets s_i will learn k and therefore $desc(f)$; thus, this obfuscator does not satisfy 1-resilience with respect to any subclass of zBoolFC.

5   Our Second Formula Obfuscator

In this section we show an obfuscator mObf for the class MonoFC of all monotone formulae $f_{\phi,s_1,\ldots,s_m}$ over point functions. (Here, ϕ can be an arbitrary m-input monotone formula). This obfuscator is obtained as a different instantiation of the paradigm described in Sect. 1. It satisfies both rrIND-obfuscation and forIND-obfuscation, and has some resiliency properties. Therefore, it is useful in applications where secret leakage cannot be ruled out and not all secrets are large enough to withstand exhaustive search attacks. Formally, we obtain the following

Theorem 3. Let EqObf be an obfuscator for the class EqFC of (secret-based) point functions. There exists (constructively) an obfuscator mObf for the class MonoFC of monotone formulae over point functions such that:

1. if EqObf satisfies composable rrIND-obfuscation with respect to a secret generator sGen then mObf satisfies rrIND-obfuscation with respect to sGen;
2. if EqObf satisfies composable rrIND-obfuscation with respect to uniform secret generator uGen then mObf satisfies forIND-obfuscation.

Moreover, there is a class of m-input monotone formulae for which mObf satisfies $\lfloor m/2 \rfloor$-resilient forIND-obfuscation.

We prove Theorem 3 by first informally describing an obfuscator for a single-gate monotone formula and then formally describe the obfuscator for any arbitrary polynomial-size monotone formula and its claimed properties.

Description of a 1-gate Obfuscator. For the base case of a single-gate monotone formula ϕ, we consider functions f_{ϕ,s_1,s_2} such that $\phi \in \{$ AND, OR $\}$. The obfuscator for such functions follows the paradigm discussed in Sect. 1. There, it was defined in terms of an obfuscator for mbo point functions, a generation labeling λ_g, an evaluation labeling λ_e, and an output test T. As obfuscator for mbo point functions, we use the scheme described in Sect. 3, along with its Theorem 1. The generation labeling λ_g consists of labels u, u_1, u_2, set as $u = u_1 = u_2$ if $\phi =$ OR, or so that $u = u_1 \oplus u_2$, for randomly chosen u, u_1, if $\phi =$ AND. Note that they satisfy the following conditions: (a) if $\phi =$ OR any one of u_1, u_2 suffices to compute u; and (b) if $\phi =$ AND, knowing both u_1, u_2 allows to compute u, while knowing only one of them leaves u undetermined. Then, for $i = 1, 2$, label u_i is computed using an obfuscator for the mbo point function associated with point function with secret s_i. Finally, the obfuscated program is defined, on input n-bit strings x_1, x_2, to compute evaluation labeling λ_e, as follows. First, for $i = 1, 2$, it computes label v_i as the output of the obfuscated program for point function with secret s_i, when evaluated on input x_i. Then, it combines labels v_1, v_2 into a third label v such that the obtained 3 labels somehow 'match' the previously generated labeling λ_g, through the output test T, here simply set as "$(u = v)$". Specifically, if $v_1 = v_2$ then $v = v_1$ else $v = v_1 \oplus v_2$. The output of the obfuscated program is then set as 1 if the test T is satisfied or as 0 otherwise. Here, a key property to prove the forIND-obfuscation property is that the code for neither λ_e nor T depend on the value of gate ϕ. Key property to prove the correctness property are the following properties of labelings λ_g, λ_e (in turn proved by a case analysis): for $i = 1, 2$, $v_i = u_i$ with probability 1 if $x_i = s_i$ or negligible otherwise; moreover, $v = u$ with probability 1 if $(x_1 = s_1)$ (gate(ϕ)) $(x_2 = s_2)$ or negligible otherwise.

Description and Properties of Obfuscator mObf. This obfuscator follows the paradigm in Sect. 1 and can also be seen as an extension of the just described obfuscator from a single gate to arbitrary polynomial-size monotone formulae. The use of the obfuscator MboEqObf for mbo point functions and the definition of the output test T are actually the same as in the obfuscator for single-gate formulae. The new components in obfuscator mObf are the definitions of labelings λ_g, λ_e.

Specifically, the labels in λ_g are generated by procedure GenLabel recursively over the monotone formula ϕ, starting from randomly choosing the top label u, and then generating labels for all subformulae, until the recursion reaches to the formula inputs. Labels in λ_g are set to satisfy the following conditions: (a) if $\phi = \phi_1 \vee \phi_2$, any one of u_1, u_2 suffices to compute u; and (b) if $\phi = \phi_1 \wedge \phi_2$, knowing both u_1, u_2 allows to compute u, while knowing only one of them leaves u undetermined.

Moreover, the labels in λ_e are generated by procedure EvaLabel recursively over the monotone formula ϕ, starting from the generation of the bottom label at ϕ's inputs, based on evaluating the obfuscated programs $D_1, \ldots, D_m$. For these labels, the following condition will hold: for any subformula of ϕ, the labels from λ_g, λ_e associated with this subformula's output wire will be equal with probability 1 if a subformula of ϕ is satisfied under input $x_1, \ldots, x_m$ or with negligible probability otherwise.

A formal description follows.

INPUT TO GenLabel: m-input monotone formula ϕ and label $u \in \{0, 1\}^\ell$

INSTRUCTIONS FOR GenLabel:

1. If $\phi = '(x_i = s_i)'$ for some $i \in \{1, \ldots, m\}$, then
   let D_i be the output of MboEqObf using secret s_i and output u, and return: D_i
2. If $\phi = \phi_1 \vee \phi_2$ then set $u_1 = u_2 = u$
3. If $\phi = \phi_1 \wedge \phi_2$ then randomly choose $u_1 \in \{0, 1\}^\ell$ and set $u_2 = u_1 \oplus u$
4. let a be the number of inputs to ϕ_1, for some $1 \leq a \leq m - 1$
5. let $(D_1, \ldots, D_a) = $ GenLabel(ϕ_1, u_1)

6. let $(D_{a+1}, \ldots, D_m) = \mathsf{GenLabel}(\phi_2, u_2)$

7. return: $(D_1, \ldots, D_m)$

Let $struct(\phi)$ denote the structure of formula ϕ; that is, the description of formula ϕ, where gates of ϕ are replaced by a special symbol that does not reveal the gate type.

INPUT TO $\mathsf{EvaLabel}$: strings $x_1, \ldots, x_m$, circuits $D_1, \ldots, D_m$ and $struct(\phi)$ for monotone formula ϕ,

INSTRUCTIONS FOR $\mathsf{EvaLabel}$:

1. If $\phi = \text{`}(x_i = s_i)\text{'}$ for some $i \in \{1, \ldots, m\}$, then set $v = D_i(x_i)$ and return: v
2. If ϕ has two sub-formulae ϕ_1, ϕ_2 then
   let a be the number of inputs to ϕ_1, for some $1 \le a \le m - 1$
   set $v_1 = \mathsf{EvaLabel}(\phi_1, D_1, \ldots, D_a)$
   set $v_2 = \mathsf{EvaLabel}(\phi_2, D_{a+1}, \ldots, D_m)$
   if $v_1 = v_2$ then set $v = v_1$ else set $v = v_1 \oplus v_2$
3. return: v

INPUT TO mObf: security parameter 1^ℓ and a circuit $C_{\phi, s_1, \ldots, s_m}$ whose description contains m-input monotone formula ϕ and secrets $s_1, \ldots, s_m \in \{0,1\}^n$;

INSTRUCTIONS FOR mObf:

1. Randomly choose $u \in \{0,1\}^\ell$
2. Let $(D_1, \ldots, D_m) = \mathsf{GenLabel}(\phi, u)$
3. let $oC_{D_1, \ldots, D_m, u}$ be the circuit that, on input $(x_1, \ldots, x_m, struct(\phi))$, does the following:
   let $v = \mathsf{EvaLabel}(struct(\phi), D_1, \ldots, D_m)$
   if $v = u$ then output: 1 else output: 0.
4. return: $(oC_{D_1, \ldots, D_m, u})$

The rrIND-obfuscation and forIND-obfuscation properties claimed in Theorem 3 for mObf reuse the main ideas in the proofs of Theorems 1 and 2, and are proved by induction over the input formula ϕ, the base case being a 1-gate formula.

For the efficiency property, one can verify by inspection that the runtime of the obfuscated program returned by mObf is dominated by m executions of obfuscator mObf and m executions of the obfuscated equality function programs D_i, for any m-input formula.

For the correctness property, the main labeling claims we prove inductively and for any label u, are: (1) if $\phi(x_1, \ldots, x_m) = 1$ then it holds that $v = u$, where $v = \mathsf{EvaLabel}(\phi, D_1, \ldots, D_m)$ and $(D_1, \ldots, D_m) = \mathsf{GenLabel}(\phi, u)$; and (2) if $\phi(x_1, \ldots, x_m) = 0$ then it $v = u$ holds with probability $\le 2^{-|u|}$.

For the resiliency property, we now show a subclass of MonoFC relative to which mObf satisfies t-resilient forIND-obfuscation, for some t linear in m (specifically, $t = \lfloor m/2 \rfloor - 1$). Specifically, consider the class of monotone formulae of the type $(w_1 \wedge \ldots \wedge w_{\lfloor m/2 \rfloor}) \circ (w_{\lfloor m/2 \rfloor + 1} \wedge \ldots \wedge w_m)$, for some $\circ \in \{\vee, \wedge\}$, where w_i denotes the equality statement $\text{`}(x_i = s_i)\text{'}$. This subclass contains only two formulae, depending on the value of the top gate $\circ$. Now, note that in order to determine the value of gate $\circ$, an adversary has access, in addition to the label u already contained in $oC_{D_1,\ldots,D_m,u}$, to all labels u_i associated with secret s_i, if known, for all $i \in \{1,\ldots,m\}$. We then observe that by the properties of the generation labeling λ_g used, the adversary obtains information about the value of the top gate $\circ$ if and only if it obtains information about one of the 2 labels v_a, v_b associated with the input wires to $\circ$. Specifically, it holds that $\circ = \vee$ if $v_a = v_b = v$ and $\circ = \wedge$ if $v_a \oplus v_b = v$, in which case, with high probability $v_a, v_b \neq v$. Accordingly, determining v_a or v_b suffices to check these conditions and therefore determine $\circ$. On the other hand, in the considered subclass of formulae, because of the properties of the generation labeling λ_g on $\wedge$ gates, label v_a remains completely undetermined unless $m/2$ labels u_i are known. This implies that knowing up to $t \leq m/2 - 1$ secrets s_i will not help the adversary determine v_a or v_b, and thus will leave $\circ$ completely undetermined.

6   Conclusions

We proposed formula obfuscation as a paradigm to achieve program obfuscation with a desirable combination of properties: correctness (i.e., a single obfuscator approach for a large class of programs), efficiency (runtime of the obfuscator program) and provability (i.e., some obfuscation notion is achievable under intractability assumptions that are standard in cryptography). Our formula obfuscation results are the first to significantly enlarge the class of programs with these properties, previously consisting of essentially variations of point functions or less than a handful of cryptographic functionalities. Several research directions remain of interest on this paradigm, including constructions with improved resiliency properties, more general boolean formulae, different intractability assumptions, and different obfuscation notions.

Acknowledgements. Many thanks to Brian Coan for interesting discussions on these results. I am still very grateful to Alfredo De Santis, Giuseppe Persiano, and Moti Yung, coauthors in past work cited here, for several enjoyable conversations on using formula labelings in constructions of other cryptographic primitives.

References

1. Bahler, L., Di Crescenzo, G., Polyakov, Y., Rohloff, K., Cousins, D.B.: Practical implementations of lattice-based program obfuscators for point functions. In: International Conference on High Performance Computing and Simulation, HPCS 2017, pp. 761–768 (2017)
2. Barak, B., et al.: On the (Im)possibility of obfuscating programs. In: Kilian, J. (ed.) CRYPTO 2001. LNCS, vol. 2139, pp. 1–18. Springer, Heidelberg (2001). https://doi.org/10.1007/3-540-44647-8_1
3. Bellare, M., Stepanovs, I.: Point-function obfuscation: a framework and generic constructions. In: Kushilevitz, E., Malkin, T. (eds.) TCC 2016. LNCS, vol. 9563, pp. 565–594. Springer, Heidelberg (2016). https://doi.org/10.1007/978-3-662-49099-0_21

4. Benaloh, J., Leichter, J.: Generalized secret sharing and monotone functions. In: Goldwasser, S. (ed.) CRYPTO 1988. LNCS, vol. 403, pp. 27–35. Springer, New York (1990). https://doi.org/10.1007/0-387-34799-2_3

5. Boldyreva, A., Fehr, S., O'Neill, A.: On notions of security for deterministic encryption, and efficient constructions without random oracles. In: Wagner, D. (ed.) CRYPTO 2008. LNCS, vol. 5157, pp. 335–359. Springer, Heidelberg (2008). https://doi.org/10.1007/978-3-540-85174-5_19

6. Brakerski, Z., Vaikuntanathan, V., Wee, H., Wichs, D.: Obfuscating conjunctions under entropic ring LWE. In: Proceedings of the 2016 ACM ITCS Conference, pp. 147–156 (2016)

7. Brzuska, C., Mittelbach, A.: Indistinguishability obfuscation versus multi-bit point obfuscation with auxiliary input. In: Sarkar, P., Iwata, T. (eds.) ASIACRYPT 2014. LNCS, vol. 8874, pp. 142–161. Springer, Heidelberg (2014). https://doi.org/10.1007/978-3-662-45608-8_8

8. Canetti, R.: Towards realizing random oracles: hash functions that hide all partial information. In: Kaliski, B.S. (ed.) CRYPTO 1997. LNCS, vol. 1294, pp. 455–469. Springer, Heidelberg (1997). https://doi.org/10.1007/BFb0052255

9. Canetti, R., Dakdouk, R.R.: Obfuscating point functions with multibit output. In: Smart, N. (ed.) EUROCRYPT 2008. LNCS, vol. 4965, pp. 489–508. Springer, Heidelberg (2008). https://doi.org/10.1007/978-3-540-78967-3_28

10. Canetti, R., Tauman Kalai, Y., Varia, M., Wichs, D.: On symmetric encryption and point obfuscation. In: Micciancio, D. (ed.) TCC 2010. LNCS, vol. 5978, pp. 52–71. Springer, Heidelberg (2010). https://doi.org/10.1007/978-3-642-11799-2_4

11. Canetti, R., Rothblum, G.N., Varia, M.: Obfuscation of hyperplane membership. In: Micciancio, D. (ed.) TCC 2010. LNCS, vol. 5978, pp. 72–89. Springer, Heidelberg (2010). https://doi.org/10.1007/978-3-642-11799-2_5

12. Di Crescenzo, G., Bahler, L., Coan, B.: Cryptographic password obfuscation. In: Naccache, D., et al. (eds.) ICICS 2018. LNCS, vol. 11149, pp. 497–512. Springer, Cham (2018). https://doi.org/10.1007/978-3-030-01950-1_29

13. Di Crescenzo, G., Bahler, L., Coan, B.A., Polyakov, Y., Rohloff, K., Cousins, D.B.: Practical implementations of program obfuscators for point functions. In: International Conference on High Performance Computing and Simulation, HPCS (2016)

14. Dodis, Y., Kalai, Y.T., Lovett, S.: On cryptography with auxiliary input. In: Proceedings of the 41st Annual ACM Symposium on Theory of Computing, STOC 2009, pp. 621–630 (2009)

15. Dodis, Y., Smith, A.D.: Correcting errors without leaking partial information. In: Proceedings of the 37th Annual ACM Symposium on Theory of Computing, pp. 654–663 (2005)

16. Freeman, D.M., Goldreich, O., Kiltz, E., Rosen, A., Segev, G.: More constructions of lossy and correlation-secure trapdoor functions. In: Nguyen, P.Q., Pointcheval, D. (eds.) PKC 2010. LNCS, vol. 6056, pp. 279–295. Springer, Heidelberg (2010). https://doi.org/10.1007/978-3-642-13013-7_17

17. Garg, S., Gentry, C., Halevi, S., Raykova, M., Sahai, A., Waters, B.: Candidate indistinguishability obfuscation and functional encryption for all circuits. In: Proceedings of 54th IEEE FOCS, pp. 40–49 (2013)

18. Goldwasser, S., Micali, S.: Probabilistic encryption. J. Comput. Syst. Sci. **28**(2), 270–299 (1984)

19. Hada, S.: Secure obfuscation for encrypted signatures. In: Gilbert, H. (ed.) EUROCRYPT 2010. LNCS, vol. 6110, pp. 92–112. Springer, Heidelberg (2010). https://doi.org/10.1007/978-3-642-13190-5_5

20. Hohenberger, S., Rothblum, G.N., Shelat, A., Vaikuntanathan, V.: Securely obfuscating re-encryption. J. Cryptol. **24**(4), 694–719 (2011)
21. Lynn, B., Prabhakaran, M., Sahai, A.: Positive results and techniques for obfuscation. In: Cachin, C., Camenisch, J.L. (eds.) EUROCRYPT 2004. LNCS, vol. 3027, pp. 20–39. Springer, Heidelberg (2004). https://doi.org/10.1007/978-3-540-24676-3_2
22. De Santis, A., Di Crescenzo, G., Persiano, G., Yung, M.: On monotone formula closure of SZK. In: FOCS, pp. 454–465 (1994)
23. Wee, H.: On obfuscating point functions. In: Proceedings of 37th ACM STOC 2005, pp. 523–532 (2005)
24. Wichs, D., Zirdelis, G.: Obfuscating compute-and-compare programs under LWE. In: Proceedings of 58th IEEE FOCS 2017, pp. 600–611 (2017)
25. Xie, X., Xue, R., Zhang, R.: Deterministic public key encryption and identity-based encryption from lattices in the auxiliary-input setting. In: Visconti, I., De Prisco, R. (eds.) SCN 2012. LNCS, vol. 7485, pp. 1–18. Springer, Heidelberg (2012). https://doi.org/10.1007/978-3-642-32928-9_1

Fault Analysis of the New Ukrainian Hash Function Standard: Kupyna

Onur Duman[(✉)] and Amr Youssef

Concordia Institute for Information Systems Engineering,
Concordia University, Montréal, Québec, Canada
o_dum@encs.concordia.ca

Abstract. Kupyna has been selected by the Ukrainian government as the new national hash function standard in 2015. In this paper, we apply two fault attacks on Kupyna. In the first attack, we assume that the attacker knows all the hash parameters and aims to recover the input to the hash function. We experiment using three different fault models which are random byte fault model, known byte unique fault model and known byte random fault model. In the second fault attack, we assume that the attacker does not know the entries of the SBoxes used in Kupyna and aims to recover the SBox entries. Our experimental results in both attacks illustrate the importance of protecting implementations of Kupyna against fault analysis attacks.

Keywords: Cryptanalysis · Kupyna · Hash · Streebog · Grøstl ·
DFA · IFA · DSTU 7564:2014

1 Introduction

GOST 34.311-95 has been used in Ukraine as the national standard hash function until 2015 [17]. It provides an acceptable level of security since it uses 256-bit keys. However, two theoretical attacks have been presented against this standard [15,16]. In [15], the authors analyzed the security of GOST 34.311-95 with respect to pre-image attacks and concluded that it has a certificational weakness. In [16], the authors presented a collision attack on GOST 34.311-95 and demonstrated that their attack is an improvement over [15]. In addition to those vulnerabilities, GOST 34.311-95 is also found to be impractical for modern platforms. Also, most Commonwealth of Independent States (CIS) countries other than Ukraine started to adopt newer standards such as GOST R 34.11-2012 [1] instead of GOST 34.311-95 in Russia. As a result, the Ukrainian government decided to adopt a new standard hash function called Kupyna under the standard DSTU 7564:2014 [17].

In this paper, we present two different fault attacks against Kupyna. In the first case, we assume that the attacker has access to the hash function output, without knowing the input, and all the hash function parameters are known including the round constants, substitution box entries, and the initialization

© Springer Nature Switzerland AG 2019
N. Zincir-Heywood et al. (Eds.): FPS 2018, LNCS 11358, pp. 225–240, 2019.
https://doi.org/10.1007/978-3-030-18419-3_15

vector. Also, the attacker is able to request the output of the hash function as many times as needed by faulting either known or random bytes at a certain state. So, the attacker knows where the fault occurs but the attacker may or may not know which byte has been faulted depending on the fault model. In the second case, the attacker is assumed to know everything about the hash function except the entries of the SBoxes. The attacker is assumed to have access to the hash function where the attacker has control over the input given to the hash function and tries to recover all 4 different SBoxes using stuck-at-0 fault model [6]. We show that even if the SBoxes are not known, the attacker can still successfully recover all 4 different SBoxes and hence secret SBoxes may not provide additional security to Kupyna.

The rest of the paper is organized as follows. In Sect. 2, a brief overview of fault analysis is given with the specification of Kupyna. In Sect. 3, we provide descriptions of two fault attacks on Kupyna. In Sect. 4, we provide our simulation results and discussions. Section 5 concludes the paper.

2   Background and Related Work

2.1   Fault Analysis

In fault analysis [12], an attacker tries to retrieve information which is not known to the attacker such as a secret key or a secret input by intervening with the computation. Intervening with the computation allows the attacker to retrieve a set of correct and faulty output pairs. By comparing those correct and faulty output pairs, the attacker recovers the secret key or the secret input. Fault attacks are mostly applied to ciphers since the security of ciphers relies on a secret key. However, hash functions also started to receive attention in terms of fault analysis since they can be used to build MAC (Message Authentication Code) schemes. In a typical fault analysis, the attacker gives a plaintext and retrieves the correct ciphertext. After that, the attacker faults the computation at a specific state and retrieves a set of faulty ciphertexts. Using the correct ciphertext and the set of faulty ciphertexts, the attacker aims to retrieve information about the secret material. In differential fault analysis, information is retrieved by comparing differences between the correct ciphertext and the set of faulty ciphertexts. In ineffective fault analysis [6], information about the secret material is retrieved when the presented fault has no effect on the output. In other words, a fault gives information about the secret material only when the correct and faulty outputs are the same. In this paper, we apply both differential fault analysis and ineffective fault analysis to Kupyna.

In order to perform fault analysis, faults need to be injected in order to intervene with the computation of the internal state of the cryptographic primitive. Fault injection can be done in different ways which include power glitches, clock pulses, laser radiation [13]. Fault analysis was first applied to retrieve the secret key in RSA-CRT algorithm [5] by Boneh et al. After that, this idea was generalized by Biham and Shamir where they introduced a concept called Differential Fault Analysis [4].

In addition to the fault attack applied on RSA-CRT algorithm [5], fault attacks were also applied to other cryptographic primitives. In [4], authors showed that differential fault analysis can be applied to DES (Data Encryption Standard) and it allows the attacker to break DES by analyzing a small number of ciphertexts generated from random plaintexts. In [9], authors apply differential fault analysis on AES (Advanced Encryption Standard) and show that AES-128 can be broken with ten faulty messages in a short time. In [19], authors introduced a fault attack which can break AES-128 with only 2 faulty ciphertexts. In [20], the authors performed fault analysis on CEASAR candidate ACORN v2 and concluded that all faults can be located and the initial step can be recovered with 41 faults. In [10], the authors performed differential fault analysis on the hash function, Grøstl, and showed that attackers are able to recover input messages. In [14], the authors performed fault analysis on SHACAL-1 and demonstrated that the 512-bit secret key in SHACAL-1 can be recovered using 120 faults. In [8], the authors performed fault analysis on the Ukrainian standard cipher, Kalyna, and showed that even though Kalyna seems to be more resistant to fault analysis compared to other standard ciphers such as AES, it can still be broken using a reasonable number of faults. For further information about the plausibility of fault analysis and different fault models, the reader is referred to [12].

2.2 Specification of Kupyna

Kupyna hash function is an **IV** (initialization vector) dependent mapping of a given message to a hash code. After the input massage is given, the result of each computation is referred as the internal state. A given hash input goes through many states until it becomes the hash output. The number of output bits can be chosen by the user and it determines the number of bytes in the state and the number of rounds. The notation Kupyna-η denotes Kupyna with η output bits, where $\eta \in \{8 \times s | s = 1, 2, ..., 64\}$. For Kupyna-$\eta$, the number of rounds ($\rho$) and the number of bytes in the internal state (μ) are given by:

$$\rho = \begin{cases} 10, & \text{if } 8 \leq \eta \leq 256. \\ 14, & \text{if } 256 \leq \eta \leq 512. \end{cases}$$

$$\mu = \begin{cases} 64, & \text{if } 8 \leq \eta \leq 256. \\ 128, & \text{if } 256 \leq \eta \leq 512. \end{cases}$$

Kupyna can be used with a known **IV** or secret **IV**, where in known **IV**, **IV** is defined as:

$$\mathbf{IV} = \begin{cases} 1 \ll 510, & \text{if } \mu = 64. \\ 1 \ll 1023, & \text{if } \mu = 128. \end{cases}$$

Kupyna can process messages with length from 1 bit to $2^{96} - 1$ bits. Each message is padded regardless of its length and the padding adds one additional block to hashing. This additional block contains single "1" bit, followed by d zero bits where d is calculated as:

$$d = (-N - 97) \bmod \beta$$

where N is the number of bits in the input block and β is the number of bits in the state which is calculated as $\beta = 8 \times \mu$. Padding ensures that number of input bits is a multiple of number of bits in the internal state ($\beta \in \{512, 1024\}$). After that, the next 96 remaining bits contain the length of the input message in terms of number of bits, N, in little endian. After padding, the message is divided into k blocks of length μ bytes each. So, the hash function processes k blocks, i.e., it involves k block operations and one truncation operation at the end.

Each block contains functions which work similar to the cipher Kalyna [18], these functions are called: $\tau^{\oplus}$ and τ^{+} and are defined as:

$$\tau^{\oplus} = \prod_{0}^{\rho-1} (\psi \circ \alpha \circ \sigma \circ \kappa) \qquad \tau^{+} = \prod_{0}^{\rho-1} (\psi \circ \alpha \circ \sigma \circ \theta)$$

where:

- ψ is a linear transformation layer which uses the same vector as Kalyna [18] which is :

$$v = (0x01, 0x01, 0x05, 0x01, 0x08, 0x06, 0x07, 0x04)$$

Row i and column j of the new state matrix are calculated as:

$$\omega_{i,j} = (v \ggg i) \otimes G_j,$$

where G_j is column j of the state matrix and $\otimes$ is Galois field multiplication in the finite field $\mathrm{GF}(2^8)$ with irreducible polynomial $\gamma(x) = x^8 + x^4 + x^3 + x^2 + 1$.
- α is the shift rows operation which circular right shifts each row. There are 8 rows in the state matrix for each column numbered as $0 \cdots 7$, and each row i is circular right shifted by i bytes except the row number 7. Row number 7 is circular right shifted by 7 bytes if block size (μ) is 64 bytes and it is circular right shifted by 11 bytes if block size (μ) is 128 bytes.
- σ is the non-linear transformation of bytes, where each byte value is mapped to another byte value based on Kupyna SBoxes. Kupyna uses 4 different SBoxes (S_0, S_1, S_2, S_3) and which SBox to use depends on the row number and for row i, SBox to use is calculated as "$i \bmod 4$".
- θ is the modulo 2^{64} addition of round constant to the current state.
- κ is XOR addition of the round constant to the current state.
- $G_{i,j}$ refers to row i and column j of the current state.

The round keys for operations κ and θ are known and are calculated as follows:

- For κ, where the round key is added to current state using XOR operation (modulo 2 addition), the round key is calculated as $\varpi(j) = ((j \ll 4) \oplus v, 0, 0, 0, 0, 0, 0, 0)^T$ where v is the round number and j is the column of current state $G_{i,j}$.
- For θ, where the round key is added to current state using modulo 2^{64} addition, the round key is calculated as $\varkappa(j) = ((0xF3, 0xF0, 0xF0, 0xF0, 0xF0, 0xF0, 0xF0, (c-1-j) \ll 4))^T$ where c is total number of columns in state which is 8 for $\mu = 64$ and 16 for $\mu = 128$ and j is the column of current state $G_{i,j}$.

For a given message M which is padded and divided into k blocks $m_1, m_2, .., m_k$, the result of the hash function Kupyna-η is calculated as:

$$h_0 = \mathbf{IV}$$
$$h_i = \tau^{\oplus}(h_{i-1} \oplus m_i) \oplus \tau^{+}(h_{i-1}) \oplus h_{i-1} \text{ for i} = 1, 2, .., k$$
$$H(\mathbf{IV}, M) = R_{l,n}(\tau^{\oplus}(h_k) \oplus h_k)$$

where $R_{l,n}$ is the truncation function which retrieves l most significant bits of input of n bits. Figure 1 shows a block diagram of Kupyna for a given message M and an initialization vector $\mathbf{IV}$.

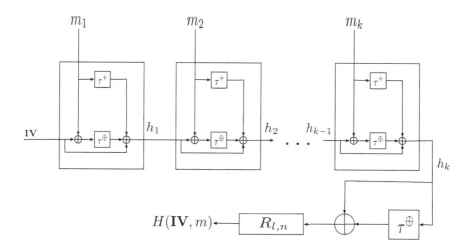

Fig. 1. Block diagram of Kupyna hashing operation

During the description of our attacks on Kupyna, we use the same notation as we use for operations to refer to states except we have two subindices which are the block number and the round number. Block numbers go from 1 to k. The last $\tau^{\oplus}$ block before the truncation is a special block and it will be referred as block number t. As an example, if we refer to block number k and the state input to the substitution layer in round $r - 1$ in $\tau^\oplus$ operation of the block, we will refer to that state as $\tau^\oplus[\sigma_{k,r-1}]$ where r is the total number of rounds. In order to refer to a specific byte in the state located at row i and column j, we use $\tau^\oplus[\sigma_{k,r-1}][i][j]$.

2.3   Existing Attacks on Kupyna

In [11], the authors present a collision attack and a preimage attack on 5 rounds of Kupyna-256 but conclude that their attacks do not demonstrate that Kupyna is not secure. Later, in [7], the authors perform rebound attacks on Kupyna and conclude that even though Kupyna contains a modular addition of some round constants rather than XOR addition, it is still vulnerable to rebound attacks.

3   Proposed Attacks on Kupyna

3.1   Differential Fault Analysis on Kupyna with Known SBoxes

Attack Goal. Kupyna can be used to build MAC schemes in secret-IV or secret prefix mode. In the secret-IV mode, the **IV** is the secret information to be recovered. In the secret prefix mode, a secret input is appended to the input message such that the message input to the hash function becomes $Prefix \parallel M$. In this attack we are going to recover all the message blocks and the value of **IV** which allows us to break the MAC scheme if the MAC scheme is used in secret-IV or secret prefix settings. Throughout the rest of the paper, we will illustrate our attacks on Kupyna-256 but our analysis can be extended to other versions of Kupyna with different message digest lengths.

Attack Procedure. Our approach contains two stages. First, we aim to recover h_k which is the input to $\tau^\oplus[\kappa_{k+1,0}]$ as shown in Fig. 1. So, $\tau^\oplus_{k+1}$ is the first block we are going to apply faults to. After recovering h_k, our next goal is to recover inputs to each block $(m_1, m_2, \cdots, m_k)$. During this process, the **IV** is also recovered. It should be noted that the size of the hash output is not the same as the size of the state since there is a truncation step in Kupyna. Hence, we first recover some bytes of the state $\tau^\oplus[\sigma_{k+1,t-1}]$, we will refer to that partial state as $\tau^\oplus[\sigma_{k+1,t-1}]'$. After that, we recover the full state of $\tau^\oplus[\sigma_{k+1,t-2}]$ which allows us to recover h_k by going backwards. In order to recover the inputs to a message block i, which are h_{i-1} and m_i, we first recover the input to $\tau^+[\sigma_{i,t-1}]$, then going backwards allows us to recover m_i. After that we recover the input to $\tau^\oplus[\sigma_{i,t-1}]$ and going backwards allows us to recover the value of $m_i \oplus h_{i-1}$. By knowing m_i and $m_i \oplus h_{i-1}$, we can recover h_{i-1}. Then the same approach is recursively applied to all the blocks until all inputs are recovered.

In order to recover the partial state $\tau^\oplus[\sigma_{k+1,t-1}]'$, we first need to find byte indices in the state $\tau^\oplus[\sigma_{k+1,t-1}]$ that propagate to the output (see Fig. 2 which shows indices of bytes that survive after the truncation step). Faults are applied to the input to $\tau^{\oplus}[\sigma_{k+1,t-1}]$. Some faults give us information about state bytes in the input to the last round SubBytes operation. However, some faults do not give any information about the input state to the last round SubBytes. As shown in Fig. 2, if a fault is applied to the byte index 0 among the indices, then this fault does not give any information about the partial state $\tau^{\oplus}[\sigma_{k+1,t-1}]'$. However, if the fault is applied to the byte index 32, this fault gives us information about the byte index 32 (row 0, column 4) of the partial state $\tau^{\oplus}[\sigma_{k+1,t-1}]'$. Using the same approach, we recover all state bytes in the partial state that propagate to the output.

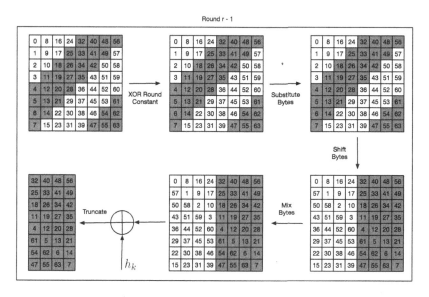

Fig. 2. Propagation of bytes to the output in Kupyna

In order to find the value of byte input in the partial state $\tau^{\oplus}[\sigma_{k+1,t-1}]'$ for a specific index among indices, which survive the truncation step, we use the following property of the SBoxes:

If x is a random input byte, and if Δ_i is chosen from the set: $\Delta = \{0x01, 0x02, 0x04, 0x08, 0x10, 0x20, 0x40, 0x80\}$ where $1 < i \leq n$, and n is the number of faults, then x is uniquely determined using only using the values for Λ_i in the following equation [2]:

$$S(x) \oplus S(x \oplus \Delta_i) = \Lambda_i \qquad (1)$$

This means that x can be recovered using n output differences Λ_i corresponding to n one-bit distinct faults Δ_i. According to our experiments, the average number of faults required to recover x uniquely is about 2.42 if known byte random fault model is used. If known byte unique fault model is used, the average number of faults required to recover x uniquely is about 2.21.

In order to retrieve the state bytes in the partial state $\tau^{\oplus}[\sigma_{k+1,t-1}]'$, first the attacker calculates the correct hash value for a given message. After that, the attacker faults the computation at $\tau^{\oplus}[\sigma_{k+1,t-1}]$ by applying one of the values among Δ to a byte value. The attacker knows which byte is faulted if it is a chosen fault model. However, in the random fault model, the attacker does not know which byte is faulted. After the attacker applies the fault, she receives a faulty result. We call the correct hash value as H and the faulty hash value as H'. After getting H and H', the attacker calculates the difference between H and H' backwards by calculating the following equation:

$$\Omega = \alpha^{-1} \circ \psi^{-1}(H \oplus H') \tag{2}$$

Figure 3 shows the propagation of a fault applied at byte index 4 in the input to SubBytes operation in the last round. Ω is calculated as the inverse MixColumns and the inverse ShiftRows operations are applied to the difference between the correct state and the faulty state. The result of this calculation will be all zeros except in one byte position and that byte position gives us which byte was faulted and the nonzero value in that byte position gives us one value for Λ. Using this Λ, we find candidates for the byte using Eq. 1. After that, we find other values for Λ and narrow down the list of candidates until there is only one candidate remaining. This allows us to recover the partial state $\tau^{\oplus}[\sigma_{k+1,t-1}]'$.

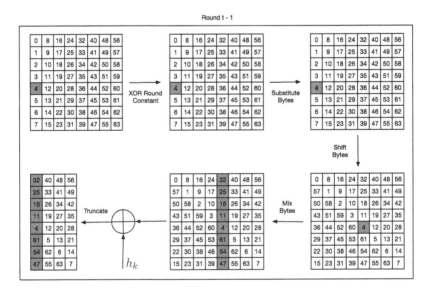

Fig. 3. Propagation of a fault applied at byte index 4 in Kupyna

Then the next step is to recover the full state just before that partial state. This state, $\tau^{\oplus}[\kappa_{k+1,t-1}]$, can be recovered directly since the round constant is known. However, recovering the input to the MixColumns operation just before the addition of the round constant in the last round $(\tau^{\oplus}[\psi_{k+1,t-2}])$ is a bit more difficult. In order to recover the input to MixColumns operation in the round $(t-2)$, we are going to use the following property of the MixColumns operation:

Let $s \in G$ be a state matrix with only one non-zero entry in row i and column j such that $G_{i,j} = s'$ and $G_{i,j} = 0$ for all other entries, then the value of s' can be determined by knowing two entries in MixColumns operation applied to G.

This means that if we give an input to the MixColumns operation a state matrix which has only one nonzero entry, we can get this nonzero entry uniquely if we know at least two bytes in the result of the MixColumns operation. Note that, this MixColumns operation changes byte values in the same column as that nonzero entry. To illustrate, as shown in Fig. 4, if we give a state matrix as input which is all zeros except byte a to the MixColumns operation, then we can find a uniquely if we know at least two entries among $A, \cdots, H$. In order to use this property, we fault the SBox input to round $(t-2)$, which is $\tau^{\oplus}[\sigma_{k+1,t-2}]$.

After faulting the SBox input at round $(t-2)$, the attacker retrieves the correct and the faulty hash results which are H and H'. Then, the attacker calculates the difference between these as $H \oplus H'$ and calculates this difference backwards by calculating the following equation:

$$\Omega' = \alpha^{-1} \circ \psi^{-1}(H \oplus H')$$

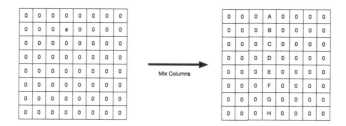

Fig. 4. Kupyna MixColumns with input which has only one nonzero byte

However, since the SBox operation is not linear, in order to calculate the difference between the correct state and the faulty state just before SBox operation, we will use the bytes of partial state $\tau^{\oplus}[\sigma_{k+1,t-1}]'$ we recovered in the previous step which corresponds to actual bytes in the correct state. Let x_i be one of the bytes recovered in the previous step, i be the byte index for x_i and $G'[i]$ be the byte at index i at the faulty state, then

$$G'[i] = S(x_i) \oplus \Omega'[i]$$

gives us the byte value of the faulty state after the SubBytes operation and before the ShiftRows operation at round $(t-1)$, $\tau^{\oplus}[\alpha_{k+1,t-1}]$. We do the same for all values of x_i we recovered in the previous step and we get the partial bytes of the faulty state after the first SubBytes operation in the last round. After that, if we go backwards, by applying the inverse of SubBytes (σ^{-1}) operation to the bytes of the faulty state, we get the state difference after addition of the round constant in the last round as:

$$G^{'}[i] = \sigma^{-1}(G^{'}[i])$$

Since we know the bytes just before SubBytes operation in the correct state and in the faulty state, we can then calculate their state difference as:

$$\Omega^{''}[i] = G^{'}[i] \oplus x_i$$

This difference will have only one nonzero byte in one column and using the property of the MixColumns operation, we are able to retrieve the location of the byte and the value of the byte at the input to the MixColumns operation at round $(t-2)$, $\tau^{\oplus}[\psi_{k+1,t-2}]$. This is the state matrix which has one nonzero byte value and applying the inverse of ShiftRows to this state matrix $(\alpha^{-1}(G^{'}))$, we get the difference after the SubBytes operation at round $(t-2)$ and using Eq. 1, we are able to get the SBox input to round $(t-2)$, so we are able to recover the full state $\tau^{\oplus}[\sigma_{k+1,t-2}]$. Then we are able to recover h_k by going backwards from the state $\tau^{\oplus}[\sigma_{k+1,t-2}]$.

After recovering h_k, our goal is to recover the inputs to each block in order to break the hash function by recovering the input message and the value of **IV**. Since the attacker is only able to observe the correct and the faulty results, we need to create a lookup table for each possible case when we apply fault analysis to recover inputs of each block. The cost of creating such a lookup table can be calculated as $\mu \times 255$ since we consider each fault applied to each byte. This lookup table is created by applying possible differences that can come from faults to h_k before applying h_k to the truncation function. In order to recover m_k and h_{k-1} for the block k, first the attacker faults $\tau^{+}[\sigma_{k,t-1}]$ and recovers the full state at the input to the SBox operation at τ^{+} block of round $(t-1)$. After that, the attacker inverts that full state and recovers m_k.

The next step is to recover h_{k-1}. In order to do so, the attacker faults $\tau^{\oplus}[\sigma_{k,t-1}]$ and recovers the full state at the input to the SBox operation at $\tau^{\oplus}[\sigma_{k,t-1}]$ block of round $(t-1)$ and inverts this state to recover $h_{k-1} \oplus m_k$ as shown in Fig. 1. Using this known input and the recovered m_k from the previous step, the attacker is able to recover h_{k-1}. The same procedure is applied for all other blocks from 1 to $(k-1)$.

For the known byte random and known byte unique fault models, each fault gives us information about the state we are aiming to recover. However, in the random fault model, some faults may end up giving no information about the state we are aiming to recover since the difference between the correct result and the faulty result may be 0 if the faulted byte was truncated by the truncation step.

So far, we have shown how to break Kupyna if it is used in the secret-IV or secret prefix mode. We recover all inputs to the hash function including the value of **IV** and m_1. If Kupyna is used as the underlying block for HMAC [3], then the output is calculated as:

$$HMAC(K, m) = H((K \oplus opad)||H((K \oplus ipad)||m))$$

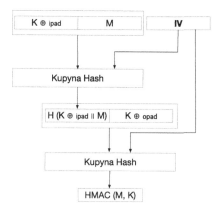

Fig. 5. Kupyna in HMAC mode

In this function, opad and ipad are known constants and K is the secret key we are aiming to recover (see Fig. 5).

In this case, we first recover the input to the hash function which is $((K \oplus opad)||H((K \oplus ipad)||m))$. This allows the attacker to know the values of $H((K \oplus ipad)||m)$ and since the value of opad is known, the attacker can determine the value of K. Using the value of $H((K \oplus ipad)||m)$, which is the output of the first hash block as shown in Fig. 5, the attacker can recover the input which is $((K \oplus ipad)||m)$. Then, the value of K can be recovered along with the value of m if the secret prefix is applied to the value of m.

In the case of NMAC, two keys are employed and the NMAC is calculated as:

$$NMAC(M) = H_{K_2}(H_{K_1}(M))$$

This is basically applying K_2 and K_1 instead of the known value of **IV** in Fig. 5. Similar to our attack in the HMAC case, we first recover K_2 which is the input to outer block, then we recover K_1 which is the input to the inner block.

3.2 Fault Analysis on Kupyna with Unknown SBoxes

In order to recover $S_i^{-1}[0]$ for a specific SBox, firstly, the attacker needs to find ineffective bytes [6], i.e., bytes values in the input for an index that make the SBox output for that index 0. In this case, the SBox fault becomes an ineffective fault since the correct calculation and faulty calculation produce the same results. Algorithm 1 describes steps used to recover the SBox inputs that produce 0 output for each SBox.

After finding the ineffective bytes, we subtract the round constants that are added to those ineffective bytes to recover the SBox inputs. After finding the SBox inputs that lead to zero, the next step is to recover all the SBox inputs and outputs. In order to do so, we fault the SBoxes in the second round and we use two nonzero values in the first column of the state, one being an SBox entry we

---

Algorithm 1. Recovering Ineffective Bytes in Kupyna

1: // RC_0 refers to the round constant matrix for round 0 in τ^+
2: Set input M to 32 bits which has all zeros. We refer to input as M = $m_1||m_2||m_3||m_4$.
3: Initialize Ineffective Bytes$[0 \cdots 3]$ to all 0s
4: **for** Each SBox index i from 0 to 3 **do**
5:     **for** Each byte value from 0 to 255, called currentByte and IneffectiveByte is not found **do**
6:         Set m_i to currentByte
7:         Set input M to all zeros except m_i which is $currentByte$
8:         Calculate the hash value without fault, called H
9:         Calculate hash value with fault to SBox $S_{1,0}[i][0]$
10:         **if** H is equal to H' **then**
11:             Set $IneffectiveBytes[i] = currentByte$ and ineffectiveByte is found.
12:         **end if**
13:     **end for**
14:     Calculate the SBox inputs which give output 0 for each SBox i as $S_i^{-1}[0] = IneffectiveBytes[i] - RC_0[0][i]$
15: **end for**

---

recovered before and the other being the byte input we would like to find and which forces the output of SBox in the second round to 0. Figure 6 shows how the attacker is able to choose the input to the hash function in a way such that the state becomes all zeros except two positions after the first round SubBytes and the ShiftRows operations.

Figure 6 also shows how the state propagates after $\sigma_{1,0}$. In this figure a is an SBox input that has been recovered and $S(a)$ is the corresponding output, and m is the byte value that propagates from 0 to 255 until an ineffective fault occurs. The attacker needs to take the ShiftRows operation into account since the input to the MixColumns operation has to be all zeros except the two bytes in the first column. The location of the fault is shown in red and faults are applied to the bytes in the state after $\sigma_{1,1}$. For S_0, we use indices 0 and 4. For S_1, we use indices 1 and 5. For S_2, we use indices 2 and 6 and for S_3, we use indices 3 and 7. Algorithm 2 explains steps to recover all SBox entries.

The above attack allows us to recover all the four SBoxes used in Kupyna. Since the round key addition is modulo 2^{64} addition, sometimes we get two candidates for $S(m)$. In this case, we ignore those candidates and only add entries when we are able to determine $S(m)$ uniquely for a given m.

4   Results and Discussion

For the first experiment, we simulate Kupyna-256 using three different fault models and using random input of 64 bytes which is processed in two blocks after padding. For known byte fault models, we estimate the number of faults required to recover SBox input for each byte, that is number of Λ (SBox difference) values

Algorithm 2. Recovering all SBox entries in Kupyna

1: Initialize RecoveredValues to empty set for each SBox.
2: // FirstIndex refers to index where m is iterated
3: // SecondIndex refers to index where a is used.
4: **for** each SBox index i from 0 to 3 **do**
5:     Initialize a to $S_i^{-1}[0]$ recovered in algorithm 1
6:     **for** each index from 0 to 7 which refers to bytes in the first column of $\psi_{1,0}$ **do**
7:         **for** each m from 0 to 255 **do**
8:             Find hash input which makes MixColumns input in round 0, $\psi_{1,0}$ to all zeros except $\psi_{1,0}[FirstIndex][0] = S_i(m)$ and $\psi_{1,0}[SecondIndex][0] = S_i(a)$
9:             Get the Hash output without fault, called H
10:            Get the Hash output with faulted SBox at $S_{1,1}[index][0]$ called H'
11:            If ineffective fault occurs, find the value of $S(m)$ according to the Mix-Columns operation that makes the output byte at index $S_{1,1}[index][0] = 0$
12:            If $S_i(m)$ is found uniquely, add $(m, S(m))$ to $RecoveredValues[i]$
13:         **end for**
14:         Set a to the next value in $RecoveredValues[i]$ and find another m,
15:         If all possible $RecoveredValues[i]$ are used for a, then go to next index
16:     **end for**
17: **end for**

that uniquely define the value of x (SBox input) in Eq. 1. For unique fault model the average number of Λ values that uniquely find x is 2.21. For random fault model the average number of Λ values that uniquely find x is 2.43. After that, we experiment each fault model 10 times and find the average number of faults

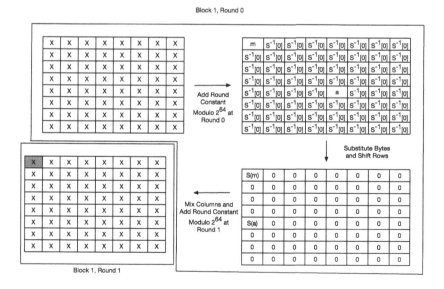

Fig. 6. Kupyna SBox fault at round 1 and recovering SBoxes

required to recover half of state at $\tau^{\oplus}[\sigma_{t,r-1}]$ (Input to last round MixColumns), than to recover $\tau^{\oplus}[\kappa_{t,r-1}]$ (Input to last round XOR addition of the round key), which are needed to recover h_k (output from the last block). After that we need to recover two inputs to each of two blocks which are input values for h and m. Our simulation results can be summarized as follows:

– For known byte random fault model, the average number of faults required to recover half of the state $\sigma_{t,r-1}$ is 79.3, the average number of faults to recover the full state $\kappa_{t,r-1}$ is 155.8 (h_2 is recovered using the full state $\kappa_{t,r-1}$). For block number 1, the average number of faults to recover the message input(m_1) is 153.1, the average number of faults to recover the hash input(**IV**) is 157.7. For block number 2, the average number of faults to recover the message input(m_2) is 154.3, the average number of faults to recover the hash input(h_1) is 155.1. So, inputs to the hash function (**IV**, m_1, m_2, h_1, h_2) can be recovered using $\approx 79.3 + 155.8 + 153.1 + 157.7 + 154.3 + 155.1 = 855.3$ faults.
– For known byte unique fault model, the average number of faults required to recover half of the state $\sigma_{t,r-1}$ is 70.7, the average number of faults to recover the full state $\kappa_{t,r-1}$ is 141.3 (h_2 is recovered using the full state $\kappa_{t,r-1}$). For block number 1, the average number of faults to recover the message input(m_1) is 142.2, the average number of faults to recover the hash input(**IV**) is 142.1. For block number 2, the average number of faults to recover the message input(m_2) is 140.6, the average number of faults to recover the hash input(h_1) is 143.9. These results are consistent in terms of the number of expected faults required to recover each byte. So, inputs to the hash function can be recovered using $\approx 70.7 + 141.3 + 142.2 + 142.1 + 140.6 + 143.9 = 780.8$ faults.
– For random fault model, not every fault results in useful information since bytes affected by the fault may be eliminated during the truncation step. In this model, the average number of faults required to recover the half of the state $\sigma_{t,r-1}$ is 454.5, the average number of faults to recover the full state $\kappa_{t,r-1}$ is 587 (h_2 is recovered using the full state $\kappa_{t,r-1}$). For block number 1, the average number of faults to recover the message input (m_1) is 535.4, the average number of faults to recover the hash input(**IV**) is 570.3. For block number 2, the average number of faults to recover the message input(m_2) is 558.5, the average number of faults to recover the hash input(h_1) is 543.1. In average, number of faults is mostly between 8 and 9 per byte if random fault model is used. So, inputs to the hash function can be recovered using $\approx 454.5 + 587 + 535.4 + 570.3 + 558.5 + 543.1 = 3248.8$ faults.

For the SBox recovery attack, our simulation results confirmed that our attack successfully recovers the entries for all the 4 SBoxes. More precisely, we experimented 10 times using randomly selected SBoxes, and we were always able to correctly recover all the SBox entries.

Table 1 summarizes our experiment results for differential fault analysis.

Table 1. Summary of experiments

Recovered values	Fault model		
	Known byte random fault model	Known byte unique fault model	Random byte random fault model
m_1	153.1	142.2	535.4
m_2	154.3	140.6	558.5
h_1	155.1	143.9	543.1
h_2	$79.3 + 155.8 = 235.1$	$70.7 + 141.3 = 212$	$454.5 + 587 = 1041.5$
IV	157.7	142.1	570.3
Total	**855.3**	**780.8**	**3248.8**

5   Conclusion

In this paper, we investigated the security of Kupyna hash function, which is a newly accepted standard by the Ukrainian government, against fault analysis. We proposed two different fault attacks against Kupyna. In the first attack, we assume that the attacker has all the information except the input to the hash function and the attacker is trying to recover the input to the hash function. In the second case, we assume that Kupyna is used with secret SBoxes and the attacker aims to recover SBox entries for all SBoxes. According to our experiments, if Kupyna-256 is using two blocks for a given input, the input and the value of **IV** can be recovered using known byte random fault model with 855.3 faults, using known byte unique fault model 780.8 faults, using random fault model with 3248.8 if fault models on average. We have also shown that making Kupyna SBoxes secret does not add any security since round constants are known and SBoxes can be recovered easily. We have also shown how our attacks can be applied to different modes which are Secret-IV, Secret-Prefix, HMAC and NMAC. Even though those attacks may not present a threat to the theoretical security of Kupyna directly, they serve as example to demonstrate the fact that it is important to protect implementations of Kupyna when utilized to build MAC schemes, even if its Sboxes are kept secret.

References

1. GOST R 34.11-2012: Streebog Hash Function. https://www.streebog.net/. Accessed 10 Nov 2017
2. AlTawy, R., Youssef, A.M.: Differential fault analysis of streebog. In: Lopez, J., Wu, Y. (eds.) ISPEC 2015. LNCS, vol. 9065, pp. 35–49. Springer, Cham (2015). https://doi.org/10.1007/978-3-319-17533-1_3
3. Bellare, M., Canetti, R., Krawczyk, H.: Keying hash functions for message authentication. In: Koblitz, N. (ed.) CRYPTO 1996. LNCS, vol. 1109, pp. 1–15. Springer, Heidelberg (1996). https://doi.org/10.1007/3-540-68697-5_1

4. Biham, E., Shamir, A.: Differential fault analysis of secret key cryptosystems. In: Kaliski, B.S. (ed.) CRYPTO 1997. LNCS, vol. 1294, pp. 513–525. Springer, Heidelberg (1997). https://doi.org/10.1007/BFb0052259

5. Boneh, D., DeMillo, R.A., Lipton, R.J.: On the importance of eliminating errors in cryptographic computations. J. Cryptology **14**(2), 101–119 (2001)

6. Clavier, C., Wurcker, A.: Reverse engineering of a secret AES-like cipher by ineffective fault analysis. In: 2013 Workshop on Fault Diagnosis and Tolerance in Cryptography, pp. 119–128, August 2013

7. Dobraunig, C., Eichlseder, M., Mendel, F.: Analysis of the Kupyna-256 hash function. In: Peyrin, T. (ed.) FSE 2016. LNCS, vol. 9783, pp. 575–590. Springer, Heidelberg (2016). https://doi.org/10.1007/978-3-662-52993-5_29

8. Duman, O., Youssef, A.M.: Fault analysis on Kalyna. Inf. Secur. J. Global Persp. **26**(5), 249–265 (2017)

9. Dusart, P., Letourneux, G., Vivolo, O.: Differential fault analysis on A.E.S. In: Zhou, J., Yung, M., Han, Y. (eds.) ACNS 2003. LNCS, vol. 2846, pp. 293–306. Springer, Heidelberg (2003). https://doi.org/10.1007/978-3-540-45203-4_23

10. Fischer, W., Reuter, C.A.: Differential fault analysis on Grøstl. In: 2012 Workshop on Fault Diagnosis and Tolerance in Cryptography, pp. 44–54, September 2012

11. Jian Zou, L.D.: Cryptanalysis of the Round-Reduced Kupyna Hash Function. Cryptology ePrint Archive, Report 2015/959 (2015). https://eprint.iacr.org/2015/959

12. Joye, M., Tunstall, M. (eds.): Fault Analysis in Cryptography, vol. 147. Springer, Berlin (2012). https://doi.org/10.1007/978-3-642-29656-7

13. Kim, C.H., Quisquater, J.J.: Faults, injection methods, and fault attacks. IEEE Des. Test Comput. **24**(6), 544–545 (2007)

14. Li, R., Li, C., Gong, C.: Differential fault analysis on SHACAL-1. In: 2009 Workshop on Fault Diagnosis and Tolerance in Cryptography (FDTC), pp. 120–126, September 2009

15. Mendel, F., Pramstaller, N., Rechberger, C.: A (second) preimage attack on the GOST hash function. In: Nyberg, K. (ed.) FSE 2008. LNCS, vol. 5086, pp. 224–234. Springer, Heidelberg (2008). https://doi.org/10.1007/978-3-540-71039-4_14

16. Mendel, F., Pramstaller, N., Rechberger, C., Kontak, M., Szmidt, J.: Cryptanalysis of the GOST hash function. In: Wagner, D. (ed.) CRYPTO 2008. LNCS, vol. 5157, pp. 162–178. Springer, Heidelberg (2008). https://doi.org/10.1007/978-3-540-85174-5_10

17. Oliynykov, R., et al.: A New Standard of Ukraine: The Kupyna Hash Function. Cryptology ePrint Archive, Report 2015/885 (2015). https://eprint.iacr.org/2015/885

18. Oliynykov, R., et al.: A new encryption standard of Ukraine: the Kalyna block cipher. Cryptology ePrint Archive, Report 2015/650 (2015). https://eprint.iacr.org/2015/650

19. Piret, G., Quisquater, J.-J.: A differential fault attack technique against SPN structures, with application to the AES and KHAZAD. In: Walter, C.D., Koç, Ç.K., Paar, C. (eds.) CHES 2003. LNCS, vol. 2779, pp. 77–88. Springer, Heidelberg (2003). https://doi.org/10.1007/978-3-540-45238-6_7

20. Zhang Xiaojuan, X.F., Lin, D.: Fault attack on the authenticated cipher ACORN v2. Secur. Commun. Netw. **2017**, 16 (2017). Article ID 3834685

Cyber Physical Security and Hardware Security

When Fault Injection Collides
with Hardware Complexity

Sebanjila Kevin Bukasa[(✉)], Ludovic Claudepierre, Ronan Lashermes,
and Jean-Louis Lanet

LHS Inria, Rennes, France
{sebanjila.bukasa,ludovic.claudepierre,ronan.lashermes,
jean-louis.lanet}@inria.fr

Abstract. Fault Injections (FI) against hardware circuits can make a
system inoperable or lead to information security breaches. FI can be
used preemptively in order to detect and mitigate weaknesses in a design.
FI is an old field of study and therefore numerous techniques and tools
can be used for that purpose. Each technique can be used at different
levels of circuit design, and has strengths and weaknesses. In this paper,
we review these techniques to show their pros and cons and more precisely we highlight their shortcomings with respect to the complexity of
modern systems.

1 Introduction

In the field of hardware security, Fault Injection (FI) is a technique to alter the
correct execution of a program in a chip. The resulting errors can be harnessed
in order to weaken the security of the device, by extracting cryptographic keys
for example. In the case of hardware security, the distinction between errors (the
internal system state is erroneous) and failures (the behaviour does not follow
specifications) is blurred. Indeed, the attacker can observe, or deduce, the state
of the device though its interaction with the environment; thus it is considered
that the attacker can observe errors and exploit them. For example, a timing
attack can leak a password during its verification. It is therefore common to use
the term *errors* to designate either errors or failures.

A fault may be caused by radiation (laser pulses, electromagnetic pulses,
alpha particles, ...), power glitches, clock glitches, abnormal temperatures, etc.
Faults are naturally found in hardware, but can also be voluntarily caused by
an attacker. In all cases, they can often be exploited for malicious activities.
Therefore faults must be mitigated.

FI can be used to infer the faults that can be created in a system, to analyse
the errors created as a consequence and whether they make the system vulnerable. The difficulty is in the trade-off between the size of the state space to
explore and the speed of the analysis. We will show that the complexity of modern system renders FI tools less precise because they cannot accurately model
the erroneous states.

© Springer Nature Switzerland AG 2019
N. Zincir-Heywood et al. (Eds.): FPS 2018, LNCS 11358, pp. 243–256, 2019.
https://doi.org/10.1007/978-3-030-18419-3_16

In this paper, after a context presentation in Sect. 2, we review the techniques and tools to assess the vulnerability of a device to FI in Sect. 3. The shortcomings of actual techniques will be presented in Sect. 4 as well as a discussion on how to improve them. Finally, the conclusion is drawn in Sect. 5.

2   Context Safety/Security

FI is an old research discipline [1–4], which originates from the study of fault tolerant systems, mainly from aerospace. FI is defined by Arlat [5] as a validation technique of dependability for fault tolerant systems. It consists in observing system behaviour in presence of faults defined with a fault model. At the beginning, FI was applied on hardware components. Consequently, corresponding fault models were comprised of effects that were deemed representative for failing logic elements, in particular stuck-at logical zero or one. One would be able to inject a fault at transistor level which models an unintended physical effect, such as a signal transition caused by a heavy ion hit and resulting in a communication error at system level for example. While this approach is close to reality, a practical implementation is barely possible.

All FI techniques aim to solve several problems:

– Injection of faults;
– Observation of their effects;
– Intrusiveness of the solution;
– Capacity to explore the entire state space.

The FI techniques have been recognized for a long time necessary to validate the dependability of a system by analysing the behaviour of devices when a fault occurs. More recently, secure devices have to face fault attacks which are similar to failure problems. Efforts have been made to develop techniques for injecting faults into a system prototype or model.

When considering information security, fault injection assumes that the attacker is able to target specific assets in the system. It means that she knows exactly what kind of behaviour she requires to reach her goal. In case of targeting cryptographic algorithms [6,7] or assets (keys, tokens, ...) several solutions have been proposed to protect them against fault injections [8]. Applications can be designed to be resilient against FI, but this resilience mainly focus on software execution of these applications, in some cases this can be a problem, indeed a complete confidence is given to hardware.

3   Fault Injection Techniques

Several techniques exist to inject faults, all of them with advantages and disadvantages. Here is an overview of these techniques.

3.1 Hardware-Based FI

Hardware based FI aims at disturbing hardware with physical and environmental parameters (heavy ion radiation, electromagnetic interferences [9], *etc.*), injecting voltage dips on power rails [10,11] laser fault injection [12] or modifying the value of some pins with circuit editing. The main advantage of this family of techniques over the other solutions is that they evaluate the final device. To achieve this kind of FI it is necessary to possess a final version of the evaluated device.

The effects of physical injections are difficult to control and repeatability of experiment is hard to achieve. To obtain repeatability, instead of injecting physically a fault, injection mechanisms emulate effects of physical perturbations on hardware such as pin-level FI [13].

Fault Injection system for Study of Transient fault effects (FIST) uses heavy-ion radiation or power disturbance faults to create faults inside a chip when it is exposed to radiation. It can cause single or multiple bit-flips producing transient faults at random locations directly inside a chip, which cannot be done with pin-level injections.

Messaline [5] is a pin-level fault forcing system. It uses both active probes and sockets to conduct pin-level fault injection. It can inject stuck-at, open, bridging and complex logical faults, among others. It can also tune the duration of the fault existence and its frequency. RIFLE [14] is also a pin-level fault injection system for dependability validation. This system can be adapted to a wide range of target systems and faults are mainly injected in processor pins. FI is deterministic and can be reproduced if needed. Different kind of faults can be injected and the fault injector is able to detect whether the injected fault has produced an error or not without specific hardware.

Obviously, hardware-based tools are also hardware dependent. Furthermore, the setup of these hardware-based injectors is rather complex.

3.2 Simulation-Based FI

Simulation based hardware fault injection techniques simulate hardware description of tested circuit using high-level models (mostly Hardware Description Language (HDL) models). It consists in injecting faults into that model to evaluate their impacts. Most of the tools modify the hardware description of tested circuit to include the components necessary to inject faults. These fault injection components can be designed to inject different fault behaviours depending on the fault model. Faults can also be injected using hardware description language simulator commands which allow variables and signals of circuit being modified.

A major disadvantage of simulation based techniques is that they are extremely slow. Simulating the register transfer level (RTL) description of a circuit is multiple orders of magnitude slower than actual circuit operation speed. Hence, even for relatively small processors, simulation based fault injection tools can only evaluate fault propagation for a very short time interval.

VERIFY [15] (VHDL-based Evaluation of Reliability by Injection Faults Efficiently) uses an extension of VHDL for describing faults correlated to a component, enabling hardware manufacturers to express their knowledge of fault behaviour on their components. Multi-threaded fault injection which uses checkpoints and comparison with a golden run is used for faster simulation of faulty runs. Proposed extension to VHDL language unfortunately requires modification on language itself. VERIFY uses an integrated fault model which cannot be extended.

MEFISTO-C [16] conducts fault injection experiments using VHDL simulation models. The tool is an improved version of MEFISTO tool which was developed jointly by LAAS-CNRS and Chalmers. MEFISTO-C uses a VHDL simulator and injects faults via simulator commands in variables and signals defined by a VHDL model. It offers to users a variety of predefined fault models as well as other features to set-up and automatically conduct fault injection campaigns.

FAUMachine [17] is a tool allowing simulation of complete systems, it was the main core for different works in the field of fault injections [18,19]. Its particularity is that it allows to simulate various types of faults and in various devices connected to the system, while making possible the observation of the impacts on the total operation of the system

3.3   Emulation-Based FI

System emulation uses hardware prototyping on Field Programmable Gate Arrays (FPGA) based logic emulation systems [20,21]. This technique has been presented as an alternative solution in order to reduce time spent during simulation-based fault injection campaigns.

This technique allows designer to study the actual behaviour of circuits in application environment, taking into account real-time interactions. However, when an emulator is used, initial VHDL description must be complete and fully synthesizable. Modified circuit contains sequences of operations which can flip their output bit based on a control signal value. Such techniques require an additional control mechanism to specify time and location of fault injection in circuit. If such a control mechanism is implemented in circuit, its complexity increases with number of fault injectable memory elements.

Antoni et al. [22] proposed a technique to inject a fault on chosen memory elements at run time on a FPGA using runtime reconfiguration. This eliminates the need for having a complex control circuit to determine injection location. However, the time required to reconfigure the circuit could be significant when compared to the total application run time.

Civera et al. [20] proposed another solution to provide a more flexible control over runtime fault injection. They used modified flip-flop circuits capable of injecting faults based on a control bit associated with each flip-flop. All these control bits are tied together like a scan-chain and at run time can be programmed to inject fault in any desired flip-flop in the circuit.

3.4 Software Implemented FI

The objective of these techniques consists in reproducing at software level errors that would have been produced by faults at hardware level. They are mostly used in order to detect and predict vulnerabilities with respect to hardware fault injection. Software implemented fault injection (SWIFI) tools use a software level abstraction of fault models in order to inject errors in software while it runs or by modifying programs before execution. This approach does not need any hardware modification. SWIFI provides a way to test complete systems including the operating system and the applicative layer. This makes SWIFI techniques quite popular and a large number of such tools exists, Table 1 summarizes some of them and explore their particularities.

Table 1. Overview of some SWIFI techniques

SWIFI technique	Fault model	Fault target	Injection point
CEU [23]	Bit flip	Variables	Runtime (interruptions)
DOCTOR [24]	Bit flips	Communications, variables	Preruntime
EFS [25]	Bit flips, code insertion, data modifications	Control flow, variables	Runtime (OS service)
FERRARI [26]	Address, data or flags modifications	Control flow, variables	Runtime (parallel process)
FIES [27]	Bit flip, bridging and stuck-at faults	Control flow, variables	Runtime
XCEPTION [28]	Bit flip, bridging and stuck-at faults	Variables	Runtime (interruptions)

The most common fault models are:

- instruction skip (one or several instructions are not executed),
- instruction modification (one or several instructions are modified according to a pattern such as single bit-flip, random change, ...).

Common software mechanisms used for run time FI, such as perturbation functions require a modification of the program. Unfortunately, this extra instrumentation causes execution overhead that will affect the system behaviour (speed, memory consumption, ...). For example, FERRARI [26] and EFS [25] tools require some context switches between its fault injection process and target system process.

A common problem with run time approach is the intrusiveness which refers to the alteration of the original system due to fault injection experiment setup (*e.g.* changes in program flow, additional components, temporal variation, ...). Depending on the actual intention of fault injection, respective tools have to cope with completely different requirements. In contrast to an ideal tool which always provides low intrusiveness, high visibility and high performance, available tools are only specialized on a subset of these requirements.

The major drawback of SWIFI is related to state space problem. The tools often generate much more faults than any other techniques (since the abstraction level has a richer representation, *i.e.* there may be 2^{32} possible instruction values in a 32-bit system and less that 2^{32} wires in the chip). Yet most of the time generated faults do not lead to failures, the error may have been silently suppressed during the execution. The challenge is to either generate only a minimal set of faults (those that can lead to a Silent Data Corruption) or to prune them while they are generated. This leads to several optimization phases during simulation and remains a difficult challenge.

In the context of information security, errors can often be exploited even in the absence of failures. An error can cause copying of a secret in a vulnerable part of memory for example. Since SWIFI tools use a software level abstraction of fault models, they cannot capture such vulnerabilities.

4   Techniques Validity

We consider ourselves as evaluators. When it comes to FI, we want to evaluate if a technique is more appropriate in order to evaluate behaviour of a device when a fault occur.

Various injection means exist and several techniques have been using them in different way and targeting several type of devices. Since simulation and emulation based techniques require a white-box model (access to HDL sources, ...) that are most of the time not available to evaluators.

In this section we limit ourselves to hardware-based and software-based injections techniques.

4.1   Experiences

In order to test the consistency of SWIFI models, in particular their software level abstraction of fault models with real observations, we conducted different experiments, which we will present here.

Faustine Platform. Our platform, called Faustine Fig. 1, is made of a Keysight 33509B pulse generator, a Keysight 81160A signal generator and a Milmega 80RF1000-175 power amplifier, connected in sequence to generate a signal. This signal then passes through a Langer RF probe RF B 0.3-3 located on the targeted chip to generate an Electromagnetic Fault Injection (EMFI).

In order to launch a fault injection, a synchronization signal (a trigger) is sent by the targeted chip General-Purpose Input/Output (GPIO) (controlled from the code) directly to the 33509B pulse generator. This experimental trick,

Fig. 1. Overview of Faustine platform

possible when the attacker has control of the code (*i.e.* only for vulnerability assessment) is not mandatory. Other synchronization possibilities include sniffing communications with the target or measuring its EM emissions to find a relevant pattern.

The location of the probe on the chip was chosen after a scan that determined the most sensitive area on the chip. The same location was kept for all experiments.

Microcontroller. We first analyse a Microcontroller (μC). The targeted board is an STM32VLDISCOVERY board with an STM32F100RB chip, embedding an ARM Cortex-M3 core running at 24 MHz (41.7 ns clock period). As shown in Fig. 2, probe is just on top of the chip.

On this board the tested software is a PIN code checker, the entered PIN code is compared with the internal PIN code if it is false (**false=1** in Listing 1.1), the status variable takes the value 0xFFFFFFFF, otherwise it takes 0x55555555. Thus in the first case, access will be denied, in the second it will be granted.

```
if(false == 1) {
   status = 0xFFFFFFFF; }
else {
   status = 0x55555555; }
```

Listing 1.1. Targeted C code

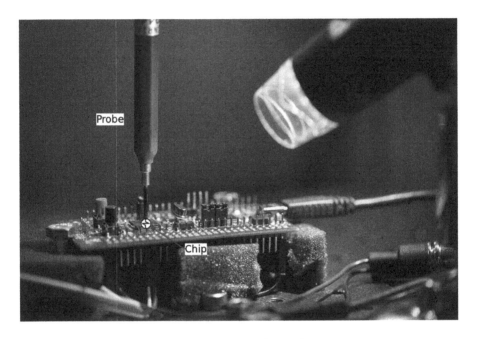

Fig. 2. STM32 under probe

```
cmp r3, #1                          ; r3 contains *false*
ite eq                              ; if then else
moveq.w r4, #4294967295    ; 0xFFFFFFFF
movne.w r4, #1431655765    ; 0x55555555
```

Listing 1.2. Resulting assembly (thumb2)

As we can see on Listing 1.2, in order to modify the behaviour of the program and thus get access without the PIN code, we can target the *if then else (ite)* instruction. If it is possible to not execute it, then the next two instructions will execute in sequence and, as their result is stored in the same register ($r4$), only the second assignment will have an impact (overwriting the first one).

In the case of SWIFI, we consider the software level abstraction of fault model by deleting (manual edition of the binary) this instruction which allows us to see that it is indeed the right target, then we target the execution of this instruction with a hardware fault.

In this way, when we inject our fault, we try to synchronize with the code snippet in Listing 1.2 and target the instruction ite eq. In 10% of the cases, the execution is faulty (status = 0x5555555), proving that the SWIFI allows us in this case to find a point of sensitivity and thus to inject our fault effectively.

However, we found that different timings (over a span of 5 instructions) were able to get our faulty behaviour. This can have several plausible explanations, such as the fact that several different skipped instructions can lead to the same impact, or that the ite eq instruction can be impacted at different levels of its execution pipeline.

System-on-Chip. We then analysed a System-on-Chip (SoC). The targeted board is a Raspberry Pi3 board with a BCM2837 chip, which embeds 4 ARM Cortex-A53 cores, running at up to 1.2 GHz (833ps clock period).

```
while(1){
  wait(x*desynch_value+x);
  turn_on_LED(y);
  wait(x*activation_duration+x)
  turn_off_LED(y);
}
```

Listing 1.3. Targeted C code

Here we want to evaluate the impact of a fault and compare it to the SWIFI models. The goal is to see if a hardware generated fault can be explained by a software abstraction of the fault model, represented by software modification. Thus we inject faults at different timings during the execution of a loop (Listing 1.3) on 2 of the 4 cores, others being used to communicate with the host, while desynchronizing them (they are not started at the same time). The 2 cores (x) are activating their own signal (y) during a given time in parameter $(x * activation\_duration + x)$, this leads to a time span visible in Fig. 3.

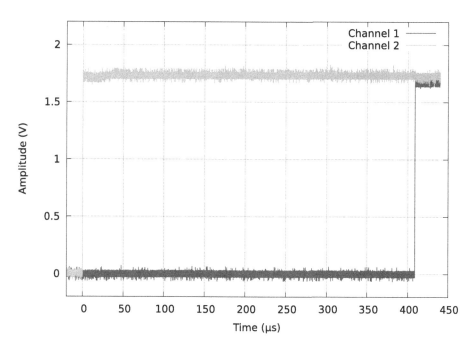

Fig. 3. Signals are desynchronized. Channel 1 for GPIO signal sent by core 1, channel 2 for GPIO signal sent by core 2. Time span between the two rising edges is due to "$x * desynch\_value + x$" in Listing 1.3.

Whatever the timing of the injection, the impact was the same: this had the effect of largely modifying the execution time of the loop on each core, alternately faster or slower in a random way. Another effect is to synchronize the different cores between them (in Fig. 4), but also to break one of the two channels of communication with our host (application channel on one core and debug channel using JTAG).

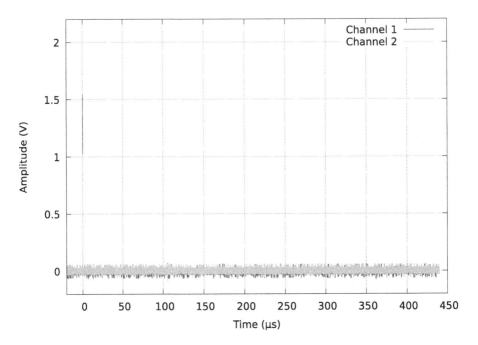

Fig. 4. Signals are shorter and synchronized. First, time span seems to have disappeared, then "$x * activation\_duration + x$" (in Listing 1.3) seems to have changed to be equal in the 2 cores.

In this case we were not able to find a match with software abstraction of the fault model as usually used in SWIFI techniques. So this lead us to question what makes the difference between a μC and a SoC and thus what prevents us from using SWIFI in the second case.

4.2 System Complexity

Abstraction Layers. A computing system is a complex device. In order to allow humans to build mental models of how such systems work, this complexity is often hidden behind abstraction layers as visible in Fig. 5.

There is a main division between these layers corresponding to the hardware/software interface constituted by the Instruction Set Architecture (ISA). On the upper side, software is constituted of a succession of instructions.

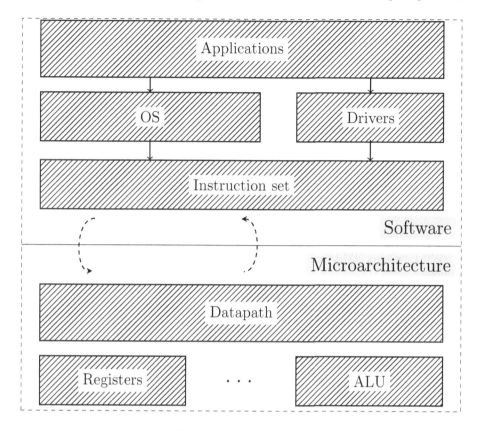

Fig. 5. Abstraction layers

On the lower side, the micro-architecture (hardware) is responsible for upholding this abstract representation.

The micro-architecture is widely different if we consider a μC or a SoC. In the first case, the instruction execution flow is quite simple, with a single core, a simple memory hierarchy, in-order execution, *etc.* In the case of a SoC, the micro-architecture can be quite complex. Several core can share the same memory space, with a complex memory hierarchy (several cache levels, shared or not). Instructions can be executed out-of-order or even speculatively. What happens in hardware differs from the simple model provided by the ISA.

SWIFI Shortcomings. The hardware part is mostly fixed, the application designer cannot modify it whereas she controls the software part of the application. In consequences, in order to protect her application, she will act on the software only. This fact remains a main reason that SWIFI techniques are quite popular: they allow the application developer to act upon the results. Therefore SWIFI techniques are preferred by software developers whereas hardware-based fault models are preferred by hardware designers in order to secure the system.

The problem is that the application still executes on a given hardware that may or may not be vulnerable to fault injection. The application developer would like to free herself from this responsibility by considering only software.

Yet SWIFI cannot capture the full extent of hardware fault injection consequences. Indeed they are not able to analyze the range of interactions and components present at the hardware level (the microarchitecture in Fig. 5) by abstracting the behaviour at the software level. Consider a Direct Memory Access (DMA) transfer for example. In this case, a section of memory is copied to another without the Central Processing Unit (CPU) involvement. Instructions are present to describe the desired memory transfer then it is enforced in parallel of the program execution. Therefore, any fault on the DMA transfer cannot be captured by a SWIFI technique.

Complexity Evolution. It can be argued that cases that cannot be captured by SWIFI, such as DMA transfers, are special cases not representative of classical applications.

But as we have show in Sect. 4.1, if these asynchronous behaviours are seldom present in simple systems, they are ubiquitous in modern SoCs. In order to squeeze the maximum performance out of modern SoCs, a lot of processing is done in parallel of the instruction flow execution.

The recent trend is in more complex systems, not simpler. As a consequence, SWIFI techniques are less and less able to capture the extent of possible errors in these systems.

5   Conclusions

FI tools are quite useful in the context of dependability and information security. They can be used to assess the security of a system with respect to fault attacks. Application developers mostly use SWIFI tools to predict the behaviour of their program in the event of a fault according to a software abstraction of the fault model. However, we have seen that the part targeted by the fault attacks is at the microarchitecture level which is the physical representation of the system, we have seen that in the case of a simple system, such as an μC (also in [29,30]), it was possible to find an abstraction at the software level of behaviour occurring at the hardware level. Nevertheless, through the experiments we conducted it appeared to us that on systems where the microarchitecture is more complex, as in the case of the SoC it became complex to find an abstraction at the software level of the models of faults corresponding to those generally considered by SWIFI methods (bit-flip, stuck-at, skip instruction, etc.). As a consequence, SWIFI is less and less relevant for such systems.

References

1. Hardie, F.H., Suhocki, R.J.: Design and use of fault simulation for saturn computer design. IEEE Trans. Electron. Comput. **4**, 412–429 (1967)
2. Armstrong, D.: A deductive method for simulating faults in logic circuits. IEEE Trans. Comput. **21**, 464–471 (1972)
3. Ulrich, E.G., Baker, T., Williams, L.: Fault-test analysis techniques based on logic simulation. In: Proceedings of the 9th Design Automation Workshop, pp. 111–115. ACM (1972)
4. Menon, P.R., Chappell, S.G.: Deductive fault simulation with functional blocks. IEEE Trans. Comput. **27**(8), 689–695 (1978)
5. Arlat, J.: Validation de la sûreté de fonctionnement par injection de fautes, méthode- mise en oeuvre- application. Ph.D. dissertation (1990)
6. Joye, M., Tunstall, M.: Fault Analysis in Cryptography, vol. 147. Springer, Heidelberg (2012). https://doi.org/10.1007/978-3-642-29656-7
7. Lashermes, R., Fournier, J., Goubin, L.: Inverting the final exponentiation of tate pairings on ordinary elliptic curves using faults. In: Bertoni, G., Coron, J.-S. (eds.) CHES 2013. LNCS, vol. 8086, pp. 365–382. Springer, Heidelberg (2013). https://doi.org/10.1007/978-3-642-40349-1_21
8. Barenghi, A., Breveglieri, L., Koren, I., Naccache, D.: Fault injection attacks on cryptographic devices: theory, practice, and countermeasures. Proc. IEEE **100**(11), 3056–3076 (2012)
9. Moro, N., Dehbaoui, A., Heydemann, K., Robisson, B., Encrenaz, E.: Electromagnetic fault injection: towards a fault model on a 32-bit microcontroller. arXiv preprint arXiv:1402.6421 (2014)
10. Timmers, N., Spruyt, A., Witteman, M.: Controlling PC on ARM using fault injection. In: 2016 Workshop on Fault Diagnosis and Tolerance in Cryptography (FDTC), pp. 25–35. IEEE (2016)
11. Tunstall, M., Mukhopadhyay, D., Ali, S.: Differential fault analysis of the advanced encryption standard using a single fault. In: Ardagna, C.A., Zhou, J. (eds.) WISTP 2011. LNCS, vol. 6633, pp. 224–233. Springer, Heidelberg (2011). https://doi.org/10.1007/978-3-642-21040-2_15
12. Buchner, S., et al.: Laser simulation of single event upsets. IEEE Trans. Nucl. Sci. **34**(6), 1227–1233 (1987)
13. Arlat, J., et al.: Fault injection for dependability validation: a methodology and some applications. IEEE Trans. Software Eng. **16**(2), 166–182 (1990)
14. Madeira, H., Rela, M., Moreira, F., Silva, J.G.: RIFLE: a general purpose pin-level fault injector. In: Echtle, K., Hammer, D., Powell, D. (eds.) EDCC 1994. LNCS, vol. 852, pp. 197–216. Springer, Heidelberg (1994). https://doi.org/10.1007/3-540-58426-9_132
15. Sieh, V., Tschache, O., Balbach, F.: VERIFY: evaluation of reliability using VHDL-models with embedded fault descriptions. In: Twenty-Seventh Annual International Symposium on Fault-Tolerant Computing, FTCS-27. Digest of Papers, pp. 32–36. IEEE (1997)
16. Folkesson, P., Svensson, S., Karlsson, J.: A comparison of simulation based and scan chain implemented fault injection. In: Twenty-Eighth Annual International Symposium on Fault-Tolerant Computing. Digest of Papers, pp. 284–293. IEEE (1998)
17. Sieh, V.: Faumachine. http://www3.informatik.uni-erlangen.de/EN/Research/FAUmachine/description.shtml

18. Potyra, S., Sieh, V., Cin, M.D.: Evaluating fault-tolerant system designs using FAUmachine. In: Proceedings of the 2007 Workshop on Engineering Fault Tolerant Systems, p. 9. ACM (2007)

19. Sand, M., Potyra, S., Sieh, V.: Deterministic high-speed simulation of complex systems including fault-injection. In: 2009 IEEE/IFIP International Conference on Dependable Systems & Networks, pp. 211–216. IEEE (2009)

20. Civera, P., Macchiarulo, L., Rebaudengo, M., Reorda, M.S., Violante, A.: Exploiting FPGA for accelerating fault injection experiments. In: Proceedings of the Seventh International On-Line Testing Workshop, pp. 9–13. IEEE (2001)

21. Leveugle, R.: Fault injection in VHDL descriptions and emulation. In: Proceedings-IEEE-International-Symposium-on-Defect-and-Fault-Tolerance-in-VLSI-Systems, pp. 414–419. IEEE Comput. Soc., Los Alamitos (2000)

22. Antoni, L., Leveugle, R., Feher, M.: Using run-time reconfiguration for fault injection in hardware prototypes. In: Proceedings of the 17th IEEE International Symposium on Defect and Fault Tolerance in VLSI Systems, DFT 2002, pp. 245–253. IEEE (2002)

23. Velazco, R., Rezgui, S., Ecoffet, R.: Predicting error rate for microprocessor-based digital architectures through C.E.U. (Code Emulating Upsets) injection. IEEE Trans. Nucl. Sci. **47**(6), 2405–2411 (2000)

24. Han, S., Shin, K.G., Rosenberg, H.A.: Doctor: an integrated software fault injection environment for distributed real-time systems. In: Proceedings of the International Computer Performance and Dependability Symposium, pp. 204–213. IEEE (1995)

25. Riviere, L., Bringer, J., Le, T.-H., Chabanne, H.: A novel simulation approach for fault injection resistance evaluation on smart cards. In: 2015 IEEE Eighth International Conference on Software Testing, Verification and Validation Workshops (ICSTW), pp. 1–8. IEEE (2015)

26. Kanawati, G.A., Kanawati, N.A., Abraham, J.A.: FERRARI: a flexible software-based fault and error injection system. IEEE Trans. Comput. **44**(2), 248–260 (1995)

27. Höller, A., Rauter, T., Iber, J., Kreiner, C.: Diverse compiling for microprocessor fault detection in temporal redundant systems. In: 2015 IEEE International Conference on Computer and Information Technology; Ubiquitous Computing and Communications; Dependable, Autonomic and Secure Computing; Pervasive Intelligence and Computing, pp. 1928–1935, October 2015

28. Carreira, J., Madeira, H., Silva, J.G., et al.: Xception: software fault injection and monitoring in processor functional units. Dependable Comput. Fault Tolerant Syst. **10**, 245–266 (1998)

29. Yuce, B., Ghalaty, N.F., Schaumont, P.: Improving fault attacks on embedded software using RISC pipeline characterization. In: 2015 Workshop on Fault Diagnosis and Tolerance in Cryptography (FDTC), pp. 97–108. IEEE (2015)

30. Riviere, L., Najm, Z., Rauzy, P., Danger, J.-L., Bringer, J., Sauvage, L.: High precision fault injections on the instruction cache of ARMv7-M architectures. arXiv preprint arXiv:1510.01537 (2015)

A Study on Mitigation Techniques for SCADA-Driven Cyber-Physical Systems (Position Paper)

Mariana Segovia[1], Ana Rosa Cavalli[1], Nora Cuppens[2],
and Joaquin Garcia-Alfaro[1(✉)]

[1] Télécom SudParis, Evry, France
{segovia,ana.cavalli,joaquin.garcia_alfaro}@telecom-sudparis.eu
[2] IMT Atlantique, Cesson Sévigné, France
nora.cuppens@imt-atlantique.fr

Abstract. Cyber-physical systems (CPSs) integrate programmable computing and communication capabilities to traditional physical environments. The use of SCADA (Supervisory Control And Data Acquisition) technologies to build such a new generation of CPSs plays an important role in current critical national-wide infrastructures. SCADA-driven CPSs can be disrupted by cyber-physical attacks, putting at risk human safety, environmental regulation and industrial work. In this paper, we address the aforementioned issues and provide a discussion on the mitigation techniques that aim to optimize the recovery response when a SCADA-driven CPS is under attack. Our discussion paves the way for novel cyber resilience techniques, focusing on the programmable computing and communication capabilities of CPSs, towards new research directions to tolerate cyber-physical attacks.

1 Introduction

Current Cyber-Physical Systems (CPSs) integrate modern computation and networking resources to control physical processes. These systems use sensor measurements to get information about physical processes, then control processing units to analyze and make decisions that are performed by system actuators, e.g., to maintain the stability of the physical processes. Supervisory Control And Data Acquisition (SCADA) is a traditional technology to build CPSs. SCADA protocols can be used to monitor and control hardware that may be separated by relatively large distances. SCADA-driven CPSs play an important role in most national critical infrastructures. This includes electrical transmission, energy distribution, manufacturing and supply chain, waste recycling, public transportation, e-health, financial services and several others.

Disruption of SCADA-driven CPSs have a direct impact in the physical world. Cyber-physical attacks may lead to negative impact on human safety, cause harm in natural environments, interrupt industrial process continuity,

© Springer Nature Switzerland AG 2019
N. Zincir-Heywood et al. (Eds.): FPS 2018, LNCS 11358, pp. 257–264, 2019.
https://doi.org/10.1007/978-3-030-18419-3_17

hence leading to large economic losses, generate legal problems and damage the reputation of the affected organizations [9,12].

Traditional protection techniques have been centered in detection and prevention methodologies, in order to build preemptive approaches that aim at identifying and responding to potential threats, even when vulnerability removal is not possible [10,11]. Attack tolerance should be enforced in such environments, in order to provide a correct service even in the presence of successful attacks against the system. The resulting systems should satisfy high availability requirements to guarantee the execution of the critical tasks. To guarantee that the whole system remain operational even in the presence of attacks, the activation of mitigation techniques shall be enforced, even if that means to work under graceful degradation modes.

Graceful degradation is the ability of a system to continue functioning even after parts of the system have been damaged, compromised or destroyed. The efficiency of the system working in graceful degradation usually is lower than the normal performance and it may decrease as the number of failing components grows. The purpose is to prevent a catastrophic failure of the system. In this paper, we address the aforementioned issue, and discuss the use of mitigation techniques aiming to ease and improve recovery response when a SCADA-driven CPS is under attack. Our discussion paves the way for orchestration and configuration of novel techniques, focusing on current capabilities of modern SCADA systems, capable of enabling programmable computing and communication functionalities.

The paper is structured as follows. Section 2 provides the background. Section 3 surveys representative mitigation techniques for SCADA-driven CPSs. Section 4 provides a discussion about a novel mitigation technique and how to optimize the response of the system under an attack using the existing mitigation approaches. Section 5 provides the conclusions of the work.

2   Background

SCADA-driven CPSs have special requirements that may affect traditional security mechanisms designed for traditional IT systems. In the following, some of these requirements are reviewed.

2.1   Cyber-Physical Systems

A Cyber-Physical System (CPS) consists of two main parts. First, a programmable (cyber) layer, containing the computing and network functionalities. Second, a physical layer, representing dynamic automation processes. Both together hold the series of distributed resources leading the environment that is expected to monitor the behavior of physical phenomena, as well as to taking the necessary actions to get control over them.

The components of the cyber layer control the behavior of the physical layer and the feedback of the physical layer affects the decisions of the cyber layer.

The CPS become smarter as the interaction between physical and cyber layers grows up. As a consequence, they get more vulnerable to attacks. The integration between layers is an important point to evaluate and determine how the information flow should be protected.

The cyber layer uses security mechanisms similar to the mechanisms for traditional information systems. The physical layer has different requirements and can be controlled in different ways. For example, considering the model of the involved physical process. However, it is important to see the system as a whole, also thinking about the information flows to and from the cyber layer and the interconnected networks to determine how to protect them.

Most of the proposals work only on the cyber layer or in the physical layer in a separate way, without keeping in mind the information flows from one layer to another or the communication patterns allowed between different components. Security solutions should work on a more general approach that takes into account attack vectors that exploit vulnerabilities of different components at the same time instead of focusing on analyzing isolated components. In addition, correlating events may help to detect security incidents that occur in different components and can not be detected analyzing the components separately.

2.2 Specificity and Characteristics of SCADA-Driven Systems

SCADA-driven systems have particular characteristics and requirements that must be taken into account with respect to traditional information systems. For instance, they may need to satisfy *real time constraints*, e.g., for the execution of critical functionality. This may include satisfying high speed communications, synchronization of tasks, etc.

A second characteristic is the priority of such systems at guaranteeing *availability* constraints. Indeed, availability and service continuity requirements in SCADA-driven systems are a crucial factor, more than any other property addressed from an information technology standpoint. The whole system may require to prove and fulfill the ability of the system in order to continue its operations through enabling redundant controls, while some mitigation patches are applied to the affected resources, even if this requires moving the system to degraded state modes.

Finally, other representative characteristics may lay on the *geographic distribution of system components* (e.g., some of the monitoring or surveyed nodes being deployed at remote locations), the *constrained nature of the computation resources* associated to some of the field devices (e.g., in terms of memory and processing power), and the existence of outdated and highly vulnerable *legacy systems*, given the lifetime cycle of SCADA resources (much longer than any other equivalent technology deployed over traditional information systems).

Attacks against SCADA-driven CPSs may exploit vulnerabilities at both the physical and the cyber layers. Regardless the layer, attacks may exploit vulnerabilities in the associated resources of the whole system, such as transport protocols, low-level transmission technologies, system-oriented monitoring languages, etc.

3 Mitigation Techniques

The main objective of protecting a SCADA-driven CPS is to enable attack tolerance while satisfying the requirements listed in Sect. 2.2. Attack tolerance assumes that a system remains to a certain extent vulnerable and attacks on components can happen and be successful. However, the CPS must ensure that the overall system nevertheless remains operational and can continue to function under graceful degradation [16].

One of the earliest techniques to respond and mitigate the effect of an attack is the use of redundancy. This technique uses alternative copies of, e.g., system components, in order to guarantee system availability. If the system finds that the output values of a primary component are not correct (e.g., according with the output values of redundant components), then the responsibility is transferred to one of the redundant components assuming that there was an infiltration or compromise. This technique is mostly used for achieving fault tolerance in case one of the components fail. However, its use for security purposes has some drawbacks. Since the replicas are identical, if the attacker manages to compromise one of them, then the rest of the replicas can be compromised too. Nonetheless, if the replicas are placed geographically distributed, then this approach may be useful for attacks that exploit vulnerabilities that require physical access to the devices. But this mitigation approach would be based on the inability of the attacker to physically reach the other locations. Regardless, this would not solve the possible malicious access through the network. For this reason, redundancy is often combined with the use of diversity. The goal is to guarantee the existence of different replicas failing in an independently manner and with non-overlapping patterns. To achieve this, replicas may hold different hardware, platform or software. Thus, the system is protected from specific infrastructure failures, errors, bugs or vulnerabilities. Authors in [4] use this approach with hardware and software diversity to achieve cyber-resilience of industrial control systems. This technique may also be used to achieve resilient web services [6,7]. This approach increases the management complexity of the platform as well as the effort required to control the vulnerabilities and keep all the components correctly patched. It also increase the required investment to acquire the redundant components.

In a similar vein, recovery techniques may also help to repair the damages caused by an attack against the systems. For instance, imagine the situation in which roll-back actions can be enforced to returning the system to a previous state that was considered as correct prior an attack. If this is possible, complementary techniques could include resuming and deploying of operations, re-execution of disrupted operations, as well as re-installation of corrupted files and renewal of cryptography [16]. Other examples include the use of periodic software rejuvenation in a proactive and reactive mode [14], in a way in which a system gets recovered automatically and periodically whenever an attack against the system is detected. However, this approach has the same problem as the redundancy technique, since the vulnerabilities are not removed, the attacker may compromise the system again.

Another example is the use of *model-based responses*, in which a model of the physical process is computed in order to generate an approximation of the normal behavior of the system prior the execution of an attack. This approach can use as input parameters an estimation of the true value of, e.g., system sensors; as well as the resulting value after the attack has occurred, i.e., right after the sensor has been tampered [3]. This approach should be used only as a temporal solution because using a simulation value instead of the real sensor measured opens the control loop and this may bring cause problems in the system behavior.

Mechanisms to detect attacks in SCADA-driven CPSs have been developed but there is very little work on how to automatically respond to them. Most of the response solutions are manual or aim at absorbing the impact of the attack through redundancy, diversity, restoration or containment techniques. However, more effective solutions that take into account the dynamic and changing nature of an attacker could be achieved, e.g. using a technique that considers dynamic adaptation of the system as a reaction, i.e. the system could deploy different defense policies depending on the attack or it could also modify the executed actions as the attack is going on. In this line, authors in [8,13] have proposed response solutions based in the network reconfiguration. In these solutions, the network controller coordinates the mitigation strategies. However, this approach could be enhanced using software reflection, in order to achieve a system capable of modifying the code to achieve state reparation. Software reflection is a technique appropriate for high-level languages. However, since the SCADA-driven CPSs controllers are located within the cyber layer of the system, they can monitor the system and apply these mitigation techniques.

4   Mitigation of Attacks Using Software Reflection

A promising technique to be fully explored under the problem domain addressed in this paper deals with the use of *software reflection* to handle attack on SCADA-driven CPSs. Software reflection is a meta-programming technique that allows a system to adapt itself through the ability of examining and modifying its execution behavior at runtime. As a mitigation technique, software reflection has the potential to allow a system to react and defend itself against availability threats. When a malicious activity is detected, the system shall dynamically change the implementation to activate remediation techniques to guarantee that the system will continue to work. During the development process it is important to do non-regression testing over the alternatives defense implementation to verify that the system is still correct according to the functional specifications.

Notice that software reflection provides the ability to analyze, inspect and modify the structure and behavior of an application at runtime. This allows the code to inspect other code within the same system or even itself. Reflection allows inspecting classes, examining fields, changing accessibility flags, dynamic class loading, method invocation and attribute usage at runtime even if that information is unavailable at compile time.

This kind of approach has been successfully explored to mitigate attacks against Internet web services [2] restoring the interface of a system to the state previous to the attack. The idea relies on enabling reflection as a remediation techniques, when attacks are detected. However, research challenges include the application of this technique in more complex scenarios as well as modeling and orchestration of the appropriate plans in order to activate the technique, while guaranteeing the availability of the service, even if offered under a degradation mode.

Software reflection can complement the list of mitigation techniques listed in Sect. 3, in order to enable an optimal management of attacks against SCADA-driven CPSs. Research work remains to be explored, in order to put in practice such a solution. Some concerns, directions and discussions to address the afore-mentioned goal is presented in the sequel.

4.1 Discussion and Research Directions

The first concern deals with *performance overhead*. Reflection involves program-ming types that are dynamically resolved. Some optimization that typically are done in advance may risk to fail performance guarantees. In addition, reflection takes execution time and memory to discover and manipulate class properties during the runtime execution of the system. Reflective operations may suffer from slower performance than their non-reflective counterparts. It should be avoided in sections of a code that are called frequently in performance sensitive applications [5]. This may be used or restricted to small code sections that are not intensively called.

The second concern is in terms of access restrictions. Reflection requires runtime permissions which may not be present when running normally. This is an important consideration for code which has to run in a restricted security context [1,5]. Reflection may allow to access and update fields, and execute methods that are forbidden by normal access or visibility rules. This is achieved due to reflection breaks object encapsulation. If this technique is not used properly, it increases considerably the attack surface of a program and may allow malicious access to information that is supposed to be hidden, access files on the local machine, allow the injection of malicious native code or load restricted classes.

Solutions to the aforementioned problem exist. For instance, the issue may be addressed by using dynamic object ownership concepts, e.g., to design an access control policy to reflective operations [15]. This policy grants objects full reflective power over the objects they own but limited reflective power over other objects. This is done through an object ownership relation to determine access rights to reflective operations on a per-object basis and based on the dynamic arrangement of objects rather than on static relations between structural entities.

In terms of complexity, reflection procedures fail more often at runtime than during compilation. For instance, changing the object to be loaded will probably cause the generated loading class to throw a compilation error, but the reflexive procedure will not see any difference until the class is used during runtime. Moreover, determining exactly what the code is doing is quite complex due to reflection can obscure what is actually going. So, the only way to truly determine its behavior is to execute the code and see how it would behave at runtime with sample data. However, to do this for every possible data combination is nearly impossible. In addition, this increases the complexity of the maintenance of the software due to the reflection code is also more complex to understand than the corresponding direct code. Many of the security problems are due to human programming errors and this approach increases the complexity of the solution. So, it also increases the likelihood of errors in the code.

Finally, languages with software reflection capabilities must to be explored under the problem domain context of SCADA-driven CPSs. Note that reflection is an advanced development technique for high-level languages such as Java, Python and Ruby. The possibility of extending traditional languages for the family of systems explored in this paper, e.g., given the low resource capabilities of some of the components, may be a barrier to our proposal. Nevertheless, the technique may certainly be applied by those component at the cyber layers, holding much less resource constraints.

5 Conclusion

This paper has surveyed some current trends in terms of mitigation techniques aiming to optimizing the recovery response of cyber-physical systems (CPSs) under attack. We have focused on CPS built using SCADA (Supervisory Control And Data Acquisition) technologies, in order to provide their computing and communication capabilities, beyond traditional physical components. We have enumerated some ongoing solutions in order to build higher resilient environments. We argued that the use of software reflection, in addition to traditional techniques such as redundancy, diversity and automated recovery is a promising way to enable an efficient response under the presence of cyber-physical attacks. We have also discussed some concerns and limitations that would deserve new research directions to enable and orchestrate such a technique, in order to drive our next steps and future work.

Acknowledgements. The authors acknowledge support from the Cyber CNI chair of the Institut Mines-Télécom. The chair is supported by Airbus Defence and Space, Amossys, EDF, Orange, La Poste, Nokia, Société Générale and the Regional Council of Brittany. The chair has been acknowledged by the Center of excellence in Cybersecurity. The authors also acknowledge support from the European Commission, in the framework of the H2020 SPARTA project, under grant agreement 830892.

References

1. Security considerations for reflection: https://docs.microsoft.com/en-us/dotnet/framework/reflection-and-codedom/security-considerations-for-reflection. Accessed 23 Aug 2018
2. Cavalli, A.R., Ortiz, A.M., Ouffoué, G., Sanchez, C.A., Zaïdi, F.: Design of a secure shield for internet and web-based services using software reflection. In: Jin, H., Wang, Q., Zhang, L.-J. (eds.) ICWS 2018. LNCS, vol. 10966, pp. 472–486. Springer, Cham (2018). https://doi.org/10.1007/978-3-319-94289-6_30

3. Cómbita, L.F., Giraldo, J., Cárdenas, A.A., Quijano, N.: Response and reconfiguration of cyber-physical control systems: a survey. In: 2015 IEEE 2nd Colombian Conference on Automatic Control (CCAC), pp. 1–6. IEEE (2015)
4. Kim, C.: Cyber-resilient industrial control system with diversified architecture and bus monitoring. In: 2016 World Congress on Industrial Control Systems Security (WCICSS), pp. 1–6. IEEE (2016)
5. Oracle, J.D.: The reflection API. https://docs.oracle.com/javase/tutorial/reflect/. Accessed 23 Aug 2018
6. Ouffoué, G., Zaidi, F., Cavalli, A.R., Lallali, M.: How web services can be tolerant to intruders through diversification. In: 2017 IEEE International Conference on Web Services (ICWS), pp. 436–443. IEEE (2017)
7. Ouffoué, G., Zaidi, F., Cavalli, A.R., Lallali, M.: Model-based attack tolerance. In: 2017 31st International Conference on Advanced Information Networking and Applications Workshops (WAINA), pp. 68–73. IEEE (2017)
8. Piedrahita, A.F.M., Gaur, V., Giraldo, J., Cardenas, A.A., Rueda, S.J.: Virtual incident response functions in control systems. Comput. Netw. **135**, 147–159 (2018)
9. Rubio-Hernan, J., De Cicco, L., Garcia-Alfaro, J.: Event-triggered watermarking control to handle cyber-physical integrity attacks. In: Brumley, B.B., Röning, J. (eds.) NordSec 2016. LNCS, vol. 10014, pp. 3–19. Springer, Cham (2016). https://doi.org/10.1007/978-3-319-47560-8_1
10. Rubio-Hernan, J., De Cicco, L., Garcia-Alfaro, J.: Revisiting a watermark-based detection scheme to handle cyber-physical attacks. In: 2016 11th International Conference on Availability, Reliability and Security (ARES), pp. 21–28. IEEE (2016)
11. Rubio-Hernan, J., De Cicco, L., Garcia-Alfaro, J.: On the use of watermark-based schemes to detect cyber-physical attacks. EURASIP J. Inf. Secur. **2017**(1), 8 (2017)
12. Rubio-Hernan, J., De Cicco, L., Garcia-Alfaro, J.: Adaptive control-theoretic detection of integrity attacks against cyber-physical industrial systems. Trans. Emerg. Telecommun. Technol. **29**(7), e3209 (2018)
13. Rubio-Hernan, J., Sahay, R., De Cicco, L., Garcia-Alfaro, J.: Cyber-physical architecture assisted by programmable networking. Internet Technol. Lett. **1**(4), 44 (2018)
14. Sousa, P., Bessani, A.N., Correia, M., Neves, N.F., Verissimo, P.: Resilient intrusion tolerance through proactive and reactive recovery. In: 13th Pacific Rim International Symposium on Dependable Computing (PRDC 2007), pp. 373–380 (2007)
15. Teruel, C., Ducasse, S., Cassou, D., Denker, M.: Access control to reflection with object ownership. In: Proceedings of the 11th Symposium on Dynamic Languages, DLS 2015, pp. 168–176. ACM, New York (2015)
16. Veríssimo, P.E., Neves, N.F., Correia, M.P.: Intrusion-tolerant architectures: concepts and design. In: de Lemos, R., Gacek, C., Romanovsky, A. (eds.) WADS 2002. LNCS, vol. 2677, pp. 3–36. Springer, Heidelberg (2003). https://doi.org/10.1007/3-540-45177-3_1

Access Control

Mining Relationship-Based Access Control Policies from Incomplete and Noisy Data

Thang Bui, Scott D. Stoller$^{(\boxtimes)}$, and Jiajie Li

Department of Computer Science, Stony Brook University, Stony Brook, USA
`stoller@cs.stonybrook.edu`

Abstract. Relationship-based access control (ReBAC) extends attribute-based access control (ABAC) to allow policies to be expressed in terms of chains of relationships between entities. ReBAC policy mining algorithms have potential to significantly reduce the cost of migration from legacy access control systems to ReBAC, by partially automating the development of a ReBAC policy. This paper presents algorithms for mining ReBAC policies from information about entitlements together with information about entities. It presents the first such algorithms designed to handle *incomplete* information about entitlements, typically obtained from operation logs, and *noise* (errors) in information about entitlements. We present two algorithms: a greedy search guided by heuristics, and an evolutionary algorithm. We demonstrate the effectiveness of the algorithms on several policies, including 3 large case studies.

1 Introduction

In *relationship-based access control* (ReBAC), access control policies are expressed in terms of chains of relationships between entities. This increases expressiveness and often allows more natural policies. High-level access control policy models such as ABAC and ReBAC are becoming increasingly important, as policies become more dynamic and more complex. This is reflected in the widespread transition from access control lists (ACLs) to role-based access control (RBAC), and more recently in the ongoing transition from ACLs and RBAC to ABAC. High-level policy models allow concise policies and promise long-term cost savings through reduced management effort.

Policy mining algorithms automatically produce a "first draft" of a high-level policy from existing lower-level data. They promise to drastically reduce the cost for an organization to migrate from a legacy access control technology to a high-level policy model. There is a significant amount of research on role mining, and

This material is based on work supported in part by NSF Grants CNS-1421893, and CCF-1414078, ONR Grant N00014-15-1-2208, and DARPA Contract FA8650-15-C-7561.

© Springer Nature Switzerland AG 2019
N. Zincir-Heywood et al. (Eds.): FPS 2018, LNCS 11358, pp. 267–284, 2019.
https://doi.org/10.1007/978-3-030-18419-3_18

role mining is supported by several commercial products, including IBM Tivoli Access Manager and Oracle Identity Analytics. Research on ABAC policy mining is much younger but growing as adoption of ABAC increases [4,7,13,14].

Mining of ReBAC policies, expressed as object-oriented ABAC policies with path expressions, has been explored in recent work by Bui, Stoller, and Li [3]. They present two algorithms, called the *greedy algorithm* and the *evolutionary algorithm*, to mine a ReBAC policy from a set of entitlements, a class model, and an object model. An *entitlement* is represented as a tuple $\langle subject, resource, action \rangle$, indicating that *subject* is authorized to perform *action* on *resource*.

The *meaning* of a policy π, denoted $[\![\pi]\!]$, is the set of granted entitlements. Both algorithms produce mined policies whose meaning is exactly the given set of entitlements. Consequently, they do not handle cases where that set is incomplete or noisy, which is often the case in practice. We propose more practical policy mining algorithms that do.

Incomplete information about entitlements is often readily available from operation logs, even when complete information is not, e.g., because the policy is not enforced by software, or because the policy is expressed using obscure *ad hoc* code. Many systems produce operation logs, e.g., for auditing or accounting. A set of entitlements can easily be extracted from a log. However, that set is typically *incomplete*, i.e., lacks some entitlements granted by the policy, because those entitlements were not exercised during the period covered by the log. We refer to these as *missing entitlements*. If the log contains entries for access requests that were denied, a set of *denials* can also be extracted from it. We represent denials as 3-tuples, just like entitlements.

Information about entitlements, even when nominally complete, is often noisy, i.e., contains errors in the form of *missing entitlements* (i.e., entitlements that should be present but aren't) and *excess entitlements* (i.e., entitlements that should not be present but are). Note that incomplete inputs typically have a much larger percentage of missing entitlements than noisy inputs.

We modify Bui et al.'s algorithms to handle incomplete and noisy inputs. Our algorithms identify suspected missing entitlements and add them to the meaning of the mined policy, so we also call them *added entitlements*. Our algorithms identify suspected excess entitlements and omit them from the meaning of the mined policy, so we also call them *omitted entitlements*.

To handle excess entitlements, our algorithms, like [14], construct a candidate policy, classify entitlements covered only by low-quality rules as suspected excess entitlements, and omit them from the meaning of the mined policy by discarding the low-quality rules.

We extend the greedy algorithm with two approaches for missing entitlements. The *validity-threshold (VT) approach* [14] modifies the algorithm to keep rules that are "almost valid", i.e., whose meaning contains a percentage of added entitlements that is below a specified threshold. The *extended quality (EQ) approach* [13] does not impose a strict cutoff on the percentage of added entitlements in the meaning of a rule. Instead, it extends the notion of rule quality with a term proportional to the percentage of added entitlements in the meaning of the rule, allowing a smooth trade-off between this and other aspects of quality. We refer to the versions of the greedy algorithm extended with these approaches as *VT greedy algorithm* and *EQ greedy algorithm*, respectively.

We extend the evolutionary algorithm to handle missing entitlements using a combination of the above approaches. We modify the fitness function so that, when the fraction of added entitlements in a rule's meaning is below a threshold, the added entitlements do not affect the rule's fitness, and when that fraction is above the threshold, the rule's fitness is redued proportionally to that fraction. We tried simpler approaches, but they produced worse results. We also modify the algorithm to use a validity threshold when deciding whether to add a candidate rule to the policy.

We evaluate our algorithms on four relatively small but non-trivial sample policies and three larger and more complex case studies. One sample policy is for electronic medical records (EMR), based on the EBAC policy in [2], translated to ReBAC; the other three are for healthcare, project management, and university records, based on ABAC policies in [14], generalized and made more realistic by translation to ReBAC. Two of the case studies are based on Software-as-a-Service (SaaS) applications offered by real companies [5,6]; one is based on a university's grant proposal workflow management system [10]. More details about these policies (other than the last one, which is new) appear in [3]. Our evaluation methodology is to start with a ReBAC policy π_0, compute the set $[\![\pi_0]\!]$ of granted entitlements, create from it a set of entitlements E_0 that is either incomplete (by pseudorandomly removing a significant percentage of the entitlements) or noisy (by pseudorandomly adding and removing small percentages of entitlements), run a policy mining algorithm on E_0 (along with the class model and object model from π_0), and compare the meaning $[\![\pi]\!]$ of the mined ReBAC policy π with $[\![\pi_0]\!]$. If the algorithm correctly compensates for the incompleteness or noise, they will be the same.

In our experiments with the greedy algorithm, the VT approach achieves better results than the EQ approach. We initially expected the EQ approach to be superior, because its quality metric is sensitive to the exact number of added entitlements. We now believe that the VT approach achieves better results because the goal is not to minimize the added entitlements, but rather to add just the right ones.

In our experiments comparing the VT greedy algorithm with the evolutionary algorithm, the VT greedy algorithm runs faster and achieves slightly to moderately better results. This is somewhat surprising, considering that, in Bui et al.'s experiments for ReBAC policy mining without incompleteness or noise [3], the evolutionary algorithm achieved somewhat better results than the greedy algorithm. It will be interesting to see if one of the algorithms can be improved to match or beat the other in both settings. One reason for favoring improvement of the evolutionary algorithm (e.g., by experimenting with new mutations) is its superior extensibility: it relies less on language-specific heuristics and hence is easier to extend to handle additional policy language features, e.g., additional data types (numbers, sequences, etc.) and associated relational operators. We plan to investigate extensibility in future work. We also plan to try to get real-world logs and associated policies to further evaluate our approach.

We also evaluated Rhapsody's approach to handling missing entitlements in the context of mining ABAC policies from logs [4]. There is no easy way to combine Rhapsody's approach with our algorithms, so we evaluate Rhapsody by running it and Xu and Stoller's EQ greedy algorithm for mining ABAC policies from logs [13] on the same data sets. We find that Rhapsody is much slower and would be usable for ReBAC mining only on small problem instances.

2   Policy Language

Since our algorithms are based on Bui et al.'s, we also adopt their ReBAC policy language, ORAL (Object-oriented Relationship-based Access-control Language) [3]. It formulates ReBAC as an object-oriented extension of ABAC. Relationships are expressed using attributes that refer to other objects, and path expressions are used in conditions and constraints to follow chains of relationships between objects. We describe the language briefly and refer the reader to [3] for details.

A *ReBAC policy* is a tuple $\pi = \langle CM, OM, Act, Rules \rangle$, where CM is a class model, OM is an object model, Act is a set of actions, and $Rules$ is a set of rules.

A *class model* is a set of class declarations. Each field has a *multiplicity* that specifies how many values may be stored in the field and is "one" (also denoted "1"), "optional" (also denoted "?"), or "many" (also denoted "*", meaning any number). Boolean fields always have multiplicity 1. Every class implicitly contains a field "id" with type String and multiplicity 1. A *reference type* is any class name (used as a type).

An *object model* is a set of objects whose types are consistent with the class model. Let type(o) denote the type of object o. The value of a field with multiplicity "many" is a set. The value of a field with multiplicity "optional" may be a single value or the placeholder $\perp$ indicating absence of a value.

A *path* is a sequence of field names, written with "." as a separator. A *condition* is a set, interpreted as a conjunction, of atomic conditions. An *atomic condition* is a tuple $\langle p, op, val \rangle$, where p is a non-empty path, op is an operator, either "in" or "contains", and val is a constant value, either an atomic value or a set of atomic values. For example, an object o satisfies $\langle \text{dept.id}, \text{in}, \{\text{CompSci}\} \rangle$ if the value obtained starting from o and following (dereferencing) the dept field and then the id field equals CompSci.

A *constraint* is a set, interpreted as a conjunction, of atomic constraints. Informally, an atomic constraint expresses a relationship between the requesting subject and the requested resource, by relating the values of paths starting from each of them. An *atomic constraint* is a tuple $\langle p_1, op, p_2 \rangle$, where p_1 and p_2 are paths (possibly the empty sequence), and op is one of the following four operators: equal, in, contains, supseteq. Implicitly, the first path is relative to the requesting subject, and the second path is relative to the requested resource.

The empty path represents the subject or resource itself. For example, a subject s and resource r satisfy $\langle specialties, contains, topic \rangle$ if the set $s.specialties$ contains the value $r.topic$.

A *rule* is a tuple $\langle subjectType, subjectCondition, resourceType, resource$ $Condition, constraint, actions \rangle$, where *subjectType* and *resourceType* are class names, *subjectCondition* and *resourceCondition* are conditions, *constraint* is a constraint, *actions* is a set of actions. For a rule $\rho = \langle st, sc, rt, rc, c, A \rangle$, let $\text{sType}(\rho) = st, \text{sCond}(\rho) = sc, \text{rType}(\rho) = rt, \text{rCond}(\rho) = rc, \text{con}(\rho) = c$, and $\text{acts}(\rho) = A$.

For readability, we may prefix paths with "subject" or "resource", to indicate the object from which the path starts. For example, our e-document case study involves a large bank whose policy contains the rule: A project member can read all sent documents regarding the project. This is expressed as $\langle$ Employee, subject.employer.id = LargeBank, Document, true, subject.workOn.relatedDoc $\ni$ resource, {read}$\rangle$, where Employee.workOn is the set of projects the employee is working on, and Project.relatedDoc is the set of sent documents related to the project.

The *type of a path* p (relative to a specified class), denoted $\text{type}(p)$, is the type of the last field in the path. Given a class model, object model, object o, and path p, let $\text{nav}(o, p)$ be the result of navigating (a.k.a. following or dereferencing) path p starting from object o. The result might be no value, represented by $\bot$, an atomic value, or (if a field in p has multiplicity many) a set of values. This is like the semantics of path navigation in UML's Object Constraint Language.

An object o *satisfies* an atomic condition $c = \langle p, op, val \rangle$, denoted $o \models c$, if $(op = \text{in} \wedge \text{nav}(o, p) \in val) \vee (op = \text{contains} \wedge \text{nav}(o, p) \ni val)$. Objects o_1 and o_2 *satisfy* an atomic constraint $c = \langle p_1, op, p_2 \rangle$, denoted $\langle o_1, o_2 \rangle \models c$, is defined in a similar way. An *entitlement* $\langle s, r, a \rangle$ *satisfies* a rule $\rho = \langle st, sc, rt, rc, c, A \rangle$, denoted $\langle s, r, a \rangle \models \rho$, if $\text{type}(s) = st \wedge s \models sc \wedge \text{type}(r) = rt \wedge r \models rc \wedge \langle s, r \rangle \models c \wedge a \in A$. The *meaning* of a rule ρ, denoted $[\![\rho]\!]$, is the set of entitlements that satisfy it. The *meaning* of a ReBAC policy π, denoted $[\![\pi]\!]$, is the union of the meanings of its rules.

3 Problem Definition

A ReBAC policy that grants a given set E_0 of entitlements can be trivially constructed, by creating a separate rule that grants each entitlement in E_0, using conditions on the "id" field to specify the relevant subject and resource. Such a ReBAC policy is no better than ACLs.

We adopt two criteria to specify which ReBAC policies are most desirable. One criterion is to use "id" field only when necessary, i.e., only when every ReBAC policy consistent with π_0 contains rules that use it, because rules that use the "id" field are identity-based, not attribute-based or relationship-based. The other is to maximize a *policy quality metric*, which is a function Q_{pol} from ReBAC policies to a totally-ordered set, e.g., natural numbers. For generality, we parameterize the policy mining problem by the policy quality metric, with the convention that smaller values indicate higher quality.

The *extended ReBAC policy mining problem* is: given a set E_0 of entitlements, a set D_0 of denials, an object model OM, and a class model CM, find a set *Rules* of rules such that the ReBAC policy $\pi = \langle CM, OM, Act, Rules \rangle$ that uses the "id" field only when necessary, denies all requests in D_0, and has the best quality, according to Q_{pol}, among such policies. Here, Act is the set of actions that appear in E_0.

We call this the "extended" problem to distinguish it from the ReBAC policy mining problem in [3], which requires $[\![\pi]\!] = E_0$ and can be viewed as a special case corresponding to policy quality metrics that give overwhelming penalty to mismatches between $[\![\pi]\!]$ and E_0.

The policy quality metric that our algorithms aim to optimize is a sum of three terms. Our algorithms do not guarantee to optimize it; that is NP-hard even for ABAC mining [13]. The first term is *weighted structural complexity* (WSC), a generalization of policy size. It is the same as in [3]. Minimizing policy size is consistent with prior work on ABAC mining and role mining and with usability studies showing that concise policies are easier to manage [1]. The WSC of a policy, denoted $\mathrm{WSC}(\pi)$, is the sum of the WSCs of its rules. The WSC of a rule ρ, denoted $\mathrm{WSC}(\rho)$ is a weighted sum of the WSCs of its components, ignoring the two types, because they always have the same size. We ignore the weights hereafter, because we always set them to 1. The WSC of an atomic condition $\langle p, op, val \rangle$ is $|p| + |val|$, where $|p|$ is the length of path p, and $|val|$ is 1 if val is an atomic value and is the cardinality of val if val is a set. The WSC of a condition is the sum of the WSCs of the atomic conditions in it. The WSC of a constraint is defined similarly [3]. The WSC of an action set is its cardinality.

The second and third terms measure differences between $[\![\pi]\!]$ and E_0. They are not needed in [3], which requires $[\![\pi]\!] = E_0$. They measure the numbers of addeed and omitted entitlements, respectively. We divide them by $|OM|$ (the number of objects), because incompleteness and noise are typically characterized by percentages, not absolute numbers, of affected entitlements, and the number of granted entitlements is typically proportional to the size of the object model.

In summary, policy quality is $Q_{\mathrm{pol}}(\pi) = w_{\mathrm{wsc}}\mathrm{WSC}(\pi) + w_{\mathrm{add}} |[\![\pi]\!] \backslash E_0| / |OM| + w_{\mathrm{omit}} |E_0 \backslash [\![\pi]\!]| / |OM|$, where the weights are user-specified.

4   Greedy Algorithm

Our VT and EQ greedy algorithms are based on the greedy algorithm for ReBAC policy mining (without incompleteness or noise) in [3]. It has three phases. The first phase iterates over the given entitlements, uses selected entitlements as seeds for constructing candidate rules, and attempts to generalize each candidate rule to cover more of the given entitlements, greedily selecting the highest-quality generalization according to a heuristic rule-quality metric. The second phase improves the policy by merging and simplifying candidate rules. The third phase selects the highest-quality candidate rules for inclusion in the mined policy.

4.1   Validity-Threshold (VT) Approach

Top-level pseudocode appears in Fig. 1. It returns a rule set $Rules'$. Entitlements covered by $Rules'$ and not in E_0 are the suspected missing entitlements. Entitlements in E_0 not covered by $Rules'$ are the suspected excess entitlements. It calls several functions, described below, after a summary of how missing and excess entitlements are handled. Note that function names hyperlink to descriptions of the functions.

Missing Entitlements. The algorithm has a parameter α that bounds the acceptable fraction of added entitlements (i.e., entitlements not in E_0) for a rule. A rule ρ is α-valid iff the fraction of added entitlements is at most α (i.e., $|\,[\![\rho]\!]\setminus E_0|\div|\,[\![\rho]\!]\,|\leq\alpha$) and the rule does not cover any denials (i.e., $[\![\rho]\!]\cap D_0=\emptyset$).

// Phase 1: Create a set Rules of candidate rules that covers E_0.
$Rules = \emptyset$
// uncov contains entitlements in E_0 that are not covered by Rules
$uncov = E_0.\mathrm{copy}()$
while *uncov* is not empty
    // Use highest-quality uncovered entitlement as a "seed" for rule creation. Quality
    // of $\langle s,r,a\rangle$ is proportional to the number of occurrences in E_0 of $\langle r,a\rangle$ and s.
    $\langle s,r,a\rangle = $ highest-quality entitlement in *uncov*
    $cc = \mathrm{candidateConstraint}(s,r)$
    // s_{sub} contains subjects with permission $\langle r,a\rangle$ and with same candidate constraints as s
    $s_{\mathrm{sub}} = \{s' \in OM \mid \mathrm{type}(s') = \mathrm{type}(s) \wedge \langle s',r,a\rangle \in E_0 \wedge \mathrm{candidateConstraint}(s',r)=cc\}$
    // Add candidate rule that covers at least permission $\langle r,a\rangle$ for subjects in s_{sub}
    $\mathrm{addCandidateRule}(\mathrm{type}(s), s_{\mathrm{sub}}, \mathrm{type}(r), \{r\}, cc, \{a\}, uncov, Rules)$
    // s_{act} is set of actions that s can perform on r
    $s_{\mathrm{act}} = \{a' \in Act \mid \langle s,r,a'\rangle \in E_0\}$
    // Add candidate rule that covers at least permissions $\{\langle r,a'\rangle \mid a' \in s_{\mathrm{act}}\}$ for subject s
    $\mathrm{addCandidateRule}(\mathrm{type}(s), \{s\}, \mathrm{type}(r), \{r\}, cc, s_{\mathrm{act}}, uncov, Rules)$
end while
// Phase 2: Merge and simplify rules.
Repeatedly call $\mathrm{mergeRules}(Rules)$, $\mathrm{simplifyRules}(Rules)$, and
$\mathrm{mergeRulesInheritance}(Rules)$, until they have no further effect
// Remove redundant rules
while *Rules* contains rules ρ and ρ' such that $[\![\rho]\!] \subseteq [\![\rho']\!]$
    $Rules.\mathrm{remove}(\rho)$
end while
// Phase 3: Select high quality rules into Rules'.
$Rules' = \emptyset$
Repeatedly move highest-quality rule from $Rules$ to $Rules'$ until $\sum_{\rho\in Rules'}[\![\rho]\!] \supseteq E_0$,
using $E_0 \setminus [\![Rules']\!]$ as second argument to Q_{rul}, and discarding a rule if it does not
cover any tuples in E_0 currently uncovered by $Rules'$ or if its quality is below τ
return $Rules'$

Fig. 1. Greedy algorithm for the extended ReBAC policy mining problem. Inputs: subject-permission relation E_0, class model CM, object model OM. Output: set of rules $Rules'$.

The usual notion of *validity* [3] corresponds to $\alpha = 0$. Candidate rules are checked for α-validity at several places in the algorithm, as discussed below.

Excess Entitlements. Excess entitlements typically result from individual errors in policy administration and hence do not fit any pattern that can be expressed concisely as rules. Consequently, excess assignments lead to the creation of low-quality candidate rules. As described in Sect. 1 and embodied in the last line in Fig. 1, our algorithm drops rules whose quality is below a threshold τ, which is a parameter of the algorithm.

The function candidateConstraint(s, r) returns a set containing all the atomic constraints that hold between subject s and resource r and that satisfy specified limits on the lengths of the path expressions. It first computes all candidate constraints that contain type-correct paths that start from type(s) and type(r), respectively, and satisfy the length limits, and then it computes and returns the subset of these that are satisfied by $\langle s, a \rangle$. The length limits mainly bound the difference between the length of the path and the length of the shortest path between the same types.

The function addCandidateRule$(st, s_{\mathrm{sub}}, rt, s_{\mathrm{res}}, cc, s_{\mathrm{act}}, uncov, Rules)$ first computes conditions sc and rc that characterize (i.e., whose meaning equals) the set s_{sub} of subjects and the set s_{res} of resources, respectively. It tries to do this using paths that satisfy the length limits and without using the path "id" (this is a path of length 1); if this is insufficient, an atomic condition on the path "id" is added. addCandidateRule then constructs a rule $\rho = \langle st, sc, rt, rc, \emptyset, s_{\mathrm{act}} \rangle$, calls generalizeRule (described below) to generalize ρ to ρ', adds ρ' to candidate rule set $Rules$, and then removes the entitlements covered by ρ' from $uncov$.

The function generalizeRule$(\rho, cc, uncov, Rules)$ attempts to generalize rule ρ by adding some atomic constraints in cc to ρ and eliminating the conjuncts (if any) of the subject condition and resource condition that use the same paths as those atomic constraints. A rule obtained in this way is called a *generalization* of ρ. It is more general in the sense that it refers to relationships instead of specific values, and its meaning is a superset of the meaning of ρ. In more detail, generalizeRule tries to generalize ρ using each constraint in cc separately, discards the generalizations that are not α-valid, sorts the α-valid generalizations in descending order of the number of covered entitlements in $uncov$, recursively tries to further generalize each of them using constraints from cc that produced α-valid generalizations later in the sort order, and then returns the highest-quality rule among them (rule quality is defined below); if no generalizations of ρ are α-valid, it simply returns ρ.

A *rule quality metric* is a function $Q_{\mathrm{rul}}(\rho, E)$ that maps a rule ρ to a totally-ordered set, with the order chosen such that larger values indicate higher quality. The second argument E is a set of subject-permission tuples. Based on our primary goal of minimizing the mined policy's WSC, a secondary preference for rules with more constraints (because constraints tend to produce more general rules than conditions), and a tertiary preference for rules with shorter paths in constraints, we define $Q_{\mathrm{rul}}(\rho, E) = \langle |\,[\![\rho]\!] \cap E|/\mathrm{WSC}(\rho), |\mathrm{con}(\rho)|, 1/\mathrm{TCPL}(\rho) \rangle$ where $\mathrm{TCPL}(\rho)$ ("total constraint path length") is the sum of the lengths of the paths used in the constraints of ρ. In generalizeRule, the second argument to Q_{rul} is $uncov$, so $[\![\rho]\!] \cap E$ is the set of currently uncovered entitlements that are covered by ρ.

The function mergeRules($Rules$) attempts to improve the quality of $Rules$ by merging pairs of rules with the same subject type, resource type, and constraint by taking the least upper bound (LUB) of their subject conditions, the LUB of their resource conditions, and the union of their sets of actions. The *least upper bound* of conditions c_1 and c_2 is obtained by combining "in" conditions with the same path in c_1 and c_2, keeping "contains" conditions with the same path and constant in c_1 and c_2, and dropping other atomic conditions in c_1 and c_2. Thus, if c_1 contains $\langle p, \mathrm{in}, val_1 \rangle$ and c_2 contains $\langle p, \mathrm{in}, val_2 \rangle$, then their LUB contains $\langle p, \mathrm{in}, val_1 \cup val_2 \rangle$; and, if c_1 contains $\langle p, \mathrm{contains}, val \rangle$ and c_2 contains $\langle p, \mathrm{contains}, val \rangle$, then their LUB contains $\langle p, \mathrm{contains}, val \rangle$.

The meaning of the merged rule ρ_{mrg} is a superset of the meanings of the rules ρ_1 and ρ_2 being merged. If ρ_{mrg} is α-valid, then it is added to $Rules$, and ρ_1 and ρ_2 are redundant and will be removed later.

The function simplifyRules($Rules$) attempts to simplify each of the rules in $Rules$ using several transformations, detailed in [3]. For example, it eliminates atomic conditions from the subject condition and resource condition, and eliminates atomic constraints from the constraint, if the resulting rule is α-valid.

The function mergeRulesInheritance($Rules$) attempts to merge a set of rules if their subject types or resource types have a common superclass and all the other components of the rule are the same. In this case, it replaces that set of rules with a single rule whose subject type or resource type is the most general superclass for which the resulting rule is α-valid, if any.

Complexity Analysis. The step with the highest asymptotic complexity is mergeRules, since the number of attempted merges is $O(|Rules|^2)$. In the worst case, each rule covers only one entitlement, and this is quadratic in log size. In practice, a rule covers many entitlements on average, and the complexity is much less. The complexity is similar as for Bui et al.'s algorithm [3], and in their experiments, measured growth in running time is less than quadratic with respect to number of entitlements.

Example. We illustrate the VT greedy algorithm on a small fragment of the workforce management case study containing only the rule "Help desk operators can modify work orders that apply to active contracts of a Primary Tenant for which he/she is assigned responsible", formalized as $\rho_0 = \langle \mathrm{HelpdeskOperator},$ true, WorkOrder, resource.contract.active = true, subject.tenants $\ni$ res.contract. tenant, {modify}$\rangle$.

The object model contains: PrimaryTenant objects telco and pp; Helpdesk-Operator objects ho1 and ho2 with ho1.tenants = {telco, pp} and ho2.tenants = {pp}; Contract objects telcoActive, telcoInactive, and ppActive whose tenant and active status are as indicated in the name; WorkOrder objects telcoWO1 on telcoActive contract, telcoWO2 on telcoInactive contract, and ppWO1 on ppActive contract.

For the policy π containing only ρ_0, $[\![\pi]\!] = \{\langle \text{ho1}, \text{telcoWO1}, \text{modify}\rangle, \langle \text{ho1},$ ppWO1, modify$\rangle$, $\langle \text{ho2}, \text{telcoWO1}, \text{modify}\rangle\}$. Suppose the input E_0 is missing entitlement $\langle ho1, ppWO1, modify\rangle$ and contains excess entitlement $\langle ho2, ppWO1, modify\rangle$.

Our algorithm selects $\langle \text{ho2}, \text{telcoWO1}, \text{modify}\rangle$ as the first seed. The first call to addCandidateRule creates a rule with conditions subject.tenants $\ni$ {Telco}, resource.contract.tenant $\in$ {Telco}, and resource.contract.active = true, and then calls generalizeRule on it. The generalization with candidate constraint subject.tenants $\ni$ resource.contract.tenant succeeds, removing the first two conditions and creating a rule ρ_1 identical to ρ_0, provided $\alpha \geq 1/3$ (to allow covering the missing entitlement). The second call to addCandidateRule generates a rule similar to rule ρ_0 except that it has additional condition subject = ho2; later, this rule is merged with ρ_1, and the merge leaves ρ_1 unchanged.

Our algorithm selects $\langle \text{ho2}, \text{ppWO1}, \text{modify}\rangle$ as the next seed. The two calls to addCandidateRule generate two rules without constraints; merging and simplification produces a rule with conditions subject = {ho2} and resource.contract.tenant = {pp}. This rule's quality is low, since it covers only 1 entitlement (the excess one). It will be discarded, provided $\tau \geq 1/6$.

4.2 Extended-Quality (EQ) Approach

The main difference in this approach compared to the VT approach is that the algorithm uses a modified rule quality metric that takes added entitlements into account. The rule quality metric Q_{rul} in Sect. 4.1 is replaced with a rule quality metric $Q_{\text{rul}}^{\text{EQ}}$ whose first component includes a factor that imposes a penalty for added entitlements, measured as a fraction of the number of entitlements covered by the rule, and with a weight specified by a parameter $w_{\text{rul}}^{\text{EQ}}$.

$$Q_{\text{rul}}^{\text{EQ}}(\rho, E) = \langle \frac{|[\![\rho]\!] \cap E|}{\text{WSC}(\rho)} \times (1 - \frac{w_{\text{rul}}^{\text{EQ}} \times |[\![\rho]\!] \setminus E_0|}{|[\![\rho]\!]|}), |\text{con}(\rho)|, 1/\text{TCPL}(\rho)\rangle$$

Also, the four functions that involve α-validity checks are modified as follows. In generalizeRule, the α-validity check is replaced with a check that the rule does not cover any tuples in D_0. In mergeRules, instead of checking whether ρ_{mrg} is α-valid, the algorithm compares the policy quality (as defined in Sect. 3, with $w_{\text{omit}} = 0$, since omitted entitlements are not determined yet) of $Rules$ and $Rules \cup \{\rho_{\text{mrg}}\} \setminus \{\rho_1, \rho_2\}$, where ρ_1 and ρ_2 are the rules being merged. If the latter has higher quality, and ρ_{mrg} does not accept any tuples in D_0, then ρ_1 and ρ_2 are replaced with ρ_{mrg}. In simplifyRules($Rules$) and mergeRulesInheritance($Rules$), instead of checking α-validity of the simplified or merged rule, the algorithm checks that the rule does not cover any denials in D_0 and that it does not cover any *new* added entitlements, i.e., entitlements not in E_0 and not currently covered by $Rules$; allowing new added entitlements in those places led to overly permissive policies.

5   Evolutionary Algorithm

Our evolutionary algorithm is based on the evolutionary algorithm for ReBAC mining (without incompleteness or noise) in [3], which is inspired by Medvet et al.'s work [7]. It is in the context-free grammar genetic programming (CFGGP) paradigm, in which individuals, which in our context are ReBAC rules, are represented as derivation trees of a context-free grammar (CFG). The main part of the algorithm is preceded by *grammar generation*, which specializes the generic grammar of ORAL to a specific input, so that rules in the language of the grammar contain only classes, fields, constants, and actions that appear in the input, and all path expressions are type-correct and satisfy the same length limits as in the greedy algorithm.

The algorithm's first phase iterates over the given entitlements, and uses each of the selected entitlements as the seed for an evolutionary search that adds one new rule to the candidate policy. Each evolutionary search starts with an initial population containing candidate rules created from a seed tuple in a similar way as in the greedy algorithm along with numerous random variants of those rules together with some completely random candidate rules, evolves the population by repeatedly applying genetic operators (mutations and crossover), and then selects the highest quality rule in the population as the result of that evolutionary search. The second phase improves the candidate rules by further mutating them.

Pseudocode appears in Fig. 2. Function initialPopulation($\langle s, r, a \rangle$, *Rules*, *uncov*) creates an initial population for the evolutionary search for a high-quality rule that covers the seed $\langle s, r, a \rangle$ and other tuples. It is implicitly parameterized by the desired population size *popSize*. Half of the initial population is generated as follows: perform the same two calls to addCandidateRule as in Fig. 1, add those rules to the initial population, and then add random variants of those rules obtained by removing some atomic conditions and atomic constraints. The other half consists of rules with subject type type(s) or one of its ancestors (selected randomly), resource type type(r) or one of its ancestors, randomly generated conditions and constraint, and action set $\{a\}$.

Rule quality is measured using a fitness function f, modified from the one in [3] to take missing assignments into account using a threshold approach: false acceptances are ignored unless they exceed a threshold specified by algorithm parameter α. The fitness function is $f(\rho, \alpha) = \langle \text{FAR}(\rho, \alpha), \text{FRR}(\rho), \text{ID}(\rho), \text{WSC}(\rho) \rangle$. The *false acceptance rate* $\text{FAR}(\rho, \alpha)$ is 0 if $\frac{\|\rho\| \backslash E_0\|}{\|\rho\|} < \alpha$ and is $\frac{\|\rho\| \backslash E_0\|}{\|\rho\|}$ otherwise. The *false rejection rate* is $\text{FRR}(\rho) = |uncov \backslash \llbracket \rho \rrbracket|$, and $\text{ID}(\rho)$ is the number of atomic conditions in ρ with path "id".

The two validity checks used in the algorithm in [3] are replaced with α-validity checks, as shown in Fig. 2. Also, to deal with excess entitlements, the algorithm returns only rules with quality at least τ.

The set *searchOps* of genetic operators used in the search phase contains the two traditional CFGGP genetic operators: a mutation operator that randomly selects a non-terminal in the derivation tree being evolved, and replaces the

// Phase 1: Construct candidate policy, using evolutionary search to create each rule.
Rules = ∅; *uncov* = E_0.copy()
while *uncov* is not empty
  seed = highest-quality entitlement in *uncov* (same quality metric as in greedy algorithm)
  pop = initialPopulation(*seed*, *Rules*, *uncov*)
  for *gen* = 1 to *nGenerationsSearch*
    op = a genetic operator randomly selected from *searchOps*
    S = set of *nTournament* rules randomly selected from *pop*
    if *op* is a mutation
      pop.add(the rule generated by applying *op* to the highest-quality rule in *S*)
    else   *// op is a cross-over*
      pop.add(the two rules generated by applying *op* to the two highest-quality rules in *S*)
    end if
    remove the lowest-quality rules in *pop* until |*pop*| = *popSize*
  end for
  ρ = the highest-quality rule in *pop*
  if α-valid(ρ);
    Rules.add(ρ); *uncov*.removeAll($\llbracket\rho\rrbracket$)
  end if
end while
// Phase 2: Improve the candidate rules by further mutating them.
for each ρ **in** *Rules*
  for *gen* = 1 to *nGenerationsImprove*
    if *gen* = *nGenerationsImprove*/2 ∧ (all attempted improvements to ρ failed)
      break *// This rule is unlikely to improve. Don't bother trying more.*
    end if
    op = a genetic operator randomly selected from *improveOps*
    ρ' = the rule generated by applying *op* to ρ
    if α-valid(ρ') ∧ ID(ρ') ≤ ID(ρ)
      redundant = {ρ_0 ∈ *Rules* | $\llbracket\rho_0\rrbracket \subseteq \llbracket\rho'\rrbracket$}
      if (*Rules* ∪ {ρ'} \ *redundant*) covers E_0 and has lower WSC than *Rules*
        Rules.removeAll(*redundant*); *Rules*.add(ρ')
      end if
    end if
  end for
end for
Repeatedly call mergeRules(*Rules*) and simplifyRules(*Rules*) until they have no effect
return the rules in *Rules* with quality at least τ

Fig. 2. Evolutionary algorithm for extended ReBAC policy mining problem. Inputs: subject-permission relation E_0, class model *CM*, object model *OM*. Output: set of rules *Rules*.

existing subtree rooted at that non-terminal with a new subtree randomly generated starting from that non-terminal, and a cross-over operator that randomly selects a non-terminal that appears in both of the derivation trees being evolved (called "parents"), and swaps the subtrees rooted at that non-terminal. It also contains a *double mutation* operator that mutates two out of the three predicates (the subject condition, resource condition, and constraint) in a rule (this enables the operator to have an effect similar to generalizeRule), and a *simplify mutation* that removes one randomly selected atomic condition or atomic constraint (this mutation is included to increase the overall probability of these mutations). The set *improveOps* of genetic operators used in the improvement phase is similar, except it also contains a *type mutation* operator that can replace the subject type or resource type with one of its ancestors.

The version of simplifyRules used in this algorithm is the same as in the greedy algorithm except extended with an additional simplification: replace the subject type or resource type with one of its children, if the policy still covers E_0.

6   Evaluation

This section presents experimental results evaluating our algorithms on the four sample policies and three large case studies mentioned Sect. 1, following the evaluation methodology sketched in Sect. 1. Our code and data are available at http://www.cs.stonybrook.edu/~stoller/software/. Parameters of the algorithms (e.g., *popSize*) have the same values as in [3]. Since the results of experiments with the EMR and project management sample policies are similar to the results for the other two sample policies, we summarize their results, omitting details due to space constraints. Each policy has handwritten class model and rules, and a synthetic object model generated by a policy-specific pseudorandom algorithm designed to produce realistic object models, by creating objects and selecting their attribute values using appropriate probability distributions.

Similarity Metrics. We evaluate the quality of the generated policy using three similarity metrics. They are normalized to range from 0 (completely different) to 1 (identical). They are based on *Jaccard similarity* of sets, defined by $J(S_1, S_2) = |S_1 \cap S_2| \, / \, |S_1 \cup S_2|$. The *semantic similarity* of policies π_1 and π_2 is $J(\llbracket \pi_1 \rrbracket, \llbracket \pi_2 \rrbracket)$. We use this metric to compare meaning of the original policy π_0 and the mined policy π. If the algorithm accurately identifies and compensates for all incompleteness and noise, the semantic similarity will equal 1. *Missing entitlements similarity* is the Jaccard similarity of the set of actual missing entitlements (removed when creating E_0 from $\llbracket \pi_0 \rrbracket$) and the set of suspected missing entitlements. *Excess assignments similarity* is the Jaccard similarity of the actual excess entitlements (added when creating E_0 from $\llbracket \pi_0 \rrbracket$) and the suspected excess entitlements.

Running Time. An organization needs to run policy mining occasionally, not frequently, so our evaluation focuses on quality of results. Both algorithms have reasonable running times, although the VT greedy algorithm is significantly faster than the evolutionary algorithm. With our implementation in Java on an Intel i7-3770 CPU, each run of the VT greedy algorithm and evolutionary algorithm take at most 8.5 and 70 min, respectively. The policies involve up to several hundred objects, a few thousand entitlements, and a few dozen rules (more details on policy size are in [3]). The evolutionary algorithm can be sped up significantly, at the cost of a small decrease in quality, by varying parameters. For example, for e-document (our largest case study), reducing the number of generations per evolutionary search from 2000 (the value used in our main experiments) to 1000 reduces the running time by 27%, with a decrease of only 0.02 (from 0.87 to 0.85) in policy semantic similarity.

6.1   Experiments with Noise

We introduce synthetic noise at a specified level into the meaning of a ReBAC policy π_0 in a similar way as [14], apply our policy mining algorithms to the resulting set of entitlements E_0 along with the class model and object model, and then compute the above metrics comparing the original policy π_0 and mined policy π. Noise level is expressed as a fraction of $|\,[\![\pi_0]\!]\,|$; thus, noise level ν means that $\nu|\,[\![\pi_0]\!]\,|$ entitlements are added to or removed from $[\![\pi_0]\!]$. To introduce a specified level ν of noise, we introduce $\nu|\,[\![\pi_0]\!]\,|/6$ missing entitlements and $5\nu|\,[\![\pi_0]\!]\,|/6$ excess entitlements. This ratio is based on the data in [8, Table 1]. Missing entitlements are selected from a discrete normal distribution on $[\![\pi_0]\!]$, to reflect that policy errors are usually non-uniformly distributed. Excess entitlements are selected from a discrete normal distribution on the complement of $[\![\pi_0]\!]$. We tune all of the algorithm parameters manually, so the experimental results reflect the capabilities of the algorithms with an experienced user.

Figure 3 shows results for the VT greedy algorithm and evolutionary algorithm. Each datapoint is the average over 10 runs (except 5 runs for grant proposal and e-doc) on inputs with different pseudorandom object model and noise. The 95% confidence intervals using Student's t-distribution are reasonably small, less than 0.13 in all cases except missing assignment similarity for grant proposal policy when running with evolutionary algorithm, for which it is 0.18. For experiments on healthcare and university sample policies (not shown in the figure), both algorithms achieve perfect values (i.e., 1.0) on all three similarity metrics at all three noise levels.

To compare the algorithms, we average the similarity metrics over all three noise levels and all seven policies. For both algorithms, the average policy semantic similarity is 0.99, and the average excess entitlement similarity is 0.98; the latter is not surprising, since the algorithms use the same approach to identify excess entitlements. The average missing entitlement similarity is 0.96 for the greedy algorithm, and 0.94 for the evolutionary algorithm. We conclude that VT greedy algorithm is slightly better than evolutionary algorithm at detecting missing entitlements. Noise detection results for the EQ greedy algorithm are significantly worse: the average excess entitlement similarity is 0.95, and the average missing entitlement similarity is 0.73.

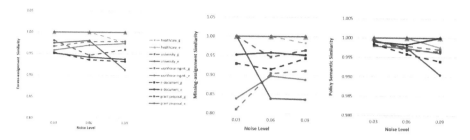

Fig. 3. Left: Excess entitlement similarity. Center: Missing entitlement similarity. Right: Policy semantic similarity. The legend is the same for all three graphs. Suffixes "_g" and "_e" indicate VT greedy algorithm and evolutionary algorithm, respectively. Results for the two algorithms are plotted with dashed and solid lines, respectively.

6.2 Experiments with Incompleteness (Mining from Logs)

Given a set of entitlements E_0, which is a subset of the meaning of a ReBAC policy π_0, the *completeness* of E_0 (relative to π_0) is $|E_0|/|[\![\pi_0]\!]|$, i.e., the fraction of entitlements in $[\![\pi_0]\!]$ that are in E_0. Given a ReBAC policy π_0 and a desired completeness level c, we pseudorandomly select $(1-c)|[\![\pi_0]\!]|$ entitlements in $[\![\pi_0]\!]$ and remove them to create E_0. We select them from a discrete normal distribution on $[\![\pi_0]\!]$, to reflect that some entitlements are used more often and hence more likely to appear in an access log. We also generate a set of denials D_0 by pseudorandomly selecting tuples from a discrete normal distribution on the complement of $[\![\pi_0]\!]$. We set the number of denials to 4% of $|[\![\pi_0]\!]|$, based on Cotrini et al.'s comment that the percentage of denied operations in logs used in their experiments is usually less than 5% [4]. For simplicity, we do not add excess entitlements as noise in these experiments, because sets of entitlements obtained from logs are expected to contain a relatively small percentage of excess entitlements, which would not appreciably affect our results.

Figure 4 shows results for the VT greedy algorithm and evolutionary algorithm. Each datapoint is the average over 10 runs (except 5 runs for grant proposal and e-doc) on inputs with different pseudorandom object model and incompleteness. The 95% confidence intervals using Student's t-distribution are reasonably small, less than 0.12 in all cases. As expected, the results are better for higher completeness. For inputs with completeness 0.7 and higher, policy semantic similarity is above 0.93, and missing entitlements similarity is above 0.8, for all policies. For the healthcare and university sample policies (not shown in the figure), for all four completeness levels, both algorithms achieve perfect values on both similarity metrics.

To compare the algorithms, we average the similarity metrics over all four completeness levels and all seven policies. The average policy semantic similarity is 0.98 for VT greedy algorithm, and 0.97 for evolutionary algorithm. The average missing assignments similarity is 0.94 for VT greedy algorithm, and 0.91 for evolutionary algorithm. Thus, the VT greedy algorithm is modestly better than the evolutionary algorithm on incomplete inputs. Since the EQ greedy algorithm was less effective in the noise experiments, we run incompleteness experiments for it on a subset of policies, namely, EMR, grant proposal and workforce management. The results are consistent with our expectation: the average policy similarity is 0.89, compared to 0.97 for VT greedy algorithm on the same datasets, and the average missing assignments similarity is 0.67, compared to 0.89 for VT greedy algorithm on the same datasets.

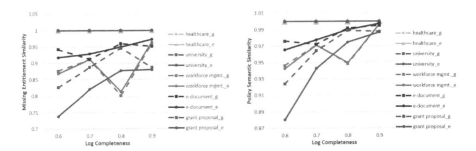

Fig. 4. Left: missing entitlements similarity. Right: policy semantic similarity. The suffixes and line styles have the same meaning as in Fig. 3.

6.3   Comparison with Rhapsody

We evaluated Rhapsody's approach to handling incompleteness by running Rhapsody [4] and Xu et al.'s algorithm [13] on some of the ABAC policies used in [13]. For the university policy with manually written attribute data [13], which involves 10 ABAC rules and 16 attributes, and a log with completeness 0.8, Rhapsody's running time (based on its progress indicator) would exceed 24 hours. In contrast, Xu et al.'s algorithm produces a policy with a perfect policy semantic similarity of 1 in less than 1 second. We created a very small version of the policy, with only 7 ABAC rules and 9 attributes. After parameter tuning based on guidance in [4], the best result is a policy with policy semantic similarity 0.65, and Rhapsody took 3.7 hours to produce it.

The implementation of Rhapsody we were given considers neither conditions involving set relations nor constraints of any kind. Extending the implementation to consider these (as our algorithms do) would significantly increase the number of atoms (predicates that can appear in rules) and hence the running time. Further extending it to support ReBAC instead of ABAC would further greatly increase the number of atoms and hence the running time, making it usable only on small problem instances.

7   Related Work

The only prior work on mining of ReBAC policies (or object-oriented ABAC policies with path expressions) is [3], which is discussed in Sect. 1. The contributions of this paper include adapting their algorithms to handle incompleteness and noise using two approaches, and extensive experimental evaluation of the accuracy and performance of the two approaches and the two algorithms in this context. Interestingly, we find that the VT greedy algorithm achieves slightly to moderately better results; in contrast, the evolutionary algorithm achieves somewhat better results in the experiments in [3].

The earliest work on mining of access control policies from logs is Molloy et al.'s algorithm to mine "meaningful" roles from logs and attribute data, i.e., roles whose membership is statistically correlated with user attributes [9]. Their algorithm is based on a reduction to the author-topic model problem. Xu and Stoller adapted that approach to ABAC policy mining and found that it is less accurate and less scalable than the validity-threshold approach [13]. Other work on mining roles from incomplete or noisy data, e.g., [11,12], uses thresholds but does not consider attribute data.

References

1. Beckerle, M., Martucci, L.A.: Formal definitions for usable access control rule sets–From goals to metrics. In: Proceedings of the Ninth Symposium on Usable Privacy and Security (SOUPS), pp. 2:1–2:11. ACM (2013)
2. Bogaerts, J., Decat, M., Lagaisse, B., Joosen, W.: Entity-based access control: supporting more expressive access control policies. In: Proceedings of 31st Annual Computer Security Applications Conference (ACSAC), pp. 291–300. ACM (2015)
3. Bui, T., Stoller, S.D., Li, J.: Greedy and evolutionary algorithms for mining relationship-based access control policies. Comput. Secur. **80**, 317–333 (2019)
4. Cotrini, C., Weghorn, T., Basin, D.: Mining ABAC rules from sparse logs. In: Proceedings of 3rd IEEE European Symposium on Security and Privacy (EuroS&P), pp. 2141–2148 (2018)
5. Decat, M., Bogaerts, J., Lagaisse, B., Joosen, W.: The e-document case study: functional analysis and access control requirements. CW Reports CW654, Department of Computer Science, KU Leuven, February 2014
6. Decat, M., Bogaerts, J., Lagaisse, B., Joosen, W.: The workforce management case study: functional analysis and access control requirements. CW Reports CW655, Department of Computer Science, KU Leuven, February 2014
7. Medvet, E., Bartoli, A., Carminati, B., Ferrari, E.: Evolutionary inference of attribute-based access control policies. In: Gaspar-Cunha, A., Henggeler Antunes, C., Coello, C.C. (eds.) EMO 2015. LNCS, vol. 9018, pp. 351–365. Springer, Cham (2015). https://doi.org/10.1007/978-3-319-15934-8_24
8. Molloy, I., Li, N., Qi, Y.A., Lobo, J., Dickens, L.: Mining roles with noisy data. In: Proceedings of 15th ACM Symposium on Access Control Models and Technologies (SACMAT), pp. 45–54. ACM (2010)
9. Molloy, I., Park, Y., Chari, S.: Generative models for access control policies: applications to role mining over logs with attribution. In: Proceedings of 17th ACM Symposium on Access Control Models and Technologies (SACMAT). ACM (2012)
10. Munakami, M.: Developing an ABAC-based grant proposal workflow management system. Master's thesis, Boise State University, December 2016
11. Vaidya, J., Atluri, V., Guo, Q., Lu, H.: Role mining in the presence of noise. In: Foresti, S., Jajodia, S. (eds.) DBSec 2010. LNCS, vol. 6166, pp. 97–112. Springer, Heidelberg (2010). https://doi.org/10.1007/978-3-642-13739-6_7

12. Vavilis, S., Egner, A.I., Petkovic, M., Zannone, N.: Role mining with missing values. In: Proceedings of 11th International Conference on Availability, Reliability and Security (ARES) (2016)
13. Xu, Z., Stoller, S.D.: Mining attribute-based access control policies from logs. In: Atluri, V., Pernul, G. (eds.) DBSec 2014. LNCS, vol. 8566, pp. 276–291. Springer, Heidelberg (2014). https://doi.org/10.1007/978-3-662-43936-4_18. Extended version http://arxiv.org/abs/1403.5715
14. Xu, Z., Stoller, S.D.: Mining attribute-based access control policies. IEEE Trans. Dependable Secure Comput. **12**(5), 533–545 (2015)

Fine-Grained Access Control for Microservices

Antonio Nehme[(⊠)], Vitor Jesus[(⊠)], Khaled Mahbub[(⊠)],
and Ali Abdallah[(⊠)]

School of Computing and Digital Technologies, Birmingham City University,
Birmingham, UK
{antonio.nehme,vitor.jesus,khaled.mahbub,
ali.abdallah}@bcu.ac.uk

Abstract. Microservices-based applications are considered to be a promising paradigm for building large-scale digital systems due to their flexibility, scalability, and agility of development. To achieve the adoption of digital services, applications holding personal data must be secure while giving end-users as much control as possible. On the other hand, for software developers, the adoption of a security solution for microservices requires it to be easily adaptable to the application context and requirements while fully exploiting reusability of security components. This paper proposes a solution that targets key security challenges of microservice-based applications. Our approach relies on a coordination of security components, and offers a fine-grained access control in order to minimise the risks of token theft, session manipulation, and a malicious insider; it also renders the system resilient against confused deputy attacks. This solution is based on a combination of OAuth 2 and XACML open standards, and achieved through reusable security components integrated with microservices.

Keywords: Microservices · Security · Confused deputy attack · Gateways · Access control

1 Introduction

Enterprise applications nowadays require using multiple, distributed and multi-owner components. While Service Oriented Architecture has been adopted for over a decade, its underlying model is now proving complex to manage given its tendency to a small number of large and complex components, referred to as monolithic applications ("monoliths") [4]. To ensure better software maintainability, faster development and deployment, and a more efficient scalability, microservice architecture is gaining popularity [22]. With Microservices, monolithic applications are replaced by a large number of loosely coupled components, yet each small and easy to maintain. By definition, microservices need to have a small role and should be designed to communicate with other services over a network [4] in a distributed fashion. Compared to monoliths, the considerable number of independent services renders enforcing security solutions and verifying every request's authenticity much more challenging.

Moreover, Microservices do introduce coordination complexity which, in turn, creates new security risks. This brings forward trust challenges as, effectively, every

© Springer Nature Switzerland AG 2019
N. Zincir-Heywood et al. (Eds.): FPS 2018, LNCS 11358, pp. 285–300, 2019.
https://doi.org/10.1007/978-3-030-18419-3_19

microservice is an independent party that, in the extreme case, cannot be trusted [22]. In particular, distributed architectures create access control problems such as the so-called *confused deputy* attacks and the use of *powerful tokens*. A *confused deputy*, referred to as the 'vulnerability du jour' [7], is a privilege escalation attack in which a microservice that is trusted by other microservices is compromised; this results in the trustees responding to the compromised microservice requests, not knowing that it is acting on behalf of the attacker [13]. *Powerful tokens*, in turn, result from the fact that, typically, one valid authorisation token is enough to have access to every microservice since requests pass through a gateway (the orchestrator) that can access all the system services with that access token. These are normally Open Authorization (OAuth) tokens that are created through one OAuth client, and their theft leads to data exposure at the level of every microservice [1].

The context of this paper is user-centred services that are multi-party and inter-domain. In particular, we consider scenarios where multiple parties are requesting access to personal data or assets; the data exchange process should be transparent to and controlled by the data owners. One example of such systems is a digital govern-ment portal: multiple administrations, that are nevertheless independent and segregated, have to coordinate to provide services for citizens, and citizens need to ensure that their data is safe, while being aware of how this data is being used, and what is being processed; on the other hand, each administration is responsible for protecting the citizens' data, and of correctly performing its role. Our solution for these requirements applies to microservice-based systems with access to sensitive data in different administrative domains.

This paper proposes a security solution for Microservices that enables fine-grained access-control policies to be deployed, thus mitigating several problems while giving the user control over their requests. Beyond globally validating a token at the entrance (the Gateway interfacing the user or another external application), we propose that each service has its own local Gateway that validates highly-descriptive and fine-grained tokens. These tokens are centrally generated, short-lived and have a narrow access scope. Additionally, these gateways include security checks that reveal and mitigate potential malicious activities, like data theft from government departments or tam-pering with government digital services, through a compromised microservice in one department. Furthermore, to enable scalability and reusability, we propose that these gateways are configurable and reuse security components that get added to microser-vices templates outside their core functionalities, and can scale with them when needed. Our solution is based on OAuth 2 and eXtensible Access Control Markup Language (XACML) open standards. To summarize, our architecture requires a user to explicitly allow actions from the multiple services engaged and belonging to different parties, while confining permissions of the services with pre-defined policies that all parties agree on.

The structure of this paper is as follows. The next section reviews related work and Sect. 3 describes the problem. In Sect. 4 we describe our solution, followed by an analysis in Sect. 5. Section 6 discusses our implementation, Sect. 6.1 shows the experimental results, and we conclude the paper in Sect. 7 with some future directions for our work.

2   Related Work

Many approaches found in the literature rely on *powerful tokens* strategy, i.e. one access token giving access to all the system's components, for access control. This results from using one OAuth client for a microservice-based application: [12] is an example of an implementation where powerful tokens are being used, and [3, 5, 6, 15] also point out to using similar approaches in their systems. OAuth token theft has been approached in literature. Ahmad et al. [2] used ID and OAuth tokens to minimise the possibility of token theft; however, the combination only reduces the chances of a successful attack and does not protect against powerful tokens theft in the service-to-service communication. Security architectures, [18] for example, recommend using standard mechanisms like OAuth 2 and XACML for API protection. XACML and OAuth 2 are discussed separately in [9, 14], and Suzic [17] mentioned the possibility of combining the two standards; however, the combination was not detailed or applied by any of them. Zhang et al. [20] based their implementation on this combination; however, their solution targets a specific use case that is not applicable to microservices. The confused deputy is another possible attack. Härtig et al. [7] call for tools to detect this attack; our work directly addresses that. Finally, work on a new OAuth grant type, Token Exchange [10], still in progress, tackles a similar problem as this paper. It is equally tailored for microservices in which the authorization server is in charge of policy decisions based on the identity of users, calling and called services, predefined action and access rules.

In short, to the best of our knowledge, this is the first attempt for designing a reusable and user-centric Identity and Access Management (IAM) security solution for primitive (only implementing functional requirements) microservices that mitigates token theft and the confused deputy problem. The reusability and configurability of our solution render it scalable and adaptable in agile Microservice Architecture (MSA) systems.

3   Problem Statement

This section presents a scenario to illustrate our security requirements. We then show our threat model for a Microservice-based system, give an overview of the principles that we are abiding by, the inadequacy of most used approaches and their common vulnerabilities, and a rationale for our design decisions.

To illustrate, we consider a digital government scenario of applying for a passport at the Department of State. The applicant needs to be a citizen to be eligible to apply for the passport service. The user logs in to a central portal, and selects the passport service; by logging in, the portal fetches the required information for access control: the citizenship status in this example. The passport service asks for further identity information required from the Department of Interior Affairs, and other data attributes from the Department of Justice to show a clean record; these attributes are already agreed on between the departments. The user needs to approve on the personal data attributes that will be shared between departments, and an access token will be produced for each consent. Each token only serves to access one specific service of one department.

3.1   Threat Model

In this threat model, we assume that traditional inter-domain security mechanisms, including intrusion detection and prevention systems, firewalls, input validation, mutual TLS authentication and encryption are placed between different security domains. We trust these security mechanisms, and that the authentication and authorisation servers are not compromised, but not the application microservices.

These microservices, and the Virtual machines (containers) which they run on, can be under the control of an attacker, or even abused by a privileged insider. This gives the adversary the ability to intercept requests and responses, steal and manipulate tokens by replacing a token belonging to a user with another, and send requests from the compromised microservice. A compromised microservice cannot generate a new access token without the user's consent on the list of scopes; this happens with a redirection to the OAuth server. Access Token theft can happen at the level of any compromised microservice, or by an insider monitoring local traffic.

3.2   Security Requirements

Considering the scenario detailed in Sect. 3, our approach uses the following as requirements:

- R1: Access policies are needed to control which services a user can access.
- R2: Every personal data attribute at each department needs user consent to be shared with another department.
- R3: Departments only share data following pre-defined and verifiable agreements with service consumers.
- R4: An access token should only serve to access the assets of a user exposed by a single service in one department.

   Where the corresponding security goals are:

- R1 requires fine-grained access policies, that must relate to the (micro-)service itself
- R2 separates control between user and service providers by allowing administrative policies on a per-service basis
- R3 verifies the authenticity of consumers and limits insiders malicious activities
- R4 protects against Powerful Token and Confused Deputy attacks.

3.3   Decoupling Security from Functional Requirements

A further requirement is to decouple the control of the microservice from the service itself. We approach this by designing our architecture using reusable and configurable gateways at the level of each microservice. These components can be added to secure primitive services, and modified to meet different policies. Figure 1 shows a primitive Resource Microservice (RMS) protected by a local Gateway (GW). In order for a request to reach the RMS, security policies enforced by GW have to be met by the requesting service or party (the consumer microservice); note that the consumer microservice should have another gateway to enforce access control policies. The Resource Microservice (RMS), which encapsulates only the primitive functionality, is

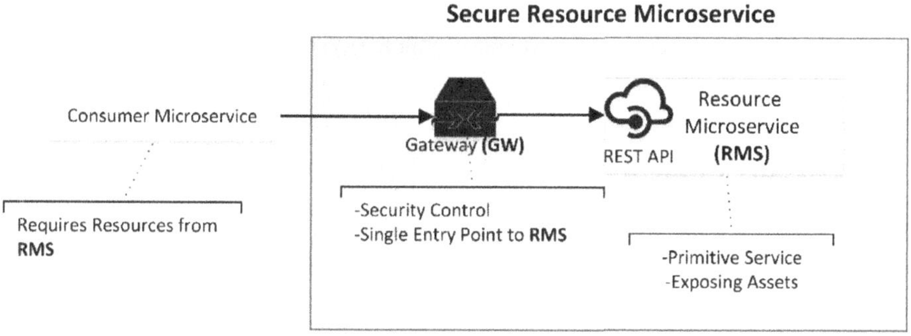

Secure Resource Microservice

Fig. 1. Gateway to secure primitive services

thus released from the verification logic and only manages the assets themselves (such as personal data).

A reusable security solution placed around services provides better consistency, simplicity, and portability [21]; adaptability and flexibility are essential requirements to follow. For different scenarios, a variety of attributes have to be considered when designing security solutions, and a trade-off has to be made between multiple variables including performance, security tightness, user-friendliness, and ease and flexibility of management.

3.4 Limitations of Current Practices

Open Authorization 2 (OAuth 2) is one of the most commonly used mechanisms in a microservice architecture for access delegation. OAuth 2 access scopes are used to define the token holder's access rights. However, the standard only gives the ability to define static, normally coarse-grained scopes, and does not provide any support for auditing and flexible policy enforcement [16, 17]. OpenID Connect, built on top of OAuth 2, is commonly used for authentication with MSA [12]; it is an enabler for identity federation by producing an ID token with end-user information, and a practice of the separation of concerns principle. Nevertheless, these approaches are not particularly suitable for MSA due to their large attack surface in such a fine-grained architecture [4]. These approaches normally rely on a single token that is used to access all parts of the system resulting in several problems, Powerful Token Theft being the most obvious [1, 2]. With this approach, any service having access to a session with a valid token can make requests to other components on behalf of the user [12].

On the other hand, we have the confused deputy problem. As explained, this consists of a component which has access to sensitive resources, and which can be manipulated by an adversary to have an indirect access to these resources [13]. In essence, the confused deputy attack arises from trusting a component based on mere identity information such as the component's IP address or an ID token [11]; in our scenario, presented in Sect. 3, the passport service is a potential confused deputy. The key point to prevent this is to have the resource services, the department of Justice and of Interior Affairs microservices in our scenario, verify that the calling microservice is acting truthfully on behalf of the user. This requires, for example, tokens to be individual to each component, and have finer granularity reflecting users' consents on access rules.

4   An Access Control Solution for Microservices

Figure 2 represents our approach for access control between consumer and resource microservices. This solution is built on a combination of XACML for administrative and OAuth 2 for user-defined policies. The architecture involves an Access Control Server (ACS) acting as an OAuth 2 and XACML server, consumer microservices (CMS) containing OAuth 2 client credentials and requiring access to resources, Resource Microservices (RMS) hosting and exposing assets, and a Gateway (GW) to secure each microservice.

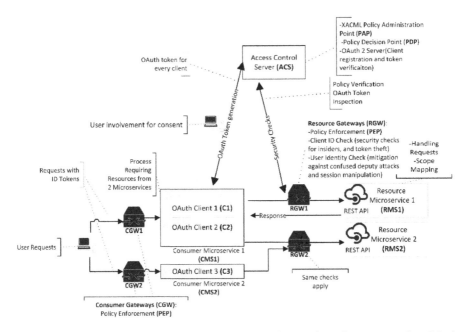

Fig. 2. Overview of our security architecture: Gateways for security enforcement, and an OAuth client per consumer-resource.

A request to CMS requires an ID token, generated by ACS when the user logs in, from the authentication session to verify the access rights of the user; to request resources from RMS, it also needs to generate an OAuth 2 token by having the user consent on the access scopes. As shown in Fig. 2, RGW1 and RGW2 are gateways to the resource microservices RMS1 and RMS2; consumer microservices also have a gateway each, CGW1 and CGW2, to enforce administrative access control policies. Typically, a central gateway in MSA sits in front of all services and can take different roles ranging from a simple address forwarder to an orchestrator. In our architecture, each microservice has its own gateway that gathers security and control functions, and is minimally dependent of the microservice; this makes it reusable as a configurable component across different microservices. Note that a central gateway is still present as a single entry point to the administrative and security domain to provide conventional network security services such as intrusion detection and prevention, firewalls, input validation, mutual TLS authentication or encryption.

The key functionality of a gateway per microservice is becoming a single entry point to each microservice that, while being fairly agnostic to the service itself, is able to validate the authenticity of the incoming requests. Our implementation of these gateways include other mechanisms for security assurance, policy enforcement, token theft detection, auditing and incident reporting; these serve to minimise blind trust between services, and therefore limit the effect of a successful confused deputy attack. The details for these checks and the requests flow of requests are explained in the next parts of this section.

4.1 A Fine-Grained Access Control

XACML is used to create access control policies. These define whether a user can interface a particular microservice. Policies are directly enforced by the GWs, each acting as a Policy Enforcement Point (PEP). The PEP component of the GW checks the user's identifier by inspecting the user's ID token in the authentication session. The ACS is the Policy Decision Point (PDP) and determines if this user is authorized to access a microservice endpoint to make a particular request. In the case of resource microservices, the request goes through other security checks discussed in Sect. 4.2.

OAuth 2 is used for users to delegate access to part of their protected data, residing at a resource microservice, to a consumer microservice. We use OAuth 2 to produce a token that maps to access scopes; these scopes are indicators for what the token gives access to. Being part of the token, scopes are used by RMS to share only the data that the owner has given consent for. Our proposal includes creating an OAuth client for every pair of consumer-resource microservices, to allow the generation of verifiable tokens with access scopes tailored for the combination.

Consider Fig. 2 OAuth clients C1 and C2 are used to send requests from the consumer microservice CMS1 to two different resource services, RMS1 and RMS2 respectively, exposing user's data. Although our approach gives the flexibility of using one OAuth client for multiple microservices, we recommend one OAuth client per consumer-resource microservices to limit the power of access tokens. Also, a microservice can receive requests from more than one consumer service as shown with RMS2 receiving requests from both CMS1 and CMS2. OAuth client creation is always done at the ACS level following the OAuth 2 common practice. Scopes are defined during creation, and client credentials (a unique identifier and a password) are generated to be used by consumer microservices for access tokens production.

4.2   Proposed Security Checks

For each request from microservices to access resources of another, an OAuth access token needs to be provided, alongside the ID token in the authentication session, by the sender of the request. The ID token is inspected by the GW of every microservice (Consumer or Resource) to verify the eligibility of access of the user, and the OAuth token is to be inspected by the RGW of the resource microservice before the request gets through to the RMS. This gateway sends the access token to an endpoint of the ACS to verify its authenticity and retrieve the information mapped to it.

To illustrate with Fig. 2, if a service CMS1 needs some of the user's personal information from RMS1, CMS1 uses C1's client credentials to produce an OAuth access token following OAuth 2 common practice. The user is required to choose the access scopes and confirm access for the OAuth token to be produced for CMS1. An access request is sent from service CMS1 to RMS1. RMS1, through its gateway RGW1, uses the token inspection endpoint of ACS to verify the authenticity of the access token and to decode it. The token would have a reference to the OAuth client ID, token scopes, the subject (user) identifier, and an expiry date. Given that the token is authentic and valid, RGW1 would perform the following security checks:

1. 'User Identity Check' by verifying that the user in the ID Token (the user that authenticated to the portal) is the same as the subject of the token
2. 'Client ID Check', by checking C1's client ID against a set of authorized client IDs to access the service

The first check reveals tokens' theft and manipulation attempts, and the second diminishes a token's power, and limits blind trust between components. If these checks pass, the gateway forwards the token information to the microservice; otherwise, the request is denied and the incidence gets reported. If the gateway lets the request through to the resource microservice, the latter returns the attributes of the user mapped to the scopes of the access token.

4.3   Operational Flow

The sequence diagram in Fig. 3 shows a representative example of our proposal. This shows the dataflow of an operation between a CMS and RMS of Fig. 2; it also reflects an access request between the passport microservice and one of the resource microservices in the scenario presented in Sect. 3. One service, the CMS, is to retrieve resources from another service, the RMS. A central ACS is used as an OAuth 2 authorization server, as well as an XACML server with policy administration and decision points. The ACS can include or be linked to an authentication server that produces and keeps track of authentication sessions with ID tokens. Each gateway (CGW and RGW) functions as a PEP which inspects the ID token, and uses the ACS PDP to check the policy rules. Access rules can be defined as a set of URLs and actions mapped to a group of users (i.e. Role-based); however, more complex policies can be defined following any policy definition criteria.

Before any attempt to access CMS, the user has to have an active session with an ID token. When the user sends a request, the PEP at CGW inspects the user's ID token

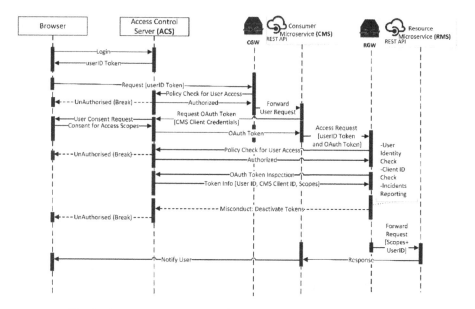

Fig. 3. Sequence diagram representing a service-to-service interaction.

with the Policy Decision Point of ACS, and if the action with CMS is allowed, this user is able to initiate a request with the service. When CMS requires data/service from an external resource (RMS), it first needs to request an OAuth access token. CMS uses its OAuth credentials, specific for RMS, to initiate the token production request with ACS. In turn, ACS requires the user to be authenticated and to choose the access scopes. At the level of ACS, an Intrusion Detection System can detect session manipulation attempts between the last two interactions with it. The produced access token is sent to CMS, and a request with the ID and OAuth tokens in the header is sent to RGW. RGW, protecting the resource microservice, checks if the user is authorized to access the service that it protects and, if so, the OAuth token is sent to the OAuth token inspection endpoint of ACS. This token gets verified, decoded, and sent back to RGW to perform the User Identifier and Client ID Checks described in Sect. 4.2. If any of the previous checks fails, an appropriate alert will be sent to the system administration and the user session and access token get deactivated. If all conditions are met, RGW sends the request with the user ID and the access scopes to RMS. This service has now the data attributes and/or methods mapped to the token scopes and the data of the user will now be sent to CMS.

5 Analysis

We now revisit the early requirements listed in Sect. 3 and discuss how our proposal addresses them.

5.1   Fine-Grained Access Control

With PEPs used at each microservice gateway level, access policies allow defining access roles for users to particular services (R1). Gateways here keep any unnecessary potential load off the microservices and act as a further defence layer. Since XACML allows to define complex policies, one can further add contextual access rules such as time and location.

Having multiple OAuth 2 clients helps to enforce transparency in the system by requiring users' consent for each access operation to their personal data, and giving them the option to choose what they want to share. Scopes are defined during OAuth 2 client creation following agreements between the resource and consumer microservices departments (R3), and having an OAuth client per consumer-resource microservice enables a fine-grained user-centred access control at the level of microservices (R2). Scope to resource mapping is done at the RMS level, and having scopes tailored to each service gives the transparency needed for systems in which privacy is key to users' trust.

5.2   Token Theft Mitigation

Having multiple OAuth 2 clients, for different consumer-resource combinations, limits the power of access tokens. With one OAuth 2 token per access task, a stolen token would only be a threat to the data of a particular person in one microservice only. These tokens can have a short lifespan since they are meant to be used once and for one particular request. Also, due to the User Identity Check at the gateway level, access to information from a stolen access token is not possible without access to the ID token of the same user. Any attempt from a conflicting user session would result in deactivating the tokens and reporting the incidence; even session hijacking can be rendered ineffective with a stolen token's short lifespan. Also, the Client ID Check diminishes the token's power, by limiting the services that accept the token. This partially fulfils the security goal of R4.

5.3   Confused Deputy Mitigation

Going back to Fig. 2, a token produced with C1, belonging to CMS1 and valid for RMS1, would not be valid for RMS2. This is also valid if service CMS1 is allowed to access both services RMS1 and RMS2, and even if RMS1 and RMS2 belong to the same department (R4). The combination of the User Identity Check, the Client ID Check, and requiring user consent for every service to service data access is a mitigation against the confused deputy attack. These security checks and practices minimise trust between services and give an assurance that a service is acting faithfully on behalf of the user. Therefore, this solution achieves the security goal of R4.

On a related note, our design mitigates some malicious insiders' activities. According to an IBM report in 2015, 60% of attacks are due to an insider [8]. If she or he manages to create an OAuth client on ACS to be used by a malicious node, the resource microservices would not accept any access token from this new client since its

ID is not in the list of trusted clients of any RGW. This approach minimises the possibility of having a service confused with a rogue/fake client (R3).

5.4 Manageability and Reusability

To help manageability, categorising services into groups, according to their security requirements is likely necessary. These requirements are decided based on the functionality of the microservices, the criticality of assets, and the trust context. This is a common approach for large enterprise software to protect their resources [19]. In our scenario, we separated consumer from resource microservices and required different gateways for each; other microservices may require encrypting their data at rest and on exchange for example. Having reusable security components helps to define configurations with security functions to meet different requirements; this facilitates securing new primitive microservices by plugging in these predefined gateways. Security gateways are extensible and can include other security functionalities including, but not limited to, logging and auditing, cryptographic roles, and throttling. However, these are out of the scope of this paper.

6 Implementation

We implemented a proof of concept using ForgeRock[1] open source components. ForgeRock Access Management (AM[2]) is used as the central access control server (ACS) for its ability to manage authentication, OAuth access delegation and XACML policies. As for microservices local gateways, ForgeRock Identity-Gateway (IG[3]) is used due to its Policy Enforcement and OAuth 2 token validation filters, and the flexibility that it provides to extend its functionality. This solution is feasible using any technological stack implementing OAuth 2 and XACML; a gateway can be written with any programming language that supports XACML, HTTPS calls, and the implementation of our proposed security checks. For the sake of clarity of this demonstration, we have used Postman[4] to play the role of a consumer microservice with an ID token, accessed by the authentication cookie, and an OAuth 2 token, sending an access request to an RMS protected behind an IG. This shows the same behaviour of a consumer-to-resource microservice call, with the resource microservice protected by RGW.

Figure 4 shows the response of an RGW on a failed User Identification Check. This is one approach to detect session hijacking and OAuth token theft. Both tokens would be deactivated in this case.

Figure 5 shows a request sent to RMS from an unauthorized OAuth client; this reflects the response of using an access token for a different consumer-resource

---

[1] https://www.forgerock.com/platform/.

[2] https://www.forgerock.com/platform/access-management.

[3] https://www.forgerock.com/platform/identity-gateway.

[4] https://www.getpostman.com/.

Fig. 4. Token theft detection

Fig. 5. Unauthorized client detection

combination, even if this resource and RMS are part of the same department. Client ID Check weakens the power of tokens, limits the trust between services to minimize the effect of a successful confused deputy attack, and mitigates creating fake OAuth clients by an insider.

In Fig. 6, we show a successful malicious request caused by the absence of our security checks. In this case, an unauthorized client, potentially created by an insider, is used to send the request, and the resource microservice responded with the data. Due to the lack of our Client ID Check, a malicious microservice with a fake OAuth client can be a threat, leading to data exfiltration from RMS. Having an OAuth client per

Fig. 6. Malicious request without our security checks.

consumer-resource combination, alongside the Client ID Check mitigates this threat. It also minimizes the trust between microservices by only allowing essential communications between them, and requiring the access control server involvement for token production and verification rather than blindly trusting a microservice or its domain. This practice minimises the impact of a confused deputy attack by limiting what can be done with a potentially compromised microservice.

Moreover, the user of the session and the OAuth token subject are not the same, which suggests using a stolen token for the request. Without our User Identity Check, token theft would not be detected. This gives this malicious user the ability to apply to services using another user's information. Our User Identity Check mitigates these attacks.

6.1 Performance

In this section, we show the overhead resulting from our proposed solution. We have conducted this experiment on an Ubuntu 17.10 running on a machine with 2.6 GHz Core i7 processor and 12 GB of RAM; we show the overhead caused by adding gateways configured for consumer microservices (CGW) and resource microservices (RGW). The line chart in Fig. 7 visualises the response time of 250 service calls for the same microservice without any gateways, with CGW, and with RGW. ACS is placed in a separate Linux container, on the same machine, to isolate the effect of data propagation over the internet. The lines show that the response time is the highest for microservices protected by RGW; the numbers confirm that, on average, an overhead of 23% results from adding a CGW, and of 32% occurs from adding RGW to a microservice. This means that a mixture of gateways protecting consumer and resource microservices should lead to an overhead of less than 32% on average. The overhead of User Identity Check and Client ID Check is minimal, given that it is all done within the GW program with no data propagation to the ACS.

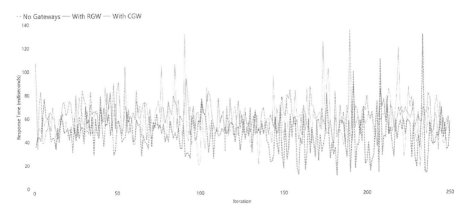

Fig. 7. Line chart showing our experimental results

As for ACS, the load factor is mostly affected by the number of exposed resource microservices due to the extra checks of OAuth 2 tokens; this is relatively easy to overcome with the cheap cloud elastic scaling.

7   Conclusions and Future Work

In this paper, we highlighted some security challenges that microservice-based applications are prone to in connection to access control and authorisation, both when the User is the trust anchor and when microservices work in conjunction. We presented a security design allowing fine-grained access control, while not compromising scalability, by proposing an access gateway at a per-microservice level. We have demonstrated the concept by implementing a prototype using XACML and OAuth 2, two leading open standards and readily available for microservices.

This work is part of a larger project that, on one hand, is looking into the chain of trust of distributed, multi-party many-component systems; on the other hand, we are developing solutions for digital governments where user control and trust are the central requirements. Several challenges are kept open. Our solution still largely depends on trusting key elements – for example, the Access Control Servers pose a risk and are able to compromise the whole system if they get compromised. On the other hand, from a user perspective, aspects such as repudiation and secure delegation of control are still open. Finally, we are also looking into the implications of having interdomain borders on which different (human) administrations sit. In other words, how to dynamically set very short-lived and on-on-the-fly trust boundaries, between multiple security administrations and environments.

References

1. Our approach to API authentication. https://gdstechnology.blog.gov.uk/2016/11/14/our-approach-to-authentication. Accessed 20 May 2018
2. Ahmad, A., Hassan, M.M., Aziz, A.: A multi-token authorization strategy for secure mobile cloud computing. In: 2014 2nd IEEE International Conference on Mobile Cloud Computing, Services, and Engineering (MobileCloud), pp. 136–141. IEEE, April 2014
3. Yarygina, T., Bagge, A.H.: Overcoming security challenges in microservice architectures. In: 2018 IEEE Symposium on Service-Oriented System Engineering (SOSE), pp. 11–20. IEEE, March 2018
4. Dragoni, N., et al.: Microservices: yesterday, today, and tomorrow. In: Mazzara, M., Meyer, B. (eds.) Present and Ulterior Software Engineering, pp. 195–216. Springer, Cham (2017). https://doi.org/10.1007/978-3-319-67425-4_12
5. Gao, X., Uehara, M.: Design of a sports mental cloud. In: 2017 31st International Conference on Advanced Information Networking and Applications Workshops (WAINA), pp. 443–448. IEEE, March 2017
6. Geisriegler, M., Kolodiy, M., Stani, S., Singer, R.: Actor based business process modeling and execution: a reference implementation based on ontology models and microservices. In: 2017 43rd Euromicro Conference on Software Engineering and Advanced Applications (SEAA), pp. 359–362. IEEE, August 2017
7. Härtig, H., Roitzsch, M., Weinhold, C., Lackorzynski, A.: Lateral thinking for trustworthy apps. In: 2017 IEEE 37th International Conference on Distributed Computing Systems (ICDCS), pp. 1890–1899. IEEE, June 2017. https://doi.org/10.1109/ICDCS.2017.29
8. IBM: An integrated approach to insider threat protection. https://www-05.ibm.com/services/europe/digital-whitepaper/security/growing_threats.html. Accessed 15 May 2018
9. Ilhan, Ö.M., Thatmann, D., Küpper, A.: A performance analysis of the XACML decision process and the impact of caching. In: 2015 11th International Conference on Signal-Image Technology & Internet-Based Systems (SITIS), pp. 216–223. IEEE, November 2015
10. Jones, M., et al.: OAuth 2.0 token exchange draft-ietf-oauth-token-exchange-13. https://tools.ietf.org/html/draft-ietf-oauth-token-exchange-13
11. Newman, S.: Building Microservices: Designing Fine-Grained Systems. O'Reilly Media, Inc., Sebastopol (2015)
12. Patanjali, S., Truninger, B., Harsh, P., Bohnert, T.M.: Cyclops: a micro service based approach for dynamic rating, charging & billing for cloud. In: 2015 13th International Conference on Telecommunications (ConTEL), pp. 1–8. IEEE, July 2015
13. Rajani, V., Garg, D., Rezk, T.: On access control, capabilities, their equivalence, and confused deputy attacks. In: 2016 IEEE 29th Computer Security Foundations Symposium (CSF), pp. 150–163. IEEE, June 2016
14. Samlinson, E., Usha, M.: User-centric trust based identity as a service for federated cloud environment. In: 2013 Fourth International Conference on Computing, Communications and Networking Technologies (ICCCNT), pp. 1–5. IEEE, July 2013
15. Suryotrisongko, H., Jayanto, D.P., Tjahyanto, A.: Design and development of backend application for public complaint systems using microservice spring boot. Procedia Comput. Sci. **124**, 736–743 (2017)
16. Suzic, B.: Securing integration of cloud services in cross-domain distributed environments. In: Proceedings of the 31st Annual ACM Symposium on Applied Computing, pp. 398–405. ACM, April 2016

17. Suzic, B.: User-centered security management of API-based data integration workflows. In: 2016 IEEE/IFIP Network Operations and Management Symposium (NOMS), pp. 1233–1238. IEEE, April 2016
18. Tang, L., Ouyang, L., Tsai, W.T.: Multi-factor web API security for securing mobile cloud. In: 2015 12th International Conference on Fuzzy Systems and Knowledge Discovery (FSKD), pp. 2163–2168. IEEE, August 2015
19. Yu, Y., Silveira, H., Sundaram, M.: A microservice based reference architecture model in the context of enterprise architecture. In: 2016 IEEE Advanced Information Management, Communicates, Electronic and Automation Control Conference (IMCEC), pp. 1856–1860. IEEE, October 2016
20. Zhang, H., Li, Z., Wu, W.: Open social and XACML based group authorization framework. In: 2012 Second International Conference on Cloud and Green Computing (CGC), pp. 655–659. IEEE, November 2012
21. Linthicum, D.S.: Practical use of microservices in moving workloads to the cloud. IEEE Cloud Comput. 3(5), 6–9 (2016)
22. Nehme, A., Jesus, V., Mahbub, K., Abdallah, A.: Securing microservices. IT Prof. 21(1), 42–49 (2019). https://doi.org/10.1109/MITP.2018.2876987

Achieving Mobile-Health Privacy Using Attribute-Based Access Control

Vignesh Pagadala and Indrakshi Ray[✉]

Computer Science Department, Colorado State University, Fort Collins, CO, USA
{vignesh.pagadala,indrakshi.ray}@colostate.edu

Abstract. Mobile Health (mHealth) refers to a healthcare-provision scheme which uses mobile communication devices for effective detection, prognosis and delivery of services. mHealth systems consists of sensors collecting information from patients, cell phones through which users access the data, and a cloud-based remote data store for holding health information of the patients. Healthcare data contains sensitive information and it must be protected from unauthorized access. Although role-based access control is commonly used for healthcare data, we advocate the use of attribute-based access control as it offers finer granularity of access and can be used across organizational boundaries. Specifically, we use the NIST Next Generation Access Control (NGAC) for representing the access control policies as it is efficient, expressive, and simplifies policy management. We propose an approach that allows constant time evaluation of access decisions based on using a graph database.

1 Introduction

The proliferation of smartphone applications provide enhanced services and functionality to users. Many healthcare smartphone applications, commonly referred to as mHealth applications, such as the one proposed by Avancha et al. [1] shown in Fig. 1, are commonly used. An mHealth system consists of several Sensor Nodes (SN) attached to a person's body, which detect health-related parameters such as blood pressure, and relay the same to a Mobile Node (MN) or a Mobile Internet Device (MID). The SNs and the MID constitute the Body-Area Network (BAN). The MID eventually transmits this information over the Internet, to a remote data store called the Health Records System (HRS), for secure, persistent storage.

Many different categories of users, including patients, healthcare providers, insurance agents, researchers, and law enforcement agencies may need to access healthcare data for various purposes. However, healthcare data is sensitive in nature. Inadvertent or malicious disclosure has grave consequences. Access control, is therefore, critical for such data [2]. Lomotey et al. [3] have used Role-Based Access Control (RBAC) [4] for their application, where access is governed by the roles of the healthcare professionals. RBAC suffers from the problem of role explosion and role management for larger institutions [2,5] and often times

© Springer Nature Switzerland AG 2019
N. Zincir-Heywood et al. (Eds.): FPS 2018, LNCS 11358, pp. 301–316, 2019.
https://doi.org/10.1007/978-3-030-18419-3_20

more finer grained access control is needed [6]. Attribute-Based Access Control (ABAC) [7] can, however, overcome these drawbacks [8–10]. Our work improves upon the performance over existing literature in ABAC for mHealth.

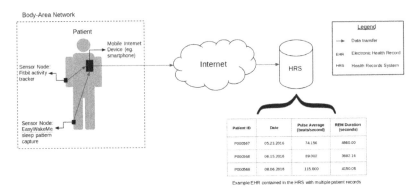

Fig. 1. mHealth architecture

Basnet et al.'s [10] is closest to ours and we use the same graph structure for representing mHealth policies. However, there is scope for investigating their algorithms further, as access-request evaluation is not being done in constant-time. In their work, they use different indexes and lists maintained at the nodes of the NGAC DAG. The time complexity of these pre-computations are also very high (cubic, in terms of number of users/objects), and is not suitable for implementation in a real-world scenario. The current work builds on this work by Basnet et al. [10] but improves upon the performance time significantly. In the current work, access-request evaluation can be achieved in $O(1)$. We give a detailed comparison in Sect. 4. The current work also provides algorithms doing incremental analysis when the graph structure changes so that the users accessing the graph are not inconvenienced. The current work is also able to handle multiple policy classes.

The rest of the paper is organized as follows. Section 2 contains a description on NIST's NGAC framework. Section 3 describes our enhanced approach. Section 4 provides complexity evaluation for the proposed algorithms. Section 5 concludes the paper with pointers to future directions.

2   Background on NIST Next-Generation Access Control

NGAC is essentially a framework for specifying and enforcing ABAC [11].

NGAC Policy Elements
Some relevant policy elements are - (1) users, (2) objects, (3) user attributes, (4) object attributes, (5) operations (6) policy classes and (7) access rights. Let us examine each of these. *Users* (u) are entities authenticated by the system and

have access to system resources. *Objects* (*o*) are the resources needing protection. *User attributes* (*ua*) are properties associated with users. *Object attributes* (*oa*) are properties of the objects. *Operations* (*op*) are actions that a user can perform and are classified into *resource operations* (ROP) or *administrative operations* (AOP). The actions that a user performs on a resource are referred to as resource operations. The operations that a user performs that operate on policy elements are referred to as administrative operations. The permitted actions are given through *access rights*, which can be *resource access rights* (RAR) or *administrative access rights* (AAR) depending on whether the operations are administrative operations or resource operations respectively.

NGAC Relationships

Two different types of relationships can exist between policy elements. *Assignment* (ASSIGN) is a irreflexive binary relation that can exist between a user and user attribute, object and object attribute, user attribute and user attribute, object attribute and object attribute, user attribute and policy class, object attribute and policy class. An ASSIGN essentially conveys a 'belongs-to' relationship. Therefore, an object attribute cannot be assigned to an object, a user attribute cannot be assigned to a user. There should also be no cycles formed by a series of ASSIGNs. Finally, every user, user attribute and object attribute should have a sequence of ASSIGNs that eventually lead to a policy class element. *Association* (ASSOC) is a binary relation between NGAC elements, which essentially represents an access privilege. An ASSOC $< ua, ar, oa >$ indicates that users assigned to user attribute *ua* have access right *ar* over objects assigned to object attribute *oa*. An ASSOC can exist only between a user attribute and an object attribute.

According to Mell et al. [12], an NGAC policy can be effectively represented as a Directed Acyclic Graph (DAG), and this feature is used extensively to optimize the complexity associated with access-request evaluation. In their work, two types of access requests are considered - (1) a single user requesting to perform an operation on a single object and (2) a single user requesting to view all privileges at the disposal. The first request performs linearly with respect to the number of operations, and the second request it's log-linear with respect to the number of operations and users. Also, this complete graph determines which authorizations are allowed, due to which it shall be referred to in following sections as the 'authorization graph'.

3   Our Approach

We use the Neo4j graph database platform for implementing the authorization graph. Neo4j allows for fast graph traversal and look-up of a record's location in constant time, using the record ID [13]. We represent an association in the form of an operation node with an out-degree of zero. An example of such an implementation is shown in Fig. 2. The authorization graph is 'indexed', meaning, we maintain a data structure at two types of nodes - users and objects, to enable fast evaluation of access decisions.

3.1   Authorization Graph Indexing

We index the authorization graph by storing every allowable access right for the user u in the form of $< op, o >$, at each user node. Every access right allowed to different users, for accessing object o, is stored in the form of $< u, op >$, at each object node. As stated before, this graph can be modified in different ways, and for some types of these changes, this indexing procedure has to be carried out on the graph. In Algorithm 1, the authorization graph is traversed using depth-first search from every user and object node, whilst keeping track of the nodes visited at each respective user and object node (lines 10–12). Once this is done, we perform an intersection across these indexes for every u and o node combination (lines 13–24). It is clear that the common nodes in the visited-node list are the operation op nodes. If such a common node is encountered, we immediately store the $< op, o >$ node combination in the *permissions* index of that particular user node, in line 18. The data structure used to construct *permissions* at each user and object node is a hash-map, with a self referencing key. We also store $< u, op >$ in the *permissions* index of the object node, in line 19.

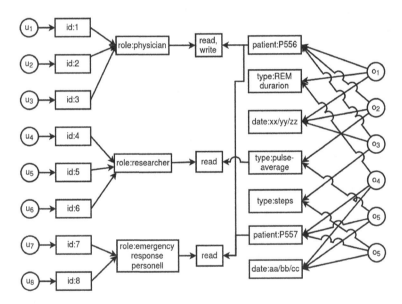

Fig. 2. Neo4j implementation of authorization graph

This approach could, however, pose a problem when multiple policy classes are involved. In our work, we shall simply consider multiple authorization graphs, one for each corresponding policy class. Algorithm 1 shall be followed for each of these graphs, and the final permissions index built at the user node would be the intersection of the permissions list associated with each user, intersected across the different authorization graphs.

It is also crucial to ensure that the storage of *permissions* does not result in a large overhead. Let us assume that each permission represented by $< op, o >$ or $< u, op >$, takes up around 20 bytes of memory. Now, even if the authorization graph consists of up to 10 million permissions in total (which is quite a stretch), the space complexity would be 20×10^7 Bytes $= 0.2$ GB. 0.2 GB does not pose a significant challenge at all, for present day RAMs, thereby allowing storage of permissions in-memory.

3.2   Access Request Evaluation

We shall take into consideration three types of queries.

Queries of the form $< u, op, o >$: A query of the form $< u, op, o >$ essentially represents a user u requesting whether they have permissions for performing operation op on the object o. Algorithm 2 shows how we shall handle this. Storing every authorized permission at the user node, renders this a simple task. We simply have to look up the *permissions* hash-map belonging to the user u, and determine if $< op, o >$ is present, in the same. If this is indeed present, we grant access, in line 4. Otherwise, the access request is denied.

Queries of the form $< u, *, * >$: Occasionally, a user might want to know every privilege at their disposal. This type of access request is represented by the query type $< u, *, * >$. As mentioned before, storing of access decisions during the indexing renders this task to be trivial. This is done in Algorithm 3, where, in response to this query type, we simply look up the *permissions* hash-map of user u, and return the same.

Queries of the form $< *, *, o >$: In some situations, the administrator may issue a query to determine which access rights are allowed to whom, for accessing an object o. We handle this using Algorithm 4, where, we look up the *permissions* hash-map of object o and return it.

4   Complexity Analyses

Indexing. We shall now assay the worst-case time complexity of the indexing procedure, being performed in Algorithm 1. Since this is not being done in real-time, and is evaluated before-hand, it is not necessary to consider the indexing time with respect to performance of access request evaluation. This procedure is performed once a change is made to the authorization graph as discussed in Sect. 3. While the authorization graph is being updated, it is unable to respond to access request evaluation. Thus, it is important to minimize the time needed for indexing the graph. The time complexity of Algorithm 1 at worst case is $O(|u|)$ and $O(|o|)$, with respect to increasing number of users and objects respectively.

Processing for $<u, op, o>$: For evaluating $<u, op, o>$, our approach achieves theoretically constant worst-case time complexity $O(1)$. While processing $< u, op, o >$, we have to perform two major look-ups which may cost time.

Firstly, in Algorithm 2, we need to look up the right user node for checking *permissions*. This can be successfully achieved in $O(1)$. The second major look-up to be performed lies in checking *permissions* itself. It is necessary to check this for the existence of $< op, o >$ for the user u. This may contain many thousands of allowed access permissions, but since we use a hash-map to store the same, this permissions check can also be achieved in $O(1)$. Therefore, theoretically, the time complexity of access request evaluation is $O(1)$.

Algorithm 1. Indexing

1: [Input: Unlabelled Graph $= (users \cup objects \cup operations, E)$ where $\forall u \in users, u.permissions = \emptyset$ and $\forall o \in objects, o.permissions = \emptyset$]

2: [Output: Labelled Graph $= (users' \cup objects' \cup operations, E)$ where $\forall u \in users', u.permissions \neq \emptyset$ and $\forall o \in objects', o.permissions \neq \emptyset$]

3: **for all** $u \in users$ **do**

4:     $u.permissions = \{\}$

5: **end for**

6: **for all** $o \in objects$ **do**

7:     $o.permissions = \{\}$

8: **end for**

9: $source\_nodes \leftarrow users \cup objects$

10: **for all** $s \in source\_nodes$ **do**

11:     $s.nodes \leftarrow$ set of all the nodes visited during DFS traversal from s

12: **end for**

13: **for all** $u \in users$ **do**

14:     **for all** $o \in objects$ **do**

15:         **for all** $nodeA \in u.nodes$ **do**

16:             **for all** $nodeB \in o.nodes$ **do**

17:                 **if** $nodeA.id = nodeB.id$ **then**   ▷ nodeA is an op node

18:                     $u.permissions \leftarrow u.permissions \cup \langle nodeA, o \rangle$ ▷ Building permissions hash-map associated with u [Output]

19:                     $o.permissions \leftarrow o.permissions \cup \langle u, nodeA \rangle$ ▷ Building permissions hash-map associated with o [Output]

20:                 **end if**

21:             **end for**

22:         **end for**

23:     **end for**

24: **end for**

25: **return** Labelled Graph

Processing for $< u, *, * >$: In our approach (Algorithm 3), it is only necessary to look up the user in the query, and return the permissions for that user. As stated before, looking up a particular user in Neo4j is $O(1)$, which leads us to establish that, the access request of the type $< u, *, * >$ can be achieved in constant time as well.

Processing for $< *, *, o >$: The worst-case time complexity of evaluating a query of this type is, once again, $O(1)$, with respect to increasing users, objects and type of policy. The complexity evaluation for Algorithm 4 is quite similar to Algorithm 3, wherein, we simply look up *permssions* for object o (which can be done in $O(1)$ in Neo4j), and return the same in constant time.

Algorithm 2. Evaluate $< u, op, o >$

1: [Input: Query $< u, op, o >$, $u.permissions$].
2: [Output: Granted or Denied]
3: **if** $\langle op, o \rangle \in u.permissions$ **then**
4:     **return** Granted   ▷ [Output] is Granted
5: **else**
6:     **return** Denied   ▷ [Output] is Denied
7: **end if**

Algorithm 3. Evaluate $< u, *, * >$

1: [Input to the algorithm u]   ▷ u is the user who want to know their capabilities
2: **return** $u.permissions$

Algorithm 4. Evaluate $< *, *, o >$

1: [Input to the algorithm o]   ▷ o is the object for which the allowed rights are requested
2: **return** $o.permissions$

4.1   Evaluation of Structural Changes in Authorization Graph

Here we look into the different types of changes possible in the authorization graph, and analyze the time complexity cost incurred with respect to performing the indexing procedure, after each change. Instead of analyzing the entire graph, we only assess the subgraphs impacted by the change.

Adding a New User/New Object. When a new user/object node is added to the system, no permissions are associated with it. The node is created, labeled as 'user'/'object', and permissions for that node is set to NULL. The user/object is uniquely identified by the node ID. This operation can be achieved in constant time.

Removing a User. When a user is removed, the *permissions* index stored at some object nodes might have to be modified. Algorithm 5 will be followed, wherein, we simply iterate through the *permissions* index of the user to be deleted u, and remove the entries for user u from the *permissions* of each corresponding object. This delete operation is affected by the number of policies stored at the user node being deleted, and in object nodes. The worst case time complexity is $O(|u|)$ and $O(|o|)$, with respect to increasing user and objects.

Removing an Object. Removal of an object might warrant the need to change the *permissions* index of some users, due to which Algorithm 6 is followed.

Algorithm 5. Delete User

1: [Input: Labelled Graph $= (users' \cup objects' \cup operations, E)$ where $\forall u \in users', u.permissions \neq \emptyset$ and $\forall o \in objects', o.permissions \neq \emptyset$]
2: [Input: User to be deleted $= u$]
3: [Output: Updated Labelled Graph $= (users' \cup objects' \cup operations, E)$ where $\forall u \in users', u.permissions \neq \emptyset$ and $\forall o \in objects', o.permissions \neq \emptyset$ and $u \notin users'$]
4: **for all** $(o_u, op_u) \in u.permissions$ **do**
5:     **for all** $(u_o, op_o) \in o_u.permissions$ **do**
6:         **if** $u_o = u$ **then**
7:             *Delete (u_o, op_o) from $o_u.permissions$*
8:         **end if**
9:     **end for**
10: **end for**
11: *Delete user u*
12: **return** Updated Labelled Graph

Similar to Algorithm 5, the stored permissions list of the object to be removed is used to find out which users' *permissions* list has to be changed. This results in a worst-case time complexity of $O(|u|)$ and $O(|o|)$, with respect to increasing user and objects.

Algorithm 6. Delete Object

1: [Input: Labelled Graph $= (users' \cup objects' \cup operations, E)$ where $\forall u \in users', u.permissions \neq \emptyset$ and $\forall o \in objects', o.permissions \neq \emptyset$]
2: [Input: Object to be deleted $= o$]
3: [Output: Updated Labelled Graph $= (users' \cup objects' \cup operations, E)$ where $\forall u \in users', u.permissions \neq \emptyset$ and $\forall o \in objects', o.permissions \neq \emptyset$ and $o \notin objects'$]
4: **for all** $(u_o, op_o) \in o.permissions$ **do**
5:     **for all** $(o_u, op_u) \in u_o.permissions$ **do**
6:         **if** $o_u = o$ **then**
7:             *Delete (o_u, op_u) from $u_o.permissions$*
8:         **end if**
9:     **end for**
10: **end for**
11: *Delete object o*
12: **return** Updated Labelled Graph

Adding a User Attribute. When a new user attribute is added to the system, no policies are associated with it yet. Due to this, changes need not be made to any of the indices, and the complexity is constant.

Removing a User Attribute. When a user attribute is removed from the system, a subset of the users and objects may need to change their *permissions*. Algorithm 9 is used to handle this. We simply run a DFS in the reverse direction to the assignments, from the user attribute to be deleted. This would give us the set of object nodes which will be affected by the change. We then use their existing indices to find out the object nodes which will also be affected. Now, we have a subset of user and object nodes on which we will do the intersection as shown in Algorithm 1, as opposed to doing in intersection on all objects and users. The average case complexity of doing this is lesser than that of Algorithm 1, but in the worst case, it is $O(|u|)$ and $O(|o|)$, with respect to increasing user and objects.

Adding an Object Attribute. When an object attribute is added, no new policies are associated with it yet, due to which no changes need to be made to the *permissions* index of any users or objects. This can be done in constant time.

Algorithm 7. Add and Delete u to ua ASSIGN

1: [Input: Labelled Graph $= (users' \cup objects' \cup operations, E)$ where $\forall u \in users'$, $u.permissions \neq \emptyset$ and $\forall o \in objects'$, $o.permissions \neq \emptyset$]
2: [Input: User $= u$]
3: [Input: User Attribute $= ua$]
4: [Output: Updated Labelled Graph $= (users' \cup objects' \cup operations, E)$ where $\forall u \in users'$, $u.permissions \neq \emptyset$ and $\forall o \in objects'$, $o.permissions \neq \emptyset$ and $u - uaASSIGN \in$ E]
5: $u.nodes \leftarrow$ set of all the nodes visited during DFS traversal from u
6: **for all** $o \in objects$ **do**
7:     $o.nodes \leftarrow$ set of all the nodes visited during DFS traversal from o
8: **end for**
9: **for all** $o \in objects$ **do**
10:     **for all** $nodeA \in u.nodes$ **do**
11:         **for all** $nodeB \in o.nodes$ **do**
12:             **if** $nodeA.id= nodeB.id$ **then**   ▷ nodeA is an op node
13:                 $u.permissions \leftarrow u.permissions \cup \langle nodeA, o \rangle$ ▷ Building permissions hash-map associated with u [Output]
14:                 $o.permissions \leftarrow o.permissions \cup \langle u, nodeA \rangle$ ▷ Building permissions hash-map associated with o [Output]
15:             **end if**
16:         **end for**
17:     **end for**
18: **end for**
19: **return** Updated Labelled Graph

Removing an Object Attribute. When an object attribute is deleted, we shall follow Algorithm 10, where the *permissions* index of only those affected user and object nodes are changed. We find out this subset of nodes to update by performing a DFS in the reverse direction, which will lead us to all the user nodes. The object nodes are discovered by examining the *permissions* hash-map of each user. After this, we intersect across all nodes visited using DFS from each user and object, to find the common operation nodes, and update the indices. In the average case, this would incur lesser complexity cost than Algorithm 1, but in the worst case, it is $O(|u|)$ and $O(|o|)$, with respect to increasing user and objects.

Adding a u to ua ASSIGN. As shown Algorithm 7, we perform a DFS traversal from the user node u, and every object node, and perform an intersection across both these sets of visited nodes, to get the common operation nodes. The worst case time complexity is $O(1)$ and $O(|o|)$ with respect to number of users and objects respectively.

Algorithm 8. Add and Delete o to oa ASSIGN

1: [Input: Labelled Graph $= (users' \cup objects' \cup operations, E)$ where $\forall u \in$ $users'$, $u.permissions \neq \emptyset$ and $\forall o \in objects'$, $o.permissions \neq \emptyset$]

2: [Input: Object $= o$]

3: [Input: Object Attribute $= oa$]

4: State [Output: Updated Labelled Graph $= (users' \cup objects' \cup operations, E)$ where $\forall u \in users'$, $u.permissions \neq \emptyset$ and $\forall o \in objects'$, $o.permissions \neq \emptyset$ and $o - oaASSIGN \in E$]

5: $o.nodes \leftarrow$ set of all the nodes visited during DFS traversal from o

6: **for all** $u \in users$ **do**

7:     $u.nodes \leftarrow$ set of all the nodes visited during DFS traversal from u

8: **end for**

9: **for all** $u \in users$ **do**

10:     **for all** $nodeA \in u.nodes$ **do**

11:         **for all** $nodeB \in o.nodes$ **do**

12:             **if** $nodeA.id= nodeB.id$ **then**   ▷ nodeA is an op node

13:                 $u.permissions \leftarrow u.permissions \cup \langle nodeA, o \rangle$ ▷ Building permissions hash-map associated with u [Output]

14:                 $o.permissions \leftarrow o.permissions \cup \langle u, nodeA \rangle$ ▷ Building permissions hash-map associated with o [Output]

15:             **end if**

16:         **end for**

17:     **end for**

18: **end for**

19: **return** Updated Labelled Graph

Removing a u to ua ASSIGN. In this case, we perform the same procedure as done for adding a u to ua assignment. We again follow Algorithm 7 for performing this.

Removing a User. For adding an o - oa assignment, we shall follow Algorithm 8, where a procedure similar to Algorithm 7 is followed, but on the objects' side. We perform the DFS from the object node o and from every user, and follow this up with the intersection. The time complexity of this algorithm is $O(|u|)$ and $O(1)$ with respect to number of users and objects respectively.

Removing an o to oa ASSIGN. We follow the same procedure as done when adding an o to oa ASSIGN (Algorithm 8).

Algorithm 9. Delete User Attribute

1: [Input: Labelled Graph $= (users' \cup objects' \cup operations, E)$ where $\forall u \in users'$, $u.permissions \neq \emptyset$ and $\forall o \in objects'$, $o.permissions \neq \emptyset$]
2: [Input: User attribute to be deleted $= ua$]
3: [Output: Updated Labelled Graph $= (users' \cup objects' \cup operations, E)$ where $\forall u \in users'$, $u.permissions \neq \emptyset$ and $\forall o \in objects'$, $o.permissions \neq \emptyset$ and $ua \notin$ Updated Labelled Graph]
4: $onodes = \{\}$
5: $unodes = \{\}$
6: $unodes \leftarrow$ set of all the user nodes visited during reverse DFS traversal from ua
7: **for all** $u \in unodes$ **do**
8:     $onodes \leftarrow onodes \cup u.permissions[1]$
9: **end for**
10: $source\_nodes \leftarrow unodes \cup onodes$
11: $Delete(ua)$
12: **for all** $s \in source\_nodes$ **do**
13:     $s.nodes \leftarrow$ set of all the nodes visited during DFS traversal from s
14: **end for**
15: **for all** $u \in unodes$ **do**
16:     **for all** $o \in onodes$ **do**
17:         **for all** $nodeA \in u.nodes$ **do**
18:             **for all** $nodeB \in o.nodes$ **do**
19:                 **if** $nodeA.id = nodeB.id$ **then**   ▷ nodeA is an op node
20:                     $u.permissions \leftarrow u.permissions \cup \langle nodeA, o \rangle$ ▷ Building permissions hash-map associated with u [Output]
21:                     $o.permissions \leftarrow o.permissions \cup \langle u, nodeA \rangle$ ▷ Building permissions hash-map associated with o [Output]
22:                 **end if**
23:             **end for**
24:         **end for**
25:     **end for**
26: **end for**
27: **return** Updated Labelled Graph

Adding a ua to ua ASSIGN. A ua - ua assignment is added using Algorithm 11. We assume the user attribute ua_1 is assigned to the user attribute ua_2. In this case, as shown in Algorithm 11, we perform a DFS in the reverse direction from ua_1, which leads us to every u node whose *permissions* has to be updated. We then perform forward DFS from this subset of user nodes, and all objects nodes, followed by the intersection. The worst case time complexity comes out to be $O(|u|)$ and $O(|o|)$ with respect to number of users and objects respectively.

Algorithm 10. Delete Object Attribute

1: [Input: Labelled Graph $= (users' \cup objects' \cup operations, E)$ where $\forall u \in users', u.permissions \neq \emptyset$ and $\forall o \in objects', o.permissions \neq \emptyset$]

2: [Input: Object attribute to be deleted $= oa$]

3: [Output: Updated Labelled Graph $= (users' \cup objects' \cup operations, E)$ where $\forall u \in users', u.permissions \neq \emptyset$ and $\forall o \in objects', o.permissions \neq \emptyset$ and $oa \notin$ Updated Labelled Graph]

4: $onodes = \{\}$

5: $unodes = \{\}$

6: $onodes \leftarrow$ set of all the object nodes visited during reverse DFS traversal from oa

7: **for all** $o \in onodes$ **do**

8:     $unodes \leftarrow unodes \cup o.permissions[0]$

9: **end for**

10: $source\_nodes \leftarrow unodes \cup onodes$

11: $Delete(oa)$

12: **for all** $s \in source\_nodes$ **do**

13:     $s.nodes \leftarrow$ set of all the nodes visited during DFS traversal from s

14: **end for**

15: **for all** $u \in unodes$ **do**

16:     **for all** $o \in onodes$ **do**

17:         **for all** $nodeA \in u.nodes$ **do**

18:             **for all** $nodeB \in o.nodes$ **do**

19:                 **if** $nodeA.id = nodeB.id$ **then**   ▷ nodeA is an op node

20:                     $u.permissions \leftarrow u.permissions \cup \langle nodeA, o \rangle$ ▷ Building permissions hash-map associated with u [Output]

21:                     $o.permissions \leftarrow o.permissions \cup \langle u, nodeA \rangle$ ▷ Building permissions hash-map associated with o [Output]

22:                 **end if**

23:             **end for**

24:         **end for**

25:     **end for**

26: **end for**

27: **return** Updated Labelled Graph

Removing a ua to ua ASSIGN. Here we follow the same procedure as done with adding a ua to ua ASSIGN, which is shown in Algorithm 11.

Adding a oa to oa ASSIGN. A oa - oa assignment is added using Algorithm 13. We assume the object attribute oa_1 is assigned to the object attribute oa_2. In this case, as shown in the algorithm, we perform a DFS in the reverse direction from oa_1, which leads us to every o node whose *permissions* has to be updated. We then perform forward DFS from this subset of object nodes, and all user nodes, followed by the intersection. The worst case time complexity is $O(|u|)$ and $O(|o|)$ with respect to number of users and objects respectively.

Removing a oa to oa ASSIGN. Here we follow the same procedure as done with adding a oa to oa ASSIGN, which is shown in Algorithm 13.

Algorithm 11. Add and Delete ua to ua ASSIGN

1: [Input: Labelled Graph $=$ $(users' \cup objects' \cup operations, E)$ where $\forall u \in$ $users'$, $u.permissions \neq \emptyset$ and $\forall o \in objects'$, $o.permissions \neq \emptyset$]
2: [Input: User Attribute 1 $= ua_1$]
3: [Input: User Attribute 2 $= ua_2$]
4: [Output: Updated Labelled Graph $=$ $(users' \cup objects' \cup operations, E)$ where $\forall u \in users'$, $u.permissions \neq \emptyset$ and $\forall o \in objects'$, $o.permissions \neq \emptyset$ and $ua -$ $uaASSIGN \in$ E]
5: $unodes \leftarrow$ set of all the user nodes visited during reverse DFS traversal from ua_1
6: $source\_nodes \leftarrow unodes \cup objects$
7: **for all** $s \in source\_nodes$ **do**
8:     $s.nodes \leftarrow$ set of all the nodes visited during DFS traversal from s
9: **end for**
10: **for all** $u \in unodes$ **do**
11:     **for all** $o \in objects$ **do**
12:         **for all** $nodeA \in u.nodes$ **do**
13:             **for all** $nodeB \in o.nodes$ **do**
14:                 **if** $nodeA.id= nodeB.id$ **then** $\triangleright$ nodeA is an op node
15:                     $u.permissions \leftarrow u.permissions \cup \langle nodeA, o \rangle$ $\triangleright$ Building permissions hash-map associated with u [Output]
16:                     $o.permissions \leftarrow o.permissions \cup \langle u, nodeA \rangle$ $\triangleright$ Building permissions hash-map associated with o [Output]
17:                 **end if**
18:             **end for**
19:         **end for**
20:     **end for**
21: **end for**
22: **return** Updated Labelled Graph

Adding a ua to oa ASSOC. Adding an association between a ua and an oa node, implies the addition of an op node. For doing this, we simply perform a DFS in the reverse direction from ua and oa, as shown in lines 7 and 8 in Algorithm 12. This gives us the subset of u and o nodes whose *permissions* has to be updated. Now, we simply iterate through each user and object node, and include every object node in the user's *permissions* hash-map, and vice verse. The worst case time complexity is $O(|u|)$ and $O(|o|)$ with respect to number of users and objects respectively.

Removing a ua to oa ASSOC. As shown in Algorithm 14, when a permission gets deleted, we first find out the subset of users and objects affected by this change, by performing a reverse DFS from ua and oa. Once we achieve this, we simply do a forward DFS from each of these nodes, and store all visited nodes. The intersection across the visited nodes from the users and objects will enable us to find the common operation nodes and update the *permisisons* hash-map of the users and objects. The worst case time complexity is $O(|u|)$ and $O(|o|)$ with respect to number of users and objects respectively.

Algorithm 12. Add *ua* to *oa* ASSOC

1: [Input: Labelled Graph $=$ $(users' \cup objects' \cup operations, E)$ where $\forall u \in users'$, $u.permissions \neq \emptyset$ and $\forall o \in objects'$, $o.permissions \neq \emptyset$]

2: [Input: User Attribute $= ua$]

3: [Input: Object Attribute $= oa$]

4: [Input: Operation $= op$]

5: State [Output: Updated Labelled Graph $= (users' \cup objects' \cup operations, E)$ where $\forall u \in users'$, $u.permissions \neq \emptyset$ and $\forall o \in objects'$, $o.permissions \neq \emptyset$ and $ua - oaASSOC \in$ operations,E]

6: $unodes \leftarrow$ set of all the user nodes visited during reverse DFS traversal from ua

7: $onodes \leftarrow$ set of all the object nodes visited during reverse DFS traversal from oa

8: **for all** $u \in unodes$ **do**

9:     **for all** $o \in onodes$ **do**

10:         $u.permissions \leftarrow u.permissions \cup (o, op)$

11:     **end for**

12: **end for**

13: **for all** $o \in onodes$ **do**

14:     **for all** $u \in unodes$ **do**

15:         $o.permissions \leftarrow o.permissions \cup (op, u)$

16:     **end for**

17: **end for**

18: **return** Updated Labelled Graph

Algorithm 13. Add and Delete *oa* to *oa* ASSIGN

1: [Input: Labelled Graph $=$ $(users' \cup objects' \cup operations, E)$ where $\forall u \in users'$, $u.permissions \neq \emptyset$ and $\forall o \in objects'$, $o.permissions \neq \emptyset$]

2: [Input: Object Attribute 1 $= oa_1$]

3: [Input: Object Attribute 2 $= oa_2$]

4: [Output: Updated Labelled Graph $= (users' \cup objects' \cup operations, E)$ where $\forall u \in users'$, $u.permissions \neq \emptyset$ and $\forall o \in objects'$, $o.permissions \neq \emptyset$ and $oa - oaASSIGN \in$ E]

5: $onodes \leftarrow$ set of all the object nodes visited during reverse DFS traversal from oa_1

6: $source\_nodes \leftarrow users \cup onodes$

7: **for all** $s \in source\_nodes$ **do**

8:     $s.nodes \leftarrow$ set of all the nodes visited during DFS traversal from s

9: **end for**

10: **for all** $u \in users$ and $o \in onodes$ **do**

11:     **for all** $nodeA \in u.nodes$ and $nodeB \in o.nodes$ **do**

12:         **if** $nodeA.id = nodeB.id$ **then**   ▷ nodeA is an op node

13:             $u.permissions \leftarrow u.permissions \cup \langle nodeA, o \rangle$ ▷ Building permissions
hash-map associated with u [Output]

14:             $o.permissions \leftarrow o.permissions \cup \langle u, nodeA \rangle$ ▷ Building permissions
hash-map associated with o [Output]

15:         **end if**

16:     **end for**

17: **end for**

18: **return** Updated Labelled Graph

Algorithm 14. Delete ua to oa ASSOC

1: [Input: Labelled Graph $= (users' \cup objects' \cup operations, E)$ where $\forall u \in users', u.permissions \neq \emptyset$ and $\forall o \in objects', o.permissions \neq \emptyset$]
2: [Input: User Attribute $= ua$, Object Attribute $= oa$, Operation $= op$]
3: [Output: Updated Labelled Graph $= (users' \cup objects' \cup operations, E)$ where $\forall u \in users', u.permissions \neq \emptyset$ and $\forall o \in objects', o.permissions \neq \emptyset$ and $ua - oaASSOC \notin$ operations,E]
4: $unodes \leftarrow$ set of all the user nodes visited during reverse DFS traversal from ua
5: $onodes \leftarrow$ set of all the object nodes visited during reverse DFS traversal from oa
6: $source\_nodes \leftarrow unodes \cup onodes$
7: **for all** $s \in source\_nodes$ **do**
8:     $s.nodes \leftarrow$ set of all the nodes visited during DFS traversal from s
9: **end for**
10: **for all** $u \in unodes$ **do**
11:     **for all** $o \in onodes$ **do**
12:         **for all** $nodeA \in u.nodes$ **do**
13:             **for all** $nodeB \in o.nodes$ **do**
14:                 **if** $nodeA.id= nodeB.id$ **then**   ▷ nodeA is an op node
15:                     $u.permissions \leftarrow u.permissions \cup \langle nodeA, o \rangle$ ▷ Building permissions hash-map associated with u [Output]
16:                     $o.permissions \leftarrow o.permissions \cup \langle u, nodeA \rangle$ ▷ Building permissions hash-map associated with o [Output]
17:                 **end if**
18:             **end for**
19:         **end for**
20:     **end for**
21: **end for**
22: **return** Updated Labelled Graph

---

5   Conclusion and Future Work

We propose the use of attribute-based access control for specifying and enforcing mHealth access control policies and provide efficient algorithms for policy enforcement and management. A lot of work remains to be done. We need to extend our approach to handle multiple policy classes and further look at techniques for optimizing the approach. We need to implement our approach on Neo4j for real-world case studies and investigate whether the model is adequately expressive and efficient to meet real-time requirements of mHealth applications.

References

1. Avancha, S., Baxi, A., Kotz, D.: Privacy in mobile technology for personal health-care. ACM Comput. Surv. **45**(1), 3:1–3:54 (2012)
2. Kotz, D.: A threat taxonomy for mHealth privacy. In: Proceedings of 2011 Third International Conference on Communication Systems and Networks (COMSNETS 2011), pp. 1–6 January 2011

3. Lomotey, R.K., Deters, R.: Mobile-based medical data accessibility in mhealth. In: Proceedings of 2014 2nd IEEE International Conference on Mobile Cloud Computing, Services, and Engineering , pp. 91–100, April 2014
4. Ferraiolo, D.F., Sandhu, R., Gavrila, S., Kuhn, D.R., Chandramouli, R.: Proposed NIST standard for role-based access control. ACM Trans. Inf. Syst. Secur. **4**(3), 224–274 (2001)
5. Elliott, A., Knight, S.: Role explosion: acknowledging the problem. In: Proceedings of the 2010 International Conference on Software Engineering Research & Practice, pp. 349–355 (2010)
6. Fischer, J., Marino, D., Majumdar, R., Millstein, T.: Fine-grained access control with object-sensitive roles. In: Drossopoulou, S. (ed.) ECOOP 2009. LNCS, vol. 5653, pp. 173–194. Springer, Heidelberg (2009). https://doi.org/10.1007/978-3-642-03013-0_9
7. Hu, V.C., et al.: Guide to attribute based access control (ABAC) definition and considerations (draft). NIST Spec. Publ. **800**(162) (2013)
8. Scholl, M., Stine, K., Lin, K., Steinberg, D.: Draft security architecture design process for health information exchanges (HIEs). Report, NIST (2009)
9. Zhang, R., Liu, L.: Security models and requirements for healthcare application clouds. In: Proceedings of 2010 IEEE 3rd International Conference on Cloud Computing, pp. 268–275, July 2010
10. Basnet, R., Mukherjee, S., Pagadala, V.M., Ray, I.: An efficient implementation of next generation access control for the mobile health cloud. In: Proceedings of 2018 Third International Conference on Fog and Mobile Edge Computing (FMEC), pp. 131–138 (2018)
11. Ferraiolo, D., Atluri, V., Gavrila, S.: The policy machine: a novel architecture and framework for access control policy specification and enforcement. J. Syst. Architect. **57**(4), 412–424 (2011)
12. Mell, P., Shook, J.M., Gavrila, S.: Restricting insider access through efficient implementation of multi-policy access control systems. In: Proceedings of the 8th ACM CCS International Workshop on Managing Insider Security Threats MIST@CCS, pp. 13–22 (2016)
13. Miller, J.J.: Graph database applications and concepts with neo4j. In: Proceedings of the Southern Association for Information Systems Conference, Atlanta, GA, USA, vol. 2324, p. 36 (2013)

Author Index

Abdallah, Ali   285
Adams, Carlisle   46
Ahmad, Tahir   131
Alshammari, Fayzah   46

Bissessar, David   46
Bui, Thang   267
Bukasa, Sebanjila Kevin   243
Bultel, Xavier   78

Cavalli, Ana Rosa   257
Chohra, Aniss   95
Ciucanu, Radu   78
Claudepierre, Ludovic   243
Cuppens, Nora   257

Dantas, Yuri Gil   173
Debbabi, Mourad   61, 95
Di Crescenzo, Giovanni   208
Duman, Onur   225

Gambs, Sébastien   17
Garcia-Alfaro, Joaquin   257
Giraud, Matthieu   78
Gong, Guang   3

Hamann, Tobias   29, 173
Hezaveh, Maryam   46

Jarraya, Yosr   61
Jesus, Vitor   285

Lafourcade, Pascal   78
Lanet, Jean-Louis   156, 243
Lashermes, Ronan   243

Le-Bouder, Hélène   156
Li, Feng   143
Li, Jiajie   267
Logrippo, Luigi   115
Luo, Xiao   143

Madi, Taous   61
Mahbub, Khaled   285
Majumdar, Suryadipta   61
Manabe, Yoshifumi   193
Mantel, Heiko   29, 173
Martinez, Erick Eduardo Bernal   143

Nehme, Antonio   285

Oh, Bella   143
Ono, Hibiki   193
Ouairy, Léopold   156

Pagadala, Vignesh   301
Pourzandi, Makan   61

Ranise, Silvio   131
Ray, Indrakshi   301

Segovia, Mariana   257
Shirani, Paria   95
Stambouli, Abdelouadoud   115
Stoller, Scott D.   267

Wang, Lingyu   61

Ye, Lihua   78
Youssef, Amr   225

Printed in the United States
By Bookmasters